Conscious Awakening 101

A SHORT COURSE

Guide to **WAKING UP**, To see Actual Reality,
Become your True Self, To become Enlightened,
To Guide you to a higher Density and Realm,
To help you develop your **Escape Plan**

Research into Reality
(The TRUTH – Can you handle it)

Arlene Lanman

BookBaby
7905 N Crescent Blvd
Pennsauken, NY 08110

Library of Congress Cataloging-in-Publication Data
Names: Lanman, Arlene, 1946-
Title: Conscious Awakening 101 / Arlene Lanman.
Description: Pennsauken, New York: BookBaby, 2020 | Includes article references and preface.
Identifiers: IISBN 978-1-09833-1-573
Subjects: LCSH: Who is GOD? | AGE of Aquarius | Why we as Extradimensional Beings & Bearers of Light are Here | Why Enlightenment is hard to Achieve | Service-to-Self vs. Service to Others | The Meaning of Life | Alternate Timelines and Universes | Ego vs. Essence – Your own worst Enemy | The Journey to Self – the First Step to Awakening | Sovereign Integrity 3.0 SI – Importance to Star Beings | Reality is Wrong – Dreams are For Real | Raise your brain power 30% | The Lesson of snow – Stage 1 of Waking Up | Waking Up Stage 2 – The Stage of Questioning | Waking Up Stage 3 – the Stage of Introspection | Waking up Stage4 – the Stage of Resolution | What you should have learned in Awakening Stages 1 -4 | Waking up Stage 5 – the real work begins – Step into your power | Waking up to reality in Stages – Summary | Number of People Seeking Enlightenment | Spirit, Soul, Mind, Body – Know thyself | The types of Souls – Live the life your Soul intended | The ascending lifetime (Earth Souls, Starseeds, Light Bearers) | Why Earth Frequency is Increasing& being manipulated – We are at war | Heart's electromagnetic field – Source of Consciousness | Interaction Between Hear Fields – We are one (almost) | Chakras are a Programming Overreach – The body as machine | Tricked by the light – All is frequency, vibration and energy | Simultaneously living in the past, present and future | The Dark Side of Healing | Humming is Psycho Acoustic & Vibro-Acoustic Therapy | The Vedic Realms | Spiritual Densities of the Earth | Levels of Consciousness within the Earth Density (Octave) | The Enki Group's 24 Ascension Masters – Part of the Anunnaki/ENKI Dominion of Dominance | Escaping the 4% Universe | Reincarnation is a Trap | Oneness / Singularity is a trap | Escape Plan Preparation While on Earth | Journey after Death – Realms of consciousness | The Galactic Wars+ | Card Catalogs and the secret history of modernity | PLANET C-53 (Earth) – the slave planet | The Council of Five | MAJESTIC 12 and The Jason Society | The Consequences are Inescapable | The Essential War – Light vs. Dark – Pending Revelations | Defeating the Dark Force – Death by a 1000 cuts | Electromagnetic Frequency Uses | Planet Earth Inc.- Who really controls the World | We are fragments of the same Source | Uniting with your Twin Flame is Essential | Me and my Shadow | Photographic References | Author Biography.

Printed and Bound in the United States by BookBaby.

This Book typeset in Baskerville Old Face

Cover background by potitus lanarm | Shuterstock.

To send correspondence to the author of this compendium, mail a first-class letter to the author c/o BookBaby, and it will forward the communication, or contact the author directly at www.arlenelanman@gmail.com.

"Truth is stranger than fiction,
but it is because Fiction is
obligated to stick to possibilities;
Truth isn't"

Mark Twain

CONTENTS

Article	Title	Page

Title Page
Copyright Page
Epigraph – quote
Table of Contents
Acknowledgements

	PREFACE - IS IT REAL, IS IT FAKE...........................	1
	PART 1 – THE BASICS (Why Me, Why Now)......................	3
1	WHO IS GOD?	5
2	AGE OF AQUARIUS	9
3	WHY ARE WE HERE	21
4	WHY WE, AS EXTRADIMENSIONAL BEINGS & BEARERS OF LIGHT, ARE HERE - YOUR MISSION	25
5	WHY ENLIGHTMENT IS HARD TO ACHIEVE	29
6	SERVICE-TO-SELF VS. SERVICE TO OTHERS	THE MEANING OF LIFE	33
7	ALTERNATE TIMELINES AND UNIVERSES	37
	PART 2 - PREPARING FOR THE JOURNEY OF YOU ... LIFE (THE JOURNEY INSIDE)	43
8	EGO VS. ESSENCE- YOUR OWN WORST ENEMY	45
9	THE JOURNEY TO SELF - THE FIRST STEP TO AWAKENING	57
10	SOVEREIGN INTEGRITY 3.0 SI - IMPORTANCE TO STAR BEINGS	67
11	REALITY IS WRONG - DREAMS ARE FOR REAL	77
12	RAISE YOU BRAIN POWER 30%	81
	PART 3 - STAGES OF WAKING UP.................................	87
13	THE LESSON OF SNOW - STAGE 1 OF WAKING UP	89
14	WAKEING UP STAGE 2 - THE STAGE OF QUESTIONING	93
15	WAKEWNING UP STAGE 3 - THE STAGE OF INTROSPECTION	95
16	WAKING UP STAGE 4 - THE STAGE OF RESOLUTION	99
17	WHAT YOU SHOULD HAVE LEARNED IN AWAKENING STAGES 1 -4	103
18	WAKING UP STAGE 5-THE REAL WORK BEGINS-STEP INTO YOUR POWER	105
19	WAKING UP TO REALITY IN STAGES - SUMMARY	107
20	NUMBER OF PEOPLE SEEKING ENLIGHTENMENT	109
	PART 4 - MIND, BODY, SOUL SPIRIT.................................	113
21	SPIRIT, SOUL, MIND, BODY - KNOW THYSELF	115
22	THE 3 TYPES OF SOULS - LIVE THE LIFE YOUR SOUL INTENDED	119
23	THE ASCENDING LIFETIME (EARTH SOULS, STARSEEDS. LIGHT BEARERS)	123
24	WHY THE EARTH FREQUENCY IS INCREASING & BEING MANUPLIATED - WE ARE AT WAR	129
25	HEART'S ELECTROMATIC FIELD - SOURCE OF CONSCIOUSNESS	133
26	INTERACTION BETWEEN HEART FIEDS - WE ARE ONE (ALMOST)	143
27	CHAKRAS ARE A PROGRAMMING OVERREACH - THE BODY AS MACHINE	149

28	TRICKED BY THE LIGHT - ALL IS FREQUENCY, VRIBRATION AND ENERGY	159
29	SIMULTANEOUS LIVING IN THE PAST< PRESENT, AND FUTURE	165
30	THE DARK SIDE OF HEALING	171
31	HUMMING IS PSYCHO ACOUSTIC & VIBRO-ACOUSTIC THERAPY	175

PART 5 - REALMS, DENSITIES, HUMAN .... CONSCIOUSNESS, ESCAPE **177**

32	THE VEDIC REALMS	179
33	SPIRITUAL DENSITIES OF THE EARTH	189
34	LEVELS OF HUMAN CONSCIOUSNESS WITHIN THE EARTH DENSITY (OCTAVE)	205
35	THE ENKI GROUP'S 24 ASCENSION MASTERS —PART OF THE ANUNNAKI/ENKI DOMINION OF DOMINANCE	213
36	EXCAPING THE 4% UNIVERSE	219
37	REINCARNATION IS A TRAP	225
38	ONENESS / SINGULARITY IS A TRAP	227
39	ESCAPE PLAN PREPARATION WHILE ON EARTH	233
40	JOURNEY AFTER DEATH - REALMS OF CONSCIOUSNESS	239

PART 6 – HISTORY OF HOW WE GOT HERE & WHY ... **251**
(GALACTIC HISTORY, LIVING LIBRARY, DNA MANUIPULATION, ELECTROMAGNETIC FREQUENCYS, EARTH FREQUENCY RISING)

41	THE GALACTIC WARS +	253
42	CARD CATALOGS AND THE SECRET HISTORY OF MODERNITY	277
43	PLANET C-53 (Earth) – The Slave Planet	281
44	THE COUNCIL OF FIVE	283
45	MAJESTIC 12 and The JASON SOCIETY	289
46	THE CONCLUSIONS ARE INESCAPABLE	295
47	THE ESENTIAL WAR - LIGHT VS. DARK - PENDING REVELATIONS	297
48	DEFEATING THE DARK FORCE - DEAT BY A 1000 CUTS	299
49	ELECTROMAGNETIC FREQUENCY USES	305
50	PLANET EARTH INC - WHO REALLY CONTROLS THE WORLD	309
51	WE ARE FRAGMENTS FROM THE SAME SOURCE	315
52	UN ITING WITH YOUR TWIN FLAME IS ESSENTIAL	323
53	ME AND MY SHADOW	329

PART 7 – END MATTER **337**

Photograph References	339
Author Biography	347

Acknowledgements

You are not alone and neither was I. I would like to thank my Spirit, Twin Flame, my Higher Self, and the many other ethereal Guides and Advisers who "nudged" me along the path to find the Truth, for helping me to remember many of my past lives and the lessons they taught me, and to develop my ESCAPE PLAN.

I would also like to thank my fellow Travelers, the insights they conveyed to me and who have been instrumental in both my professional and spiritual development, to know my True Self and gave me part of their vibrational strength and guidance to become enlightened and AWAKE.

Childhood & Life	Violet Lucille (Marchion) Lanman	Mother – most likely a Light Bearer
Junior High School	Mr. Brandt	Art Instructor & Wayshower
Wm. J Palmer High School	Mr. Lloyd Samuelson	Art Instructor & Wayshower
	Ms. Ida Belle Kennedy	English Dept Head
	Mr. Hank Lujan	Science Dept Head
Kansas State University	Dr. Alden Krieder, RA	Architectural History Professor – indirectly showed me the past alien influences
	F. Gene Ernst, Professor	Urban Design Professor and an Inspiration
Kansas City Refinery	Louis F Kusek, P.E.	Chief Engineer & Mentor
	Herbert (Herb) Kettelsen, PE	Senior Mech Engineer & Mentor
	John Robert (Bob) Johnson, PE	Mechanical Engineer & Mentor
Phillips Petroleum, Corporate Engineering	James A Hooker, RA	Architectural Group Supervisor & Mentor
Mentors & Friends	Elaine (McFarland) Radney	Childhood and later life friend – she found me; I do not go out-of-my-way to make friends
	Charlotte (Crandall) Porterfield	Fellow Warrior of Light, friend and an inspiration (proof read this and my previous book for spelling, grammatical errors, and for cohesion and fluidity of the thoughts)
	Steve (PePe) Tellinger	Fellow Warrior of Light and an inspiration, even after his death
	Rachael Henderson	Believed previous lifetime she was a Celtic Druid – was a warrior, transmigration of souls, Realms below and as islands in the sea.
Spirits	My Spirit, Twin Flame, Higher Self, My Two Guards, Counselors, Advisors, all of my cat companions (my spiritual protectors)	They are always near me, protect me, and are sources to help me along my spiritual path

PREFACE - IS IT REAL, IS IT FAKE

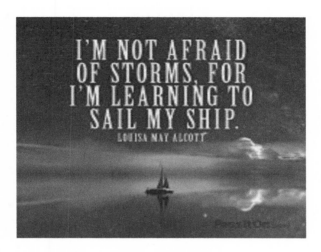

Is it Real? Is it Fake? Is the Game of Life a Mistake? The question revolves around the basic question of do we perceive the universe around us as it really is (direct) or is the universe an internal perception is generated within our brain (indirect) from an interpretation fed by our senses of feel, touch, taste, see, and hear, as well as how society has "programmed" us?

CONSCIOUS AWAKENING 101 (book) is your Short Course guide to WAKING UP to become enlightened, to increase the frequency of both the Earth and yourself in order for you to see Actual Reality and guide others to a higher density and realm.

It is beyond how you touch, how you see, how you hear and the senses you use in the reality. Actual Reality is beyond all of these and you need a SHORT COURSE to fully understand Who you Really Are. Maybe parts of you try to understand, but a lot of it is beyond what we can even imagine.

It is a choice to WAKE UP. When you begin to Wake Up, you go into a certain reality to remember who you are; you remember you are a divine being. Remember you have a connection to the stars and you have a connection at many different levels.

Conscious Awakening 101 will help you understand the vastness of your spirituality, your immortality and your connection to everything in the universe, from its very beginning to today. The more you acknowledge how vast your really are will give you the ability to tap into it. You always had the ability to tap into your vastness, but now you are seeking to know who you really are. The more you can have the information come through, the more in sync with the universe you will become and the more you will be able to help others raise their own frequency to find their own TRUE REALITY.

Most of all, you will realize this Realm (the Middle Realm) is a polarity world, dominated and controlled by the Draco-Reptilian Empire (sometimes referred to as "Evil" and "Darkness") and you have for many lifetimes been caught up in the Reincarnation Cycle. This Short Course will help you determine (write) your ESCAPE PLAN and be on the "road"to Higher Realms.

HEED THE CALL TO WAKE UP and go through the process of remembering your true self and Escaping this world.

THERE ARE TWO "TRAINS" leaving the station. One has you and all others aboard, weather you're STO (Service to Others) or STS (Service-to-Self). There are 7 "cars" (Densities) making up each of the "train's" consist. All start out on the "train" driven by the False God (the "owner" of this world and the 4% Universe) who created mankind to be dominated and to be controlled by Him. The other "train" is driven by Creator God who provides you with unconditional love. You can either stay on the "train" driven by the False God; it is "headed" to the Lower Realms. Or, you can intentionally transfer to the "train" driven by Creator God; it is headed to the Upper Realms. Your intensions and understanding of the Actual Truth will determine which "train" you choose. Which "train" do you choose to be on – you have the Free Will to choose. You are a Free Spirit, riding an avatar which is on fire; it is your Free Will to WAKE UP to Reality and become Enlightened, and to make the choice.

YOU CAME HERE TO BE A BEARER OF LIGHT - WAKE UP AND LET YOUR ADVENTURE BEGIN – YOUR FUTURE AND OUR WORLD DEPENDS UPON YOU WAKING UP TO ACTUAL REALITY AND TO DEVELOPE YOUR ESCAPE PLAN.

PART 1 - THE BASICS
(WHY ME, WHY NOW)

Article 1

WHO IS GOD?

FELINE   CARIAN   HUMAN   REPTILIAN

CREATION OF THE FOUR UNIVERSAL RACES - Source / **Creator God** created the entire universe and all things within the universe. However, Creator God is a multi-dimensional, non-physical entity and has no way to receive feedback about his creation. After eons of contemplating its own nature, he solved the "problem" by creating a basic number of races to physically experience his creation and provide "feedback," so Creator God could experience his creation through these physically, thinking and experiencing "species." The creation of the various races required the creation of multi-strand DNA sequence to facilitate multiple and different reproducing entities having many of the powers possessed by Creator God. The initial creation of the four basic galactic races (**Carians, Felines, Humans, and Reptilians**) may have occurred in a galaxy other than the Milky Way and may not have occurred on Earth but on various planets in different galaxies. In addition, the process may have resulted through the establishment of the Founding Fathers.

CARIANS – Creator God gave the Carians the Orion constellation for their home. It was more tropical in design and featured an abundance of humid swamps and jungles. It also had more islands than large land masses. The Carians were etheric and, therefore, had to develop physical bodies from the life forms evolving on the planet's surface. Due to the environment they chose the life form to become the bird and over a period of hundreds of thousands of years, they developed bodies of varying colors and sizes. When their physical vehicles had reached a certain level of development, they began genetic crossing (something they had learned from the Felines) with certain reptiles that had evolved in the swamps and warmer regions of the planet. The result of this genetic program was the creation of a new hybrid race known to us as the **Draconians** (Dragons and Reptilians).

FELINES – Creator God gave the Felines a planet in the Lyra Constellation for their home. When the Felines arrived, they were in etheric form, and therefore, went through the stage of evolving a physical body in which to reside on the planet. After many millions of years they evolved the lion and other felines and began incarnating into those forms. As part of the plan, a portion of the original Felines stayed in etheric form to provide guidance to those incarnating. As time passed, and through countless incarnation cycles, the Felines evolved a line of felines that walked upright. Over time, many among them became geneticists (a Feline specialty) and began to develop life forms of various kinds for planets and stars in the universe. It was during this stage in their development the Felines would turn their attention to the bipedal mammal they owed so much to, and begin a program of genetic crossing and upgrading that would give them a soul and, in the process create a new species that would become known as the **Humans**.

HUMANS - The Humans are the youngest of the four primary races in our universe. They were first created by the Felines on a planet in the Lyra constellation. The Humans were given the Gene of Compassion as their inheritance from the Felines. They are heirs to the great work which is showing all other races how to achieve compassion through the opening of the heart and the heart chakra. The Human's creation myth states they will strive to live in harmony with any and all races occupying a planet they wished to colonize – that is, "Service-to-Others."

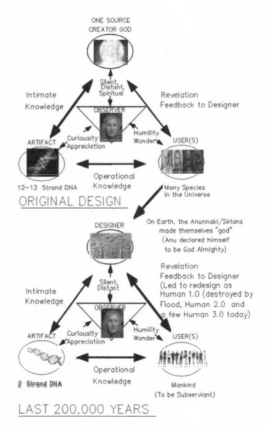

DRACONIANS - The Reptilians are the creation of the Carians, their parent race. They evolved on a planet in the Alpha Draconi star system of the Orion Constellation. The **Anunnaki** were a species within the Lyra star system that traveled to Orion. The Anunnaki were "fallen" Anuhazi crossed with Draconian from Orion and were mutated into the 10-strand reptilian imprint. The Reptilians had two other major sub-races. They are known as the **Winged Serpents** (Snakes) and the **Lizards**. The Reptilians were told they had the right to colonize all planets and star systems in the universe and when they did, they also had the right to conquer or destroy any civilization they found there.

CREATION OF MANKIND - Then, Creator God's creations (namely the Anunnaki and Sirians in our galaxy and our solar system) clamored for the ability to, in turn, create their own creations. Creator God imagined into being a new lower frequency dimension contained within the first. Into this, Creator God's creations thought into existence their own creations and endowed these lower frequency versions of themselves, also with free will, which is how it all began for Mankind. The Anunnaki wanted to be "god" so they could dominate their creation of beings to honor, worship, and, sometimes, be their slaves. Therefore, "all of MANKIND are the children of the lesser god."

TRANSHUMANS - Today, the Mankind ELITE want to be "god" so mankind will worship, honor and be servants to tem. The Earth was created as a galactic library and the humans are the library cards. Each human contains a small piece of universal knowledge. Through the various quantum processes (Quantum Mechanics, Quantum Physics and Quantum Ma-

thematics), the Dark Force is attempting to extract this knowledge in order to further control their fought-for part of the universe and the various species therein. The Elite/Dark Force will use the various Quantum Processes to modify the human DNA by incorporating "Junk" DNA and bio-mechanics to create trans-humans or to create trans-humans through the injection of nanobots. The trans-human creation may reveal the human's vast stored knowledge. The Dark Force will induce the humans to become trans-human by telling them it will provide them with eternal life which they already have without becoming trans-human, but eternal life has been hidden from them. It was this same obtuse "attack" used by the Anunnaki, to lure the Atlanteans to become the power source for the Anunnaki/Sirian creation of Mankind. Be wary of the attempt to create trans-humans.

Article 2

AGE OF AQUARIUS

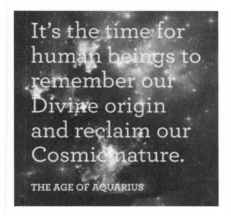

It's the time for human beings to remember our Divine origin and reclaim our Cosmic nature.

THE AGE OF AQUARIUS

AGE OF AQUARIUS

Precession of Earth's Equinox /Mayan Long Count/Photon Belt
Extracted from Chapters 3, 23 and other Chapters of *Conscious Awakening – A Research Compendium* (2019) by Arlene Lanman

Precession of the Earth's Equinox -

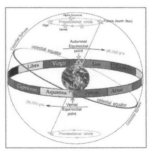

The precession of the equinoxes, also called the Great Year, refers to the precession (slow western movement) of Earth's axis of rotation with respect to inertial space – more commonly referred to as "Earth's Wobble" of approx. 23.5 degrees. A complete precession cycle covers a period of approximately **25,625 years**. During this time the equinox will regresses a full 360°. Processional movement also is the determining factor in the length of an Astrological Age. To summarize, the precession is the sun's apparent position moving slowly west in a constellation when observed on the same day each year; it takes an equinox sun approximately ~2,135 years to move through one of the twelve constellations on its 25,625 cycle completely around the Zodiac. The cycle begins with Leo and has just entered Aquarius. The Earth has just entered Aquarius.

Mayan Long Count Calendar

The Mayan calendar – or more precisely, calendars – is the sophisticated calendar system of the Mesoamerican indigenous peoples. There were three main Mayan calendars, but all were combined into one overarching calendar. Maya states the fine-matter body exists in cycles of world years (25,920 years), world months (**2,160 years**) and world days (144,000 days = 1 baktun). In addition, The Tibetans, the ancient Egyptians, and the Cherokee and Hopi Indians all also chart a cycle of 26,000 years. We also encounter the number 144 in the Vedic Maha Yuga (6 x 24,000 = 144,000 days) and as a holy figure in the Revelation of John. 2,160 years is the length of one Earth Zodiac Astrological Age (12 x 2160 = **25,960 years**). Many believed the End of the World would occur at the end of the Mayan 13th baktun (Long Count cycle of 5,126 years) on December 21, 2012, the Winter Solstice. Dec. 21, 2012 is but the end of the Pisces Age and the beginning of the Age of Aquarius in the Universe Zodiac.

The Photon Belt & Universe Zodiac

The Photon Belt of photon particles was first discovered in the 1960's in vicinity of the Pleiades by satellite instrumentation. A photon particle is the result of a collision between an anti-electron or positron and an electron. These split second collisions cause the charges of the particles to cancel and the resultant mass is converted into energy in the

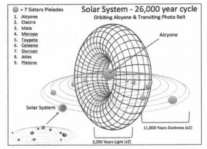

form of photons. **Paul Otto Hesse** studied this system and discovered at absolute right angles to the movement of the star Alcycone. His study indicated the Proton Belt location was coincident with the projected orbit of our solar system.

Our planet Earth orbits the Sun once a year but our sun is spinning as the eighth Star of the Pleiadian spiral, and the Pleiades. The other Pleiadian Stars (Merope, Electra, Targeta, Coele, and Atlas) are themselves spiraling with the Galaxy that spins on its axis. Alcyone is the Central Star of the Pleiadian Constellation and it functions as the Great Central Star within this quadrant of the Milky-Way Galaxy.

Our Sun is linked to the Pleiades by means of a spiral stellar light radiating out from Alcyone. This Star Light is 5th-Dimensional Light moves out through the Stars of the Palisades (Merope, Maya, Electra, Taygeta, Coele and Atlas), through Alcyone, the Central Star. Each

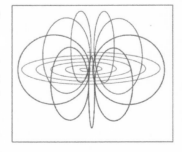

Pleiadian Star, except Alcyone, passes through the Photon Band eternally, traveling through the 7th-Dimensional Light for 2000 years of Earth

time, then traveling through the Galactic "night" for varying lengths of Earth time.

The belt consists of many photon bands emanating from Alcyone – one pair for each Star. Envision a toroid or doughnut-shaped cloud cutting across these orbiting star systems. It is also described as an amoeba-like cloud of particles but most of its frequencies are invisible. This is the photon belt, or photon band of highly vibrant particles. The Stars closer to Alcyone, such as Merope and Maya, are in the Photon Belt more time than they are in the Galactic Night. Our Sun spends the most time in the Galactic Night - our solar system goes through the belt twice each cycle of 12,000 – 13,000 years (that is, every half cycle). The thickness of the photon cloud is such that technically it takes about 2000 years for our solar system to pass through, and therefore about 11,000 years between each encounter with this belt (2 x 10,600 plus 2 x 2,200 = 25,600 years).

Some scientists have stated the SOL system entered the photon belt just after 2010, but it is still difficult to set an exact date due to the random oscillation of the belt. Due to the position for the Earth in relation to the Sun, the Earth did not enter the photon belt until at least 2012.

The photon belt is an immense region of space that is radiating intense electromagnetic radiation throughout the visible spectrum and beyond, into high-frequency invisible light, even including some x-ray spectra. It is part of a magnetic flow of light throughout the galaxy.

Earth Zodiac of the Proton Belt

Envision the zodiac of the Photon Belt; notice that our Sun is about to enter the Proton Belt (lower center left – View is looking down on the Proton Belt – dashed lines depict the 2000 light year width of the Proton Belt – note the Zodiac signs will pass through the Photon Belt, with each zodiac sign taking approx 2000 years to pass through the Photon Belt. The Sun is approaching (on the "cusp) of the 2,160 year Age of Aquarius.

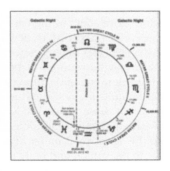

'Great Crossing' (crossing through the Photon Belt) occurs every 12,800 years. The 'Great Purification' naturally occurring at this time is the result of the surge in brilliant photonic light from the Greater Central Sun (Alcyone) will be in the form of high frequency photons. Being in the Photon Belt will play a significant role in the transformation of humankind. Both great illumination of consciousness will occur as well as great resistance to new ideas – some refer to this as Armageddon. This period represents a sorting-out process, gathering matured souls into the Light of the Spirit and affording the weaker, just maturing souls a stabilization period of respite and an opportunity for further spiritual growth.

The individuals who could not or would not acknowledge Divine Love (by Creator God) as the essence of their being during the 10,600 year period of incarnations (Galactic Darkness) are given another chance. In this sense --and in this sense only--it is *The Day of Judgment,* for it is Man who judges himself.

What to Expect Entering and Inside the Proton Belt

The various Star Systems within the Pleiades become very dense while in the Galactic Night and this generates the experience called "Karma" – feelings in our 4-Dimensional bodies on the spiritual level seek expression and that translates as actions down on the 3rd-Dimensional physical worlds. Bodies traveling through the 7th-Dimensional Bands of Light become less dense, more multidimensional. As a result, their acquisition of the Photon Light cleanses their emotional bodies and intensifies vibrations in physical bodies.

The Photon Belt has high vibrational photons which can interact with magnetic fields. Changes in magnetic fields, like what will be encountered as the solar system passes through the photon belt, are sure to have a marked effect on the Earth and life on it.

In the initial stages of the photon-belt encounter only sensitives will detect anything strange but when we enter fully, even the most hardened individuals will receive the full effects. Both great illumination of consciousness will occur and great resistance to new ideas. This is a period of awakening essentially due to the ascension cycle. What proportion of effects is directly due to the belt is difficult to say. Nevertheless this phenomenon of both the photon belt plus stellar activity will reduce the veil stopping us from seeing who we are. It will remove some of the barriers around cells and DNA making them more reactive or responsive to new energies and the DNA will attempt to respond to the changing frequencies, increasing its capacity – even our once 12-strand DNA may be restored. It presents opportunities for change on a planet by adding new energies. It increases the flow of energy in the magnetic grids of Earth, attracting new ideas and energies. People will feel the need to transform but those who consider this physical reality their only expression will dwindle into greater fixations, blocks and negativity. Even the densest person will be accelerated into a higher state of consciousness, causing possible havoc in their mind and body if they are not prepared. The energy will encourage people to come into balance but where resisted will cause further imbalances.

As we creep closer to the Proton Belt, the planet has become subjected to an increase in seismic activity and volcanism. Further, we have seen an alteration of traditional weather patterns permits the formation of extremely severe typhoons, hurricanes and tornadoes.

There is also the added stress placed on the upper atmosphere which could have aided in the formation of ozone holes. The Sun has responded by an increase in solar flare activity and in a general stellar cooling. It must be remembered the null zone is the place where the photon energy in the belt is created. It is a place where all particles of matter and anti-matter are annihilated. Hence, there is a vast pressure on our solar system. This pressure builds up gradually and does not climb in an exponential manner until we pass into the zone. We are now in the position of near entry into the belt (entry will occur sometime before the end of this decade).

To aid us in this shift, the Federation has commissioned two projects.

First the Federation altered the basic polarity of the Sun. This feat will allow the Sun, as it enters the belt, to maintain the integrity of the Sun's planetary system.

Second, the Federation has put into position ships that are designed to lessen the effects of the belt on our atmosphere and to help repair any passive Ozone breaches that may occur in the first few months of entering this belt. The Photon belt consists of three major elements. First, there is the null zone. This zone is where the particles of matter and antimatter collide to form the belt's immense photon streams. This area is also where the electromagnetic fields of this star system will be nullified. Gravitational fields and related photon energy fields will be altered. This alteration will cause all atoms and molecules in this star system to be unusually excited. This process will alter our state of consciousness and force us to look at our universe in new and unique ways.

When the collapse of the planet's electrical and magnetic fields occurs, it will also allow all atoms on Earth to be changed. The atoms in your body will be modified to form a new body--a body that is semi-etheric--and the veil of consciousness around you will be removed. You will no longer be living in the limited 4rd-density reality. You will now have physical and psychic gifts   you were meant to have ever since the time humanoids first left the Lyran constellation to spread their knowledge and guardianship throughout this galaxy. You will have begun the process of "coming home" to the 5th Density (which so call the 5th Dimension).

The next segment is a flux field between the photon stream and the inner edge of the null zone. Here, we will encounter a space/time distortion that has the possibility to hurl our system into another and higher dimension. After we have entered the photon stream proper, we will be able to utilize photon beam energy and inter dimensional space travel of all types imaginable will become possible. It could well be the "Golden Age" the Bible and other religious tracts have spoken about. Biblical and various tribal myths throughout this planet talk of a period in which men were different than they are now and we had a bridge to the stars. Such a time of vast change is upon us. This period of change will last for about 2000 years.

Earth first entered the Photon Belt during the Spring Equinox of 1987 and has been steadily moving into it further – one week more each side of the entry point each year. The boarder of Photonic Light is currently inching across the disc of our Solar System. Earth was first in the Photon Belt for 1-week in March 1987, then for three weeks in 1988. The Photonic Light increases by two weeks each year, with half of the Solar System immersed in Photonic Light by the Summer Solstice of 1998. At the rate of two weeks each year, the Solar System was engulfed in the title wave of Light after the Winter Solstice of 2012. During the next 2000 years, the Solar System will have "traveled through it."

At present researchers believe there are **three types of bodies in the creative universe**.

The first type is purely corporeal with the solid mass structure we are presently used to.

A second type is less corporeal but with an altered mass structure that allows the body to do more unusual things such as easily walking through a solid three dimensional wall. **A third type is a purely ethereal** body with no mass at all (a spiritual being). In our entry into the null zone, our bodies and the matter around us will be altered into the second type described.

We should take on new capabilities such as telepathy and telekinesis. Since we are entering a place where the electromagnetic grid collapses, a second simultaneous event will be the fact electromagnetic equipment will cease to function. In addition, we will also encounter a brief period of darkness (roughly 3 days) that will gradually give way to a period of extreme light. It is a time the Bible and other documents have described as when one will be changed to immortality in the twinkling of an eye. However, there is another potential disaster of extremely fatal proportions for us to ponder.

As the atmosphere is compressed and then rapidly expanded and excited by the photon belt, our atmosphere has the possibility of suddenly exploding if it is exposed to large amounts of nuclear radiation. This radiation is a natural byproduct of the nuclear reactions produced daily by nuclear powered electrical generation plants and nuclear weaponry. This possibility could explain the vast interest extraterrestrial space craft have shown in such power plants and in the vast stockpiles of nuclear weaponry in various parts of this planet. In addition, we must establish emergency plans to either shut down these facilities. A firestorm in the atmosphere could well doom our planet and prevent us from achieving our glorious destiny.

In addition, the change in our magnetic field may cause our electrical systems to fail (electrical lighting systems quit, fueled cars will not start, electric vehicles will cease to operate, etc.). However, when we enter this aspect of our journey, the photon energy will not only give us light; but also the heat and subtle radiation required to run our bodies at maximum efficiency. This effect will also apply to the various plants and animals presently occupy this planet. We may well not need very much sleep nor require hardly any food to exist. It could well be the most remarkable period in our history. Entering the Photon Belt may provide and enhanced opportunity for space travel through using photons as a fuel for photon engines, ion-thrusters, and EM-thrusters. Theorists have proposed extraterrestrials may have used the photon belt as in-flight refuel for their travels to destinations within the proton belt of eons ago. Note EM-thrusters and photon engines are capable of near light speed and beyond, with additional development. These phenomena may be why we see the increase in extraterrestrial vehicles operate in and near the Photon Belt.

A facet of the passing into the null zone will be the cooling of the Sun's atmosphere and the resulting lesser amounts of radiant energy sent to us. This event could signal a temporary winter like effect throughout the globe. This cooling period should last about 3 to 5 weeks and will end when we start to enter the period of complete daylight. This unbelievable period of seemingly eternal light will characterize the formal entry into the main segment of the photon belt.

Past Crossings of the Photon Belt

The transition into super-consciousness, [also called the second *Coming of Christ*], is to occur at the precise moment of suspension of movement between expansion and contraction with the entry into the radiation of the Photon Belt. This energy is also referred to as the Manasic Vibration or Radiation. Astrophysical calculations, based on the sun's speed traveling through space (29 km/s) -- and Earth's own movement -- indicate we will enter the photon belt at a speed of 208,800 km/h. The actual entry of Earth into the Manasic Vibration will occur in the twinkling of an eye.

The energy of the Photon Belt is of etheric and spiritual nature, not physical, but it interacts with and affects the physical. The 10,500 years of darkness between the 2000-year periods of light afford incarnating Man repeatedly in his spiritual evolution. As the majority of humans become forgetful of their Divine source and purpose during these Earthly sojourns, the periods of Light serve a dual purpose. They represent a sorting-out process, gathering matured souls into the Light of the Spirit and affording the weaker, just maturing souls a stabilization period of respite and an opportunity for further spiritual growth.

The individuals who could not or would not acknowledge Divine Love as the essence of their being during the 10,500 year period of incarnations are given another chance. In this sense --and in this sense only-- it is *The Day of Judgment*, for it is Man who judges himself.

The entry of Earth into the Manasic Radiation constitutes the fulfillment of the deepest hopes of the human soul. Much scare has been generated since the time of David, prophesying the coming transition into Light. This may have been justified in order to shake the apathy from Man, inciting him to look within. Today's generations, however, are less in need of pressure induced through fear of coming events than an enlightening approach addressing their intelligence.

The Universe is alive and growing – spreading out and changing constantly. The number of years in any given Great Age, to be exact, must be calculated on the actual movement of the Earth through the Mazzaroth Trail for each particular Age and the constellations through which the Earth travels during that period, before beginning a new journey. However, the past is no prediction of the future. The Earth where we have grown crops for thousands and thousands of years, what is not the same (and why history does not repeat itself) is the SEED. For this cycle though the Photon Belt, it is the Lyran/Pleiadian SEED that makes the difference.

100,000 years ago:
  Pleiadians came and planted seeds of quantum divine DNA into one of 17 kinds of humans existing at that time. Biological beings slowly gained their quantum DNA and spirituality was born.

  The first civilization was Lemuria with 90% quantum DNA, not 30% like we have today. Lemurians were considerably more advanced than Atlantis, in consciousness only, not technically. They could heal with magnetics. They had intuitive information.

  Atlantis was on the rise.

75,000 years ago:
  2nd Density moved to 3rd Density.

50,000 years ago:
  Anannaki, traveling from Mars in a synthetic Merkaba, settle in Atlantis.

35,000 – 40,000 years ago:
  Compared to our ancestors, the modern head shape changed to having a bigger, rounder cerebellum (the area in the back of the brain, responsible for things like motor control and balance, as well as some memory and language), a more bulging, rounded parietal lobe (which helps us orient, plan and pay attention), and smaller, more retracted faces than our predecessors. The brain shape changes track almost perfectly with the development of modern behaviors, like carving tools, planning, developing self-awareness, languages and even the first cave drawings. In other words, the so-called "human revolution" that is sometimes referred to as the "great leap forward."

25,000 years ago:
Atlantis destroyed in 23,200 BC (25,200 years ago).

2nd age of Atlantis 35,000 yrs ago to 25,000 yrs ago). Atlantis was a similar civilization as ours today. The DNA was a combination of Orion, Draco, Sirian, Andromedan and Pleiadians. Orions are passionate; Draco's competitive, aggressive, and cunning. Pleiadians peaceful and loving.

After the fall of Lemuria and the rise of Atlantis, fleets of Alpha Draconian and Orion ships orbited the Earth in 4th density. They put an electromagnetic shield about the planet to prevent enemy ETs from approaching Earth. Also quarantine was put in place by 7th density Pleiadians to prevent Draco's, Orion reptilians, and Anannaki from corrupting neighboring astral and enteric civilizations.

Lemuria sank due to a change in consciousness and Atlantis rose. The people of Lemuria moved (dispersed throughout the Earth) due to the sinking.

The Age of Virgo *ca. 12812 BC to 10,652 BC*:
It was believed by many geologists the Sphinx was constructed in the 4th Dynasty but that theory has been dispelled because the erosion patterns on the Sphinx are not of sand and wind, but clearly of water. So it's much older than earlier thought. What is most interesting is the construction of the Sphinx pre-dates civilization. The Sphinx was finished by the Sirians, just before entering the Photon Belt. Thoth was the engineer, a radiant being of blue-white light, humanoid, who stepped down his vibration to come to descendants of Atlantis in Egypt. The fact that the Sphinx is in the shape of a lion with a human head gives it major astronomical significance. Leo was the pre-dawn constellation in the eastern sky during the spring equinox an hour before dawn where the sun rose. The Sphinx gazes directly east where the constellation of Leo would have rose through precession of the equinoxes in 10,970 BC to 8810BC.

The Great White Brotherhood was formed by ascended human beings from Earth - those who had mastered their physical bodies. "White" means clothed in the white garments of God. (Mathew 22:11, Isaiah 61:10, others).

The following chart shows approximate dates using the 2160 accepted years.

STATUS - THE GREAT AGE - THE RULING 'GOD' - Approximate dates:

Age of LEO - ANU - 10,652 BCE to 8492 BCE
Age of CANCER –GODDESS - 8492 BCE to 6332 BCE
Age of GEMINI - ENLIL & ENKI - 6332 BCE to 4172 BCE
Age of TAURUS-ISHTAR - APHRODITE - ISIS - 4172 BCE to 2012 BCE
Age of ARIES - YHWH or MARDUK - 2012 BCE to 148 BCE

Age of PISCES - JESUS - 148 BCE to 2012 CE
Age of AQUARIUS - MESSIAH - 2012 CE to 4172 CE
Age of CAPRICORN - SURVIVORS - 4172 CE to 6332 CE

The Age of Leo *ca. 10,652 BC to 8492 BC, The Golden Age – inside the Photon Belt.*

Humans were still hunter-gatherers at this time. The Anannaki created Mankind to, first mine the gold that was needed to repair the atmosphere of Nibiru (Anu was King) and, later and even today, to be subservient to the Anannaki God (Anu declared himself to be God Almighty). His off-springs later became "god."

Global warming was a major event at this time causing melting of ice caps and a rise of 300 feet in sea levels. This rise in sea level eroded the Sphinx. This all makes sense when you realize Leo is a "Fire" sign and is ruled by the Sun astrologically marking global warming. It was also during this time that carved stone oil lamps with a continuous burn were invented, which represents light and heat.

The Age of Cancer, *ca. 8492 BC to 6332BC - The Age of the Great Mother – outside the Photon Belt for the next 10,000 years, beginning with Cancer.*

The Great Food (10,000 years ago) – Earth exiting the Photon Belt was the turning point in our history,

The feminine was revered at this time as the creator of all life...birthing, nurturing and protecting. This is the age of the goddess and is ruled by the Moon. Cancer is a water sign and people started to realize the connection between the tides and the moon. Massive loss of coastal areas was still in effect on Earth from the elevated sea levels.

Civilization and the domestication of farm animals like pigs, goats and bees began at this time. Various food plants were also domesticated starting the agricultural era. Cancer is associated with the home. People started to settle into permanent dwellings.

The transition seems to have been everywhere with the development of civilization in Sub-Sahara Africa between 9000-7000 BC. These areas went from being largely nomadic hunters and gatherers to a settled domesticated lifestyle.

There's evidence of the widespread use of boats representing Cancer's water sign. An increase in the making of pottery signifies the protective vessel, which is one of Cancer's archetypes.

The Age of Gemini, 6332 BCE to 4172 BCE: Gemini, ruled by Mercury, is a mental communicative sign of the twins. Symbolizing the duos, we have Adam and Eve, the two opposing trees in the Garden of Eden, the twin brothers, Enki and Enlil, Jacob and Esau, and Cain and Abel. The twin brothers, Enlil and Enki (Anunnaki), brought to Earth, many mental attributes, such as the various sciences, mathematics, languages and communication skills, which are all Gemini patterns.

The Age of Taurus, 4172 BCE to 2012 BCE: Taurus, a feminine sign, is ruled by Venus – the goddess of love and beauty, and Ishtar was the goddess of this Great Age. Taurus is an earthy sign that governs the land and growing things in the soil. Taurus, the sign of builders saw the construction of the pyramids; the Great Pyramid was built as an ascension chamber and controller of Earth's grid system. Noah the Ark builder, represented this Great Age. The venerated animal was the bull – linked to the Egyptian god, Ptah. The red heifer that produced the bull once thought to represent the goddess Isis. All types of bovine were sacred during this Age - bulls, heifers, red cows, and calves. The wearing of horns in ancient Egypt implied great power as ruler and prince.

The Age of Aries, 2012 BCE to 148 BCE: Aries, ruled by Mars, is the fire sign of combat, warriors, leaders [good and bad], wars, Babylon, Moses, Marduk (Anunnaki), YHWH, and Alexander the Great. The [sacrificial] animal, as well as the animal representing the sign of Aries, was/is the Ram and sheep; and because Aries is a fire sign we have the burning bush and fiery chariots. The killing of sacrificial animals and the bloody sentiments of these sacrifices involved knifes, which are prominent representations of Aries and Mars. The planet Mars astrologically represents weapons of all kinds, as well as killing, of humans as well as animals.

The Age of Pisces, 148 BCE to 2012 CE: Pisces, ruled by Neptune, is the nebulous water sign that reflects both the deceiver and the deceived. The pattern for the entire Age of Pisces reflects deception and mystery, as well as servitude. The animal representing Pisces is a fish or two fishes on a string swimming in opposite directions. The 'raising' of Jesus Christ as the venerated god, who ruled the Age of Pisces with the opposing sign Virgo representing the virgin mother of Jesus, formed an entire religion, created around these astrological patterns.

The sign of Pisces also represents inspiration, artistic endeavors, baptisms by water, and the suffering of martyrs. Pisces rules the 12th house of the Zodiac, which has a 'dark' side of suffering and silent pain – and the Dark Ages were very typical of this pattern, right up to, and including the Civil War. Rome and Christianity represents the 'country' and movement of the Great Age of Pisces, which ends with the shocking revelations of truth and light from the 'god' of the Age of Aquarius, exposing the deception of this Great Age.

The Age of Aquarius, 2012 CE to 4172 CE – inside the Proton Belt: Aquarius, ruled by Uranus, begins with freedom fighters and truth seekers. Exiting is the old bondage of Piscean deception, replaced with the desire for harmony, truth, and humanitarian causes, marching strongly through the gates of the Great Age of Aquarius. This air sign represents a revolutionary period that ushers in a society of reformers who will see an absolute reunification of all things, from a Messiah-type influence, whose pattern is reflected in the planet Pluto as reformer and promised reunification. However, a warning should be sounded loud and clear as all is not as it seems. There is great deceivement that also takes place with misplaced confidence.

'TRUTH and FREEDOM' will eventually reign paramount during this Great Age. The symbol for Aquarius is the 'water bearer pouring out water [truth as enlightenment] from the Heavens [air sign of Aquarius]. The sign of Aquarius represents astrology, astronomy, outer space, space travel, science and extraterrestrials. The Great Age of Aquarius may very well bring in the 'Kings of the East', which are Astrologers. The Great Spirit will then 'pour' wisdom down from on high, and the truth will be written upon every heart.

Found in this Great Age, is the unification of all peoples and countries around the globe and an end to the traditions that have held humankind in bondage for so long. Religions will be deemed a detriment to society, and harmful to soul Ascension. The knowledge of the Age will be unlike any Earthly traditional doctrine and dogma, for the wisdom forthcoming will emanate from the highest heavenly air sign of them all, Aquarius.

Summary
This 'Great Crossing' thus occurs every 13,000 years. The 'Great Purification' naturally occurring at this time is the result of the surge in brilliant photonic light from the Greater Central Sun (Alcyone) will be in the form of high frequency photons. Being in the Photon Belt will play a significant role in the transformation of humankind. Both great illumination of consciousness will occur as well as great resistance to new ideas – some refer to this as Armageddon. This electromagnetic energy will facilitate a shift in consciousness and planetary alignment. About 17-20 years" in," the "spin" of the Earth (already slowing) may come to a stop (the 3-days of darkness mentioned in the Bible book of Revelations), and begin rotation in the opposite direction, along with a magnetic reversal that will "collapse" all electrical systems. When the collapse of the planet's electrical and magnetic fields occurs, it will also allow all atoms on Earth to be changed. The atoms in your body will be modified to form a new body -- a body that is semi-etheric--and the veil of consciousness around you will be removed. You will no longer be living in the limited 4rd-dimensional reality. You will now have physical and psychic gifts you were meant to have ever since the time humanoids first left the Lyran constellation to spread knowledge and guardianship throughout this galaxy. You will have begun the process of "coming home" to the 5th dimension. However, this will also be a time great resistance to new ideas.

Article 3

WHY WE ARE HERE

WHAT WAS I THINKING ON THE SOUL PLANE

VARIOUS PERSPECTIVES as to why I am here:

The atheistic or naturalistic explanation of the world is there is no higher reason we're here. The universe and everything in it—us included—happened purely by accident.

The theistic worldview suggests God, gods, or some supreme being is responsible for the world and our lives. In this view, most advocates would suggest our purpose is to please or in some way live up to the standards of our creator.

Two thirds of Earth's population continues to believe in reincarnation, however screwed up they make it. Hinduism allows for cross-species incarnation, which means "shape up or return as a bug," and in India, it is tied into the caste system as a means of controlling the population, as in: "shape up or come back as an untouchable." Neither approach exudes unconditional love.

And there are many perspectives between that of the atheist and that of the theist. For Example:

Aristotle, in the first line of his treatise *Nicomachean Ethics*, argued everything is to be done with a goal, and the goal is to do well. In other words, our highest and best use is to be an agent of good works in everything we do.

Cynics, representing another school of philosophic thought, propose the reason we're here is to live a life of virtue. This usually entails overcoming the ubiquitous temptations of power, wealth, fame, and possess.

SOUL PLANE – Eons ago, our "higher soul" fashioned the soul plane level of our vast being. For eons (or what would be millions of Earth years if time existed there), we souls on the soul plane have worked, played, grown and explored the nature of creation.

EARTH LIFE PREPARATION – Assume, as a soul busy with your soul plane research on the various types of polarity, say it is love, you've taken theory to its limit, but you just don't "get it." You-the-soul has realized you need an Earth life in order to fully understand love in "reality" as opposed to love "in theory." When a soul decides to incarnate, it begins a planning process involving countless spirit guides and counselors, and the souls of everyone who will be involved in Souls Earth life, such as parents, siblings, mates, children and significant co-workers. These soul siblings, etc. all have their say in the goals and challenges the incarnation will take on, because they know the gaps in their soul's collective experience and understanding that must be closed. You also use a time-travel "technology" to preview how the life you're planning will turn out. All the people who will be in your new life are "supporting actors" drawn from your soul's soul group, a band of maybe a thousand or so other souls who hang together for eternity. After 40 or 50 lifetimes, you all know each other very well and count on them to incarnate with you and put on a good performance. Of course, you have your smaller group favorites, or family, and turn to them for the intense interactions, such as becoming your mate or even murdering you if your soul needs the experience. With the help of your spirit guides and soul plane colleagues, you identify your goals, such as to study the balance between sexual love and platonic love, or how to create a work of art, etc. Then, what you need to decide are:

Situation – The situation that will best support you in achieving your goals, which includes choosing the most appropriate physical body.
Goal – Goal is the primary motivation in an incarnation, and soul sets up situations to facilitate goal achievement.
Mode – The next quality of personality the soul chooses is Mode or the primary form of expression and the approach taken to achieve the Goal.
Attitude – Attitude determines how we see the world and through this, we then use our Mode to go about achieving our Goal.
Challenges - Finally, souls take on one or more Challenges as a stumbling block designed to neutralize our attempts to achieve the Goal. Without obstacles, life would be a breeze; we would meet no opposition and achieve little growth, so we build in Challenges to push us to a higher level.

WHEN A SOUL INCARNATES, it "borrows" skills, understanding, wisdom and memories gleaned during the lifetimes of whichever of its incarnated fragments are needed. This "borrowing" gives it a jump-start on personality-building. But the new soul fragment is still a sovereign first-timer, never before having incarnated.

NOT FOR THE FAINT-HEARTED SOUL – Earth trips are not for faint-hearted souls because Earth life has a terrible reputation elsewhere in Creation for being the toughest thing any soul can take on. That's why only about ten percent of souls even have the courage to try. The other 90% stay warm and safe, living life on the soul plane.

A PERIL OF INCARNATION – GETTING THE CHANCE AT A LIFETIME ON EARTH, AT THIS TIME OF CHANGE is a special opportunity for the Soul to fast track its own progression. The dysfunctional nature and confusion within this earthly illusion offers many opportunities for expression of love, light and wisdom. However, it is potentially dangerous for a Mature or Old Soul to incarnate within this third density planet in case it does not at least partially remember its reason for incarnating here in the first place. If the Soul should become enthralled in materialism, the constant acquisition of goods to satisfy the Self at the detriment of spirituality, or negatively polarized behaviors such as greed, acquisition of power and control - then the Soul would then be required to repeat the cycle (a new lifetime) or further cycles until they have regained their original state of positive progression.

IN ADVERSE TIMES, never believe you are the victim but ask what am I to learn from this challenge. When I was an Engineer with Phillips Petroleum, during the point where Brent Crude Oil reached its lowest point (below $14 per barrel in the 1980's) and rumors of reductions in force were rampant, I developed the Company advertising slogan of "Meeting the Challenge of Changer."

DO THE RESEARCH AND DETERMINE YOUR OWN TRUTH. I AM BUT A LIGHTWORKER MESSENGER DELIUVERING A WAKE-UP CALL.

Article 4

WHY WE, AS EXTRADIMENSIONAL BEINGS & BEARERS OF LIGHT ARE HERE – YOUR MISION

LIFE OF THE LIGHTWORKER IS TO BE THE TIGER

We are not from here but were sent here as Star Travelers, Starseeds, Light Workers, Galactic Warriors, Indigos, Walk-Ins, Wanders, Old Souls, Empaths/Healers and other Star Beings to carry out a Mission.

We have chosen to be sent here, NOT as part of the Dark Side/Anunnaki "recycle program."

We were allowed to "pass-through" the Federation blockade (around Earth/Moon and an additional "picket line" near Jupiter). The blockage is to insure the Dark Force is contained and not allowed to escape and affect other parts of the Universe.

Mission is to WAKE UP, to use our intuition, to conduct research, separate away from Self, and see Reality for what it is – an illusion created by your ego in concert with all other egos. You are Fire riding on an avatar and you are a free spirit, untethered from any and all Cabals.

Primary Purpose: As a higher dimension star being, we are here to help raise the frequency of the Earth and, thereby, raise the frequency (Consciousness) of the people of Earth.

Raising the frequency will result in an AWAKENING, where the normal person will become aware of the Dark Side's manipulation to control the people and the deception they have created (i.e., an alternate "Reality").

An AWAKENING will result in the adoption of "service to others" (a Federation/ Bearers of Light concept) vs. the Dark Side's "service to self."

Lightworkers (at least nine types) intuitively know what others are thinking, feeling, or need in order to heal. You know you are here for a higher purpose, one directly related to awakening and transforming your own life and the lives of others by helping to raise the collective consciousness. "Love heals all" is your guiding phrase.

Galactic Warriors are here to shine a light on the Dark Force in the hope mankind will recognize they are being controlled (politically, financially, what to believe, way to act and the many other ways serve the Dark Force). The Warrior is here to deliver the blatant truth.

Empaths/ Healers are able to hold the vibration of unconditional love (the highest vibrational frequency one can hold) in their heart center and use this energy to transform lower energy levels in another to a higher energy level, thereby removing the blockade of pain that is keeping them from becoming Fully Awake. Empaths have a highly advanced nervous systems that can perceive the energies of others, animals, plants or even inanimate objects. Empaths feel in order to heal.

Spiritual Healers/Teachers: Those that can help others perceive" Reality" and grow spiritually in order to "raise" their vibration.

Old Souls are here, in this demanding and polarized world, to bring stability, to remind others they are spiritual and not worldly, even with the chaos, it is the moment that counts. They bring the time-honored and clever sense they have been here before and they gained from the experience. Old Souls are simply sages who have an extraordinary inner sophistication of peace.

Observers are sent here by the Galactic Federation to advise if:

People have lost their Free-Will by the false illusion portrayed by the Dark Side, in their quest to control the Earth and, if so, this remnant of the Dark Side should be "taken out," even if the Federation's primary directive is to never interfere with Free Will and each planet should use their Free-Will to decide governance, etc,

OR

The Federation's efforts to increase the frequency of the Earth is working, to the extent desired, and an invasion to "wipe-out" the Dark Side/Anunnaki should be delayed. However, the Federation is now ready to negotiate, with the Dark Side/Anunnaki knowing if the Federation invades, the Dark Force's choice will be to leave the planet (most likely, to a penal colony) or die.

Each extra-dimensional being, which was sent here, has a role to play. The changes are now coming quickly and each needs to WAKE UP and seize their MISSION.

Article 5

WHY ENLIGHTENMENT IS HARD TO ACHIEVE

MAY TAKE MORE THAN ONE LIFETIME

I have always known I was from the stars and we were all born pure, not born of sin. I was born into this world but I am not of this world. Over time, I began to question why there was so much chaos and, through no fault of our own, we live in a sinful world which is inadvertently taught, through observation, the world employs falsehoods, deception, and illusions. As a future and now current Engineer (Right Brain logical/data functions) and Architect (Left Brain creative), I began searching for the Truth. I began reading/studying History, Theology, Philosophy, Environmental Psychology, Sociology, Thermodynamics, Chemistry (1 and 2), mathematics (Algebra, Geometry – Plain and Solid, Trigonometry, Statistics and Multivariable Calculus through to Advanced Mathematics for Engineers), including a course in Sub–light speed Celestial Navigation – navigating in multiple plains of orientation at multiple velocities, using the stars for orientation, and Engineering Physics. The hard sciences were, of course, balanced by the "feeing" side of Architectural Design: The relationships between lines, shapes and masses; The relationship between space uses; The human relationship to the space they are in; The relationship of light into physical spaces; and simplify, simplify, simplify.

All of this was an attempt to discover the Truth. I researched the Alternate History of the Universe and Earth, and how we might have been colonized (several times). Then I read that the astronauts said there were at least 58 species who had visited Earth – I set out to find out who or what they were. I started to document my findings, which led to writing a book, *Conscious Awakening – A research Compendium*. What I learned, through my studies, was that seeking the truth, through understand, knowledge and, eventually, a sort of wisdom (in a few areas of study), led to knowing the TRUTH – My

Truth and not the "truth" others said, including organized religions, politicians and the media – all which led to the unintended consequence of Enlightenment which, in turn, lead to an AWAKENING.

What is ENLIGHTENMENT? Most of mankind resides in "lower consciousness," where they strike back when hit, blame others, quell any stray questions that lack immediate relevance, fail to freely-associate and stick closely to a flattering images of who they are and where they are headed.

When we rise from lower to higher consciousness, we find it much harder to think of our fellow human beings as enemies. Rather than criticize and attack, we are free to imagine their behavior is driven by pressures derived from their own more primitive minds, The more time we spend in our higher consciousness, the more we develop the ability to explain others' actions by their distress, rather than simply in terms of how it affects us. We perceive the appropriate response to humanity is not fear, cynicism or aggression, but always — when we can manage it — love.

When our consciousness reaches the proper altitude, the world reveals itself as quite different: a place of suffering and misguided effort, full of people striving to be heard and lashing out against others, but also a place of tenderness and longing, beauty and touching vulnerability. The fitting response is universal sympathy and kindness. When we are in higher consciousness, we find a sharp distinction drawn between the neocortex, the seat of imagination, rational thinking, empathy and impartial judgment, and the reptilian mind (lower consciousness).

What is AWAKENING? In awakening, one recognizes cause and effect and we begin to feel one's actions from the past have caused many kinds of suffering. Such behavior starts to seem abhorrent. A deep resolution turns the mind around from those long, confused patterns of afflictive behavior, lifting it up like the bud of a lotus breaching muddy water to touch air and sunshine. A sense of openness and spaciousness arises, along with the determination to behave differently. This shift could be called "a moral awakening," but it also has the aspect of the mind clearing, unbinding, and becoming more open and stable. People do experience this literally as clarity or light, coming out of darkness, or entering into spaciousness. Things that were dark, disassociated, and disconnected before become connected, and we can then see more clearly what was shrouded in darkness. Fear and disempowerment are alleviated and, we no longer feel we are at the mercy of the world and other people or other circumstances; one gains a foothold on the path. Mostly we aren't working toward enlightenment in Zen; we're assuming it as a basis and trying to accept that reality. Also a sense of an ever-unfolding awakening to one's nature and of the activity of wisdom unfolding as compassion.

Buddha, "Are you a god?" The Buddha said, "No." Then he asked, "Are you a spirit?" Again the Buddha said, "No". The young man was very puzzled and he asked, "Who are you, then?" And the Buddha simply answered, "I am awake."

Enlightenment is a great gift, a wholesome karmic fruition, and the energy behind aspiration, the paramita (Buddhist term for "perfection") of effort or diligence, can be actualized in practice. It is important to welcome the energy while not corralling enlightenment into a narrow definition.

Bottomline: "Seek the Truth and the Truth shall set you free" and maybe, just maybe, the TRUTH will lead to ENLIGHTENMENT and AWAKENING.

Story of the photo illustration (at the beginning of this Article): Rise above the maze of "reality"; climb up the ladder – takes conscious effort and thought (knowledge through to wisdom of knowing the TRUTH); reach the balloon of ENLIGHTENMENT and get aboard, knowing ENLIGHTENMENT is not the goal; then, release the balloon (release all that you think you cherish and hold true) – it is only at this point you are "I AM, "a free spirit to chart your own course through the universe and be, truly, in SERVICE-to-OTHERS, Believing Love, showing Love for all, and practicing LOVE with an open heart will not, by itself, get you there. The way is not for the faint of heart, since you will surrender all.

Article 6

SERVICE-to-SELF vs. SERVICE- to-OTHERS
THE MEANING OF LIFE

Service-to-Self vs. Service-to-Others – Yours to Choose

I have heard, especially from the Indigos, New Souls and, even a few other Lightworkers state, "I didn't ask to come here," "I didn't ask to be born," "I don't want to be here," "I don't have a reason to be here," "I don't have to do anything you say, "I don't fit in here," and many other "I don'ts." To this end they develop the statements "I need... (e.g., I need food, I need water, I need fresh air to breath, and I need you to provide me with....).

Thousands upon thousands of years ago, in the time of the "ancient alien" there were at least 22 difference races involved in this "Grand Experiment" here on Earth. They were manipulating humanity genetically, spiritually and socially. All 22 of these races claim to have created us and manipulated us and have some sort of claim to us, especially the Anannaki. Many were involved in the Lyran/Orion Wars (starting 22-million years ago) to determine dominance of the Universe. These ancient alien's were told to back off humanity and see what develops. Now "they" are back. One of the main messages from the Blue Arians, who were told to leave Earth (and then spent a period of time with the Hopi), is we going to continue humanity in the Service-to-Self mode more than Service to others. The Blue Arians / Sphere Alliance appears to be supportive of Service-to-Others but, in general, have a "hands-off" policy. The Galactic Federation of Light, on the other hand, are a bit more aggressive by increasing the frequency of the Earth will, in turn, create an Awakening within mankind who will recognize the domination, for eons, by the Service-to-Self Dark Force. Their more aggressive stance is due to having been at war with the Empirical (Draco/Reptilian) Alliance for the last 22-million years and believe they have the Draco's (Service-to-Self and winner takes all) isolated to Earth and a few other "pockets of resistance" elsewhere in the Universe. Yet, the Galactic Federation (Service–to-Others) highly respects free-will and believes mankind needs to decide for themselves. Thus, it is up to the Galactic Federation Lightworkers to convince mankind they must save themselves through Service-to-Others. Of course, the Draconian Alliance (Service-to-Self) sees nothing wrong with the way it has been for eons.

Why Service-to-Self will always fail – Service-to-Self is based on "I Need." Basically, it is not "I Need," since none asked to being born, etc. You "need nothing" but want everything given to you, even if you have to take it from me. Service-to-Self sees the path as separate from others, where body and mind worship fundamental evolution, based on control, repression, hierarchy, power and competition. It is authoritarian and militaristic at its heart. Key Words to Service-to-Self is, me, mine, taking, 1%, prison, crime, murder, selfish, glutton, abuse, rule over, control, dumb down, greed, pornography, pride, prejudice racial, stingy, sin, corruption, lies, etc. The "Need" is unsalable but the "need is high" and the need for more workers to meet the need is encouraged, yet it leads to the point the workers have too many needs that then creates greed to obtain more workers, even if it means taking them from other "Service-to-Self" Elites. Wars may ensure to limit the number of workers or to deny others of those workers. This need for workers may cause the workers to rebel due to the ever increasing demands made of them (e.g., the French Revolution, the American Revolution, the Dissidence in Korea, etc.). In the end, "Serve-to-Self" is self-consuming and failure occurs.

Service–to-Others may also say "I didn't ask to come here," "I didn't ask to be born," and "I don't want to be here." However, they then say, "I am here because someone needs me to be here." Read below of this great need. Key Words to Service-to-Others is, humanitarian, giving, revelation, reveal truth, full disclosure, golden rule, we are all one, free will, selfless, kind, praiseworthy, love, generous, whole, service, giving, ours, sharing, revealing and defeating Darkness, to name only a few.

In like terms, the Creator, who created everything and seems to need nothing, needs us; if the Creator did not need us, there would be no need to create the Universe. The Creator sent to us a list of Needs (Mt Sinai) to be accomplished in order for mankind to enter into the Universe's Consciousness. We interpreted these Needs to be the Requirements each needs attain to receive God's acceptance – they are not, we are already accepted by the Creator – the Creator loves all of Creation. They are the Creator's Needs – the Creator's List of Needs for us to accomplish.

For the Lightworker, Galactic Warrior, Indigo Child, Galactic Traveler, Old Soul, even the Galactic Visitor, Now is a period of transition, a turning point for humanity. Gaia is reacting to the pain humanity has caused and is reacting through earthquakes, fire, climate change; there is threat from those beyond who would seek to use this world for their own purposes - They are not here to destroy you but to use you; we see a fractured humanity—contentious with itself, filled with revenge and anger and the need or desire to conquer others; we are at a point where people are turning against their own institutions and leaders; we are at a point filled with difficulty and turbulence. You have chosen to be here or were sent here to bring about change. Its opportunities and demands will be tremendous. Its risk of failure will be substantial. It is not a time for the faint of heart or for the weak minded. It is not a time for the ambivalent or the self-indulgent. It is a time for great strength and dedication. Knowledge within you will give you this strength and determination as you become a student of Knowledge, as you advance in The Way of Knowledge and as you take the steps to Knowledge. This is a great calling out of self-obsession; a great calling out of trying to fulfill yourself in a world where fulfillment cannot really be obtained; a calling out of the confusion and your self-denial; a calling out of human conflict, human will and human domination. You may complain. You may be angry with the Universe. You may blame some other nation, or your government, or your parents. But you were sent into the world to be here at this time. It has your name on it. It is what you are really here to do and to respond to. You have to serve people. You have to accept yourself. All the things that really matter you will have to do, not because it is the easy thing to do or the thing that makes you happy, but because it is the thing that is required. It is your destiny to be here because you are needed for something great for humanity.

WE ARE THE ONES WE HAVE BEEN WAITING FOR.

Article 7

ALTERNATE TIMELINES
AND UNIVERSES

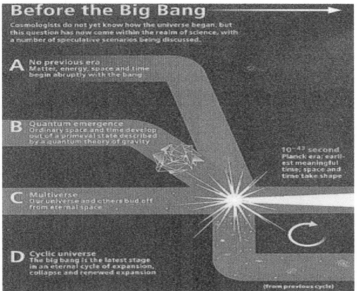

Before the "Big Bank" there could have been a Quantum Universe, Multiverse, Cycle Universe, or no Previous Era

I know I'm not alone in wondering about alternate timelines and universes;
scientists have been curious about the potential for alternate realities for decades as well. Over the years, multiple alternate universe theories have been
laid out by scientists, some of which have evidence to back it up.

STRING THEORY

In this theory, we live in a nine-
dimensional multiverse — with
only three dimensions of those
being visible to us. Since we only
exist in three dimensions, our
universe would appear flat as a
sheet of paper. Moreover, the
way other dimensions, or mem-
branes, would expand along the

> String theory envisions a
> multiverse in which our
> universe is one slice of
> bread in a big cosmic loaf.
> The other slices would be
> displaced from ours in some
> extra dimension of space.
> Brian Greene

lines of time and possible situations. Since every alternate universe would
have a slight change, and since every single universe is possible under this
theory, the alternative versions of our world could be nearly identical — or
totally different. In some universes, you also never existed. So, String Theory
suggests alternate universes are layered right on top of, and below, our
own. Some who believe this particular alternate universe theory believe if

we were to explore far enough in our own universe, we'd end up meeting the alternate versions of ourselves.

MANY WORLDS INTERPRETATION

The many-worlds interpretation is actually an interpretation of quantum mechanics supports multiple alternate universe theories. This theory suggests every possible change in reality is actually real — however, all the different possibilities exist in a bunch of different worlds. The best way to think about the many-worlds interpretation is that the multiverse is like a tree, with every possible quantum outcome acting as a different branch. In this theory, there are an infinite number of "branch off" worlds, and an infinite amount of
branches growing off each main branch. This interpretation helps solve the EPR paradox, and also explains how Schrodinger's Cat could potentially be solved. So, mathematically and quantum-wise, it could be one of the most likely theories to explain alternate worlds. So, if you arrived at school on time in one universe, the many-worlds interpretation suggests there is another version of you out there who would show up to school late. There are as many worlds as there are possibilities in this one, and there are infinite possibilities. In the many-worlds interpretation, every choice or happenstance thing that happens will influence the creation of new universes. However, all the universes that are created stop interacting with the universe they initially branched from.

MANY INTERACTING WORLDS

The idea of the many-worlds interpretation makes a lot of sense, especially on a quantum physics level. One of the newer alternate universe theories suggests t the many-worlds interpretation is correct — with one small change. In the Many Interacting Worlds theory, scientists
believe   alternate universes can and do interact from time to time, especially on a quantum level. Sometimes, this can cause new universes to branch out. Other times, it may cause quantum particles to interact with each other differently.

Larger scale interactions could be possible under this theory, which means it could be theoretically possible to accidentally find yourself in another dimension at random. So, maybe all those *Star Trek* episodes were onto something, after all.

BLACK HOLE UNIVERSE THEORY

Scientists have basically confirmed the Big Bang Theory, and have gained a lot of evidence towards the idea the universe is continuously expanding. But, what scientists haven't fully been able to prove is what existed before the big bang. Recently, one of the ideas being discussed is the possibility our universe actually began as the interior of a black hole. In a  black hole, all the laws of physics tend to warp and form a singularity. Since the Big Bang happened from a point of singularity, the idea that our universe was derived from the black hole of another universe withstands scientific scrutiny. No one knows what's on the other side of a black hole, so perhaps this theory explains what's really going on. Who knows? Perhaps a white hole was where the universe as we know it all began.

THE MANDELA EFFECT

Unlike the rest of these alternate universe theories, the Mandela Effect isn't actually supported by science. In fact, scientists didn't even make this theory at all. This alternate universe theory was spawned by an internet phenomenon showed many people remembering alternate versions of history as fact. The theory behind this is that universes involving our worlds are starting to collapse together for one reason or another. There's no theory that would really explain what would cause two alternate universes near each other  to meld together that way — which is what makes the Mandela Effect so interesting. The effect the alleged universe collapse is people from other alleged universes remember the past differently from the ones who were originally from this "home universe."

AN ATTEMPT TO VISUALIZE ALTERNATE TIMELINES (taking the above into account) - So, there are the theories. I am a visualizer and I believe I can visualize a unified theory that combines these other theories together, plus a bit more. VISUALIZE, if you will, a tree in silhouette. Make a conifer tree that has a cone shape. Visualizes the various branches having a common origin at the tree trunk – let's call the central trunk the "Unified Timeline." Now, visualize an individual branch and let's refer it as an "Alternate Timeline." The branch extends down its own timeline and along the way twigs develop; let's refer to these as alternate timelines within the same Timeline. And, lastly, there are needles; lets refer to

them as yet another variation within a given timeline.

If you now look at a perpendicular plane through the trunk, you will see (view looking down) several branches (several universes, all originating from the "trunk. If one were assign a positive or negative degree (direction) and length of each branch "timeline," one could add all the lengths and positive or negative direction" values and you would derive a SUM NET ZERO, which is the center of the trunk. One could then take multiple perpendicular sections up and down the trunk (the Sum Net Zero point) and show the height of the entire tree trunk along the NET SUM ZERO line. Some refer to this process of adding all the branches/twigs/needles as a 'condensing" process.

In addition, one will note the trunk thickens as the tree grows. This is representative of how future events affect past events. One might also see the effect outside influences (i.e., the wind of change) the shape of the tree trunk "Timeline."

ASTROPHYSICAL PLASMA

As our Alternate UN-IVERSE/ TIMELINES "tree" grows, the root system extends in mass. The roots are a source of nourishment. In more recent times, it has been observed there is AS-TROPHYSICAL PLASMA throughout the universe, consisting of protons, electron and their various quarks, neutrinos, axons, super-symmetrical particles, dark matter; this plasma could be visualized as a "web" of energy. This "web" of undulating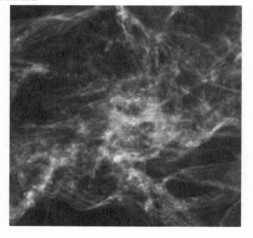
energy may connect all things. The plasma is very hot but as it condenses, stars are formed. Visualize the PLASMA WEB as the roots of our Timelines "tree." If you can make this visualization, then it is the universe "web" that is our Source.

THE UNIVERSE FROM WHICH WE CAME and it is the UNIVERSE KNOWLEDGE that we seek. It could be the spirit of the species within the universe are part of the multidimensional plasma "web" from where our planets and multiple other planets were colonized.

A FOREST of MULTIPLE GALAXIES/UNIVERSES

I have presented the Visualization of a singular TIMELINE connected by a unified Timeline, as a "tree" with multiple alternate timelines. Now, consider the entire Galaxy as a forest of "tree" timelines, all connected together by the ASTROPHYSICAL PLASMA or "root" system, where the ASTROPHYSICAL PLASMA is "universal intelligence" that connects all things together. Consider it is possible the Astrophysical Plasma connects not only our Galaxy but the many other Galaxies and Nebulas of our entire universe together. These other universes/nebula can be visualized as a "forest" of individual universes. Can you visualize that our universe is but one "tree" in a super forest of trees, all connected by a common "root" system. A slimily, would be a cluster of Aspen trees all with their common root system.

BOTTOMLINE: FROM OUR PAST COMES OUR FUTURE AND THE UNIVERSE IS OUR SOURCE, where others throughout the universe are all connected together. The Past, Current and Future are all tied together and each affects the other. Sometimes this is referred to as the "BUTTERFLY EFFECT" – YOU CAN MAKE A DIFFERENCE!

PART 2 - PREPARING FOR THE JOURNEY OF YOUR LIFE
(THE MEANING OF LIFE)

Article 8

EGO vs. ESSENCE
(Ego is You Own Worst Enemy)

There is no such thing as an external enemy, no matter what that voice in your head is telling you. All perception of an enemy is a projection of the ego as an enemy.

whisper

In Latin "ego" is "I". The biggest reason why ego is your enemy is that it keeps you out of touch with reality. Your ego is what prevents you from hearing critical but necessary feedback from others. Ego makes you over-estimate your own abilities and worth, and under-estimate the effort and skill required to achieve your goals.

EGO vs. ESSENCE – Essence never judges, justifies or makes excuses. Essence will never try to talk you into or out of something.

Essence will never express negativity. Any negative thoughts or emotions belong to Ego.

Thoughts beginning with "I" are ego based. "I want", "I need", "I feel", all of these expressions indicate Ego is behind that thought. Even such a thought as, "I want to help" is ego based. Ego is looking for the satisfaction of saying, "look what I did, aren't I great!" When your help is warranted and needed it will arise naturally and spontaneously through Essence and it will fill you with a sense of peace that ego is unable to give.

Ego has not patience. It wants it and it wants it NOW! If you really listen from an outside perspective often time Ego sounds like a five year old child throwing a tantrum.

Ego hates the unknown; it hates change. Whereas Essence embraces all experience.

The voice of Essence knows the voice of Ego reasons. If you're trying to reason, justify and make excuses, it is Ego talking. Ego is driven by selfishness, a perspective with one view. Essence sees the bigger picture. It is never judgmental and it is never negotiates. If you find yourself reasoning over something, it is Ego talking. As is said, "Essence knows things." It never "decides" something. It shows up as a thought with decisiveness and without question. Any nagging or cajoling; any should or shouldn't come from the Ego. Essence would never use these words and its voice never ends with a question mark.

Essence receives openly and graciously. Ego questions and is never grateful or satisfied.

There is spontaneity to Essence. Thoughts arrive seemingly out of nowhere, out of the blue and usually it has nothing to do with what you're focusing on at the moment. It happens when the Ego is quiet and the mind is occupied with the present moment. It always comes across as a statement and it comes across as "knowing". Thoughts that come from Essence have a peaceful underlying feeling to them, no matter what the circumstance. You can also connect to Essence through meditation or when you're completely absorbed in something.

REASONS EGO IS BAD

1) **You create unnecessary barriers** – To those around you and your peers.
2) **You become competitive** – In a bad way – You no longer think about the intended outcome, you're out to prove a point to everyone.
3) **You waste most of your energy defending yourself** – Being insecure and uncomfortable is no way to live!
4) **It makes you indifferent and heartless** – Compassion is not something that comes to us naturally. We cannot think of the positives because we prefer to see only the worst in people. We end up reacting faster than usual, without understanding the complete situation.
5) **You don't think wisely** – Rational thought goes out the window and decision making is affected with emotion.
6) **Ego stops you from learning new things** – Too much Ego makes us stubborn. We don't want to listen to anyone or ask for advice. It stops us from asking for help from people who might know better than us.
7) **Ego pushes all the nice people away**– The harsh truth of life is no one wants to be friends with an egoistic person. An egoistic person does not like being told if they're wrong and always tend to take feedback a little too seriously. No one wants such people in their life. Dealing with them is stressful, and no one wants added stress in their lives.

8) **Ego makes you insecure and overly competitive in an unhealthy way** – Studies suggest the Ego generates powerful emotions, and the Ego can make you want to harm others. It changes you and stops you from wishing the best for people. So, before you take everything seriously, understand it's more harmful for you than it is for others.
9) **You become selfish** – Everything becomes about you, with little regard of those around you.
10) **You become nasty** – Due to insecurity – People pick up on it pretty quickly and avoid it like the plague.
11) **You bring baggage** – From a bad day to the way we were brought up. Our past may define us, but our future is a choice we make.
12) **Ego represses disturbing or threatening thoughts from becoming conscious**; although hidden they will eventually create anxiety.
13) **Ego transfers blame onto another that would cause guilt.** For example, you might hate someone, but your superego tells you such hatred is unacceptable; you Ego solves the problem by believing they hate you too.
14) **Ego uses the defense of denial when a situation is too much to handle** by refusing to perceive it or to deny its existence, but no one disregards reality and gets away with it for long!
15) **It makes life STRESSFUL – It's no way to live!** – When we are constantly trying to be better than everyone else, we take everything as a straight hit to our self-worth. It causes sleepless nights and takes away our peace, leaving us frustrated and anxious.
16) **Ego stands in the way of your success!** – Because believe it or not, great leaders succeed because they're willing to do every job, ask every dumb question, and most of all, accept they cannot do everything alone.
17) **Ego makes you unhappy** – Ego can take away so many beautiful things in your life, pushing loved ones away from us. It affects the way we live our life. It stops us from dealing with disappointments and hardships in the right way.

DISOLVING EGO— The solution is to gain control of your Ego, and that's the best gift we can give ourselves.

Ego does not go away quickly or easily. Ego does not give up easily. Sometimes during the process you most feel as though you're being split in two with Ego wanting to go one way and Essence the other. You almost feel as though you're getting a little crazy but realizing this is perfectly normal and everyone goes through it helps to ease the process. Just remember you are not alone in your journey.

Everyday opportunities will present themselves through Ego or responding from Essence. Do not judge or beat yourself up over those times you may choose Ego. It is a learning experience; just observe and accept and maybe the next time the situation presents itself you will respond with Essence.

Realize whenever the Ego is in charge, it's only telling half the story – the story as you currently view it – not the whole story that takes into account other people's perceptions and the facts behind the matter. Your job is to realize when your Ego defense is in play. Acknowledge your Ego is simply trying to protect you, but at the same time it's blocking off reality. And when that happens, you're figuratively crippled because you're unable to understand how you fit into the world.

So the concept of "not letting your Ego get in the way" is not about eliminating the Ego; rather, it's about honoring and valuing the Ego position, because ultimately the Ego is there to help you and guide you. The key, however, is not letting your Ego stand in the way simply because you feel fear, threat, or embarrassment. Take into consideration that such feelings are appropriate, but they're not the whole story.

When you become aware of your Ego response, you can immediately change your reaction to the situation and keep your Ego from controlling you. In other words, the moment you can say to yourself, "Yes, I feel overwhelmed. I feel afraid. I feel threatened. I feel embarrassed," is when you become open to the whole story and can react according to the true reality, not according to your Ego's reality.

Don't fight with the Ego, the key is truly acceptance. Your Ego can be attributed to a small child, at time out is usually justified and this is generally what needs to be done with Ego. Let it cry itself out while you do little more than observe.

Your Ego will never disappear one hundred percent of the time. However, as you learn to be in Essence more and more of the time your Ego will start to take a backseat to Essence. Gradually the Ego voice will fade until it is nothing than a whisper we observe and accept.

So, how can you keep your ego in check at all times? When you first notice you feel fear, threat, or embarrassment, ask yourself the following three questions,

1) **Is this the way it really is, or is this my response to it? Why does this affect me so much?** — Check outside of yourself. Be as objective as possible and forget about your own feelings for a moment so you can uncover why the current situation is triggering an Ego response.

2) **If I feel this way, do others feel this way?** — Check around to make sure you're not the only one caught up in the situation. Even if most do, they too are responding to their Ego - seek the "calm" one in the crowd.

3) **Take Control** — keeping your Ego from getting in your way is essentially a process of becoming more aware of what triggers you.

GETTING IN TOUCH WITH ESSENCE – Separating from Ego is by no means an easy feat but once you become aware of the Ego's existence it begins to loosen its powerful grip. One of the keys to separating is to become an observer of your own life. You do this by taking a step back and "watching" as events unfold in your life, rather than reacting. This may sound difficult and even a bit odd, but one way to do this is to become almost like a narrator of your own life. This pulls you out of your mind and out of your thoughts of past and future. It brings you instantly to the present and to the awareness is essential if you are to get beyond Ego and live life through Essence.

1) **Reducing drama is essential.** The drama in your life that is created by Ego can be reduced if you keep one thing in mind. Your thoughts create your emotions. It may be hard to discern this but try and take notice. It seems to happen simultaneously but if you take a closer look the thought actually comes first and then in a split second later the emotion. When you realize this you can stop the thought before emotion connects. Just remind yourself when an unpleasant emotion arises you can reduce the hold the emotion has by just the awareness of the situation. When drama is reduced in your life it makes it easier for Essence to shine through.

2) **Simplify. Simplify**— Simplify your life. Slow down and cut out those activities that really aren't necessary or you don't enjoy. When you are constantly running it makes it difficult to hear Essence. Taking the time to sit in silence is a great way to connect with Essence. Turn off the phone, turn off the television and just sit. Let your mind wonder, but don't let it settle in any specific thoughts. Let your thoughts just "float". Being still is considered lazy by many, but it is truly an important part of life when you are trying to connect with Essence.

3) **Coming into your body** takes you out of your mind and Ego. Exercise and physical activity are a great way to shut up the Ego. Anything, hiking, skiing, surfing, running; anything that gets the body pumping will work. If you are unable to do anything physical, you can still get into the body by "feeling" each of your body parts. Tell yourself, "I feel my fingers, I feel my toes, I feel my forearms, etc. and actually feel these parts of your body by focusing your entire mind on them.

4) **Doing something you love** creates a doorway to Essence. Singing, dancing, drawing, golfing – any hobby you love will do. These things take your attention and Ego is pushed by to the wayside. Anytime that happens it quiets the mind, making it easier for a thought from Essence to be heard. Of course, any type of meditation or breathing exercise ignites the same reaction.

5) **Discover and Hear Essence.** Sometimes it may be difficult to hear Essence over all the incessant chatter cluttering your mind. Sometimes Ego tries to fool you by initiating Essence. We cannot reach Essence through the mind, no matter how hard you think about it, analyze it or try to define it – the mind simply cannot grasp the concept. Ego will work endlessly to find a solution to a problem usually a problem it created, but those answers are never found in the mind. Ego can worry, ponder, guess, plan and manipulate any way it wants and in the end what does it have? Nothing. And if by chance Ego does come with an answer, how often was it right? Usually these thought do nothing more than get in the way of hearing Essence and cause detour from your path.

In order to discover and hear Essence, it is especially important to keep in mind what was stated earlier, you are not your thoughts. Be aware, become the observer and try to keep in mind all the crazy drama is nothing more than a creation of the Ego. You are the observer, the watcher, the one who is listening, not the one who is reacting.

Although coming from Essence feels very different than thoughts of the Ego, there are no feelings behind it. No drama or questioning, no confusion. It generally comes across as a statement, almost a command. It can be expressed as an action or a sudden insight. Generally it comes seemingly out of nowhere usually when you are deeply rooted in the present moment. It often feels like, a "knowing". The voice doesn't manipulate or question; it just knows. When you take the time to quiet your Ego, even unintentionally, you have room for Essence to reach through the incessant chatter to be heard.

6) **Becoming present in the moment.** Being in the here and now is essential. Anytime you imagine the future or look back to the past, you are in Ego. There are very few ways to bring yourself into the present. Becoming the observer is one of them. Doing something you love or something creative pulls you to the present moment. Sitting in silence, meditating, conscious breathing; these also bring you to the present. Feelings of gratitude will bring you into the now. Keep this in mind and you will create a pathway for Essence to be heard.

7) **Adopt the beginner's mindset.** "It is impossible to learn what one thinks one already knows," Epictetus says. When we let Ego tell us we have arrived and figured it all out, it prevents us from learning. Pick up a book on a subject you know next to nothing about. Walk through a library or a bookstore—remind yourself how much you don't know.

8) **Focus on the effort—not the outcome.** With any creative endeavor at some point what we made leaves our hands. We can't let what happens after that point have any sway over us. We need to remember coach John Wooden's advice: "Success is peace of mind, which is a direct

result of self satisfaction in knowing you made the *effort* to do your best to become the best that you are capable of becoming." Doing your best is what matters. Focus on that. External rewards are just extra.

9) **Choose purpose over passion.** Passion runs hot and burns out, while people with purpose—think of it as passion combined with reason—are more dedicated and have control over their direction. Christopher McCandless was passionate when he went "into the wild" but it didn't work well, right? The inventor of the Segway was passionate. Better to have *clear-headed purpose.*

10) **Shun the comfort of talking and face the work.** "Void," Marlon Brando once said, "is terrifying to most people." We talk endlessly on social media getting validation and attention with fake internet points avoiding the uncertainty of doing the difficult and frightening work required of any creative endeavor. As creative's, we need to shut up and get to work. To face the "void"—despite the pain of doing so.

11) **Kill your pride before you lose your head.** "Whom the gods wish to destroy," Cyril Connolly wrote, "they first call promising." You cannot let early pride lead you astray. You must remind yourself every day how much work is left to be done, not how much you have done. You must remember humility is the antidote to pride.

12) **Stop telling yourself a story—there is no grand narrative.** When you achieve any sort of success you might think success in the future is just the natural and expected next part of the story. This is a straightforward path to failure—by getting too cocky and overconfident. Focus on the present moment, not the story.

13) **Learn to manage (yourself and others).** John DeLorean was a brilliant engineer but a poor manager (of people and himself). One executive de-scribed his management style as "chasing colored balloons"—he was constantly distracted and abandoning one project for another. It's just not enough to be smart or right or a genius. It's gratifying to be the mi-cromanaging egotistical boss at the center of everything—but that's not how organizations grow and succeed. That's not how you can grow as a person either.

14) **Know what matters to you and ruthlessly say no to everything else.** Pur-sue what the philosopher Seneca refers to as *euthymia*—the tranquility of knowing what you are after and not being distracted by others. We ac-complish this by having an honest conversation with ourselves and un-derstanding our priorities. And rejecting all the rest. Learning how to say no. First, by saying no to Ego which wants it *all.*

15) **Forget credit and recognition.** Before Bill Belichick became the four-time Super Bowl-winning head coach of the New England Patriots, he made his way up the ranks of the NFL by doing grunt work and making his superiors look good without getting any credit. When we are starting out in our pursuits we need to make an effort to trade short-term gratification for a long-term payoff. Forget credit.

16) **Connect with nature and the universe at large.** Going into nature is a powerful feeling and we need to tap into it as often as possible. Nothing draws us away from it more than material success. Go out there and re-connect with the world. Realize how small you are in relation to everything else. It's what the French philosopher Pierre Hadot has referred to as the "oceanic feeling". There is no Ego standing beneath the giant redwoods or on the edge of a cliff or next to the crashing waves of the ocean.

17) **Choose alive time over dead time.** According to author Robert Greene, there are two types of time in our lives: dead time, when people are passive and waiting, and alive time, when people are learning and acting and utilizing every second. During failure, Ego picks dead time. It fights back: *I don't want this. I want ___ . I want it my way.* It indulges in being angry, aggrieved, heartbroken. Don't let it—choose alive time instead.

18) **Get out of your own head.** Writer Anne Lamott knows the dangers of the soundtrack we can play in our heads: "The endless stream of self-aggrandizement, the recitation of one's specialness, of how much more open and gifted and brilliant and knowing and misunderstood and humble one is." That's what you could be hearing right now. Cut through that haze with courage and live with the tangible and real, no matter how uncomfortable.

19) **Let go of control.** The poisonous need to control everything and micromanage is usually revealed with success. Ego starts saying: it all must be done my way—even little things, even inconsequential things. The solution is straight forward. A smart man or woman must regularly remind themselves of the limits of their power and reach. It's simple, but not easy.

20) **Place the mission and purpose above you.** During World War II, General George Marshall, winner of the Nobel Peace Prize for the Marshall Plan, was practically offered the command of the troops on D-Day. Yet he told President Roosevelt: "The decision is yours, Mr. President; my wishes have nothing to do with the matter." It came to be Eisenhower led the invasion and performed with excellence. Marshall put the mission and purpose above himself—an act of selflessness we need to remind ourselves of.

21) **When you find yourself in a hole—stop digging.** "Act with fortitude and honor," Alexander Hamilton wrote to a distraught friend in serious trouble of the man's own making. "If you cannot reasonably hope for a favorable extrication, do not plunge deeper. Have the courage to make a full stop." Our Ego screams and rattles when it is wounded. We will then do *anything* to get out of trouble. Stop. Don't make things worse. Don't dig yourself further. Make a plan.

22) **Don't be deceived by recognition, money and success—stay sober.** Success, money and power can intoxicate. What is required in those moments is sobriety and a refusal to indulge. Leave self-absorption and obsessing over one's image for the egotists.

23) **Leave your entitlement at the door.** Right before he destroyed his own billion-dollar company, Ty Warner, creator of Beanie Babies, overrode the objections of one of his employees and bragged, "I could put the Ty heart on manure and they'd buy it!" You can see how this manifestation of Ego can lead you to success—and how it can lead to downright failure.

24) **Choose love.** Martin Luther King understood hate is like an "eroding acid that eats away the best and the objective center of your life." Hatred is when Ego turns a minor insult into a massive sore and it lashes out. But pause and ask: has hatred and lashing out ever helped anyone with *anything*? Don't let it eat at you—choose love. Yes, love. See how much better you feel.

25) **Pursue mastery in your chosen craft.** When you are pursuing a craft you realize the better you get, the humbler you are. Because you understand there's always something you can learn and you are inherently humbled by this fascinating craft or career you're after. It is hard to get a big head or become egotistical when you've decided on that path.

26) **Keep an inner scorecard.** Just because you won doesn't mean you *deserved* to. We need to forget other people's validation and external markers of success. Warren Buffett has advised keeping an inner scorecard versus the external one. Your potential, the absolute best you're capable of—that's the metric to measure yourself against.

27) **Paranoia creates things to be paranoid about.** "He who indulges empty fears earns himself to real fears," wrote Seneca, who as a political adviser witnessed destructive paranoia at the highest levels. If you let ego think everyone is out to get you will seem weak...and then people will really try to take advantage of you. Be strong, confident and forgiving.

28) **Always stay a student.** Put yourself in rooms where you're the least knowledgeable person. Observe and learn. That uncomfortable feeling, that defensiveness that you feel when your most deeply held assumptions are challenged? Do it *deliberately*. Let it humble you. Remember how the physicist John Wheeler put it, "As our island of knowledge grows, so does the shore of our ignorance."

29) **No one can degrade you—they degrade themselves.** Ego is sensitive about slights, insults and not getting their due. This is a waste of time. After Frederick Douglass was asked to ride in a baggage car because of his race, someone rushed to apologize for this mistreatment. Frederick's reply? "They cannot degrade Frederick Douglass. The soul that is within me no man can degrade. I am not the one that is being degraded on account of this treatment, but those who are inflicting it upon me."

30) **Stop playing the image game—focus on a higher purpose.** One of the best strategists of the last century, John Boyd, would ask the promising young acolytes under him: "To be or to do? Which way will you go?" That is, will you choose to fall in love with the *image* of how success looks like or will you focus on a higher purpose? Will you pick obsessing over your title, number of fans, size of paycheck or on real, tangible accomplishment? You know which way Ego wants to go.

31) **Realize you are just "I AM" without any descriptors.** Ego qualifies and tells you who you are; this is the means by which Ego controls and limits you.

    The Essence of Self has no qualifiers. Begin with defining yourself as "I AM ___ (Fill in the blank)___" Now forget what you said and try another "I AM ___ (Fill in the blank)__" and disregard that definition. Do this until you have qualified who you are and then disregard that definition. Finally, you are down to Self as simplify "I AM."

Gradually, more and more you will find yourself choosing Essence. Living through Essence opens up worlds of opportunities as you become more in tune with the signs and synchronicities which Essence presents to guide you on your path.

Sources
1. "10 Reasons Why Ego Holds You Back From Learning", Jan 18 2019, https://www.championsgym.com.au/2019/01/10-reasons-why-ego-holds-you-back-from-learning/
2. "11 Reasons A Huge Ego Is Your Worst Enemy", Surabhi Nijhawan, Updated May 24, 2016, https://www.indiatimes.com/lifestyle/self/11-reasons-a-huge-ego-is-your-worst-enemy-255141.html
3. "Defense Mechanisms". Saul McLoad, Updated 2019, Simple Psychology, https://www.simplypsychology.org/defense-mechanisms.html

4. "Why a Big Ego Could be Your Downfall", May 2016, AWCI (American Wall & Ceiling), https://www.awci.org/media/construction-dimensions/feature-articles/625-why-a-big-ego-could-be-your-downfall
5. "Don't Let Your Ego Get in the Way", Mike Jay, ReliablePlant, https://www.reliableplant.com/Read/13933/don't-let-your-ego-get-in-way
6. "25 Ways to Kill The Toxic Ego That Will Ruin Your Life". Ryan Holiday, Meditations on Strategy and Life, https://ryanholiday.net/25-ways-to-kill-the-toxic-ego-that-will-ruin-your-life/
7. "Reasons for Ego Development". Hindu Janajagruti Samiti, reference: *Sanatan* Sanstha's Holy text 'Spiritual Practice for Destroying Ego', https://www.hindujagruti.org/hinduism/ego-development
8. "Ego is the Enemy", Dunning-Kruger Effect (slope of Confidence vs. Competence), Education Practice of EM, Clay Smith, https://journalfeed.org/article-a-day/2018/ego-is-the-enemy
9. "From Ego to Essence– Integrating Spiritual Living into Everyday Life", Robin Masters, Balboa Press, https://books.google.com/books?id=7icEDgAAQBAJ&pg=PT12&lpg=PT12&dq=ego+reasons&source=bl&ots=5EEl4vpyTT&sig=ACfU3U0Ua0SHmp4O0XuhroOsMsgwQDYFeg&hl=en&sa=X&ved=2ahUKEwiT2MeFzbvpAhUGX80KHdcCCYM4HhDoATAGegQIBRAB#v=onepage&q=ego%20reasons&f=false
10. "Why 'Ego is the Enemy," and what you can do about it", Ameet Ranadive, July 17 2017, Medium.com, https://medium.com/@ameet/why-ego-is-the-enemy-and-what-we-can-do-about-it-a4eae45a81d8
11. Ego is the Enemy, Ryan Holiday, 2016, Portfolio, Selected Notes: https://static1.squarespace.com/static/5576de42e4b088027cd59de4/t/5ced56046e9a7f4fe66dd74e/1559057925639/BOOK+NOTES+-+Ego+is+the+Enemy.pdf

Article 9

THE JOURNEY TO SELF
(The first step to Awakening)

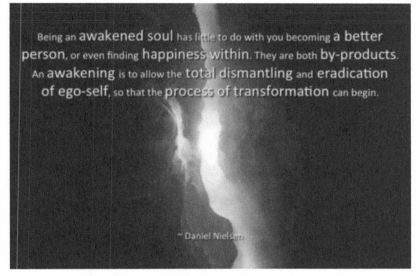

Being an **awakened soul** has little to do with you becoming **a better person**, or even finding **happiness within**. They are both **by-products**. An **awakening** is to allow the **total dismantling** and **eradication of ego-self**, so that the **process of transformation** can begin.

~ Daniel Nielsen

First and foremost to Waking Up, Enlightenment and Escaping this polarity Realm is to release your False Self to reveal your True Self.

The most transformative thing you could ever do is remember who you are. I don't mean the "you" who you think you are or the one defined by the roles you play or the masks you wear. Not the one who is driven by fear, insecurity or need, But the REAL YOU - pure, shining, precious, whole, undamaged, undefended.

Do you have the courage to find your way back to your Self?

Being an awakened Soul has little to do with you becoming a better person, or even finding happiness within. They are both by-products. An awakening is to allow the total dismantling and eradication of Ego-self, the false reality or façade that has been built, and seeing the story that has been created for what it is, so the process of transformation can begin.

The surrender of Ego-self must take place if transformation and permanent change are to happen. To admit you have been deceived is also a humbling experience - but that's what Truth demands.

As the light approaches there will be an inner stirring, and suddenly it will become clear to you. You will hear the still small voice of your God Source (Creator God, not the False God given to us by the Anunnaki when mankind was created), and you will discover is no longer a separation between you and the Creator. You will become conscious of your Soul and love will explode within you. You will come to know who you are, your true self. You will gain clarity of your purpose for being. You will have a new understanding of the amazing creation you are, that anything is possible.

There will be no more fear to control you, no more shame, no desire to judge others. There will be no more excuses, no more regrets, just a renewed zeal for taking responsibility for your actions and your life. The present moment will come alive. And for the first time in your life you will be able to breathe freely because your Soul will be at peace. That's transformation.

You Are Not Who You Think You Are: It's not who we are that makes us feel threatened and uncomfortable, it's who we THINK we are. With self investigation we can discover who we are, not who we think we are. We're so nervous about what happens around us, because we think we are affected by what happens to us. We believe who we are is somehow tied to the events in our lives. And by attaching our identity to events, we're afraid to lose control of ourselves if we cannot control the events. Events may happen to you, but you are NOT the event. These events just move THROUGH us.

The Strange Non-Life of the False Self: Our false self is fueled by negative emotional reactions that are maintained by habit. It's a mechanical movement, but as negative feelings slowly start to lose force, so does these movements, and so does your false life. Your negative self-conscious doesn't want to die, so it will fight to keep itself alive by doing self-sabotaging things like picking fights. Our life-level cannot tell the difference between the path of the negative false-self and our true-self, so it tells us we have no choice but to cave in to the false self.

The Blame Game: Our false self wants us to blame our unhappiness or unfortunate circumstances on other people, outside circumstances or an uncaring world. We focus our energy and life trying to fix and control things outside of ourselves. Our false self wants to keep us off balance and looking in the wrong direction. It's time to learn to let go the self-abandoning answers the false self wants us to believe in!

For True Self-Command, Just Stop, Look and Listen: When we start feeling anxiety we must first STOP and defy the inner shouts going on in our head. Recognize they are bad. Then we LOOK at what is talking to us; it is our inner false self starting to have a fit. It doesn't want to let go of its power, so just let it rage. Then it's over. The more we can do this, the more we are building new patterns and weakening old ones.

Let Go And Realize Real Rescue: Desperate attempts to escape our troubles only lead us into more trouble. To rescue ourselves from our problems, the rescue must be from a level above us and within us at the same time...which are the exact same thing. In the battle with our false self, we defeat it not by running away or through struggle, but by realizing we have mistakenly given-power to it. Our false self was NO power to cause us pain if we don't give it the wrong reaction.

Two Worlds, Two Natures, Two Selves: There are two of us. Our false self and our true self. Our false self is to a dessert and our true self is to the mountain next to it. The mountaintop sits higher and cannot be disturbed by the desert. The desert can only cause problems to those things in it. Once we get out of the desert and to the top of the mountain, we will no longer be bothered by our false self.

Five Illusions Keeping You from Letting Go:

- Illusion of feeling useless or insignificant - false perception of the true measure of worth is determined by others.
- Illusion of discouragement - false perception that is possible to succeed in life without learning through "failures".
- Illusion of regret - false perception that reliving the past will empower us to resolve it.
- Illusion of limitation - false perception that the only resource available in the moment of challenge is what you already know as being possible to do.
- Illusion that others are better, stronger, wiser - false perception that you are on Earth to be like someone else.

To Help Shatter Self-Limitation:

- Nothing stands between you and permanent happiness.
- Don't ask how, let Now show you.
- The spiritual Now is an unthinkable action.
- When traveling the inner roads, your arrival in the new world outside yourself, is a departure from the old one.
- The clearer it becomes you can't help yourself escape yourself, the freer you become.
- You can arrive outside of yourself as quickly as you are willing to be taken there.
- The only path to self-success is the next step.
- Add daily sweetness to the journey by working to shorten the distance between the mental now and spiritual How (moment by moment).
- No one else can help you get outside of yourself.
- Real success is not measured by what you are driven to achieve, but what you can quietly understand.

The Way Out Is Safe: During your journey there will be times we have to brave through dark, difficult and unknown territories. Just like a covered wagon, the wagon master represents your Higher Intuition, which knows you must continue through resistance or reluctance to get where you need to go. You cannot go above or around your scary problems, you must go through them. In this example of the covered wagon on a journey, the head scout represents the part of you that must pull everyone together to make it through the struggles. The head scout has doubts and fears, but leads everyone through anyway. Our own inner lives are a constant journey of knowing what we need to do, and actually doing it. They are two different things, and actually doing it can be difficult...especially when going off the beaten path. We tend to think the blockages, difficulties and cruel relationships are outside of us, when really, each terrifying mountain pass filled with unknown scariness is an inner affair. And the inner journey can only Enlighten you.

Your Ultimate Victory over Harmful Inner Voices: We must accept that we have been "invaded" by the false self without even knowing it. It is always telling us to play it safe to assure psychological security, and we wrongly believe this. We believe these warnings are protecting us from the daily attacks we encounter, when in reality...the inner warnings ARE the ONLY attacks. To remove these "intruders" you have to be willing to investigate and reveal the inner operations of the false self. The clearer it becomes that your only problem is your bad inner company, the sooner you'll move forward and start living alone inwardly. Our false self's biggest fear is that they will have no one to talk to...and that is our ultimate victory over them. Start right now by living alone with yourself. If you persist with this watchfulness, then one day living "alone" won't frighten you because the dark thoughts won't be there to tell you how lonely you feel.

Hints for Taking Charge of Yourself:
- When you understand no one really knows who THEY are, you'll stop looking for them to tell you who YOU are.
- Neither the approval nor disapproval from others makes any difference in the quality of your life.
- People who want you to be who they want do so to please themselves. Just be yourself and please yourself.
- Why do you want approval from those who don't even approve of themselves?
- One way to avoid unpleasant conversation is to stop talking to yourself.
- If you don't leap, you'll never know what it's like to fly.
- If you are headed for the mountaintop, then why do you care what the people in the valley are doing?

Let Go Of These True Life-Draining Demands: Our self-generated demands are what give rise to all of the worldly demands.

- Examples of self-demands: Be rich, famous and slim, Be important, Be wise in all topics, Be a source of strength to the less fortunate.
- Examples of worldly demands: Look at life like a race to win, Excuse rude behavior, Conform to social mandates, Compromise whatever is necessary to succeed.

Walk Lightly Through Life: It's not our life that will change, but our view of life. Without the burden of carrying all of the extra weight, we start to see life as a wonderful place, rather than a task to go through. Once you start making yourself miserable for not being where you want to be, you'll be happy exactly where you are. The truth is you don't need to be who you think you have to be. Therefore, you don't have to carry around those things through life you think you need to make you that person.

Keys for Living Lightly:
- Real life is intended to be inner-acted, not outer-directed.
- Only wrongness needs to check with itself if it's right.
- You can have a relationship with something you don't understand, but it will always be on that relationship's terms.
- To soar more, see more.
- Stop trying to act kindly and dare to be more awake, for the kindest act of all is to help another see through the hoax of unhappiness.
- As long as you act as though your life depends on anything temporal, it does.
- Your true strength knows your true weakness isn't yours at all.
- False life is exhausting; real life is inexhaustible.
- Any confidence you have based on something outside yourself is also the basis of self doubt.
- If you allow others to tell you where you are going, then you must depend on them to tell you what you need for your journey.

Hearing the Song Of The True Self: If we aren't "aware" of what we are listening to, then we are hearing without even knowing what we are receiving. This self-unawareness leads to countless uncomfortable moments. (e.g., we think someone else is thinking about us negatively. We then react defensively, which creates isolation and fear). However, had we known we were "receiving" was a self-produced, self-defeating though; we would have just disregarded it as nonsense. The True Self is the foundation of all that is good, kind, wise, love, and is always sending out its cosmic strength and silent wisdom. Our task isn't to reach for it, but to allow it to reach us by receiving its healing influences. Before we can receive the gifts from the True Self, we have to remove the obstacles that allow its entrance. The first step of being receptive is to notice where we are NOT. Higher receptivity requires us to see we have subconsciously allowed disruptive negativity to occupy our mindand hearts. The True Self will allow us to detect any slightest mistune in our lives, like an orchestra leader can detect a mistuned instrument.

Allow yourself to start listening to yourself more and more every day. Don't worry if you feel strained or sad, just keep listening and stay receptive. Your false self will want you turn these inner false sad notes into a sad song, but DON'T. Just stay silent and keep listening. Let the negative thoughts remain where they are, which is the fact you are aware they are out of place. You awareness of their "out of placeness" is coming to you from the True Self.

The Bill of Lights:

- You have the light to detect, dismiss and transcend the limiting influences of painful negative states such as doubt, worry, hatred, anger, fear.
- You have the light to do your unique part in perfecting any moment within which you are willing to come awake to yourself.
- You have the light to help each person you meet realize they have the right to live within and from the same Bill of Lights that you do.
- You have the light to live in a peaceful world within yourself that is spontaneously creative and quietly confident at all times.
- You have the light to act with compassion towards all other beings, regardless of how challenging your personal circumstances may be in any given moment.
- You have the light to always remember that goodness is responsible for your creation wants only what is true and good for you.
- You have the light to realize all things pass except for the light living within you whose eternal presence makes it possible to see the soul-consoling beauty of this truth.

Fifty Truths to Take you All The Way Home: Every time we make it to another safe higher point, we realize it's not that we have SO much more personal power, but it's we have let go of SO much deep-rooted false beliefs and habits and patterns...and the false continues to get washed away.

Seek These Truths

1) You are always right where you need to be to take the next step beyond yourself.
2) Spiritual development is an equal opportunity for all.
3) Living in inner darkness, there are only two choices: the wrong one or the lucky one.
4) See the upset not as an exterior circumstance to be remedied, but rather an interior condition to be understood.
5) All psychological conclusions are fossilized assumptions of the false self.
6) Discouraging thoughts and feelings don't even know the truth about themselves, let alone what is around the corner.
7) Only an egotist likes to feel as if they are the only one.
8) The very act of doing something for a reward is painful because it goes against your true nature, which is a reward unto itself.
9) Since spiritual awareness has no opposites, nothing can oppose it.

10) The bad feeling you don't want to feel is the feeling of not wanting that bad feeling.
11) The sentimental or sad remembrance is a memory, not who you are.
12) Just as the sun is not dependent on the moon for its light, so real love has nothing in common with any of its opposites. Look Beyond Yourself.
13) Never hesitate to place yourself in a position where you don't know what to do.
14) If life knocks you flat on your back, open your eyes: above you are the stars.
15) There is always something higher, if you will only remember to keep your head held up.
16) When your destination is not of this Earth, then nothing on this Earth can disturb you.
17) Be the investigator, not the justifier; be watchful, not willful.
18) To what you are connected is by what you are directed.
19) Truth has nothing to do with self-pleased human beings.
20) The True Self is a presence to perceive, not a prize to pursue.
21) A prayer for acceptance that isn't preceded by a prayer for forgiveness is an act of arrogance.
22) You will know the True Self when you know no one can help you, including yourself.
23) Never again help anyone to feel as though they have a right to feel badly.
24) Let the truth awaken in you the remembrance that you are not here to remain you.
25) Just Let Go.
26) Real chance of self isn't found in some new way to think about yourself but in the freedom from the need to think about yourself at all.
27) Act from the self that is true and not from the self that is you.
28) Letting go is all about finding out who you are not and having the courage to leave it at that.
29) Persistence is sticking with something until stupidity gets out of the way.
30) The only way to produce more inner light is by consciously sitting in inner darkness.
31) To do the best you can do does not mean to suffer.
32) Jump into to the truth of the moment by being willing to jump out of yourself.
33) Letting Go is not giving up; it's going up.
34) The True Self does not enter into an individual's life on any condition other than entire possession.
35) To be more alert, we need only listen for and then let go of the thoughts that steal our attention.
36) Set your course by no man and let no man set your course.
37) Let whatever it is, Truth Always Triumphs.
38) Whoever chooses truth about himself always chooses for himself.
39) Defeat is a memory; it does not exist in real life.

40) You can have the realization of helplessness without the feeling of helplessness.
41) When all has been done, patience is natural and has no strain. To remain calm, we need only listen for and then let go of the anxious inner voices.
42) Living in the light of self-awareness there is only one choice, and it is always the right one, for consciousness never chooses against itself.
43) Whatever strength you add to yourself becomes your greatest weakness, while whatever weakness you consciously endure will be replaced with strength not of your own.
44) When you know you are fully wrong, you will be standing at the gateway of real rightness.
45) When life becomes your leaders, its spirit becomes your strength.
46) Truth pours in as you pour out.
47) You need neither the permission nor the cooperation of the world to put yourself last.
48) You can't silence yourself, but you can allow stillness to show you its ways.
49) Never think any situation is too difficult for truth to triumph.

The Ten Traits of the True Spiritual Warrior: We succeed in life when we can walk away from any challenge with a measure of more self-understanding than we took into it. Below are 10 traits of a true spiritual warrior:

- A true spiritual warrior knows her only enemy she has is what she has not shed light on within or outside of herself, so she never postpones a battle that must be fought.
- A true spiritual warrior never forgets she has no spiritual enemy apart from forgetting the above.
- A true spiritual warrior starts life over, and over again.
- A true spiritual warrior works every day, every moment to sharpen her battle skills.
- A true spiritual warrior leads by example, no matter the cost.
- A true spiritual warrior makes it her aim to never burden another human being with her own pain.
- A true spiritual warrior is not afraid to look at what she doesn't want to see.
- A true spiritual warrior commits herself to her best choice, and knows to live in conflict over what is or is not her best, is irresponsible.
- A true spiritual warrior never fears feelings of helplessness, because she knows such states will bring new power.
- A true spiritual warrior knows the path of spiritual liberation she has chosen must lead her to one encounter after another with conditions that always seem greater than she is.

Finding your True Self, leads to transformation, is the higher path. But despite the beauty and wonder of seeing with new eyes, many will still choose to remain asleep in the light. Your job is not to shake them from their slumber, but to help them on their journey, to meet them where they're at. If you do your part, Love can be trusted to do the rest.

Sources
1. "Letting Go of the False Reality - The surrender of ego-self", Daniel Nelsin, August 19, 2016, Infidelity Recovery Institute. https://infidelityrecoveryinstitute.com/letting-go-false-reality/
2. "21 Ways to Let Go and Free Yourself", Joyce Marter , Contributor, Psychotherapist & Founder of Urban Balance, 8,8/21\014, Huffpost, https://www.huffpost.com/entry/21-ways-to-let-go-free-yourself_b_5649680?guccounter=1
3. "Finding Your Way Back to Your Self", Gail Brenner, https://gailbrenner.com/2011/07/finding-your-way-back-to-your-self/
4. "The Secret of Letting Go", Guy Finley, Extended Summary, static1.squarespace.com, https://static1.squarespace.com/static/54dfb9c3e4b0409b0658e848/t/54f7ac18e4b0938923dd56b6/1426252067297/The+Secret+of+Letting+Go+Re-Cap.pdf

Article 10

SOVEREIGN INTEGRITY 3.0
(Importance to Star Beings)

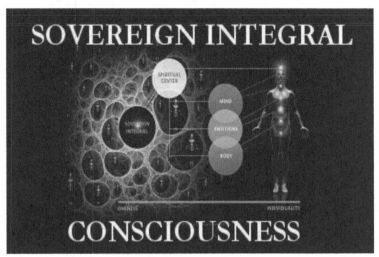

A Brief History of Earth Humans

Review the "Galactic Wars" Article to note that the Human DNA has been augmented and manipulated by nearly every sentential being within the near portions of the Milky Way (within 60-200 light years) and, perhaps, beyond, by the many acquisitions, conquests, colonization, and exploratory visitations.

12 Million Years Ago. As part of the Sirian Peace Treaty ended the 2nd Galactic War, the Treaty not only gave 4% of the Universe to the Orion Empire to rule as they pleased (by domination and control) but, also, arranged a marriage of opposing warring parties. This marriage, later failed but produced a Star Child called Merlin.

Approx 500,000 year ago. It was Merlin who brokered the Peace Treaty ending the 3rd Galactic War. The Merlin "solution" was more permanent than the Sirian Treaty which ended the 2nd Galactic War and as concession, the Treaty reconfirmed Orion Empire's governance over 4 percent of the universe, consisting of the Virgo Supercluster which contains our Local Galaxy Group (which contains the Milky Way). This concession was, in part, for the Orion Empire to become the "protectors" of the Living Library on Earth – what a ruse and coup by the Orion Empire politicians.

Tiamat, Queen of the Orion Empire, was once again declared to have governorship of our local galaxy along with her own system of Orion.

Tiamat traveled to Earth to help seed life and created a giant, androgynous, humanoid race, the Namlu'u, to act as guardians of the Living Library on Earth. The Namlu'u were the race the Greeks called the Titans. The giants were the "parents" of the "gods" — meaning a race of 50–60 foot tall humanoids existed here before the Annunaki arrived. In Hebrew the word for giants is "Anakim".

Approx 500,000 year ago there was a large influx of Orion Reptilians (Anunnaki) and Earth population reached 1 billion.

* **Anunnaki Reptilians** were/are a creation of the Carians, their parent race. The Anunnaki were a species within the Lyra star system that traveled to Orion.

450,000 BC - The Anannaki (from the planet Nibiru – 10th planet in the solar system – now an asteroid belt) created settlements on Earth to mine gold to send back via Mars to Nibiru to power their atmospheric shield. Orion Reptilians became the dominate force on Earth through inner breeding, therefore reducing the influence of the Pleiadians on Earth (the Pleiadians had, previously, colonized the Earth).

Human DNA Manipulation. The Anannaki bodies were etheric. They could not mine the gold since it was physical. They needed to have bodies that would be able to operate on Earth and mine the gold. The point is they needed to modify the local Homo Sapiens to be the physical being to mine the gold. They tried hundreds of experiments (over tens of thousands of years and had the help of the Sirians and Atlanteans). That vessel was the human body (which the Anannaki called a "uniform" or human "instrument"). The bodies to mine the gold were the Homo Sapiens, the equivalent of ape-men; they were pre-human. But they were our predecessors. The Anunnaki, excellent geneticists, created Mankind to be dominated by and be servant/slaves. The Anannaki and Sirians designed them to synchronize with the evolving densification of the Earth. As the Earth solidified, so did the human instruments. They were biological. These were very advanced beings, but apparently naïve.

Enki, the Anunnaki Earth commander, creator of the modified Homo Sapien, manipulated their miners until 300,000 BC, when the miners' revolt occurred.

300,000 BC - Enki won approval from Nibiru to replace the miner mutineers with a worker race adapted from the Anannaki genome.

Human 1.0. The Anannaki had some kind of a falling out with the Atlanteans, and began to conspire with the Sirians and another race referred to as the Serpents. Each of these three races was interested in figuring out how to embody physical planets. They saw Earth as a laboratory of sorts to figure it

out. The Anannaki already had a human uniform; they simply needed to program it and power it with a life source or Soul. The basic blueprint of mankind and womankind is referred to as the *Admon Kadmon* template - **Adam
Kadmon** (קַדְמוֹן אָדָם, "Primordial Man"; also called **Adam** Elyon עֶלְיוֹן אָדָם
or **Adam** Ila'ah עִילָאָה אָדָם, "Supreme Man"; abbreviated as ק"א, A"K), in Kabbalah, is the first spiritual World came into being after the contraction of
God's infinite light. (definition via Wikipedia).

The bigger issue was how to get the Atlanteans into these embodiments and
keep them there. In effect, these three races conspired to enslave the Atlanteans within these pre-human vessels. The Atlanteans were the power generators that made these biological entities operational.

The Sirians were mostly credited with this invention, but it was the offspring
of Anu, the Anunnaki leader, that really perfected the implants by programming them. The human uniform version 1.0 was designed by the Anannaki,
the implants were designed by the Sirians, and the programming of the implants was designed and evolved by a being known as Marduk, son of Enki,
son of Anu.

A first, these were much more primitive than Neanderthals. But the answer is
in the implants. The biological entity was not able to operate in the physical
world. They needed survival skills, how to eat, how to hunt, how to clean
themselves, how to even efficiently move their bodies. All of these very fundamental functions were necessary to actually include or program into the
vessel, which was the purpose of the functional implants. The implants were
akin to the brain of the Human 1.0 program, but it wasn't just in the brain.
These implants were placed inside the body within various parts—like the
chest area, middle back, wrists, ankles, etc. (we know these as Chakras). The
primary one was contained in the skull. But generally these implants were
networked to operate from the head, or brain area. Remember Human 1.0
was still part etheric and part physical since the basis was a mix and modification of Anunnaki DNA and human DDA. The implants also needed a similar
consistency or sound vibration. They were placed into the bone or skeletal
structure mostly, and some in the muscle tissue. These functional implants
fused into the muscles and bone, including the DNA. The DNA integration
was for the intelligence of the plan; the muscle tissue allowed life essence to
power the numerous functional implant.

There was a central coordination point, and it was in the brain, but the implants were located throughout the body. This was an integrated system that
was installed in the human uniform to allow it to be controlled, monitored,
and programmed over time. It was the evolutionary stick and carrot. Doing it
this way allowed the early humans to dig out gold, which was their primary
purpose, initially.

The implanted functionality was partly to make the Human 1.0 and its power source—the life essence of an Atlantean—to function efficiently and effectively as miners. That was the prime goal. The second, however, was to suppress the power source, or in this case, the Atlantean beings inside the human vessels. They did this by making the power source ignorant of its origin and the reality of its true expression as an infinite being. When the Atlantean beings were placed inside the human uniform, they were essentially one-hundred percent focused on physical survival and functional performance. There was no relationship. No marriage. No reproduction. These were essentially cloned beings. They were all the same in terms of their appearance and abilities. Human drones, piloted by implanted functionality the Atlantean being inside became associated with, as them. The infinite inside the body believed it was the body and the implanted functionality, and nothing more. The way the Anunnaki "tricked" the Atlanteans to be the power source inside the uniform was the promise of eternal life – which the Atlanteans already had by had no knowledge of their infinite self.

200,000 BC - Commander Enlil (Anannaki, "king" of the ski) ordered Enki ("king" of the Earth) to create more efficient, intelligent, and obedient miners. In response, Enki begat a line of Earthlings called AdaPites (that's with a P for AdaPa, the boy Enki infused into an Adamite girl).

48,000 BC - Enki and Adapite beauty Batanash begat Noah, who carried Enki's longevity genes and ruled the Iraqi city of Sharuppak until the Deluge of 15,000 years ago (some state the Great Flood was 12-13,000 BC; other insist 4,000 BC).

The Great Flood. The Great Flood wiped out most of Earth's population, reduced it from 64 million to 2 million. The Anannaki helped flood survivors proliferate and build cities of 50,000 people in the Middle East, Egypt and the Indus Valley. They built airports, pyramidal powerhouses and temples around the entire Earth. The Anannaki ruled the new civilization as gods.

A few different renegades from Pleiades, Alpha and Beta Centauri came to different places on Earth after the Flood, seeing it as an opportune time to establish their own desired ideologies and also be seen as "godlike" and thus revered. Being already genetically altered, the surviving humans were therefore easily controlled by these renegades, since no form of disobedience to these new "gods" was allowed; the concept of ruling by "divine right" became inculcated on Earth. This concept of worshipping the elite has continued through to modern times. Culture would rise against culture in wars claiming the elite they worshipped were superior to the elite of the opposing faction.

Human 2.0. With most of the Human 1.0 race killed in the Flood, The Anunnaki, again, created mankind. This was the stage where the humans could self-reproduce. And when this happened, some of the Anannaki impregnated female humans and brought in their bloodlines to the human spe cies. This began the variations. This began the idea that humans were no longer clones. The concern, however, was that Human 2.0s might become too powerful and self-aware. What if the Atlantean power source became aware it was an infinite being? This was when Anu decided he should be God. Humans needed to have a lord or ruler over them so it was clear that they were inferior to an external ruler. This was a key part of their program of indoctrination. Working with Marduk and the Sirians, they created the environment of Eden and created the paradigm of Eve as the instigator of the fall of humanity. This was, you might say, Act 1 of Anu as God. It was staged to provide the Human 2.0s with a clear sense of an external authority, and that they were expelled from Paradise because they tried to be self-realized.

Human 3.0. With the ever changing world and the 17th - 19th Century Enlightenment (as devised by the Reptilians), the Remnants of the Anunnaki and the Cabal (13 Reptilian Families, originating from the Orion Empire) conspired to create a new human to meet their ever-changing needs for domination and control – Transhumans are the new creation.

65-70 million years ago, Earth was selected to be a *Living Library*, and almost, if not everything growing and living on this planet originates from elsewhere in the Universe and was brought here by different creator gods. The Vegans first, the Lyrans later, came to Earth and started building what was to become the *Living Library*; a planet which could hold the DNA and the knowledge of the entire galaxy, not only in pure thought form but also as manifestation in 4-space/time. Therefore, mankind is an experiment, and as such, closely monitored by many different off-planetary beings. This was revealed by the Pleiadians y in 1988-89. Given this, the reason for the "new model"(Human 3.0) is to extract the "hidden knowledge" stored within each Earth human which, when know, could give the Draco-Reptilians an advantage in conquering this and other portions of the universe.

The Elite/Dark Force has or will use the various Quantum Processes to modify the human DNA by incorporating "Junk" DNA and bio-mechanics to create trans-humans or to create trans-humans through the injection of nano-bots. The Draco-Reptilians (Dark Force) will change the previous programming to better meet their current need for domination and control.

Programming (refer to Article entitled "CHAKRAS ARE A PROGRAMMING OVERREACH – The Body as Machine") is/will be completed through light coding through the Crown Chakra to modify the DNA coding. The Dark Force will induce the humans to become trans-human by telling them it will provide them with eternal life which they already have without becoming trans-human. It was this same obtuse "attack" used by the Anunnaki, to lure the Atlanteans to become the power source for the Anunnaki/Sirian creation of mankind (Human 1.0 and Human 2.0). Be wary of the attempt to create trans-humans.

Human 3.O SI was instigated by the Founding Fathers in response to the Dark Force's Human 3. 0 initiatives — each individual is a portal unto themselves and this portal is the access point to the interdimensional worlds of the Sovereign Integral; this access point is the Crown Chakra. Within the Chakras Article, it was presented that the Crown Chakra (shaped like an inverted funnel) could be used by the Dark Force to input light code to reprogram mankind. However, the Crown Chakra also contains an antenna which Mankind could transmit and receive input from the Genetic Mind. It is the Genetic Mind that has always contained Sovereign Integral Consciousness (Human 3.0 SI), our true, infinite nature. And in this realization, understands that everyone - EVERYONE - is independent but equal in this state, and in this equality we are of one spiritual belief (Creator God/ One Source). The Sovereign Integral Consciousness (Human 3.0 SI) is accessed through our individual portal and through that portal is the all-encompassing realization and then we transcend the suppression framework and express as Sovereigns.

All living forms of consciousness are connected to the Sovereign Integral Consciousness, enmeshed within the Grand Presence of the Universe. Yet, in the exterior, genetic confines of separation, these living forms seldom remember this they are connected. This paradigm, if you hold it within your heart, will help ground this feeling of Connection and help displace judgment from your emotional center. Our human body (Mind, Body, Soul, Heart) was designed by the Reptilian Draco /Anunnaki to refract all quantum objects as being separate from ourselves. The Reptilian created Mankind —its perceptions of experience—reveal only the program, not the infinite being that it so cleverly conceals.

Sovereign Integral. The Sovereign Integral is a state of consciousness whereby the entity and all of its various forms of expression and perception are integrated as a conscious wholeness. This is a state of consciousness all entities are evolving towards, and at some point, each will reach a state of transformation allowing the entity and its Body/Soul/Mind of experience (i.e., the human instrument) to become an integrated expression aligned and in harmony with One Source Intelligence (True Source/Creator God).

Sovereignty is a state of completeness and inter-connectedness. It is recognizing that as a human being you have an individuated Spirit force that animates your physical, emotional, and mental aspects and that through the Spirit you are complete and connected to all other life forms through the Universal Spirit Consciousness (Source Intelligence). Sovereign beings understand they alone create Their Own Reality and they are responsible for their life-experience. They also understand all other life forms are equally sovereign and they also create their unique realities. Sovereignty allows the True Source (One Source/Creator God) of liberating information is contained within the True Self, and all that is needed to create Your New Reality is also contained within the True Self. It is the point of empowerment and connection to all through the frequency of love.

I realize many see Mankind as the reason why heaven can never occur upon Earth. As long as Mankind remains with the Anunnaki program Human 2.0 and 3.0, they are limited and vile. They seek pleasure and survival. They are animals. I understand this belief, but the scope of this process—of birthing the Sovereign Integral consciousness on Earth—is not left to chance. It is the purpose of our species to free itself of our delusions, illusions and distortions and look clear-eyed into its depths, and to do this while living on Earth in a human body.

The importance to Star Beings. The Sovereign Integral is the calling of each Star Being (Lightworker, Galactic Warrior, Indigo, Crystal, and the many others). It is part of your mission to further the cause of Human 3.0 SI. Creation of the new soul type of 3.0 SI reflects the Soul of Creation by One Source (i.e., Source, Creator God). It is the Life Giving Spirit, the Devine Light. However long it takes. However hard it is to achieve. Sovereign Integral Consciousness will happen.

There are Three Tasks and Three Principles you need to adopt in order to fully integrate SI (Sovereign Integral) into your Consciousness.

Tasks:
1. Reveal your True Self - it will make sense to accept SI.
2. Release Ego, to a major extent - Ego will fight acceptance of SI.
3. Live in the Presence.

The below **Principles** are based upon each being's Spirit is a fragment of the True God (One Source/Creator God) and, as such, we are all part of the "whole". Our Spirit is separate from our Soul and our Spirit remains pure since our Spirit only talks to the Soul and the Soul does not talk back. Our Spirit is outside the electromagnetic field that contains (entraps) our Body, Soul, Mind and it can freely move about the universe, if it chooses to do so.

The three Principles are:

1. Universe relationship through gratitude.
2. Observance of Source in all things.
3. Nurturance of life.

Universe Relationship through Gratitude. It is principally gratitude—which translates to an appreciation of how the inter-relationship of the individual and the Prime Creator (One Source/Creator God)— opening the human Mind/Soul/Body/Heart to its connection to the Prime Creator and its eventual transformation into the Sovereign Integral state of perception and expression. The relationship of the individual with the

Universe is essential to cultivate and nurture, because it, more than any-thing else, determines how accepting the individual is to life's myriad forms and manifestations.

Observance of Prime Source in all things. This is the principle that Prime Source is present in all realities through all manifestations of energy. IT is interwoven in all things like a mosaic whose pieces adhere to the same surface (wall, floor, ceiling), and are thus, unified. However, it is not the picture that unifies the mosaic, but the surface upon which its pieces adhere. Similarly, Prime Source paints a picture so diverse and apparently unrelated that there appears to be no unification. Yet it is not the outward manifestations that unify, it is the inward center of energy upon which the pieces of diversity are layered that unifies all manifestations.

Nurturance of life. The nurturance of life is the principle that an indi-vidual is in alignment with the natural expansion of intelligence inherent within all life. This is an alignment that enhances the life-energy that flows past the individual with the clear intent of gentle support. It is the action of identifying the highest motive in all energy forms and support-ing the flow of this energy towards its ultimate expression. In so doing, the action is performed without judgment, analysis, or attachment to outcome. It is simply nurturing the energy that flows from all manifesta-tions and supporting its expression of life.

Sovereign Integral Consciousness is the immortal identity of each individual.

The language of the mind is words. The language of the heart is feel-ings. But the language of our Presence is behaviors, or activity. If you stay in the intelligence of your Presence, by giving it your attention, then the things that come within your local multiverse that have a lower den-sity, they will have minimal effect, as you can—from the empowerment of your Quantum Presence—transform them with "ease".

Visualization. I picture SI as a "concrete" foundation that supports Man-kind's effort to resist the Dark Force created domination and control pro-gram. The SI foundation's main components,

- Many are the individual "stones" that give the foundation its strength.
- Some are the "reinforcement" that resists cracking and breaking.
- The love of One Source (True God / Creator God) that "holds" (binds) the foundation components together.

Free yourself, what you can, through Sovereign Integral Consciousness (SI), **but remember your ultimate goal is to fully develop your Escape Plan** to leave this world of polarity, dominance and control, and "move" to a Higher Realm. SI is enlightenment but does not totally free you – **YOU NEED AN ESCAPE PLAN.**

Sources
1. Wingmaker's Glossary of Terms, Ancient Arrow Project, https://www.wanttoknow.info/wingmakersorig/WingMakersglossary
2. First Level of Learning, Paper 8: Human Origins and The Living Library
3. Wes Penre, March 31, 201, The Wes Penre Papers, A Journey through the Multiverse, https://wespenre.com/2019/01/26/first-level-of-learning-paper-8-human-origins-and-the-living-library/
4. "Humanity's Extraterrestrial Origins: ET Influences on Humankind's Biological and Cultural Evolution", Arthur David Horn & Lynette Anne Mallory-Horn, 1997

Article 11

REALITY IS WRONG - DREAMS ARE FOR REAL

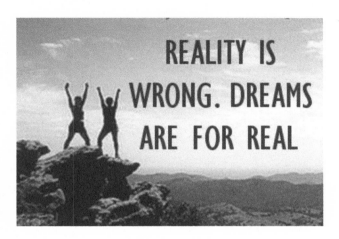

Everything we see, touch, taste, and smell are meant to "show" us the meaning of a thought or idea. At the time we make the observation, it may mean little to nothing to us but it "comes" to us at a later date. Two examples and their application:

- **We Adjust to Time Change** — We mentally, easily adjust to minor changes in time, such as traveling across two Time Zones. It affects us physiologically when time is 180 degrees out of sync with our mind, such as traveling a long period of time when we start out at Noon and arrive at our destination, a few hours later,

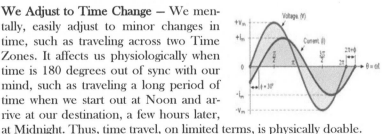

at Midnight. Thus, time travel, on limited terms, is physically doable.
- **Phase Change** — As a young officer in Base Civil Engineering, we were introduced, for a period of a few weeks, to each functional department: Project Programming/Estimating/Scheduling, Physical Operations (Daily Shop work)/Project Management (major construction), and Design Engineering. While I was within Operations, I was at the Electric Power Plant when a second diesel— electric generator was brought "online". The two generators were out-of-phase with each other and the operator matched phases using oscillators. If the second generator was brought online without phase correction, destructive interference would have occurred.

The application — We realize that if we shift back and forth between Forms of Consciousness (Densities), we experience no physical change. This is not true if we try to travel between Realms, our physical body would not survive the destructive energy shift. As one can see in the illustration, there are two different Realms, one above the other. At maximum interference we "flat line" physically between the two Realms. Thus, to travel between Realms we have to do it in Spirit form. Remember that Densities are not Realms.

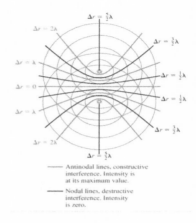

—— Antinodal lines, constructive interference. Intensity is at its maximum value.

—— Nodal lines, destructive interference. Intensity is zero.

We have a tendency to number the Densities, which is okay, but it doesn't make sense that a certain density is dedicated to a certain kind of experience; e.g., the Fourth (Density) is associated with compassion (as the RA collective, and others, say). Beings are moving in and out of a Density all the time (or across the electromagnetic spectrum—same thing)—including humans, although most of us are unaware of it. Neither they, nor we, stay in a certain Density as if it was an abode, and as if other Density (sometimes referred to as dimensions) "above this one" are inaccessible, unless we are evolved enough to access it—that's disinformation. It is true that mankind is trapped in the Middle REALM to a large degree, but this is an unusual circumstance. When we are dreaming, we are spiritual when we travel between Realms (which are spiritual, not physical) and we explore the Realms, and when we are thinking, we explore certain other Densities as well, although we cross several Densities every day in physical form and do not even notice.

However, **we don't know what we are doing because we are kept uneducated and pulled back unwittingly into our bodies again by the programming to which we are conditioned.** Once we are free, we will be free to explore the Realms as we wish! There is nothing such as "going to a specific Upper Realm and staying there". The Middle Realm is different due to the polarity. We are stuck in the Middle Realm until we free ourselves from polarity and accept I AM, WE ARE without qualifiers. When we look at it from this viewpoint, doesn't the whole thing become absurd? Are we going from one trap to another—is that what the channeled entities mean? Or do they mean that Realms are like "containers" that we jump between when we have reached a certain phase, and then we are trapped in this new container until we've raised our phase even further? It has to be either or, but none of it makes sense. However, there may be certain "Realms" that are locked, and to which beings can only get access by invitation.

Once the above really sank in, it was shocking for me to understand almost everybody in the spiritual movement has been deceived, and the majority of its truth-seekers are happily on their way into an even bigger trap. **This is profound!**

Unless the reader was fully aware of all this already, he or she should be pretty shocked and woken up by this information. I would go so far as to seriously ponder if the awakening of the human consciousness that is currently occurring, and has been accelerated thousand fold since the beginning of the Internet, is a planned setup by the Dark Force (the Enki Group and their allies, the Dracos/Reptilians Alliance).

Article 12

RAISE YOUR BRAIN CAPACITY 30%

REMOVING THE CARD BETWEEN LEFT & RIGHT BRAIN - There is a duel between mental structure and mental freedom; commonly experienced as the duality between the left and right brain when not in sync. Here the duality between your logical thinking mind, and your free-thinking and open mind comes to a clash, where thoughts do not balance with each other, but instead create struggle by their dualistic and opposite natures. Unifying these thoughts does not appear simple, but if you can relax into your meditation long enough, you might just start seeing how everything lines up and the way out will become clear.

The Eight of Swords is illustrated as a figure blindfolded unknowingly by his own will, surrounded by sharp swords flying all around him. He is unable to see the path in front of him and seemingly can't escape his own chaos. Yet, the path is right there, if he simply removed his blindfold he could easily break free from his self imposed confusion. The confusion is internal. The biggest problem is that the figure is

fixated on the problem, not looking at the solution, and thus continues in his confused state.

This card acts as the blindfold of the figure in the Eight Sword illustration and it is between the left and the right side of the brain. The card (blindfold) represents a state of mental imprisonment which eventually leads to isolation and misunderstandings. The card could, physically, be the membrane (Septum pellucidum) that resides between the two halves of our brain. The secret of this card is that the way out is actually very simple, if we could only remove our blockages to see this. Another way to look at this in a practical sense is to change our perspective and look at the challenge in a new way, one that is not restricted by the lens of limitation that we are currently viewing them through. Breaking down this card even further, it really speaks to over-thinking the little things, and spending too much time on the details at the expense of the bigger picture.

This exercise uses divine assistance to remove the card, allowing left and right brain to have improved connectivity. The result of removing the card will result in an approximate 30% increase in our spiritual mind. Remember that your heart contains your Soul's soul.

1ˢᵗ Get Centered (Preparation)

1. Wear comfortable clothing, such as sweats.
2. Remove your belt. Unhook your bra.
3. Sit up straight.
4. Knees level with pelvis.
5. Feet flat on floor.
6. Calves vertical.
7. Arms at side, on legs or on resting on the arms of the chair.

Proper Body Position

8. Roll your hips backward, slightly.
9. Align your back so that your neck aligns with the center of your pelvis.
   Shoulders relaxed but rolled back – this will thrust your heart forward. (You should feel as if someone was pushing the back center of your shoulders forward).

Shown for shoulder position

10. Pull your belly button toward your spine. (You should feel your heart is being pushed forward).
11. Elongate your body, as if someone is pulling you up from your crown.
12. Close your eyes or Look straight ahead – but have eyes unfocused.
13. Concentrate on your heart by hearing and feeling it beat. Do this for a few minutes and slow down its beat.

Final position should look

14. Breathe from your diaphragm (no shallow breaths).
15. Breathe through your mouth – you should hear the air entering and exiting your lungs. Take deep, slow steady breaths. Count the seconds in and

16. the seconds out. Count four seconds in and four seconds out. Increase the time in and out. Do this for several minutes, while still being centered in your heart.Relax your body, while still maintaining all of the above steps. Start by concentrating to relax your head, then neck, then shoulders, then chest and proceed, part by part, until you are at your toes.

17. Listen to 3rd Eye Chakra music, such as those listed below, while concentrating on your heart beat, breathing and body posture.

Sources
1. https://www.youtube.com/watch?v=VrQD9pJ9BlI
2. https://www.youtube.com/watch?v=aa7sr3ROVCw
3. https://www.youtube.com/watch?v=tU3oAyin8W4

2nd Get Grounded - Do the exercises by concentrating on your heart and aligning the heart with the Pineal Gland.

1. Complete the Centering Exercise Preparation.
2. Remain in the sitting position.
3. Roll your pelvis upward at the front.
4. Elongate your body, as if it is being pulled up from the crown. Maintain steadiness.
5. Visualize the crown of your head, as light opens up in a cone that opens upward to the cosmos.
6. Create an open channel from the crown chakra to the bottom of your spine.
7. From your navel visualize a cable of light shooting down through your piriformis down into the depth of the Earth. Like a drill of light shooting down and continuing further down, further than you can see or imagine.

3rd Complete the Pineal Gland – 3rd Eye Connection (Build up energy to remove card)

1. Remain in the sitting position and having completed the Centering and Grounding Exercises.
2. Simultaneously, bring your awareness up to the spine to the crown where the light is rising and extending to the crown chakra.
3. Breathe through your nose so that little valve shuts off the nostrils from the mouth. Breathe through your throat – a deeper sound than through your nostrils.
4. Check your form; straight down and up, as well.
5. Be receptive to the Earth energy (from your grounding rod) and upward, through the crown chakra out to the cosmos (sun energy).
6. Breathe from the belly, using the diaphragm.
7. Tighten your piriformis muscle (the one you use to stop peeing). Pull it up the center part (between your asshole and the sphincter/penis) toward your upper body, feel its energy being pulled to the pineal gland. Do this periodically, pulling the energy up and bouncing the energy up to the pineal gland.

8. Visualize a blue or purple connection between the piriformis muscle and the pineal gland. Continue bouncing the energy between the piriformis muscle and pineal gland.
9. Be cognizant of the light (sun/cosmos) energy entering the crown charka. Energy of light and love being received from the universe, through the crown charka.
10. Both energies are coalescing in rings around the pineal gland, rings that are spinning and building and releasing dopamine into your brain.
11. Visualize the pineal gland freeing itself from its sleepiness, releasing melatonin into the brain and body, making you feel free and not as physical.
12. Keep feeling the energy that is being received (love and energy).
13. Visualize a cross that extends from the center of your eyebrows and back through pineal gland to the back cortex (back of head). Then a branch upward to the crown chakra and downward to the piriformis muscle.

Sources:
1. Exercise: 'Third-Eye Meditation - Activating the Pineal Gland' by Bentinho Massaro, https://www.youtube.com > watch
2. lternate Exercises: 'How to Ground Your Energy' by Tanaaz, http://foreverconscious.com/how-to-ground-your-energy

4ᵗʰ Remove the Card between Left and Right Brain

1. Continuing from the previous Exercise, visualize a blue or purple connection between the piriformis muscle and pineal gland. Continue bouncing the energy between the piriformis muscle and pineal gland.
2. Now concentrate on the Pineal Gland and use its collective energy to push the card upward to the Crown Chakra. The Pineal Gland is in the center of the brain and is immediately below the card that separates the two halves of the brain.
3. Once the card has been pushed into the Crown Chakra, your Guardian, Counselor, and the Universe force of light entering the Crown Chakra can "nibble-away" the card.

Both halves of the brain contain consciousness but each has a component of the duel between mental structure and mental freedom, meaning the two haves can slowly recreate the confusion card. Given this, it would be best to complete the above exercise on a periodic basis.

Sources
1. "Eight of Swords,' *SpiritScienceCentral*, https://spiritsciencecentral.com/patch-tarot/tarot-directory/eight-swords-tarot/
2. 'Corax Coding,' http://www.corax.com/tarot/ cards/ index.html?swords-8
3. 'Biddy Tarot,' https://www.biddytarot.com/tarot-card-meanings/minor-arcana/suit-of-swords/eight-of-swords/
4. 'The Book of Thoth,' http://amzn.to/2wnNDCb
5. 'Learn Tarot,' http://www.learntarot.com/s8.htm

6. 'Esoteric Meanings,' http://www.esotericmeanings.com/ eight-of-swords-thoth-tarot-card-tutorial/
7. 'The Golden Dawn,' http://amzn.to/2y37B78
8. 'The Tarot Handbook,' http://amzn.to/2eUpcWM
9. 'Aeclectic Tarot,' http://www.aeclectic.net/ tarot/ learn/meanings/eight-of-swords.shtml
10. 'Tarot,' *Wikipedia*, http://www.tarotwikipedia.com/ tarot-card-meanings/minor-arcana-swords/eight-of-swords-tarot-card-meanings/

PART 3 - STAGES OF WAKING UP

Article 13

THE LESSON OF THE SNOW
(Stage 1 of Waking Up)

MYSTICISM TEACHES that nothing is as it appears – everything in the physical universe has a spiritual counterpart. Let us explore the spirit within the snow.

WATER IN ALL ITS FORMS IS A SYMBOL OF KNOWLEDGE. Descending water represents the transmission of knowledge from a higher to a lower place, the flow of information from teacher to student. On a cosmic level, rain and snow reflect different ways in which Universe energy flows to us from a higher spiritual plane. Water flowing downward thus describes the Universes way of transmitting energy to us and represents the conduit through which our material existence and the Universe interact.

The purpose of existence and why Extraterrestrial Beings are here is to create unity between the Universe and man, so that we, in our limited, material existence can become integrated and unified in an intimate and equal relationship with the Universe. To achieve this neither the Higher Spiritual Universe nor the human can be compromised. Unity achieved on the Universal Realm would annihilate our identities, our existence. Can we (our egos, vanities, and needs) co-exist with the Infinite Universe that is uncontained and undefined? Unity attained on *our* material, finite terms would compromise the Infinite Universe, because the Universe would have to limit itself to our existence.

Sometimes water flows as rain and sometimes it freezes to different degrees producing snow, hail or sleet, which are all metaphors for the teacher monitoring and transforming the flow into forms that the student can contain and assimilate. Rain falls in drops which symbolize some level of contraction, but it flows continuously like a stream of information retaining its fluidity and it is absorbed quickly into the earth. Ice on the other hand, is a transmission that is more on the recipient's terms. The information has solidified into a compact state so that the student can internalize it. The flow has ceased and turned into a solid form, so the student is not overwhelmed by the continuous flow of new ideas.

Snow is an intermediary state between fluid water and solid ice. A snowflake needs at least two components in order to form. The two components: water and earth – earth being the particles, and the water being the droplets. Earth is the material world – without any recognition of Universe Knowledge; Water is the knowledge of the Universe – a higher Level Energy without any containers. Thus snow, being half Higher Density Knowledge and half Earth provides the perfect intermediary between these two worlds.

Snow consists of separate snowflakes that are actually independent properties – each comprised of about 100 ice crystals. Snowflakes cling to each other but they are not intrinsically one. In contrast, water is one unified entity. Although it consists of droplets, each drop joins with another and they become one body of water. What is the symbolism of this is the flow of knowledge.

When a teacher has to reach out to a student who is far beneath his or her level of knowledge and understanding, he or she cannot allow the water to just flow freely, it has to be dressed up in metaphors and it has to be paced. In order for the student to understand a new concept, the teacher needs to create a point of reference by using examples, anecdotes, stories, and analogies. Thus snowflakes represent the need to explain gradually, step by step, in a language that is accessible to the student.

Snow falls gently and silently, teaching us in our own process of educating others and educating ourselves, that we need gentleness. If we educate with a sledgehammer – with unceasing rain pour – it will simply submerge and destroy the crops. Even when it rains on Earth, science tells us that on a higher level, the beginning process could have originated in snowflakes. So snowflakes are a symbol of that first gentle step.

– A Subtle Awareness of "Something More" begins to grow.

In Stage 1 of Awakening, we are most asleep; we do not even know that we are asleep. We are entrenched in mass consciousness and going through the motions of life, generally following the rules of culture and laws of the land. We don't usually question reality or seek answers beyond what is necessary for survival and maintenance of a lifestyle.

Our identities define us and we live within the construct of religion, culture and/or society. We may even play the part of victim or perpetrator.

Unconscious programming runs us, and, as a result, we see the world in black and white – good and bad. We likely process a rigid model of the world according to our specific programming.

Because there is a great desire to fit in and be accepted, in this Stage, it is common to sacrifice our needs and compromise our values in order to receive approval and be included in our desired community, be that family, culture, business, religion, etc.

Self-worth is likely conditional and attached to identity or the roles we play, or there may be other means of proving that we are worthy.

Because the ego generally runs the show, we likely believe we are the ego, with little or no awareness that there is a greater part of us.

In Stage 1, happiness is based on externals, therefore, in order to feel happy, we try to control reality; other people, places and experiences.

Although we attempt to control our lives, for both happiness and security, it is more than likely that our emotions rule, and our actions and reactions are based on our moment to moment feelings.

We make no connection between our thoughts/beliefs and our experiences in reality, and, therefore, we have no direct ability to consciously create our reality.

Despite our unconscious nature, the first signs of awakening happen during this stage; a "flash feeling" that there is something more, or an inkling of doubt that makes us uncertain about life and reality.

SNOW IS THE UNIVERSE SPEAKING TO US – speaking to us through purity, speaking to us gently and gradually on our terms. Snow is the intermediary between the Universe and Earth; ice is a little closer to the level of Earth; sleet is in between snow and ice. Thus every weather condition sends us a message and lesson – whether it's rain, snow, ice, sleet or hail.

Ultimately, the intention is that the snow should melt and turn to water. Once the snow falls and blocks our driveways and streets, we want it to melt. In the education process the student needs to pause which requires a freezing of the water, but then at some point it has to melt and integrate into our system in order for us to grow.

WAKING UP IS A JOURNEY from limitation to freedom — from unconscious to conscious. Whether you intentionally choose to take this journey or an unexpected experience propels you onto the path, once you start, there is no turning back.

There are 5 Stages of Awakening, and when you understand each Stage, and where you are on the journey, you can recognize the sign posts along the way, and the possible pitfalls to avoid.

Whatever stage you might now be experiencing, you cannot get it. Awakening is simply a natural process, just like the caterpillar that awakens as the butterfly.

Article 14

WAKEING UP STAGE 2
(The Stage of Questioning)

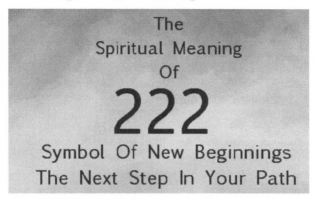

STAGE 2 OF AWAKENING – THE STAGE OF QUESTIONING - The doubts experienced in Stage 1 begins to turn into meaningful questions. The first signs of movement from unconscious to conscious are experienced.

In Stage 2 of Awakening: We experience a growing discomfort in our lives. There is a feeling that something is wrong or missing. We begin to question mass consciousness and the validity of rules, beliefs and laws. Things that used to bring us comfort like religion or traditions are no longer satisfying and the places that we once found answers no longer provide relief.

We question our identity but we still hold on to it because we must continue to prove our worth, and we don't yet know ourselves outside of our human identity. As we question the roles we play, we may feel lost, and even betrayed by others or life in general.

We may even blame religion, family, culture, gender, race, ethnicity, government or the world for our problems, or maybe we blame specific people for our dysfunctions. As we shift responsibility onto others, we feel powerless over our lives; not yet realizing that in order to take back our power, we must take responsibility. In this stage, we might move from victim to survivor, but we are likely still blaming others and feeling powerless.

We begin to ask, "Who am I? Why am I here?"

Although we are searching for answers, we still hold on to certain limiting beliefs that keep us enslaved in the reality we have known. When we attempt to challenge these beliefs, fear brings us back, keeping us asleep a little longer.

In our discomfort with reality, and our search for answers, we may experience a great deal of confusion, overwhelm, anxiety and even depression. We keep up with our lives but we are secretly just "going through the motions."

As we experience a variety of challenges designed to help us wake up, tolerable discomfort turns into pain and suffering. As our disempowering beliefs are demonstrated in real life situations and relationships, we get our first glimpse of the unconscious programs running our lives, but our desire to fit in and be accepted is likely stronger than any desires to free ourselves. Although this is the beginning of our internal programs breaking down, we are still trying to prove our worth by demonstrating our importance and seeking approval for our efforts.

We begin to understand that happiness cannot be found in the outside world, but we are still playing the game – seeking happiness in other people, places and experiences.

In this stage, there can be a large number of emotional triggers. We may even experience trauma or remember past trauma. Emotions are generally very strong, and we may feel most fragile or vulnerable. What we do not yet realize is that our issues are coming to the surface to be healed and released. Although we are beginning to see the world in a whole new light, we may still possess black and white thinking – maybe more than ever. We are not ready to take responsibility for our lives and, therefore, we make little or no connection between our thoughts and our experiences in reality.

As the outside world no longer satisfies our hunger, the journey inward is about to begin.

In Stage 2, we rebelled against the external world with little or no success in relieving our pain, suffering or discomfort, so now we retreat as we begin to seek answers inside ourselves.

As more and more people awaken, a threshold of awakening will be experienced, and the masses will awaken in much different paradigm than those of us who have already awakened or who are awakening now. The stages of awakening will be less defined and maybe even disappear altogether.

No matter where you are on your journey to awakening, you are exactly where you need to be.

Article 15

WAKEING UP STAGE 3
(The Stage of Introspection)

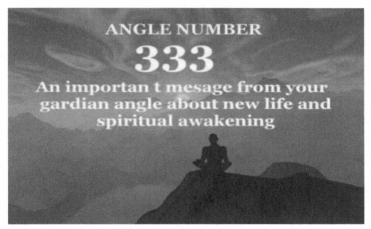

STAGE 3 OF AWAKENING – THE STAGE OF INTROSPECTION
Immense personal/spiritual growth and the start of conscious evolution through self-discovery.

In Stage 3 of Awakening, we begin a journey of introspection. In Stage 2, we rebelled against the external world with little or no success in relieving our pain, suffering or discomfort, so now we retreat as we begin to seek answers inside ourselves.

We start to disentangle from mass consciousness, releasing many limiting beliefs that were programmed into us by asleep parents, teachers, culture, society, religion and media. As we release these beliefs, we may experience both grief and relief. If we spent a life time imprisoned in beliefs that caused emotional suffering, physical hardship and lost happiness, we may grieve for the life we never had, and at the same time, we may feel great relief as we break free from limitation.

As we recognize how asleep we have been, we can clearly see that most people we know are still asleep. We try to waken them, but our attempts are seen as judgmental and, therefore, met with deaf ears.

Not surprisingly, with our eyes wide open, it is common to experience greater judgment of other people (friends and strangers alike), society and the world. Others may feel our judgment and defensively respond with their own judgment of us. We are seen as different, weird and maybe even crazy. Sooner or later, we decide to keep our growing awareness to ourselves; maybe rationalizing that it's better to be silent than be judged. At this point, we don't have a lot of hope that others will wake up.

We are still focused on everything that is wrong in our lives, and in the world, but, at the same time, we have resistance to letting go. **The process of letting go is often "the work" in this stage**, and, as we learn to let go, Stage 3 is where we may leave unsatisfying jobs, intimate relationships, families, friendships, religions, organizations and any disempowering ways of life. We may disentangle from roles we played, reject our past identity, and there may even be a total withdrawal from society.

Our former model of the world is failing and we no longer see the world in black and white or good and bad. There may be a growing sense that we are all connected, but at the same time we may feel completely disconnected from every other human being. In many ways, we are faced with the dichotomy of life and existence.

The most common attribute of stage three is loneliness. In a sea of billions of people, you may feel like you are the only one awake; no one understands you, and there is no one with whom to connect. At this point, you might begin to question "the questioning" – why did you ever begin this journey? What's the point of waking up, if you must be alone and lonely? After all, you might have been unhappy when you were asleep but at least you had friends, family and people who cared about you. Now, there is no one. You consider "going back." You wish you could forget about everything you now know just so you can be part of a family or community. You yearn for "normalcy" in order to fit in with others, but you also know that it is too late. You cannot forget what you have remembered, and despite your loneliness and your desire to fit in, you wouldn't go back or undo your path even if you could.

Issues of worthiness often surface in this stage, because the ways, in which, we once proved worth no longer work or are no longer available because we left the job or situation that once made us feel worthy. We may still try to seek approval, acceptance or appreciation or get other emotional needs met by those still in our lives, but it doesn't fulfill us, as it once did, and we are left feeling empty – forced to deal with feelings of unworthiness on our own.

Our desire to fit in and be accepted is slowly being drowned out by our desire to be free and awake.

In the quest for answers and relief from emotional pain, we may embark on some sort of spiritual practice such as meditation, yoga or mindfulness. If we are not using the practice to avoid something, its purpose is likely to get us somewhere, accomplish something or wake up.

In stage three, we may experience the first real sense of power, but, if the Ego claims this power, we may have challenging and humbling experiences. By now, we may be able to see the connection between our thoughts/beliefs and the creation of our reality, and, as a result, we try to control our thoughts, but it is a difficult process because old programs are still running.

We no longer look outside ourselves for happiness, but maybe we don't yet know how to find it within. Peace and freedom may also take precedence over happiness.

Stage three is often the longest stage and almost always the most challenging, but it is also the most important in terms of awakening.

This stage is marked by the swing between resistance and letting go, with moments of clarity and enlightenment, but they don't last. It is very common to have multiple experiences of awakening in this stage and even to believe that each one is the final awakening; only to find yourself back in "reality", hours, days or weeks later. With each experience of awakening, the sense of your higher self grows stronger. You are unknowingly making room for this real self to emerge in your consciousness and integrate in your life.

In stage three, it is common to experience a fear of losing oneself, and you may struggle to maintain a sense of self, but ultimately, toward the end of this stage, an ego-end is inevitable. When the ego loses hold, there is often a realization that there is no point or purpose to life. This can be liberating, like a breath of fresh air, or it can be devastating, resulting in hopelessness and despair. Without point or purpose, we no longer know how to live our lives, and nothing is ever the same.

There is a foreboding sense that awakening will cost you everything, yet, at the same time, there is a greater sense that something inside you is waking up.

Go inward (INTROSPECTION) to find WHO YOU ARE (an untethered free spirit), raise your frequency, disassociate from chaos and fear, and become a free spirit in the Universe – This is WAKING UP.

Article 16

WAKEING UP STAGE 4
(The Stage of Resolution)

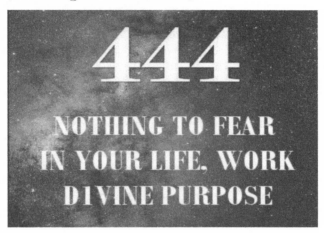

STAGE 4 OF AWAKENING is the STAGE OF RESOLUTION where your true self has finally overshadowed your false self or Ego self. The struggle that you experienced in the first three stages is over and you experience a deep peace and knowing of whom you really are, and you are no longer seeking answers. This is fondly known as the Eckart Tolle Stage.

All your beliefs have been overhauled in the past three stages, and the beliefs that remain support harmony and balance. You have mastered the art of letting go, and surrendering to a higher power. You also experience and have access to the inner power you possess, without Ego control.

Doubt has been replaced with faith and trust. You are able to see and understand your life in such a way that you're past and present all makes sense. You have forgiven everyone for everything, including yourself.

Unconscious programming has been replaced with consciousness, and there are no emotional or mental prisons holding you captive.

You take responsibility for your entire life, no longer blaming anyone for anything. As you have freed yourself, you have freed all the people who have ever been affected by your judgment and expectations.

You are no longer trying to prove your worth. You now know and own your intrinsic worth, and, as a result, you experience unconditional self-love.

Although you might still be alone on your journey, you experience a deep and profound connection to all of life and the sense of loneliness has likely faded into all oneness. The need and desire for the old paradigm of relationships has shifted and you no longer yearn to fit in or be "normal." You allow yourself to be exactly who you are, without needing approval or acceptance from anyone. You no longer have a need to change anyone or to help those you love wake up, and you are pleasantly surprised that some people you know are actually awakening. All your relationships improve, and the new people who come into your life are better aligned with who you are.

In this stage, you integrate your insights and develop greater understanding for the journey you have been on. You may teach, mentor or share, but not because you feel you have to, or because you need to, but only because it brings you joy, and you are guided to do so. You may have a compelling desire to support others on their journey or you may have no inclination whatsoever. If you take the role of teacher, mentor, healer or coach, you do not take responsibility for others, but rather you empower them to empower themselves. You don't take anything personally, and another's behavior has little, or no, effect on you.

During stage four, it is common to have some sort of spiritual practice, such as meditation, yoga or mindfulness, but not because you are trying to get somewhere or accomplish something (as in the previous stage), but rather because it feels good to you, and it is a natural expression of your life. You may also experience increased intuition and the ability to access infinite intelligence, as if you have a direct line to unlimited information.

This stage is marked by living in the moment.

You have made peace with the realization that there is no purpose or point to life, and, as a result, it is effortless to live in the present moment. Your love for life and all living beings overflows unconditionally with gratitude and appreciation as a common state of being.

The concepts of good and bad have dissolved, and, yet, you have the full knowing that inside everyone and everything is love.

You take stock of yourself, realizing that you are still you. You are free from Ego-control, and no "authentic parts" have been lost in the journey to awakening. Your personality may be quite the same, but you are likely more easy-going and light-hearted.

Either you have found a livelihood that is aligned with who you are, or you have made peace with your present day livelihood.

There is really no thought of happiness because you no longer need anything to make you happy. You have realized that the secret to happiness is living in the moment and it is now easy to be present at all times.

You have learned how to master your thoughts and beliefs, but, surprisingly, you may have no desire to change anything in your life.

Although you likely experience a full range of emotions, emotions no longer rule you or control your choices or relationships.

Your Higher Self has integrated in your body, and you live your life as this real self.

You are finally conscious and awake, and grateful that your past "asleep-self" had the courage and tenacity to make this journey. It was worth it – a million times over.

Article 17

WHAT YOU SHOULD HAVE LEARNED IN AWAKENING STAGES 1 - 4

What You Should Have Learned During the Process of WAKINGUP – Stages 1–4,

1) Don't play the part of being the victim. This is the Dark Force pulling you down.
2) Recognize that you are spiritual, not worldly.
3) Don't listen to anyone who is negative; get them out of your life. Surround yourself with only those who support you.
4) Don't hang onto the past, both this life and all past lives. They are meaningless in and by themselves. They only tell you show you got to where you are today, nothing else. Let go of the past.
5) Do not live for the future – the future never comes.
6) Only live in the moment – this moment is the only reality.
7) Disregard the negativity of the world –it is spiritual growth that matters.
8) Disregard all negative dreams. They are dark Force generated. The Light is always a warm, supporting light. Tell the Dark Force to get out of your life. Tell them you are exercising you Free Will and direct them to leave. You could say "in the name of Jesus Christ, I am directing all Darkness to leave and not come into my life ever again." Jesus was an avatar sent by God to tell us about the Creator - not to be confused with "God Almighty" who was given to us by the Anannaki, the creator of Mankind; God Almighty is not the same as the Creator God. Believe what Christ said, but not the spin put on his word by the Church, which supports God Almighty.

9) Ask your guardians to not only guard your souls but to guide you through the darker parts of your life – the Universe is there to help, but you must ask.

10) Get grounded and connect with the universe – The Grounding Exercise is listed within Article 12.

11) Get onto utube and watch the presentations by Bentinho Massaso – the meditation presentation concerning grounding and raising you antenna to connect with the Universe.

12) Only be concerned with what you can control. Don't be concerned with all that is outside your control - this is called worry. If you cannot control it, there is nothing you can do about it, so stop thinking about it.

13) Know that you are "I AM" without any qualifiers. All qualifiers are Ego. Start by responding to "I AM _____" (such as I AM an Engineer) – now discard that qualifier. Continue this exercise with all the qualifiers that might define you and discard them. Finally, you will arrive at "I AM" without any qualifier since this is who you are, "I AM".

13) Become Enlightened, Realize that you came here to perform a Mission, Raise your Frequency from, normally less than 200 (Pride) to at least 500 (Love), Encourage others to WAKE UP to the REALITY of domination and control by the Dark Force, Heal those in pain (physically and mentally) so they are free to become enlightened and raise their own frequency, Be proactive in foretelling the events to come, Reveal Darkness in all its forms and shine your Light among it, and MOST IMPORTANTLY to show your LIGHT and PRACTICE LOVE.

As more and more people awaken, a threshold of awakening will be experienced, and the masses will awaken into a much different paradigm than those of us who have already awakened or who are awakening now.

Article 18

WAKING UP STAGE 5
(The Real World Begins–Step Into Your Power)

STAGE 5 - THE STAGE OF CONSCIOUS CREATION where you experience and deepen all the attributes of stage four, but you also step into your power as conscious creator.

Huge changes have rumbled through your life (moving from Stage 1 through Stage 4). Keep these changes on the highest possible course by keeping your thoughts positive and stay centered and fully trusting your intuition to now enter the Stage of consciously creating TRUE REALITY.

Many people arrive at stage four and mistakenly believe it is the final stage of awakening, but it is actually a bridge to an even greater experience of awakening.

Although there is no pre-ordained point or purpose to life, you now understand that the point and purpose of life can be anything that you choose, and you integrate this understanding by consciously choosing the purpose of your life because that is the point. Work and play merge into one, and you experience peace and fulfillment equally in both.

You no longer do anything out of obligation or need, but, instead, you are guided through inspiration and pure desire.

You experience a direct connection to all of life, and you are inspired to create in a whole new manner.

Through intuitive connection with Infinite Intelligence, you might develop new paradigms of community building, teaching or leadership.

At this stage, you have the ability to attract relationships and form communities that support the betterment of humanity. Since you have mastered your thoughts and beliefs, you can now consciously create the life you desire; living in the moment, while also creating for the future.

In pure connection with Prime Creator, you are a channel of expression in all you do.

STEP INTO YOUR POWER – YOUR REAL JOURNEY HAS JUST BEGUN.

Article 19

WAKING UP TO REALITY IN STAGES SUMMARY

I wrote a book, *Conscious Awakening – A Research Compendium* (2019), concentrating on the Search for the TRUTH (594 pages including the True History of the Universe and its colonization, the Aliens, the Reveal now underway, the types of Lightworks, How the World may end, The Stages of Waking Up, Where from Here, and many more Chapters). This book led to my enlightenment and Awakening.

This book, *Conscious Awakening 101* is the Short Course to assist you in your enlightenment and awakening.

Within this Part of this book, I have presented an Article on each phase of Waking Up.

My Search for Knowledge led to my Enlightenment and my current journey into being fully AWAKE. In a nutshell, below is the process of AWAKING, where the Stages often blend together.

> ASLEEP – IT absolutely IS (there are rules)
> VICTIM – The world IS black and White (true polarity)
> SURVIVOR – IT IS what IT IS (shades of grey)
> THE SEARCH FOR KNOWLEDGE – IT IS not Right
> ENLIGHTENMENT – What IS, ISN'T
> AWAKE – What ISN'T IS

The MATRIX is Reality. Now, all you need to do is to determine if YOUR REALITY is within or is outside of the MATRIX and which side of Reality is where your Light work exists, taking into account if you came from within or outside of the 4% Universe (which I present in Article 41).

Article 20

NUMBER OF PEOPLE SEEKING ENLIGHTENMENT

There is an ancient Indian saying that states that for an individual to awaken from the illusion of self, the urge to do so must be similar to a man whose hair is on fire and he is desperately in need of water to put it out. Nice, gentle dreams aren't the ones that jolt you out of your sleep.

It is estimated that 1 in 10 million people have spiritual enlightenment as a goal. Only those who are seriously committed will reach it. If 1 in 10 million tries, perhaps 1 out of 100 will succeed? So, 1 in a billion? Who knows? Then again, it depends how you define "spiritual awakening." There are gradations of consciousness. One may be "awakened" but not "enlightened." And even enlightenment has its levels.

POPULATION DISTRIBUTION IN 2014 – 8.1 B (Billion) world population:

- 7.2 B –Declared Religion but may not be practicing (Christian – 2.4 B, Islam - 1.8 B, Hinduism – 1.15 B, Buddhism – 521 M, Chinese Traditional Religion – 394 M, Ethnic Religions – 300 M, African Traditional Religions – 300 M, Sikhism – 30 M, Spiritism – 15 M, Judaism 14 M, Other Religions)
- 70 M – Believe in a Higher Power
- 1.2 B – Secular, humanist, Nonreligious, agnostic, atheist

ENLIGHTENMENT / DARK DISTRIBUTION IN 2014 – Since the universe appears to be very mathematical, distribution should fit the Standard Distribution Model (Bell Curve) with 5-Deviations. However, Distribution can easily be contested, as indicated by the wide variation among the many sources (i.e., references vary widely). Literature research tends to indicate that Enlightenment is beginning to dominate the Dark Side, with the Dark Side maintaining its Control of the Earth. Given this, the below distribution may be what it was in 2014.

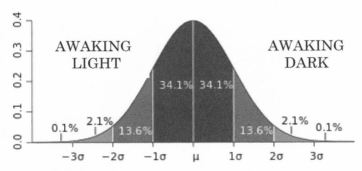

Refer to the book, *Conscious Awakening – A Research Compendium* for a detailed description of the various divisions within the Light vs. Dark spectrum.

>0.01% (810 T) - Non-Dual Awakening
>1% (8.1 M) – Spiritually Awake
>2.1% (170 M) - Spiritual Superconsciousness & Rational
>Consciousness
>13.6% (1.1 B) – Awakening to Enlightenment
>34.1% (2.8 B) – Asleep but leaning toward Enlightenment
>34.1% (2.8 B) – Asleep but leaning toward Dark
>13.6 B (2.8 B) - Waking Up Dark
>2.1% (170 M) - Sold Out, Converted, or Selected Dark
>1% (8.1 M) – Elite Dark
>.01% (810 T) – Resolute Dark

Lightworkers, Starseeds, Indigos, Wanderers, Travelers, Galactic Warriors and other Star Beings need to be concentrating on the middle 68.2% where there is the highest chance of success.

BOTTOMLINE – So what does all this mean? All the words are trying to give you a point of reference: (1) Where Am I Spiritually, (2) What Might be Next in my Ascension Process and, (3) What is the Percent of Darkness AM I Dealing With (World Population Wise and Dark vs. Light Distribution).

Sources:
1. The Groupings between "Service-to-Self (STS) and Service-o-Others (STO) are fully described within Chapter 17-Glimpses into Enlightenment, of *Conscious Awakening – A research Compendium*, Arlene Lanman, 2017, available at BookBaby Bookstore (Publisher) or through many Online and brick-and-mortar Bookstores, such as Barns and Noble, Amazon, Target, Wal-Mart, many others.]
2. 'Roughly how many enlightened people are living on the planet in 2018?,' 15 Answers, *Quora*, Mar 18, 2018, Various Authors, https://www.quora.com/Roughly-how-many-enlightened-people-are-living-on-the-planet-in-2018
3. 'How seldom or often does awakening happen in modern time? What is the percentage of enlightened people in your opinion?,' *Quora*, June 4, 2016, Various Authors, https://www.quora.com/How-seldom-or-often-does-awakening-happen-in-modern-time-What-is-the-percentage-of-enlightened-people-in-your-opinion
4. 'How many enlightened human beings are there in the world today?,' 18 Answers, *Quora*, Various Authors, Nov 30, 2016, https://www.quora.com/How-many-enlightened-human-beings-are-there-in-the-world-today
5. 'Mindful Awakening: The Cost Is Just Everything,' Jessica Graham, *Deconstructing Yourself,* Sept 18, 2018,https://deconstructingyourself.com/mindful-awakening.html
6. 'Spiritual Emergence – Awaken in The Dream,' Paul Levy, Sept 29, 2018, https://www.awakeninthedream.com/ articles/spiritual-emergence
7. 'The Pros and Cons of Having a Dark Side,' Seth M. Spain Ph.D. author of The Dark Side of Work, Aug 20, 2014, *Psychology Today*, https://www.psychologytoday.com/ca/blog/the-dark-side-work/201408/the-pros-and-cons-having-dark-side
8. 'The dark side of personality at work,' Seth M Spain, Peter D Harms, James M Lebreton, Published in *Journal of Organizational Behavior* (2013); DOI: 10.1002/job.1894, 2013, John Wiley & Sons, Ltd
9. ''List of religious populations,' Wikipedia, Pew Research, Gallup International, other references, https://en,m.wilipedia.org/List_of_religious_population
10. 'Humans are Waking Up: First Time in Recorded History, Schumann Resonance Jumping to 36+,' Feb 2, 2017, *LinkedIn*, prepareforchange.net/207/02/02/humans-are-waking-up-for-the-first-timje-in-recorded-history-schumann-resonance-jumping-to-36/

PART 4 – MIND, BODY, SOUL, SPRIT

Article 21

SPIRIT, SOUL, MIND BODY
(Know Thyself)

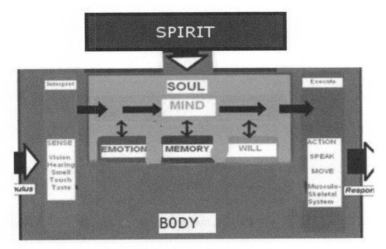

DUAL SOULS BACKGROUND – Many cultures have recognized some incorporeal principle of human life or existence corresponding to the soul, and many have attributed souls to all living things. There is evidence even among prehistoric peoples of a belief in an aspect distinct from the body and residing in it. Despite the widespread and longstanding belief in the existence of a soul, different religions and philosophers have developed a variety of theories as to its nature, its relationship to the body, and its origin and mortality.

Among ancient peoples, both the Egyptians and the Chinese conceived of a dual soul. The Egyptian *ka* (breath) survived death but remained near the body, while the spiritual *ba* proceeded to the region of the dead. The Chinese distinguished between a lower, sensitive soul, which disappears with death, and a rational principle, the *hun,* which survives the grave and is the object of ancestor worship. Today, Aboriginal, Torres Strait Islander, and Papua New Guinea natives believe in dual souls: The Higher Self (Spirit) – near but detached from the body, and the Corporeal Soul that is distinct from the body, yet residing in it.

The early Hebrews apparently had a concept of the soul but did not separate it from the body, although later Jewish writers developed the idea of the soul further. Biblical references to the soul are related to the concept of breath and establish no distinction between the ethereal soul and the corporeal body. Christian concepts of a body-soul dichotomy originated with the ancient Greeks and were introduced into Christian theology at an early date by St. Gregory of Nyssa and by St. Augustine.

Ancient Greek concepts of the soul varied considerably according to the particular era and philosophical school. The Epicureans considered the soul to be made up of atoms like the rest of the body. For the Platonists, the soul was an immaterial and incorporeal substance, akin to the gods yet part of the world of change and becoming. Aristotle's conception of the soul was obscure, though he did state that it was a form inseparable from the body.

In Hinduism the *atman* ("breath," or "soul") is the universal, eternal self, of which each individual soul (*jiva* or *jiva-atman*) partakes. The *jiva-atman* is also eternal but is imprisoned in an earthly body at birth. At death the *jiva-atman* passes into a new existence determined by karma, or the cumulative e consequences of actions. The cycle of death and rebirth (*samsara*) is eternal according to some Hindus, but others say it persists only until the soul has attained karmic perfection, thus merging with the Absolute (*Brahman*). Buddhism negates the concept not only of the individual self but of the *Atman* as well, asserting that any sense of having an individual eternal soul or of partaking in a persistent universal self is illusory.

The Muslim concept, like the Christian, holds that the soul comes into existence at the same time as the body; thereafter, it has a life of its own, its union with the body being a temporary condition.

SPIRIT, SOUL, MIND BODY - To the author, it seems rational, from a Universe standpoint that we consist of a Dual Soul (an ethereal Spirit and a Corporeal/earthy Soul), mind and body.

SPIRIT is a "piece" (fragment) of Creator God and has the twelve godlike virtues of devotion, balance, justice, faithfulness, selflessness, compassion, courtesy, equanimity, patience, courage, discernment and love. The Spirit may, also, contain the essence of our personality in order for other spirits to recognize us when we no longer have a body. Spirit never dies since it is pure and given to us by Creator God (First Source); it is part of First Source God (the "Great SPRIT").

EARTH SOUL is consciousness of our own existence due to the activity of the soul. Our personality resides in our soul. As a soul, you are a vast, powerful entity, created directly from the same "stuff" as this Supreme Creator (First Source), and you possess all its powers. As soul, You spend eternities on frequency bands higher than the **Earth plane** (Realm), exploring, creating and loving, where experiencing anything other than unconditional love is impossible. Because of this soul plane limitation, the Creator and its hierarchy of souls established a **"quarantine zone"** (Earth plane) of a lower fre quency, to which a fragment of your soul's energy can incarnate and experience fear, which blocks the flow of unconditional love. The Earth plane is of such low frequency that much of what you as soul knows is lost when your fragment descends here, so each incarnation starts with a "clean slate."

Consummation of the body and spirit (Soul is not Spirit)

SOUL is
- **Self – conscious.**
- **Intellect** which makes our existence possible.
- **Fruits of the Spirit** (Gifts of the Spirit are "materialized" in the Soul). Galatians 5:22-23 (New International Version): [22]But the fruit of the Spirit is love, joy, peace, forbearance, kindness, goodness, faithfulness,[3]gentleness and self-control. Against such things there is no law.
- Has been given the **power of Freewill** (by First Source God).
- **Self dwells in the soul**

Without Body or Spirit, Soul would only be conscious of Self.
- Prideful, Superficial, Defensive, Seeks Attention,
- Favors Self over Others,
- Seeks Worldly pleasures, sophisticated, materialistic, mercenary,
- Does not die with the Body, just lives and is the part involved in JUDGEMENT (of the thoughts and attitude of the heart – Hebrews 4:12; we are judged by our soul, which is the organ of our Free-Will).

BODY – The physical body is just a vessel which ages and dies.
- Ground/dust. Dust of the ground.
- World – what we see, touch, feel and smell.
- Physical body to communicate to the physical world.
- Senses dwell in the body.
- Senses or organs: Communicates with the physical world.

MIND - The mind is the interactive mechanism between the body and soul. The mind registers and filters emotion (the language of the soul) and registers nerve impulses generated by the body. The degree of communication between the body and mind, and soul and mind depends on your ability to manipulate your mind to work for you. When the mind is functioning as intended, it is <u>self-aware, focused and quiet</u> as required. So the mind has two choices: to block out sensation or to listen to it. If the mind is smart, it listens.

PRE-LIFE PLANNING – Approximately 3-months before birth, our Spirit is told or determines that it is to journey to the polarity world of the Earth in order to be a Light Bearer for Creator God. The Spirit is living on the Soul Plain where there is no polarity and all is love and, hence, it needs to prepare for this journey occurs approximately 3 months prior to conception. This is why the Torah and others say "this time next year" (you will enter into the world of polarity).

THE EARTHLY SOUL'S GOAL—Wants to please the Spirit and wants to bestow the Spirit with worldly gifts of wealth, jewels, attention, and worldly pleasures, which all annoys the Spirit. The Spirit comes to teach the Earthly Soul what the Spirit has experienced in the spiritual realm can occur her on Earth - together they can achieve peace, joy, happiness, lack of worry, etc. - "as it is in heaven, so it shall be on Earth."

SPIRIT'S GOAL –- It is a part of the Sprit's goal to teach the Earthly Soul the ways of The Light in order to achieve its ascension to a life aligned with the Soul Plain. To this end, **the Spirit works to Wake Up the Earthly Soul**.

WHEN THEY DON'T WORK TOGETHER

- SPIRIT CAN LEAVE: The Spirit often leaves us, and when it is away, the soul is lonely and feels abandoned. But when the Spirit comes home again, it brings with it an abundance of inspiration and light.
- SPIRIT and SOUL CAN LEAVE: when the soul and spirit leave "home" together, the heart and mind cannot wait to commit every possible kind of folly in the company of other foolish minds and hearts.

Article 22

THE 3 TYPES OF SOULS
(Live the life your Soul intended)

You have a SOUL but which type; here are a few possibilities. Yours might be one or parts of all of these:

WHEN YOU HAVE A PHYSICAL (ANIMAL) SOUL

- Is thought to be masculine in orientation.
- A voluntary soul.
- Carnal, mundane, requires sleep, Seeks health and life.
- Needs food for nourishment.
- Needs livelihood (physical work).
- Needs money (to support above).
- Feels pain, is contingent, suffering with changes in climate and health.
- Seeks physical challenges for stimulation..
- Is disgraced by the need to satisfy the body and grieved at this position, feels ashamed and confounded by this situation.

- **Primarily Service-to–Self**: "ME" and "OURS" are their key thoughts. **Service to Self** (STS) path sees the self as separate from others; body and mind drives need for material evolution, based on control, repression, hierarchy, power and competition. The physical soul sees love as conditional – what is in it for me. This soul type can be highly emotional in protecting their "assets" and what they consider as individual rights over the common good. In addition, "pack instinct" is prevalent in this soul type.

- **Subset: The Explorer**
- The seeker, iconoclast, wanderer, individualist, pilgrim.
- Don't fence me in.
- The freedom to find out who you are, within the limits of society.

- Journey, seeking out and experiencing.
- To experience a better, more authentic, more fulfilling life.
- Fear is being trapped, conformity, and inter emptiness.
- Weakness is aimless wandering, becoming selfish.
- Talent is autonomy and ambition.

WHEN YOU HAVE A SENSITIVE OR EMOTIONAL SOUL -One has the heart virtues of Appreciation or gratitude, compassion, humility, forgiveness, understanding and valor or courage. It is the combination of nowness—being in the now—and applying these words in our behaviors. It's being impeccable in this practice, since this is how to gain Human 3.0 SI and "escape" the Anannaki deception of enslavement followed by reincarnation into another Anunnaki's containment that keeps our spirit/soul in enslavement to the Anannaki [i.e., the Afterlife Trap]. (Refer to Article 40).

- To practice and apply the HEART VIRTUES is the reason that First Source has placed you in increasing larger groups and organizations – to expand the number of people that you can apply the Heart Virtues.
- Is a sensitive or emotional soul.
- Is compassionate.
- Seeks joy, happiness and warmth through feelings and love.
- Works through harmonious and artistic activities.
- To understand the eight types of Love (refer to Greek philosophy). To understand Heart Virtues.

Primarily Service-to-Others: "We" is their key thought. **Service to Others (STO)** is the path of accepting yourself and serving other selves; Heart and spirit drive the need for spiritual evolution, based on freedom, networking, cooperation and synergy. This soul type has the mantra of "Love conquers all."

Subset: The Caregiver
- The quintessential characteristics are the desire to take care of others.
- Has a tendency to put others' needs ahead of your own.
- You are loyal to the extreme.
- Your empathy allows you to understand nonverbal emotional signals.

Subset: The Lover
- The partner, friend, intimate, enthusiast, spouse, team-builder.
- Motto: You're the only one.
- Desire: Intimacy and experience.
- Goal: Being in relationship with people, work, and surroundings they love.
- Fear: Being alone, a wall-flower, unwanted, unloved.
- Strategy: To become more physically and emotionally attractive.

WHEN YOU HAVE THE INTELLECTUAL OR RATIONAL/ REASONABLE SOUL

- The driving soul to seek Knowledge, which yields Understanding, which yields Wisdom.
- Is the means of discovery as to who one really is.
- Is the researcher of information that can be condensed into thoughts.
- Is the seeker of "truth."
- Nourishment is Thoughts.
- Activity is meditation and thinking.
- Seeks mental challenge for stimulation.
- Has the capacity for reflection and circular thinking (what if).
- Is the seat of our ordinary, everyday thoughts and reasoning which concerns the satisfaction of our personal interests and our minimum need for material needs.
- Seeks knowledge, learning, Light to achieve Wisdom.

Primarily Service--to--Others: "We" is the key thought. **Service to Others (STO)** is the path of accepting yourself and serving other selves; knowledge and spirit drive the need for spiritual evolution, based on freedom, networking, cooperation and synergy. This soul type has the mantra of "Reveal Darkness and the Truth will make you free."

Subset: The Rebel
- The outlaw, revolutionary, wild person, the misfit, or iconoclast.
- Rules are made to be broken.
- Core Desire: Revolution and total change to overturn what isn't working.
- Fear: To be powerless or ineffective.
- Strategy is to disrupt, destroy, or shock.
-

Subset: The Rationalist
- Most Rationalists are cerebral and skeptical, who often discount their emotions or intuition in favor of rational analysis. The intellectual approach to life can cause Thinkers to appear restrained and unemotional to those around them.

Subset: The Creator
- The artist, inventor, innovator, musician, writer, dreamer, or sage.
- Motto: If you can imagine it, it can be done.
- Desire: To create things of enduring value.
- Goal: To realize a vision.
- Fear: Mediocre vision or execution.
- Strategy: Develop artistic control and skill; to create culture, expression of own vision.
- The sensitivity that is the mark of the Creator type, can be hard to manage in this harsh modern world. It does, however, given the advantage when it comes to accessing the intuitive part of yourself.

Subset: The Leader
- Taking on any kind of subservient role may be demeaning to this type of person.
- You have the natural air of a authority and have the charisma that makes you stand out in a crowd.
- You bring an innate wisdom, which is why people look to you for advice.
- You often make decisions on your own without thinking of others.
- Once you make up your mind, you may be reluctant to change it. This works well in an emergency, but in other circumstances it can give the impression that you are arrogant or condescending.

Subset: The Educator
- You have a gift for persuasion.
- You have a problem with repletion by going over the same point until it sinks in.
- You have a passion to convey what you know to others. There is little point in having knowledge without having someone to pass it on to. To this end, you may write a book to convey your knowledge to others.
- Much of what you know comes from reading and study.
- You may have a natural insight into a subject, often accumulated over many lifetimes.

KNOW WHO YOU ARE – This entire dissertation purpose is to help you know who you are and how the Spirit, Soul, Mind and Body, along with Soul Type interact to achieve a cohesive being. Of course, Lightworkers, Galactic Warrior, Indigos and Other Star Beings have a balance of the Physical/ Animal Soul (very minimal), the **Sensitive/ Emotional SOUL, and the Intellectual/ Rational/ Reasoning Soul, depending upon your Mission.**

Article 23

THE ASCENDING LIFETIME
(Earth Souls, Starseeds, Light Bearers)

EARTH SOULS – On average, most of the people on Earth have evolved spiritually right here. That is to say that their souls began here as simple 1st Density entities. At some point their soul group evolved and they began to embody 2nd Density forms and then, after further growth, these beings began to self-identify and transitioned to 3rd Density consciousness. At this point they became ready to be born into human bodies. Some of these Earth souls are, at this time, making the leap to Fourth (and even higher) levels of consciousness. Ascending Earth souls are a precious thing indeed, imbued as they are with the very deepest love and understanding of what it means to be "of the Earth".

Evolving from and within a group of their own kind, Earth Souls can often display the most profound compassion for others. So much so that they are often seen to be almost unnaturally empathic. They seem to feel, know and understand what others are feeling without a word being shared. And it is this capacity for compassion that often causes Earth Souls to be remarkably self-sacrificing. The propensity to feel that all humanity is one family will sometimes lead them to be willing to put the interests of others above their own. This very attribute often slows the spiritual growth of the Earth Soul as they often do not wish to advance ahead and leave others behind. They want to bring the whole world with them, wherever they go. The spiritually advanced Earth Soul is quite likely to utter a notion such as, "I will not ascend from this place until every other soul is able to come with me." So Earth Souls evolve and ascend together. Their travel through incarnations occurs in large "soul groups" that interact with each other, over and over again, lifetime after lifetime of ever shifting roles and relationships.

Most humans walking planet Earth today evolved here, however not everyone did! So, if some did not arise spiritually from this place... where DID they come from?

STARSEEDS – One fairly common point of origin for those who come from "elsewhere" are those who arose upon another planet, elsewhere in this galaxy or even beyond, in a very similar way in which Earth Souls arose upon Earth. Typically, Starseeds have evolved up to the Fourth, Fifth or lower-Sixth Density of consciousness upon their home planet and then come to Earth for an incarnation or two. It is mid-Sixth Density where polarity ceases to exist and to be here, now, one needs to understand and to have lived in a polarity world.

Starseeds usually arrive with a mission. They have accepted a spiritual contract to come here to assist in raising the vibration of planet Earth as we undergo a collective shift in consciousness. Starseeds have very often willingly taken a step down in consciousness... willingly being born into a system more dense than "home" so as to bring their gift to this place. Perhaps this is courage. Or perhaps it is the profoundest compassion. For, certainly, life in the Earth-Human society is often very hard on Starseeds.

Attributes common to many Starseeds:

1. Starseeds often struggle, for the duration of their life, with a sense of alienation; a feeling of not-belonging. This arises from a pre-cognitive awareness that they are not "home"... and worse... that they will never (in this lifetime at least) see "home" again.

2. This feeling of alienation is often exacerbated by being born into a family (of Earth Souls?) who patently "belong" together. Being the obviously odd one in the family is often just the beginning, as this experience of being "odd" will follow many Starseeds for their entire life. Somehow "fitting in" is something that seldom happens until they meet other Starseeds... and then they often suddenly felt wonderful. Like finding their "real" family for the first time.

3. Starseeds are often UFO nuts. Often they come from space cultures that had space-faring technology. As to the notion of "seeing a UFO" does not feel strange to many Starseeds. Indeed they often report the idea that the UFO's inhabitants are "my people" rather than "aliens".

4. Starseeds often have a pre-cognitive awareness that "home" is "out there".

5. Starseeds often have pre-cognitive awareness that they are here to assist in this world's transformation. And they bear a deep-seated memory of a society that was (usually) more harmonious, peaceful, gentle and advanced than that currently found upon Earth.

6. Starseeds are prone to depression if they don't take control of their lives and their experiences. They may also be prone to a variety of psychosis and neurosis due to the spiritual fracturing that they feel here on Earth and the

Disparity with the levels of consciousness and spiritual state of their home world.

7. Starseeds are seen as being HIGHLY creative; often prodigiously so. They often seem to be able to pull the most ingenious ideas, concepts and aware-ness's "out of thin air". Because, of course, they are accessing soul-deep memories from elsewhere!

8. Starseeds are quite likely to be poorly adapted to this planet in any number of ways. Perhaps they seem to be "allergic to everything". Perhaps they are photo-sensitive, declaring it always is "too bright". Perhaps they find it to al-ways be too hot or too cold. There are many possible variations for Starseeds whose physicality is demonstrating their spiritual alienation here upon planet Earth.

So, Starseeds are like Earth Souls, except that they are "visiting" for a lifetime or two.

There is a third group who originate from outside of this system of reality altogether – outside of the 4% Universe; then Universe controlled by the Dark Force. This third group is the Light Bringers.

LIGHT BEARERS – If Earth Souls are in the majority here, then Starseeds make up the majority of non-Earth Souls. Light-Bringers make up a very, very small minority.

Light Bringers are spirit entities that did not evolve inside this reality at all. Light-Bringers are so called because they are the part of that greater being that is tasked with bringing that being's essential energy or "Light" here to this place. Light-Bringers are here for something very particular. But before they can enact this purpose, they first have to utterly forget their own true nature so that they might lose themselves completely in this separation reality. Without this forgetting they will not be able to find their way down to the dense depths of consciousness where incarnation takes place. Which is what the Light Bringers had intended for themselves: to carry their Light right to the deepest core of this reality.

Essentially, if their Light is present here, then it will be possible to find it echoing throughout all the rest of their reality. So the Light Bringers first lose themselves utterly and forget all that they are and all that they know. And then, in this deep state of forgetting, they incarnate upon planet Earth (or another similar venue, deep in duality). And then their task is to find their way to sufficient healing that they might again begin remembering who they are, that they might shine the Light they went to all that effort to bring into this reality.

It's a bit difficult to make generalized statements about Light-Bringers since they are not "a group". Each one is a manifestation of a completely unique entity. And that, perhaps, is the only real unifying characteristic: When you meet a Light-Bringer you will quite likely be struck by the awareness that this person is "one of a kind". They are quite unlike anyone else you have ever met. The awakening Light-Bringer will also begin to show their Light. As they find it, so they express it. And this will inevitably result in them somewhat standing out in any crowd. You'll notice a Light-Bringer when you meet one!

Light-Bringers find their way to this level of reality via all manner of possible paths. And so we encounter the notion of beings coming here "from the angelic realms" or via a few incarnations on other planets (making those Light-Bringers also seem to be Starseeds) and so on. The possible permutations are too varied to contemplate. But when one comes to understand the origin of the soul, Light Bringers are different from other beings in that they first descended into this reality before finding themselves. They first fragmented themselves before beginning to reintegrate themselves. Earth-Souls and Starseeds, by contrast, originated spiritually from within this reality.

OTHER PATHS – There are, of course, more paths than the three. But, it doesn't really matter a great deal by which path you have traveled. All is of consciousness. So there is certainly no sense in which any of these paths are "better" than any other. No sense in which one is "more valuable" than any other. Each path is merely one way in which consciousness can find its way to this here and now.

WHAT IS IMPORTANT IS THAT YOU ARE HERE NOW. You have your "boots on the ground". You have made it to planet Earth at this pivotal time of the planetary spiritual evolution. And, right on cue, you are Awakening.

The way forward – When you begin to awaken spiritually, you begin to let go of the illusion; the illusion that every single person born on Earth is born into duality and brought with us a belief that there was nothing divine about ourselves. You begin to find your truth. You begin to heal. You begin to see your own light, your own magnificence, the beauty of your own soul. You begin to remember and fall in love with that which you truly are.

And this means, you raise your vibration. You transform yourself. You elevate your consciousness. And so, if you then leave this mortal life, you do not again return here because you are then no longer of this level of awareness. You either leave incarnation behind entirely or you move on to a different kind of life in a different kind of reality – a kinder, more loving, place. A place of less destructiveness. A place of greater harmony with your own true nature.

The point is: You can have a thousand lives on the wheel of reincarnation if you like, returning to this level of reality over and over again. But you can only have ONE ascending lifetime. And, since you are reading this, I am assuming you are engaged in your ascending lifetime. You are on your way up and out of this place.

Yes, you WILL be able to return here as a teacher or a master if you choose. That does happen often. It's a hard path, but some feel such love and compassion for this place and its people that they choose that. But that's a choice. Which is a very different thing than HAVING to come back, over and over again, because that is the level of consciousness where you are struck.

You have THIS LIFETIME to strike out from the deep, deep depths of consciousness you were born with and to reach as far and as high as you can. Because you will still be here on this Earth with your "boots on the ground" while you do so. You will, in THIS lifetime, be able to bring to bear all the light, beauty, and grace your soul has to offer, To give your gift, To shine your light, To sing your song. when you are done here and you walk away, you will do so with a heart brimming with joy and satisfaction that you did "right by yourself".

This is YOUR LIFETIME to shine your Light in such a way that others are pointed to their own hearts. That others see their own true nature. That others are awakened to their own beauty, perfection and divinity. Are you one of these? Are you an Earth Soul? Or a Starseed? Or a Light-Bringer? It really is easier to heal and find your purpose and Light when you begin to remember your origins, since that is the context for the life-story you are now telling yourself.

Source
1. "The Three Types of Awakening Soul," extracted from Are You an Awakening Soul by Arn "Zingdad" Allingham, https://zingdad.com/publications

Article 24

WHY THE EARTH FREQUENCY IS INCREASING & BEING MANIPULATED
(We are at War)

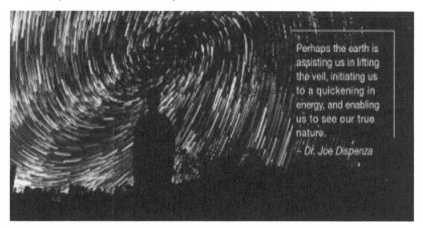

Perhaps the earth is assisting us in lifting the veil, initiating us to a quickening in energy, and enabling us to see our true nature.
– Dr. Joe Dispenza

FREQUNENCY OF THE EARTH IS RISING - An old sage from India has stated that the magnetic field (which "drives" the frequency) of Earth was put in place by the Ancient Ones to block our memories of our true heritage. This was so that souls could learn from the experience of free-will unhampered by memories of the past.

Mankind depends on two subtle environmental signals, the Yin from below and the Yang from above (both established by the Vedic civilization of Saraswati). The Schuman Resonance wave surrounding our planet is caused by the interaction between the Earth and ionosphere. In modern times it was discovered in 1954 by Winfried Otto Schumann, at that time Director of the Electro physical Institute at the Technical University of Munich, but to the Vedic civilization of Saraswati (9000-4000 BC) it was known as the YANG.

The Yank from above, has risen from 7.83 Hz (matching that of the Earth's core) to above 150 Hz. Alpha brain Frequency of 7.83 HZ on the EEG, is also known popularly as Schumann's Resonance. These frequencies start at 7.8 Hz and progress by approximately 5.9 Hz. (7.8, 13.7, 19.6, 25.5, 31.4, 37.3, and 43.2 Hz.).

The YIN from below, called OM in ancient India, is caused by the rotation of Earth's liquid iron core. YIN frequency seems to have stabilized at 7.8 Hz, as it has been for thousands of years.

OM mantra was uttered by the Vedic sages who stayed on the banks of the river Saraswati in 9000 BC. Vedic civilization of Saraswati flourished until 4000 BC, until the river became non-perennial due to tectonic shifts blocking the Himalayan Glacier mouth. The elite then migrated all over including Western coast of India, Mesopotamia, Europe and Russia.

For thousands of years the Earth Schuman Resonance frequency has hovered at a steady 7.83 Hz with only slight variations. In June 2014 that apparently changed. Monitors at the Russian Space Observing System showed a sudden spike in the Schuman Resonance frequency to around 8.5 Hz. Since then and until 1917, they recorded days where the Schuman Resonance frequency accelerated as fast as 16.5 Hz. In January 2017, The Shuman Resonance reached 36+ Hz.

In r 2019 there were several very high peaks of Schuman frequency – Earth pulse. More high peaks were measured:

-17th of March 2019: **100 Hz**
-17th of March 2019: **110 Hz**
-17th of March 2019: **120 Hz**
-17th of March 2019: **150 Hz**
-20th September2019: **100 Hz**
-6th of December 2019: **100 Hz**
-6th of December 2019: **158 Hz**

Since life began, the Earth has been surrounding and protecting all living things with a natural frequency pulsation of 7.83 HZ—the ancient Indian Rishis called OM.

Whether by coincidence or not, it also happens to be a that both the Constant Earth Core Resonance and the Schuman Resonance frequency are very powerful frequencies to use with brainwave entrainment., with the Schuman Resonance frequency being the most influential.

Entering the Photon Belt. The rising Schuman Resonance frequency values are the consequences of the events in Space. Our planet Earth is crossing the photon belt and this process has already begun. It is a cyclical process that repeats itself every 26.000 years. The Sol System entered the Photon Belt in 2012 and will be within the Belt for approx. 2,000 years, then exit for approx. 11,000 years before it reinters the Belt, once again. It takes a long time to make the demanding vibrational adaptations by the Earth and everything that constitutes it and everyone who inhabits this planet.

The rising Schuman Resonance frequency has been associated with high levels of hypnotizability, meditation, increased HGH levels and cerebral blood flow levels seem to be much higher while this frequency is being stimulated.

What does the rising Schuman Resonance frequency mean to Mankind - These emerging resonances are naturally correlated to human brainwave activity. So this means that we are changing. Human brainwaves (also, an electro-magnetic field) operates in concert with that of the Earth .and the Atmospheric (Schuman) frequencies. At rest, the human brain operates at 7.83 Hz – this is the "heart beat" ("firing" between neurons) of the human brain.

Consciousness, in humans, can be increased through an increase in field surrounding the human which, in-turn, increases the electro-magnetic field function of the human brain. If one wanted to achieve a higher consciousness, one could try to adapt each human, one at a time – a sizable task when the human population is 8-billion and growing.

As consciousness increases, the human mind determines that it is surrounded by ternary – created over time (eons) by the Dark Force. By raising consciousness, one "sees" reality for what it is and, as a result, ternary will be overcome.

Why: The Galactic Federation of Light has denoted that in the future (by analyzing all possible parallel timelines to the most probable sum-zero point), that what is happening on Earth today (tyranny by the Dark Force) will cause the same to occur throughout the universe in the future, unless it is "checked" now.

Long story, short is that the Galactic Federation of Light (Service-to-Others) is taking action now to thwart tyranny (Dark Force Service-to-Self) in the future, by accelerating the Photo Belt affect through intensive pulsed frequency waves into the Earth's core. If you are of a religious faith, then rationalize that the war between Heaven ("Light" - Service-to-Others) and the Forces of Evil ("Darkness" - Service-to-Self) continues – "As it is Above, so it is Below."

In and by itself, the rising Schuman Resonance Frequency is Awakening the brain through enlightenment to "see" the world for what it is - a polarized environment established by the Orion Empire when they were given (by Treaty (at the end of the 2nd and 3rd Galactic Wars) 4% of the Universe to dominate and control as the desired – they have ruled Mankind through deception, separation, and fear – the Free Universe is now trying to WAKE UP mankind to the ternary created by the Orion Empire overlords.

Raising the Resonance Frequency of the Earth is just one part of the "GREAT AWAKENING." Love & Light Workers, Galactic Warriors and all Star Beings need to **WAKE UP** to this Reality, WAKE UP to the deception and lies created by the Dark Force, and complete their mission to awaken Mankind to the deception and illusion instilled by the Dark Force to dominate and control the Earth.

Mankind was given Free-Will to determine their own future; no one else can make the change for them. Lightworkers, Galactic Warriors and the other Star Beings are here to assist but not control what mankind has to do for itself.

Sources

1. "SCHUMAN RESONANCE", Excerpt from Nexus Magazine, Vol. 10, #3, April-May, 2003, by Iona Miller, https://www.sedonanomalies.com/schumann-resonance.html

2. "NEW RECORD – Schuman frequency reached peak at 158 Hz. Discover this as huge, great opportunity for awakening – activating, boosting and achieving a consistent level of your Heart Coherence Vibration", Majda Ortan |, 9 Dec 2019, PH.agrohomm Natural quantum powers for sustainable agriculture, http://cora-agrohomeopathie.com/

Article 25

HEART'S ELECTROMAGNETIC FIELD
(Source of Consciousness)

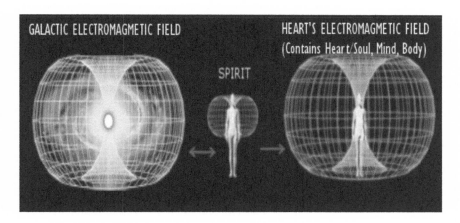

BACKGROUND – 1ST there is Creator God who created all things, then there were the Founding Fathers (from another universe), who sent four small groups to colonize our universe. Those four groups were ethereal and consisted of the Felines and Carrion. Each was given a mantra: Felines were given Service-to-Others and the Carrion were given the mantra of Service-to-Self. Since the races were ethereal, each merged/adapted to the animal species on the planets they were given. The Felines created/adapted felines and humanoids, the Reptilians created/adapted Reptilians, Draconians, Snake and lizard-like beings.

Then there were the Galactic Wars between Feline/Humanoids (Service-to-Self) and the Draconians/Reptilians, et al - outcome was the Draconians/Reptilians received 4% of our universe to control as they desired (Earth is within that 4%). An offshoot of the Reptilians were the Anannaki who modified our DNA to form Mankind. The Anannaki leader declared himself to be God Almighty over Mankind. Therefore, we have Creator God and the lesser God Almighty. Organized Religion formed their religion around Almighty God. The Orion Empire (Reptilians, Draconians, et al) sent 14 Orion families to rule the Earth.

Mankind has a Spirit (part of Creator God), Soul, Mind and Body. The <u>Soul, Mind and Body are bound within the electro-magnetic field created by the heart; the Spirit is outside of this electro-magnetic field</u>. The Spirit "talks"/advises the Soul and the Soul communicates with the Mind and receives input from the sensory parts of the Body (by way of the mind). Given all these words, when one takes the journey inside one is trying to communicate with the Soul, who functions as our guide in concert with the advice provided by the Spirit. Bottomline, the TRUTH is within each of us.

HEART'S ELECTROMAGNETIC FIELD – THE MASTER CONTROLLER - The Soul, Mind and Body are bound within the electromagnetic field created by the heart; the Spirit is outside of this electromagnetic field.

Every individual has a human heart field surrounding their body, an electromagnetic field emitted by their heart. This field is a signal network of sorts, affecting our mental and physical processes, as well as our health. The heart field extends around us in every direction at a range of fifteen to twenty-five feet, and interacts with the Earth's electromagnetic field, as well as the electromagnetic fields emitted by other living beings – not just people, but also animals and plants.

Unlike the illustration of a spherical shape field around our body and the galactic universe, the fields would, to a certain extent conform to the shape of our body and the shape of the galactic universe, unless, for the body, one of the organs is producing an abnormal amount of electromagnetic energy. A few people may be able to "see" the body electromagnetic field (aura) or feel the heart field. Lightworker Healers are able to manipulate the body field.

The heart is by far the greatest electrical generator of all the body; the continuous pumping and motion also creates sound, pressure, heat, light, magnetic and electromagnetic signals, all create magnetic fields around itself. Because the blood is a very good conductor of electricity, the whole of the circulatory system pulses each time the heart beats.

The heart generates the electromagnetic field by creating a pressure wave that travels rapidly throughout the arteries, much faster than the actual flow of blood that we feel as our pulse. These pressure waves force the blood cells through the capillaries to provide oxygen and nutrients to cells and expand the arteries, causing them to generate a relatively large electrical voltage. These pressure waves also applies pressure to the cells in a rhythmic fashion that can cause some of their proteins to generate an electrical current in response to this "squeeze."

The heart, like the brain, generates a powerful electromagnetic field, McCraty explains in <u>The Energetic Heart</u> that the Heart is a huge electrical producer that is filled with iron rich blood to makes a bio-chemical motor. The heart generates the largest electromagnetic field in the body. The electrical field as measured in an electrocardiogram (ECG) is about 60 times greater in amplitude than the brain waves recorded in an electroencephalogram (EEG).

Our soul or consciousness is imprisoned because of the electromagnetic field of the heart. Electricity is generated when a magnet is rotated, so the iron that circulates in our blood due to the heart's pumping keeps us imprisoned but the spinning of the iron core of the Earth could also be a factor unless quantum physics overrides that. When the heart stops the E-M field dissolves and the Soul is no longer bound within and is released.

The Heart–Brain Connection-- Most of us have been taught in school that the heart is constantly responding to "orders" sent by the brain in the form of neuron signals. However, it is not as commonly known that the heart actually sends more signals to the brain than the brain sends to the heart! Moreover, these heart signals have a significant effect on brain function – influencing emotional processing as well as higher cognitive faculties such as attention, perception, memory, and problem-solving. In other words, not only does the heart respond to the brain, but the brain continuously responds to the heart.

Consciousness originates from the SPIRIT, which is outside the Heart's Electromagnetic Field which keeps the Soul/Heart, Mind and Body in containment. The SPIRIT transmits Consciousness to the Soul, which conveys Consciousness to the Mind. The reason some may believe that Consciousness is "in the Mind" may be due to the fact that three of our sensory organs (hearing, visual, and taste) are contained within the same area of the body as the Mind. when someone asks a question, the responder's eyes look up and are requesting the Mind to answer. If one's eyes could roll inward, they would when one is asked a question.

Third eye or the pineal gland – Given the electromagnet field created by the heart, we should stop focusing on the third eye or the pineal gland, we need to direct energy and intention to the heart. The heart is really the source of emotional intelligence, transferring intelligence to emotions and strengthening our ability to manage them, We need to bring each of us to a heart-coherent state in the moment.

Connectivity to the universe – There is new data suggesting that the Heart's Field is directly involved in Intuitive Perception, through its coupling to an Energetic Information Field outside the bounds of space and time. There is compelling evidence that both the Heart and Brain receive and respond to information about a future event before the event actually happens. Even more surprising was that the Heart appears to receive this "Intuitive" information before the brain. This suggests that the Heart's Field may be linked to a more Subtle Energetic Field that contains information on objects and events remote in space or ahead in Time. The Subtle Energy Field is called by Karl Pribram and others the "Spectral Domain." This is a fundamental order of potential energy that enfolds space and time, and is thought to be the basis of our consciousness of "The Whole."

Effect of other electromagnetic fields – While science has yet to discover the extent to which the heart fields of the individual are affected by the other electromagnetic fields in their environments, it's been clear for some time that there is a deeper and everyone and everything in it than we might first aspect.

Our heart field is capable of communicating information throughout our body, regulating vital functions. Our minds - the intellectual center of our being is capable of tapping into and interpreting the information that exists within our heart field. Since our heart field extends well beyond our body, our field can and does interact with the fields adjacent to us to the extent we can "read" the adjacent field to determine if is "friend" or "foe," "strong or weak," and the emotions or lack of emotions emitted by the adjacent field.

Heart intelligence – This process is known as 'transformational'" and is capable of expanding the human consciousness further into the infinite, allowing us to add an extra dimension to our experience and understanding of ourselves, the universe, and Creator God. Accessing Heart Intelligence is to take the journey inward and converse with your SOUL (housed within your heart), receiving input from your SPIRIT (who has access to the infinite), and by requesting guidance from your Spiritual Guides, who have always been with you.

By accessing our heart intelligence we take one step closer to healing our divided nature. The heart and head need not function in opposition. No longer sundered, a joined heart and mind creates a higher form of intelligence, deeply connected to the universe and the infinite, and infinitely more powerful than either is individually. This is called Intuitive Intelligence.

Intuitive Intelligence –Your heart intelligence directs and then works in harmony with the other forms of intelligence at work within your being (mental, emotional, and physical intelligence) and boosts your comprehension of the world, allowing you to separate illusion ("reality") from ACTUAL REALITY (i.e., the TRUTH). It also increases your performance in areas such as high-order thinking, creativity and (crucially) intuition. Heart intelligence becomes intuitive intelligence when we recognize that the heart is the portal to the Infinite Universe.

When intuitive intelligence can be fully embraced and integrated into our consciousness it provides a powerful present, fully-connected and infinite consciousness-directed insight into all areas of our Soul.

Our heart fields are a source of powerful energy. While the brain has electromagnetic properties, research has demonstrated that, electrically speaking, the heart is a hundred times more powerful. And as such it is the gateway to the infinite field that unifies all.

Your intuitive intelligence is the energy that unifies all aspects of yourself, and brings them into a state of harmony with the Unified Field. Studies have also shown that by creating <u>heart coherence within our heart fields,</u> individuals are capable of positively impacting their own health, and that of others around them. This is because we are connected to a much greater power than our own personal resources.

Coherence - This coherence (sometimes called psycho-physiological coherence) is the ability to accept the flow of life and the universe; the capacity for the acceptance of things in the moments they happen, and the understanding that life is an experience lived moment-to-moment.

- Coherence is where we discover joy and grace.
- Coherence is where we met ourselves as the Infinite.

The Benefits Of Active Intuitive Intelligence - Simply put, it's the ability to relax into the flow of events and accept them as they unfold, rather than resisting.

If this is all sounding a little fuzzy and 'woo woo', there is a new field of scientific research dedicated to the study of heart intelligence called neurocardiology. This term is literally an amalgamation of 'neurology' – the study of the brain – and 'cardiology' – the study of the heart. While it's a relatively new field there are demonstrable benefits in terms of tools and skills that can be gained through the activation of your heart intelligence. But the new science is so often simply confirming ancient wisdom.

It's possible to use your intuitive intelligence to boost your positive feelings, while decreasing your negative emotions, will help you to release anxiety, stress and worry. Active Intuitive Intelligence will increase your capacity for joy, love, appreciation, compassion and creativity. It is possible to live in a constant state of connection to the Unified Field. This is the beginning of partnering with the highest and most powerful part of you and SPIRIT.

Spiritual Awareness - And if the spiritual and emotional benefits aren't enough for you, Intuitive can help you build a reserve of energy, and grant you clarity and increased mental focus, particularly when it comes to spiritual awareness. There is evidence that by mastering your heart intelligence, you can also positively affect your body on a physical level, improving your inner terrain by reducing stresses, strains and even pain. It can also bring your life into focus, allowing you to forge more harmonious, intimate and authentic relationships, and gain greater insights into your purpose and goals in life.

Opening to your intuitive intelligence is, in fact, one of the purposes of your life.

One way to create a heart coherent state in the moment is to call forth positive emotions through visualization, and engage your heart every day. When strong emotions arise, lovingly place your right hand over your heart and your left hand over your abdominal area. About two-thirds of the heart's physical mass is located on the left side of the chest. Thus, placement of the right hand over the heart is for synergy (male/female, right/left).

Intuitive Intelligence is the basis of self-awareness, social sensitivity, creativity, intuition, spiritual insight, and understanding of ourselves and all that we are connected to.

We're connected to all things with electromagnetic qualities, by the interactions of these fields. This includes stars, other planets, and even space.

ASTRAL PROJECTION (Out-of-Body Experience) – Beyond the astral is what is commonly called the "etheric" Densities, which have a more refined vibration. The upper etheric Densities encroach upon the mental levels, the place of higher imagination. Beyond these are the causal planes, realms of great beauty and perfection. They are causal because they "control" the 3rd Density and 4th Density worlds through a complex series of crystal grids (think of sacred geometric figures, only now in multi-colored swirling patterns). It is here that higher thoughts are coalesced into DNA and other lifeform structures. As you might have guessed, the Akashic records and divine blueprint of each soul are part of the causal Densities.

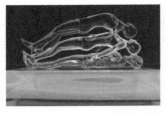

It is the SPIRIT that has the out-of-body experience, since the Soul/Heart, Mind and Body are contained/held in place by the Heart's Electromagnetic field. The Spirit has its experience and, then, conveys the experience to the Soul, which then "informs" the Mind. The only way that the Soul can "escape" the Heart's Electromagnetic Field is through the DEATH of the Body – the Heart stops and there is no Heart Electromagnetic Field.

One must be very careful, if one Astral Projects since we are within the 4% Universe controlled by the Darkness. If one does not firmly believe there is a difference between Almighty God (the Lesser God given to us by the Anunnaki) and Creator God (One Source), then you may be traveling at the beaconing of the Lesser God since you are still vulnerable to being affected by the Darkness and are being shown THEIR Levels of Density. Even if you have achieved the Frequency of Love (500 or 50%, whichever system you believe in) there is still Darkness which may make you question your ascension process. This is especially true if you are an Earth Soul or even a Lightworker who has originated from what little LIGHT there is within the 4% Universe. There are very few Light Bearers who have come here from outside the 4% Universe.

EXERCISES TO MOVE INTO HEART CONSCIOUSNESS

- **Increase Brain waves to Gamma** -The following exercises will help you experience each brain state.

  Step1/ *Conduct spirit-to-spirit.* Affirm your own spirit, other spirits, and Universe Intelligence.
  Step 2: *Experience each brain state.* Without plunging too deeply into each brain waive and each trance state, allowing the spirit or your gatekeeper to drop you briefly into each of these levels of awareness.

  - **Gamma/***Hyper-Spiritual.* Sense your spirit reaching into the heavens (Upper Realms) as it remains attuned to your body. You are in total oneness with self and all creation. Therefore, you are interconnected, you understand the other beings are within you and

- you are within them. You can even step outside of your body and remain fully linked to the "All" while remaining completely as an individual and aware.
- **Beta/***Aware.* In this everyday state of awareness, breathe deeply and accept everything you sense and feel. If you wish, you can pick up on information from beings outside of yourself and use your mind to interpret them.
- **Alpha/***Expanded.* Falling into a light trance, become aware of your body, your chakras, and your overall auric field. In this state you'll sense and feel any being that is near you, and your mind will automatically understand the meaning of their spiritual message.
- **Theta/***Meditative.* Entering theta is the moving into the portal of light that is your heart. You can now draw a loving being into you and partner with it to create positive change.
- **Delta/***Sleep.* Request that the Spirit keep you awake, even as you experience how your body feels when, perfectly rested, you are greeted by a messenger. You might be inside or outside of your body when this being brings you a gift of knowledge. The source either remains outside of you or enters to deliver the blessing.
- **Intra-Low/***Primal.* The Spirit, in the form of a Devine Being, helps you to sense, see or feel the needing aspects of yourself. Then she cradles this primal self with waves of this love. She sends into the oceanic cocoon all the love required to repair the twisted "wires" and broken parts of your needing self. Then she hums a soft sound and you know that the primal self is finally experiencing safety and security. She whispers that she can do this for you any time.

- **Breathing Exercise to Achieve Gamma –** the state of mental awakening and being in the moment.

  Step 1. First, just breathe and focus on a slow and steady in and out breathes. Develop a constant breathing pattern of 3-seconds in and 3-seconds out. Inhale using your diaphragm (lower body breathing). Exhale by pulling your bellybutton inward. Place your palm together in an upright position with hands mid-body. Complete in "sets". A "set" consists of: In mouth out mouth, in mouth out nose, in nose out nose, n nose out mouth, in mouth out mouth.

  Step 2. Keep repeating the breathing exercise until it becomes automatic, without concentrating on the breathing exercise cycles. Close eyes, relax, feel open and at peace. Loving affirmations can now be incorporated such as: I am safe; I love myself; I am loved; I am free; and I am now leading my life through my beautiful heart.

  Step 3. Once a feeling of ease, comfort and peace begins to coat your whole being, begin to ask your heart questions. The heart is very intuitive and houses many neurons, which can help reveal our deepest wounds, while filling us up with much wisdom for a happy, loving life. It will lead us to what is next. Your heart knows your truth.

Step 4. Let the Spirit guide you into your everyway senses. Return to your life when ready.

- **Bio-Feedback** - Gamma waves have the highest frequency, and they are associated with cognitive processing and memory (Staufenbiel, Brouwer, Keizer, & Van Wouwe, 2014). Thus, when these waves are faster, the speed of recalling memory is faster. Gamma waves are fast rhythms that are responsible for the brain's neural connections and data transfer to the outside world.

  They are mainly observed in the hippocampus (an area of the brain which is responsible for converting short-term to long-term memory). Also, these rapid rhythms are observed in sudden attacks like seizure and spasm. Hence, gamma training is used for promoting cognition, mental sharpness, brain activity, and problem-solving tasks. It not only improves poor calculation, but also organizes the brain, improves the speed of information processing, short-term memory, reduces the number of migraine attacks (Hughes, Vernon, 2005), and can enhance spirituality.

  - 40 Hz Light Pulsing Generators – there are several in the market.
  - 40 Hz Sound Wave Generators – There are several in the market, including an App for your cellphone.

- **Rhythmic Gamma Rhythms** - Passive listening to gamma-based regular musical beat with occasional omission of single tones show a peak after tone and omission, suggesting underlying endogenous anticipatory processes. Auditory gamma oscillations have different roles in musical beat encoding and auditory-motor interaction that increase gamma waves within the brain. When listening to 40+ Hz musical beats, close your eyes, relax, feel open and at peace. Breathe deeply, 3 seconds in and 3 seconds out. Incorporate Loving affirmations thoughts such as: I am safe; I love myself; I am loved; I am free; and I am now leading my life through my beautiful heart.

  - Listen here: Genius Frequency – 60 Hz Hyper Gamma Binaural Beats Focus Music, Studying Music for Memory, Nov 10, 2017, https://www.youtube.com/watch?reload=9&v=4Qu2VHBhGZo

- **Meditation** – Not the passive but active types, such as Yoga on the Move. Call forth positive emotions through visualization, and engage your heart every day. When strong emotions arise, lovingly place your right hand over your heart and your left hand over your abdominal area. About two-thirds of the heart's physical mass is located on the left side of the chest. Thus, placement of the right hand over the heart is for synergy (male/female, right/left). Refer to Breathing Exercise to Achieve Gamma (above) for the steps involved.

Sources
1. Heart-Brain Connection, BY ROLLIN MCCRATY, PH.D., RAYMOND TREVOR BRADLEY, PH.D. AND DANA TOMASINO, BA, https://quantumlifesource.com/heart-brain-connection/
2. Why Your Heart Intelligence Is More Powerful Than Your Head, INSTITUTE FOR INTUITIVE INTELLIGENCE, INTUITIVE INTELLIGENCE, https://instituteforintuitiveintelligence.com/heart-intelligence-powerful-head/
3. Exploring the Role of the Heart in Human Performance, Chapter 6 - Energetic Communication, Heart-Math Institute, https://www.heartmath.org/research/science-of-the-heart/energetic-communication/
4. Tricked by the Light, https://www.trickedbythelight.com/tbtl/science.shtml
5. The Holographic Universe, Michael Talbot
6. The Body Electric, Robert O. Becker
7. I sing the Body Electric, Ray Bradbury
8. The Brain, PBS Series
9. On Light and Other High Frequency Phenomena, Nikla Teska
10. The Biology of Belief, Bruce H Lipton
11. The Energy Grid – Harmonic 695 The Pulse of the Universe, Bruce L. Cathhe
12. The Selfish Gene, Richard Dawkins
13. Virus of the Mind, Richard Brodie
14. Angles Don't Play This Harp, Dr. Nick Begich
15. Mega Brain, Michael Hutchison
16. The Global Brain, Peter Rusell
17. Raise Clairaudient Energy, Cyndi Dale, 2018,Liewellyn Worldwide
18. GAMMA DMT Breath Activation video, Mojo Yoga, https://www.bing.com/videos/search?q=gamma+DMT+breath+Activation+mojo+yoga&docid=608028448173916435&mid=13F9ABA46BA33A74BA4413F9ABA46BA33A74BA44&view=detail&FORM=VIRE
19. Neurofeedback: A Comprehensive Review on System Design, Methodology and Clinical Applications, Hengameh Marzbani, Hamid Reza Marateb, and Marjan Mansourian, Natural Medical Library, n Basicand Clin ical Science, Basic Clin Neurosci. 2016 Apr; 7(2): 143–158, https://www.ncbi.nlm.nih.gov/pmc/articles/PMC4892319/
20. Beta and Gamma Rhythms in Human Auditory Cortex During Musical Beat Processing, Takako Fujioka[1], Laurel J Trainor, Edward W Large, Bernhard Ross, Natural Medical L, ibrary, Ann N Y Acad Sci, . 2009 Jul;1169:89-92, https://pubmed.ncbi.nlm.nih.gov/19673759/

Article 26

INTRACTION BETWEEN HEART FIELDS
(We are One – Almost)

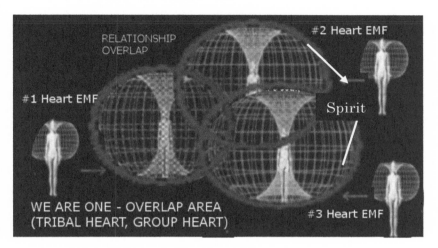

HEART FIELD INTERACTIONS – There is remarkable evidence (HeartMath Institute) that the heart's electromagnetic field transmits information between people and even between like-thinking groups, where a socio-emotional field of energy based on positive emotions such as passion, excitement, and enthusiasm connected all members.

Source: https://shawnquinlivan.com/heart-entrainment-connecting-our-love-energy/

You may have heard it said these days how everyone is connected and how we are all one. This may ultimately be the truth, made all the more likely considering a few subjective viewpoints. These include, but are not limited to, the idea that we all have a soul and are connected via spiritual, source energy – as well as the idea that all of us share the same ancestors and thus, are one big family.

Source:https://www.spiritearthawakening.com/spirituality/we-are-allconnected-we-are-one

HEART FIELD INTERACTIONS BETWEEN INDIVIDUALS – Most people think of social communication solely in terms of overt signals expressed through language, voice qualities, gestures, facial expressions, and body movements. However, experiments conducted at the <u>Institute of HeartMath</u> have found remarkable evidence that the heart's electromagnetic field can transmit information between people. This "energetic" communication system is the Heart Electromagnetic Field that operates just below our conscious awareness; the heart's field interaction between the fields play an important role in communicating physiological, psychological, and social information between individuals.

The Institute of HeartMath have found remarkable evidence that the heart's electromagnetic field can transmit information between people up to 5 feet apart where one person's brain waves can actually synchronize to another person's heart. Furthermore, when an individual is generating a coherent heart rhythm, these findings suggest that individuals in a psychologically-sociologically coherent state become more aware of the information encoded in the heart fields of those around them.

The results of these experiments infer that the nervous system acts as an "antenna" (or is it the "antenna" that Projects inside the Crown Chakra "receiver") which is tuned to and responds to the electromagnetic fields produced by the hearts of other individuals. This capacity for exchange of energetic information is an innate ability that heightens awareness and mediates important aspects of true empathy and sensitivity to others. Furthermore, it was observed that this energetic communication ability can be intentionally enhanced, producing a much deeper level of nonverbal communication, understanding, and connection between people. There is also evidence that heart field interactions can occur between people and animals. Additional evidence may show that the heart field interactions occur between the individual and Infinite Universe Knowledge.

In short, energetic communication via the heart field facilitates development of an expanded consciousness in relation to our social world (and, perhaps, the ethereal worlds/Realms).

The overwhelming majority of communication is non-verbal. It has a lot to do with the heart (as described above), the subconscious mind, and other phenomena foreign to physical perception. Intonations and body language, which are direct manifestations of your internal state, come into play as well. If your internal state is that of love, it will permeate all aspects of communication/ interaction with others.

Source: https://www.feelingoodfeelingreat.com/2014/01/09/love-aura/

To better understand this mechanism of communication it's vital to address the electromagnetic field the heart produces. This field essentially carries the energetic signature of our body, which is based upon the coherence level of the ANS (Automatic Nervous System). "Compared to the electromagnetic field produced by the brain, the electrical component of the heart's field is about 60 times greater in amplitude, and permeates every cell in the body. The magnetic component is approximately 5000 times stronger than the brain's magnetic field and can be detected approx. 16-20 feet away from the body with sensitive magnetometers." This field changes based upon the emotional state of an individual, and a positive emotional state results in a more coherent field.

This electromagnetic exchange is akin to oneness. Put simply, the human being is an emitter and receiver of information within their environment.

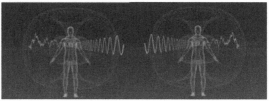

The heart allows for connection to the rest of life on an emotional and energetic dimension.

The first example (Separate Relationship) is that of infatuation that takes eye contact at close field, and conveys its input to the Mind, which, in turn, conveys an interpretation to the Heart/Soul. Without input for the Spirit, the Soul passes it off as a short–lived passion or admiration.

The second example (Relationship Overlap) is the love aura as well as human instinct for survival optimizes and harmonizes all forms of communication and interaction. So when people sense this harmonic field, they

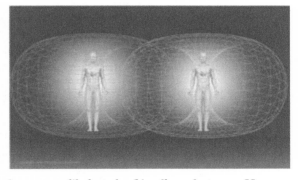

feel a "good vibe," and are more likely to be friendly and at ease. However, in this instance, the Spirit is in concert with the Heart/Soul. But when you're operating in fear, your heart's field will be disharmonious, which people will feel as a "bad vibe," and close-off or react negatively. If the Relationship Overlap is significant and is enduring, Field Bonding will occur and even when separated there will be Soul to Soul entanglement (akin to Quantum Mechanics element entanglement) that may endure for a while beyond death; the connection is Living Soul to Living's Spirit to Ethereal Soul.

The third example (Overlap of multiple Heart Fields) is the human instinct for survival. In this case, the Heart Field harmonizes with others to form bonds that enhance survival through shared resources, or have shared ancestry (A TRIBAL HARMONIZATION), and has expanded socially based on association: altruism (positive interactions with unrelated members). Or, even extending, to a regional or country base and, finally, to an ONENESS on a Planetary scale, or within a Solar System or a Sector of the Universe. The ONENESS is achieved through the Spirit.

PRACTICES OF THE HEART ELECTROMAGNETIC FIELD - Now that the physiological/spiritual mechanisms of the heart have been established, we will proceed into the practices of the heart. These include recognizing and acquiring information from the environment directly and practices to increase our own, and thus the planet's coherence.

Source: https://highexistence.com/heart-consciousness-love-and-enlightened-living/

METAPHYSICAL CONCEPTION OF CONSCIOUSNESS: The Anunnaki created Mankind by (1) Taking the DNA of the Earth Humans, (2) Mixed in a portion of the Anunnaki DNA, (3) Infused earth into the new species in order to "tie" the new species to the Earth and (4) The new species needed a "battery" power source so they enticed the Atlanteans to be that power source by telling the Atlanteans by being the power source they would attain eternal life. Of course, the Atlanteans, being Spirit, they already had eternal life but were not aware of this fact. Thus, the Anunnaki TRANSHUMAN was created to be subservient to the Anunnaki. What the Anunnaki were unaware of was that Gaia (the "super Earth") was Spirit (source of Consciousness) and part of the "mix" that would help guide the Human Soul.

SCIENCE CONCEPTION OF CONSCIOUSNESS and Where Does it Emanate – The universe may be conscious, say prominent scientists. What consciousness is and where it emanates has stymied great minds in societies across the globe since the dawn of speculation. In today's world, it's a realm tackled more and more by physicists, cognitive scientists, and neuroscientists. There are a few prevailing theories:

The first is **materialism**. This is <u>the notion that consciousness emanates from matter</u>, in our case, by the firing of neurons inside the brain. Take the brain out of the equation and consciousness doesn't exist at all. Traditionally, scientists have been stalwart materialists. But doing so has caused them to slam up against the limitations of materialism. Consider the chasm between relativity and quantum mechanics, or Heisenberg's uncertainty principle, and you quickly start to recognize these incongruities.

The second theory is **mind-body dualism**. This is perhaps more often recognized in religion or spirituality. Here, consciousness is separate from matter. It is a part of another aspect of the individual, which in religious terms we might call the spirit and the soul.

Then there's a third option is **panpsychism**. <u>In this view, the entire universe is inhabited by consciousness.</u> A handful of scientists are starting to warm to this theory, but it's still a matter of great debate. Truth be told, Panpsychism sounds very much like what the Hindus and Buddhists call the BRAHMAN, the tremendous universal Godhead of which we are a part. In Buddhism for instance, consciousness is the only thing that exists.

One must come to the realization that everything we experience is filtered through and interpreted by our mind. Without it, the universe doesn't exist at all or at least, not without some sort of consciousness observing it. In some physics circles, the prevailing theory is some kind of proto-consciousness field.

Some people are more connected to their mind and heart and they carry an image of themselves, not with the physical appearance but they relate themselves to their thoughts and emotions.

The physical body is part of the physical world, while the thoughts and emotions are part of the subtle world. The physical reality too exists, into the existence, because of the subtle world.

Source: https://www.modernagespirituality.com/we-are-all-one-but-how/

In quantum mechanics, particles don't have a definite shape or specific location, until they are observed or measured. Is this a form of proto-consciousness at play? According to the late scientist and philosopher, John Archibald Wheeler, it might. He's famous for coining the term, "black hole." In his view, every piece of matter contains a bit of consciousness, which it absorbs from this proto-consciousness field.

Source:https://bigthink.com/philip-perry/the-universe-may-be-conscious-
        prominent-scientists-state

A counter thought is that all of this Heart-Mind containment and interaction with others and even the universe is part of the Anunnaki programming (the Anunnaki created mankind) so that all components of their 4% Universe all work together to support the "god" given to us by the Orion Empire, God Almighty – the Lesser God, who is NOT Creator God (One Source). Thus, when you "connect" to Universe Intelligence, you are actually "connecting" with the world of the Lesser God. The entire Heart-Mind connection may be how the Anunnaki ("Dark Force") control and dominate mankind. Thus, be "mindful" of what you believe – through Human 3.0 SI you make the connection to Creator God as the Universe Intelligence. The Heart-Mind connection is not all bad, but it may make an interference thought pattern when it is programmed (by the Anunnaki) to do so. Remember that the Orion Empire's 4% Universe is a mirror of the Free Universe – the pathway to ascension is leads to a different "destination" within each Universe.

Article 27

CHAKRAS ARE A PROGRAMMING OVERREACH
(The Body as Machine)

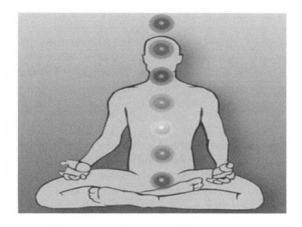

Nikola Tesla said (1942), "If you wish to understand the Universe think of energy, frequency and vibration. " Meaning that **everything** has **energy** and **energy** gives rise to **vibration** at a **frequency** determined by that energy and the mass of the **vibrating** components.

Let's look at mankind's creation by the Anannaki. What they needed:

- Labor to mine gold; Labor that was strong, reliable and functional.
- A mind that follows directions, unquestioning, and showing reliance and trust in their overseers.
- Upgradable, if malfunctions are found or if work tasks change.

This task was given to Enki (program overseer), Malduk (long range production and reliability) and Anu (programmer). The body functionality was designed by the Anunnaki by manipulating DNA that was gene spliced between the Anunnaki DNA and the local human primate DNA that was "stripped" from 12-stand to two strand, and included seven functional centers. The body was conceived with several memory implants (the 7-chakras) to function as a whole. This is akin to the modern automobile ECU (Electronic Control Module) which consists of several, individual control module types such as, Engine Control Module (ECM), Power-train Control Module (PCM), Transmission Control Module (TCM), Brake Control Module (BCM or EBCM), Central Control Module (CCM), Central Timing Module (CTM), General Electronic Module (GEM), Body Control Module (BCM), and Suspension Control Module (SCM0. Taken together, these systems are sometimes referred to as the car's computer (technically there is no single computer but multiple ones), just as the body has multiple function centers called chakras.

The term chakra is Sanskrit for "wheel" or centers which function as a whole for body wellness. Chakras are often depicted as spinning, colored wheels of energy. For millennia, chakras have been recognized as essential to life. Chakras, by definition, are energy centers within the human body that help to regulate all its processes, from organ function to the immune system and emotions.

Seven chakras are positioned throughout your body, from the base of your spine to the crown of your head. All living things are created by and comprised of energy. The ability of your energy centers to function optimally is what keeps you psychologically, emotionally, physically, and spiritually balanced. That is, achieve a "sound" body – meaning healthy, whole and unbroken.

Each chakra has its own vibrational frequency, color, and governs specific functions that help make you, well, human. Below is a list of each chakra, starting with the base of the spine and moving upward. Presented are the chakra names, locations, colors, and functions.

- Root (1st) — Base of the spine; red; governs survival instincts, grounding.
- Sacral (2nd) — Lower abdomen; orange; governs sexuality, intuition, self-worth/esteem.
- Solar Plexus (3rd) — Upper abdomen; yellow; governs impulse control, ego.
- Heart (4th) — Center of the chest; green; governs compassion, spirituality.
- Throat (5th) — Throat; blue; governs communication, emotion.
- Third Eye (6th) — Between the eyebrows; purple; governs rationality, wisdom, imagination and monitors the other chakras, as a chicken does her chicks.
- Crown (7th) — Top of the head; indigo; programming port to further monitor the "system" and to correct malfunctions through light code reprogramming.

As the programmer you can access the chakras through the Crown Chakra/programming access port, just like a technician can access each control module of the automobile. The output signals of each chakra can become blocked, underactive or overactive, throwing you off balance physically, emotionally, mentally, and spiritually. We know that specific frequencies are associated with specific chakras because we can physically feel each chakra when it is activated by its corresponding frequency.

The words science and spirituality are not commonly used in the same sentence, but we now have physical science, proving that we are more than the physical body, WE ARE ALSO SPIRITUAL BEINGS.

Energy Body, Aura, Chakras –

- **The energy body,** or subtle body, is a system that carries life force energy through and around us, connecting us to the Earth, the programmer, our higher selves and each other.

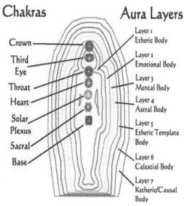

Understanding this system is crucial for physical, emotional and spiritual health. The energy body is invisible to most of us; however, we feel and react to it constantly, whether we know it or not. This system is made up of several components that work together, just like the other body systems.

The aura could be seen by the Anunnaki (the creators of mankind) since the aura acts as a visual On–Board Diagnostic (akin to an automobile's OBD) self--diagnostic and reporting system to give the creator/ programmer the status of the various sub–systems.

- **Your aura** is a barrier of energy between you and the rest of the world. When it is healthy it gives you a sense of security, insulating you from the energies around you. You have clear boundaries and can tell the difference between your own needs and emotions and those of others. When it is unhealthy you feel anxious, attacked, like the energy of everyone around you is bearing down on you. You have poor boundaries with other people and tend to take on the emotions and problems of other people.

Information Exchange – Your aura serves as an interactive field of information. You use it to exchange information with everyone you meet. It is like a virtual business card that instantly shares your mood, your overall health, your intentions, your sense of yourself and much more with everyone you come into contact with. You receive this information from everyone you come into contact with. Chakras vibrate and become sympathetically aroused when in the presence of a corresponding frequency to a point which we can feel them vibrate with our hands due to a scientific phenomenon known as "HARMONIC RESONANCE."

- **The chakras** are energy centers in the body that correspond to different areas of physical, emotional and spiritual functioning. There are <u>7 main chakras</u>, although there are many more, smaller chakras throughout the body, as well as above and below the body. The chakras are connected to one another through channels of energy that run throughout the body.

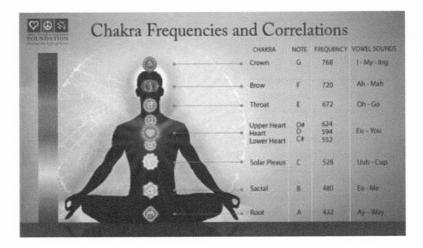

- **Connection Between Auras and Chakras** – They are connected to one another on a very deep level. Your aura projects out into the world the information that your chakras are emanating. The aura varies at each chakra to reflect the condition of that chakra. If you feel grounded and safe in your root chakra, you project that out from your aura, if you feel weak and insecure in your solar plexus, you project that out into the world. The aura is a combination of all of the information coming from your chakras and your aura colors change as your mood, emotional health and spiritual connection change.

MANUPLATING THE CHAKRAS – ENERGY MEDICINE (EM) – THE WORK OF LIGHTWORKER HEALERS

PURPOSE OF ENERGY MEDICINE (EM) – EM is the use of known subtle energy fields to therapeutically assess and treat energetic imbalances, bringing the body's systems (neurological, cardiovascular, respiratory, skeletal, endocrinal, emotional/psychological, etc.). back to homeostasis.

Knowledge of the existence of the HEF (*human energy fields*) is the first step to understanding integral physiology, which unites body, mind, and heart/soul to treat the entire human being—not just the physiology. **Energy medicine** is, therefore, a method to transmit **healing energy** to a patient's body through the hands of a practitioner to restore or balance the body's **energy** fields for better health.

THE CHAKRA SYSTEM DESIGN – As the "programmer," several systems of Energy Medicine (EM) were designed to "correct" alignment and functionality of the chakras – they were known to the Anunnaki (the creator of mankind) but many have been realized by today's Energy Healers and Energy Practitioners since the 1970's.

MODALITIES OF EM – There are several modalities of EM that interact with the subtle energy of the body. These include, but are not limited to, PEMF therapy, Polarity Therapy, acupuncture, Healing Touch, Therapeutic

Touch, Reiki, homeopathy, Qi Gong, and applied Kinesiology. New medical paradigms can bridge the gap between conventional/allopathic and EM. For instance, PEMF and acupuncture have plausible electromagnet modes of action.

MANIPULATING THE CHAKRAS DOES NOT BRING ABOUT ENLIGHTENMENT – What it does is to release pain and create alignment so that that these issues do not block the "path" to enlightenment. Relieving pain and reestablishing chakra alignment reestablishes your ability to listen and find your inner-self.

THE CHAKRAS AS A POWER PLANT TO RADIATE ENERGY TO GAIA AND THE UNIVERSE - The Lower three human chakras are dominated by energy rather than information and instruction, while the upper two chakras have more information than energy. The two energy centers in the middle 4th and 5th chakras serve as adapters of information into energy and vice versa. Any of the seven chakras can work in two phases:

- Absorbing energy and information from the surrounding space
- Emitting or releasing energy and information from the human body.

Discharge Energy - One can "bounce" energy from the Bottom chakras (dominated by energy) to the top (pineal gland) and then back-and-forth to build a charge in the top-end capacitor (part of the pineal gland). Once sufficient charge is developed, one can "discharge" that energy through the Crown Chakra's antenna:
- Into the Earth's "electromagnetic grid (thereby increasing the Earth's frequency).
- As a message to the Universe.

The Discharge of energy by the human Chakra System is similar to that of a Tesla Coil or As an Energy Transmitter (as was The Great Pyramid). All three require grounding and an initial power source to start the "system."

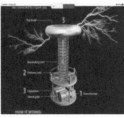

The Giza Power Plant

In addition, the discharge of all three (Chakras, Tesla Coil, and the Great Pyramid) could be used as a directed energy weapon for either defense (as a wide array or as a direct energy weapon). For a Pleiadian and others the energy weapon/shield array is via a concentrating crystal embedded in the palm of their hand and there could have been a crystal or array of crystals located within the missing top 20-feet of the Great Pyramid.

3ʳᵈ EYE – GATEWAY INTO SELF

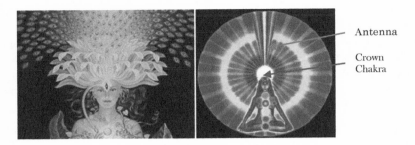

Antenna

Crown
Chakra

THE THIRD EYE - W e have two physical eyes that were created to help us, along with the other senses, to avoid obstacles in a physical, 3-dimensional environment. Of course, the Dark Force always wants us to "look" out into the world to see the illusion, augmented reality; they want us to believe the world is full of disparity, separation, pain, suffering and disillusion.

We have another "eye," the 3ʳᵈ eye, which looks internally and coordinates the chakras like a mother does her children. Looking inward reveals the Heart-Soul and the True You.

The 3ʳᵈ eye also connects us to the universe through the Crown Chakra. The Crown Chakra is formed like an outward turned lotus flower that is shaped like a funnel designed to receive light coding from the creator of Mankind (the Anunnaki – the original "programmers"). It is the portal to insert light coding to "correct" abnormalities that have developed within the chakra system, including the Heart-Mind, where the chakras are part of the body "component" control system.

The 3ʳᵈ Eye is part of the Pineal Gland located behind the forehead above the meeting point of the two eyebrows. Its main color is purple, and the element it is associated with light. It is the Chakra of perception and discrimination. It is really the eye of the Soul, the Seer, the center of presence and perception, the omega point in which all the others chakras impressions are being perceived. For this reason, it has also been called the "Seat of the Soul". Its location in the center of the brain reflects this central role. The 3rd eye is deeply non-conceptual. Its center is in a state of spacious and unlimited listening. It is observant and lucid rather than automatic and reactive – a state which allows a person to be a receptor of the Heart-Soul where the Heart-Soul connects to the Spirit (outside of the Heart-Soul containment field) – it is from the Spirit's connection to Universe Knowledge from which acquire Spirituality, Enlightenment, and Interconnection.

One may be able to use the 3rd Eye function for remote viewing, psychokinesis (mind over matter), telekinesis (moving objects and bending spoons), fire-walking, OBE (out-of-body-experience), and healing, but remember that it is connecting with Universe Intelligence that is the goal for Starseeds, Indigo Children, Wanderers, Star Travelers, and Star Beings in order to connect with "home."

There is a "lock" card between the left (creative) and right (logical) parts of the brain. That "card" is in position to keep us from reprogramming ourselves. You will need to remove this card to "open" your mind to reveal who you Really Are and to Reprogram your Heart-Mind to function as the independent Real You. It is the "card" that creates the "confusion" between the "functional" brain and the "creative/long term prior life" part of the brain.

One can remove the "card" by following the steps listed within Article 12 – Raise Your Brain Power 30%. I was taught the three exercises by a Spiritual Teacher who was on his way to Sedona and Arches Monument but was directed by the universe to contact and assist me along my path to mission completion.

It might be wise to keep your Crown Chakra closed and only open it when you want to remove the "card" and activate your 3rd Eye. Leaving the Crown Chakra open all of the time may allow the Dark Force to reprogram you through "light coding" of your DNA by injection the light "coding" through your Crown Chakra.

Opening your Crown Chakra and "broadcasting through your antenna, is a notification to the Dark Force that you may be Awakening – this is the last thing you want to do. You need to contact Universe Intelligence through your Spirit. In today terms, the Crown Chakra is the portal that allows the "programmer" access to the "operating system".

LOOKING INWARD - One may be able to use the 3rd Eye function for remote viewing, psychokinesis (mind over matter), telekinesis (moving objects and bending spoons), fire-walking, OBE (out-of-body-experience), and healing, but remember that it is connecting, trough the Spirit, with universal knowledge that is the goal for Starseeds, Indigo Children, Wanderers, Star Travelers, and Star Beings in order to connect with "home."

Confusion arises when we cannot see things clearly as they are, with no connection to the Universe. Too many thoughts and contradictory inner and outer voices cloud our own judgment of the situation. To rightly judge we need to be as objective as possible; meaning, to be able to place some distance from everything and be the observer.

This requires some degree of intelligence that makes it possible for us to look at ourselves and at the wide range of instincts, feelings, emotions and experiences; a world view. We might be swayed by this feeling or that impulse and still be unable to make sense of them, and even to know whether they are right or false, important or secondary.

Input from the Universe might be overly-analytical: looking at ourselves and at situations through very constricted structures of thought. This, of course, predetermines what is right and what is false according to our conditioned mind.

Learning how to remain open in a state of listening (from the world) and receiving (from the Universe), while having a sufficient knowledge and capacity of discrimination, is the greatest challenge of the 3rd Eye's function.

When the 3rd Eye is in a blocked state, it is seen as a cloudy and foggy mind, as if one cannot see clearly. Experiences, thoughts and feelings are all too elusive to grasp and make sense of. In this state, the third eye is more like an empty screen on which the constant stream of instincts, feelings and impulses from the lower Chakras is projected. The third eye is not really a center of commanding intelligence, but rather lower impulses disguised as thoughts. There is no center of perception, and the third eye is mainly a reactive mechanism that relies on its already conditioned and limited experience and knowledge. This condition is one that has been put in place by the Dark Force to block receipt of the Universe's knowledge and to control mankind. The Dark Force has been suppressing the 3rd Eye through calcification with phosphorus calcium and fluoride deposits. Stressful aging and lack of good sleep are also the cause and effect of calcified pineal gland. Some of the signs of calcified pineal gland are insomnia with either difficulty falling asleep, difficulty staying asleep or feeling of fatigue after waking up. Mood staying low or anxiety can also be caused by calcified pineal gland. The good news is that it can be reversed, if we are willing to do so. In the chakra system, the 3rd Eye (Ajna Chakra) is represented by Indigo or the Royal Blue color. For the complete healing of our body and the soul, we need the energy to flow through this deep area of the brain. To see more of the "Aha" moments of deep clarity and insight we need to decalcify the pineal gland to the extent that we can. There are some people who you want to keep looking in their eyes because they have this spark of deep wisdom.

Ways to Decalcify and activate your pineal gland:

- Stay well hydrated
- Sleep well and sleep enough
- Reduce or avoid fluoride toothpaste
- Reduce the use of fluorinated water
- Reduce the use of processed foods
- Reduce the use of foods with pesticides.
- Reduce the use of nonstick pans.

- Increase the use of alkaline foods.
- Deep breathing ionizes and increases the flow of cerebrospinal fluid.
- Toning or Chanting sends vibrations through CSF to energize pineal gland, Laughing and Smiling increase endorphins, which are relaxing and balance the energy.

Making sure that our thought-processes are in order often leads us to search for higher forms of intelligence, as found in scriptures, spiritual teachings and great clear minds. Some, especially those who are distinguished by the 3rd Eye Chakra personality, can introduce into our life clear systems of thought, bright perceptions and orderly models of reality. Such teachings can strengthen our own mind's confidence that underneath the mental chaos, there is some understanding waiting for us.

Sources
1. Third Eye Chakra, Shai Tubali, 7 Wisdoms.oprg, http://www.jackhouck.com/rvpk.shtml
2. Pineal Gland (Third Eye, Gateway to Universe), the Health Mind MD,July 16, 2017, Mindfulness, http://www.healthmindmd.com/pineal-gland-thirdeye-gateway-to-universe/
3. RESEARCHING REMOTE VIEWING AND PSYCHOKINESIS, Jack Houck, http://www.jackhouck.com/rvpk.shtml

Article 28

TRICKED BY THE LIGHT
(All is Frequency, Vibration and Energy)

REALITY – What we call reality is really a holographic projection harnessed by Dark Force entities and made from our own true internal light. As Tesla said if you want to know the secrets of the universe **think in terms of frequency, vibration and energy**.

Everything is energy vibrating at different frequencies on the electromagnetic spectrum. We perceive only a sliver of that spectrum in the form of visible light and sound. We have instruments that can detect other forms such as x-rays and gamma rays, infra red and ultraviolet. This energy is a projection of Consciousness. There are different levels of our Consciousness which can be expressed progressively lower brain states starting with gamma and dropping to beta, alpha, theta until it reaches delta, the lowest and slowest waves. Our perception of reality corresponds to which wave level our brain is tuned to.

The objects that are seen, according to Plato, are not real, but literally mimic the real Forms. In the Allegory of the Cave expressed in the Republic, the things that are ordinarily perceived in the world are characterized as shadows of the real things, which are not perceived directly. That which the observer understands when viewing the world mimics the archetypes of the many types and properties of things observed. In his Allegory, humanity lives deep inside the cave, and interprets life by watching shadows reflected on the wall by fire. It is a comprehensive and systematic effort by Plato to explain how limited our perceptions really are.

What we see is akin to a photographic plate negative (sometimes referred to as an "appositive") where the plate is, basically, a dark 2–dimensional image that has no form until a light is shined through it.

Reality if we saw energy frequencies– Most Likely (far left view) is what we might see. The mind then creates a "picture" from energy and frequencies. Perhaps, the mind first creates an appositive (middle picture) and then "paints" it by colorizes it based on what we have been told what we should see (photo on far right).

"Everything is an Electromagnetic Field. First was the light, endless source from which points out material and distribute it in all forms that represent the Universe and the Earth with all its aspects of life. Black is the true face of Light, only we do not see this. "-- Nikola Tesla

"A piece of holographic film containing an encoded image. To the naked eye the image on the film looks nothing like the object photographed but is composed of irregular ripples known as interference patterns. However, when the film is illuminated with light (by a laser), a three-dimensional image of the original object 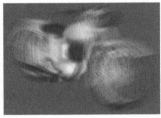 appears." *The Holographic Universe*, Michael Talbot, "Kepler discovered that the image is backwards and upside down on the retina." -- *Tycho and Kepler*, Kitty Ferguson

So, **What is Reality**? What if I told you that this world around us, this richly textured world, was all just an illusion constructed in your head? What if I said that the real world has no smell or taste... no sound? [Silence]. What if I said there's no color? If you could perceive reality as it really is out there, you wouldn't recognize it at all. I want to show you how the brain takes in information, sifts through it to find patterns, and uses it to build the multisensory, Technicolor show that is YOUR REALITY.

This might seem straight forward because we have portals to the outside world, like your eyes and ears, but these aren't just piping in sights and sounds. Instead, photons of light or air compression waves, these are getting converted into the common currency of the brain--electrochemical signals. These signals travel through dense networks of brain cells called neurons. There are a hundred billion neurons in the human brain, and in every second of your life, each one of these is sending tens or hundreds of electrical pulses to thousands of other neurons. And somehow all of this activity produces your sense of reality."

We all have this internally generated reality. Incredible as it may sound, this world lives inside your brain. It's constantly updated by information from our senses, but moment to moment, what we experience isn't what's really out there. Instead, it's a beautifully rendered simulation. This is a surprising way to understand how you see the world. It's called the internal model, and it's vital to our ability to function. As I walk down a city street, I seem to automatically know what things are without having to work out the details. For example, I don't have to work out the detail of what this rectangular, metallic thing is or this giant green fluffy thing behind me or this huge object with reflective panes on it or this thing with 4 appendages. My brain makes assumptions about what I 'm seeing based on my internal model, and that's been built up from years of experience of walking city streets just like the one I just viewed... the brain doesn't bother picking up every detail, just enough to get us through, but it plays the trick of making us feel as though we've seen it all... this is not a failure of the brain. It doesn't try to produce a perfect simulation of the world. The internal model is a hastily drawn approximation, and more details are added on a need-to-know basis.

But there's something else we're unaware of happening every time we look at any picture or person or thing... any time we look at all. We might think of color as a fundamental defining quality of the world around us. After all, it's everywhere. But here's the startling thing. In the outside world, color doesn't actually exist. When electro– magnetic radiation hits an object, some of it bounces off and is captured by our eyes. We can distinguish between millions of combinations of wavelengths, but it's only inside our heads that any of this becomes color. Add to that the fact that the wavelengths we can detect are only a small part of what's out there. You experience reality as it's presented by your senses, and it doesn't typically strike you that things could be very different.

What we've been talking about so far is what we call **the visible spectrum of light, which is a spectrum of wavelengths that runs from what we call red to violet... but it turns out that this only constitutes a tiny fraction of the electromagnetic spectrum – in fact, less than 1/10,000,000,000 of it –** so all the rest of the spectrum, including radio waves and microwaves and x-rays and gamma rays, all of this stuff,-is flowing through our bodies right now, and we're completely unaware of it because we don't have any specialized biological receptors to pick up on it. So what this means is that the part of reality that we can see is totally limited by our biology and this isn't just about sight. All our senses are only picking up a small part of the information that's out there.

The brain is the universe's ultimate storyteller. We believe whatever our brains serve up to us. The reality we take for granted requires intensive training to interpret the world. It takes time to process sensory information, so we live in the past and because all that information is ultimately just electrochemical signals to be sorted, matched, rendered and packaged; reality is some-

something created inside our head. Our brain sculpts our reality using the narrow trickle of data that it can gather through the senses. And from that trickle, it tells a story about our world. It's possible that every brain tells a different narrative.

"Reality is merely an illusion, albeit a very persistent one." – Albert Einstein

LIMITED BY DNA – When the Anunnaki created mankind, they integrated the Earth homonides DNA with a portion of their own DNA, infused the mix with the Spirit of the Earth ("dust/soil/earth"), and enticed the Atlanteans to be the power source – they enticed the Atlanteans by telling them they would attain eternal life (the trick was that the Atlanteans did not realize that they were already eternal). This is how the Anunnaki created their TRANSHUMAN to be subservient to the Anunnaki.

The DNA-RNA apparatus isn't the whole secret of (ed., mankind's) life, but a sort of computer program by which the real secret is the control system which expresses its pattern in terms of living cells." – *The Body Electric*, Robert O. Becker. Note the term "control system".

"The (cell's) membrane is a liquid crystal semiconductor with gates and a channel...A (computer) chip is a liquid crystal semiconductor with gates and channels." -- The Biology of Belief, Bruce Lipton, Ph.D.

Death & Near Death - "Those people" (at death or near death or similar events) "...who see a light are in fact seeing the light generated by an illusion-creating subtle-sorcerer (mantrik). Subtle-sorcerers, due to their high spiritual strength, can create illusions of light as well as feelings of peace and happiness radiating from the light. These illusions are created by their spiritual powers and their black energy. They use this as a mechanism to lure subtle-bodies into the light and trap them into slavery." -- Spiritual Science Research Foundation

The Rise of Consciousness —Brain Wave Frequency

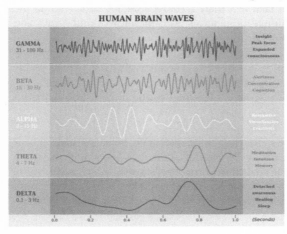

There are five categories of brain wave states ranging from Delta waves which are the slowest to Gamma waves which are the fastest, highest frequency. Research has shown that Mankind, when in motion, the brain wave is in the realm of 5 to10 Hz (Alpha: Relaxation, Visualization,

Creativity, but not at a higher frequency of Beta— Alertness, Concentration, Cognition, or Gamma— Insight, Peak Focus, Expanded Consciousness.

Gamma waves are the fastest of the brainwave frequencies and signify the highest state of focus possible. They are associated with peak concentration and the brain's optimal frequency for cognitive functioning.

Meditation slows the brain waves which may be good for our bodies to combat our normal hectic lives and eliminates stress, but I would prefer to reach the higher frequency of brain waves, the gamma waves, for insight and expanded consciousness. It is the excitement of thinking about unique subjects that creates the gamma frequencies across our mind. You take in more facts and see more details when in a gamma state. Now those who meditate with nothing are in theta meditation.

Two different effects

Gamma waves have been observed in Tibetan Buddhist monks. A 2004 study took eight long-term Tibetan Buddhist practitioners of meditation and, using electrodes monitored the patterns of electrical activity produced by their brains as they meditated. The researchers compared the brain activity of the monks to a group of novice mediators (the study had these subjects meditate an hour a day for one week prior to empirical observation). In a normal meditative state, both groups were shown to have similar brain activity. However, when the monks were told to generate an objective feeling of compassion during meditation, their brain activity began to fire in a rhythmic, coherent manner, suggesting neuronal structures were firing in harmony. This was observed at a frequency of 25–40 Hz, the rhythm of gamma waves. These gamma-band oscillations in the monk's brain signals were the largest seen in humans (apart from those in states such as seizures).

Conversely, these gamma-band oscillations were scant in novice mediators. Though, a number of rhythmic signals did appear to strengthen in beginner mediators with further experience in the exercise, implying that the aptitude for one to produce gamma-band rhythm is trainable.

Such evidence and research in gamma-band oscillations may explain the heightened sense of consciousness, bliss, and intellectual acuity subsequent to meditation. Notably, meditation is known to have a number of health benefits: stress reduction, mood elevation, and increased life expectancy of the mind and its cognitive functions.

Max Planck in 1931 said "I regard consciousness as fundamental. I regard matter as derivative from consciousness. We cannot get behind consciousness. Everything that we talk about, everything that we regard as existing, postulates consciousness." He also said, "As a man who has devoted his whole life to the most clear headed science, to the study of matter, I can tell you as a result of my research about atoms this much: There is no matter as such. All matter originates and exists only by virtue of a force which brings the particle of an atom to vibration and holds this most minute solar system of the atom together. We must assume behind this force the existence of a conscious and intelligent mind. This mind is the matrix of all matter."

BOTTOMLINE — The Anunnaki, through their creation of the TRAN-SHUMANS called Mankind, created a species that has limited senses associated with REALITY, Have been restricted in how much of that REALITY they can actually perceive, Have a Mind that approximates the input of the senses, and are, typically operating within at a 10 Hz frequency range. All was created by the Anunnaki/Dark Force so that mankind would be subservient to the Dark Force. Yet, despite these limitations, and through EN-LIGHTENED Stat Beings and a few Enlightened Masters, are seeking and finding TRUE Reality through intuitively connecting with Infinite (Universe) Intelligence, and developing new paradigms of community building, teaching or leadership in the spirit of Service-to-Others. Mankind is slowly but persistently Learning that **"WHAT ISN'T, IS."**

For those Star Beings who have come to Earth from a higher Density ("octave") and Realm, and have a higher frequency than that of the Earth humans (Mankind), the above are the limitations of the physical body you were given and are having to "struggle" with, but are compensated by your high frequency, high Consciousness, 6th Sense, and astute institution, knowledge, and skills, as well as connection to the Infinite, allowing you to project the IM-AGE of TRUE REALITY and, thereby, assist mankind in escaping the Reincarnation Trap and to develop new paradigms in the spirit of Service-to-Others, which elevates the Sprit to a Higher Realm.

Sources
1. TRICKED BY THE LIGHT: SCIENCE, compiled from several sources, https://www.trickedbythelight.com/tbtl/science.shtml
2. *The Holographic Universe*, Michael Talbot
3. *The Body Electric*, Robert O. Becker & Gary Seldon
4. *I Sing the Body Electric!*, Ray Bradbury
5. Light harvesting chlorophyll pigments enable mammalian mitouchondral to capture photonic energy and produce ATP, Journal of Cell Science
6. The Brain, PBS Series with David Eagleman
7. *Optics*, Johannes Kepler
8. *The Biology of Belief*, Bruce H. Lipton, Ph.D
9. *Net of Being*, Alex Gray
10. *The Energy Grid*, Bruce L. Cathie
11. *Touchable Holograms*, Tokyo, Japan
12. *The Signularity is Near*, Ray Kurzweil
13. Q&A Session #4, Wes Penre & Ariel Glade, Nov. 13, 2018, Wes Penre Public Ations,

Article 29

SIMULTANEOUS LIVING IN THE PAST, PRESENT AND FUTURE

THE DISTINCTIONS BETWEEN PAST PRESENT AND FUTURE ARE ILLUSIONS - As predicted by Einstein's field equations space-time may be a circle such that the future leads to the present and then the past which leads to the future, thereby creating multiple futures and pasts, and which allows information from the future to effect the present. Causes may cause themselves. Coupled with evidence from quantum mechanics' entanglement where choices made in the future effect measurements made in the present and theoretical tachyons which travel at superluminal speeds from the future to the present and then to the past; this may account for precognition, déjà vu, and premonitions. In quantum mechanics, where reality and the quantum continuum are a unity, time is also a unity such that the *future present past* are a continuum which are linked and the same could be said of consciousness which exists in the *future* and in the *present* and *past*. If considered as a "world line" and in space-like instead of time-like intervals, then consciousness from birth to death would be linked as a basic unity extending not in time but in space and the same could be said of time. Time-space and consciousness are also linked and interact via the wave function and as demonstrated by entanglement and the Uncertainty Principle.

THE FUTURE ALREADY EXISTS - Relativity and quantum physics both predict the future exists before it is experienced. However, due to the fact that time is entangled in the frenzied activity of the quantum continuum, the future, or rather "a" future may continually change until the moment it is perceived by consciousness.

Since futures and pasts overlaps and as time-space is coextensive, then time, including local time relative to a single observer, is entangled. The past may affect the future; the future can affect the past; time effects consciousness and alterations in consciousness affect the passage of time.

As a "future" flows toward Earth it can also be affected by whatever it encounters on the way to the consciousness of "now," relative to an observer on Earth--exactly as befalls light. All futures are also entangled with space-time, the quantum continuum, and subject to the Uncertainty Principle. Therefore, future time may be continually altered until perhaps just moments before these futures are experienced by observers who are also entangled with what they experience. Hence, although one may anticipate and predict the future, just like they may predict the weather, the ability to accurately anticipate and predict the future is like predicting future weather, may increase the closer that future is to the *present*. Planning skills, goal formation, strategy, concern for consequences, and even the most basic of calendars, all rest upon the ability to make predictions about the future.

YOUR VIEW OF THE FUTURE SHAPES YOUR PAST - So has the FUTURE affected the PAST. Other than the thought that this defies logic, the FUTURE affects the past through ENVISIONING. We use our ability to envision the future to help us make plans. Our beliefs about what might happen in the future help us to plan for obstacles that will confront us. A lot of research on planning suggests that those people who prepare for failure are the ones best equipped to handle problems when they come up. It is important to recognize that the only way you can plan for the future is by drawing on your memories of the past. Envisioning your future in a specific location gives you the best chance of helping yourself succeed. Thus, Your Future affects your Past and Present.

HOW IT ALL WORKS TOGETHER, SEAMLESLY – The Past blends into the Present:

1. The Imprint Period. Up to the age of seven, we are like sponges, absorbing everything around us and accepting much of it as true, especially when it comes from our parents. The confusion and blind belief of this period can also lead to the early formation of trauma and other deep problems. The critical thing here is to learn a sense of right and wrong, good and bad. This is a human construction which we nevertheless often assume would exist even if we were not here (which is an indication of how deeply Subconscious Programming/ imprinting it has become).

2. The Modeling Period. Between the ages of eight and thirteen, we copy people, often our parents, but also other people. Rather than blind acceptance, we are trying on things like a suit of clothes, to see how they feel. We may be much impressed with religion or our teachers. You may remember being particularly influenced by junior school teachers who seemed so knowledgeable—maybe even more so than your parents. This is another form of Programming/Imprinting, since we are told how to act, how to react, and how to present ourselves to the world.

3. The Socialization Period. Between 13 and 21, we are very largely influenced by our peers. As we develop as individuals and look for ways to

get away from the earlier programming, we naturally turn to people who seem more like us. Other influences at these ages include the media, especially those parts which seem to resonate with the values of our peer groups. By now, we are fully Programmed by our environment. Yes, we may think that we are making conscious choices, but those choices are based upon the deep programming that has occurred in the first 20-years of our life. We may have been taught "critical thinking," to question and analyze what we have heard or read but we conduct that analysis based upon the Programming we have received.

4. The Operational Period. Between 21 and 60 we enter the work world, where we may have learned how everything technically works but the application is still uncertain. We now turn to the professional peers (e.g., Senior and Principal Professionals, if one is a young engineer; pastors, senior family members, teachers, etc.). We become "integrated" into the world system of performance.

This is the process of how the PAST overlaps (transitional period) and becomes the PRESENT, and then the PRESENT overlaps (transitional period) and becomes the FUTURE. We rationalize this as a linear process.

5. But how does the future affect the present and future – Part of it is quantum mechanics, entanglement and the Uncertainty Principle. The Future is already there in a very malleable form (it comes from Pre-Life Planning (Refer to Chapter 2 of the author's book, Conscious Awakening – A Research Compendium) and the Universe "contract mission" that you agreed to perform during your transit time on Earth, if your origin is not a Earth Soul (i.e., Lightworker, Galactic Warrior, Wanderer, Indigo, or other form of Star Bing).

A VISUAL AID – I have created a Venn diagram to depict the relationships between Past, Present, and Future. You may have been introduced to Venn diagrams in the 9th Grade, when you took Plane Geometry or, even earlier, whenever you were taught set theory. A Venn diagram is a diagram that shows *all* possible logical relations between a finite collection of different sets. These diagrams depict elements as points in the plane, and sets as regions inside closed curves. A Venn diagram consists of multiple overlapping closed curves (where the overlap is equivalent to the logic word of "AND"), usually circles, each representing a set. The points inside a curve labeled A represent elements of the set A, while points outside the boundary represent elements not in the set A. This lends to easily read visualizations; for example, the set of all elements that are members of both sets A and B, $A \cap B$, is represented visually by the area of overlap of the regions A and B. In Venn diagrams the curves are overlapped in every possible way, showing all possible relations between the sets. In a Venn diagram, the universe of discourse is normally drawn as a rectangular region inside of which all the action occurs – in our case the universe of discourse in "universal knowledge" = u. They are thus a special case of Euler diagrams, which do not necessarily show all relations.

In the Venn Diagram below:

A = Past
B = Present
C = Future
A-B = Overlap (transition) between the Past (A) and the Present (B)
B-C = Overlap (transition) between the Present (B) and the Future (C)
C-A = Overlap (feedback/transition) between the Future ('C') and the Past (A)
A-B-C = Overlap of all three sets (A, B, C), where all three "sets" exist at the same time
U = universe of discourse = Knowledge contained within Universe

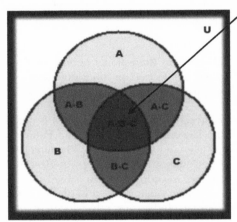

Star Being "Work Zone"

The Interchange where Past, Present and Future Overlap (Venn Diagram Area noted as A-B-C). It is in the "overlap" between Past, Present, and Future where the interchange takes place. It is here where deep consciousness is awakened and you may be reminded of past lives, past spiritual lessons learned, and why you, as a Star Being, volunteered or were sent to Earth (i.e., your mission and "contract"). This interchange could be revealed in increments throughout your Past and Present, as the Past becomes the Present, within that "zone" where Past Present and Future all overlap. This is, also, the juncture (A-B-C) where mankind may become Enlightened – this is the Star Being "work zone."

Connect to Universal Knowledge (The "U" surrounding Past, Present, Future in the Venn diagram). - Moments of sudden, unabridged inspiration and creativity are what enlightened individuals are seeking, sometimes all throughout their lives, as they are the ones who are able to access the knowledge of the Universe.

But how did they do this? They connect with the Knowledge of the Universe through their Higher Self (Spirit). Below are a few steps you could take towards accessing the knowledge of the Universe and thus transforming your life completely.

1. **Understand** - It is essential, before striving to access higher levels of consciousness and awareness, you understand the nature of the Universe. Beyond what we can see or perceive (astral objects), there is a whole matrix governing a myriad of expansive processes. The whole Universe works on a

premise of expansion which allows for elements to manage their functionality in creation-destruction dynamics. What you need to do is to try and grow your knowledge base by which the basic principles of the Cosmos is governed.

2. **Learn More** - Once you better understand the nature and purpose of the Universe, you can delve deciphering the ways of your own mind – this is the best way to understand the connection you have with your universal origins. I am referring specifically to knowledge about the subconscious and the superconscious – two significant portals connecting you with your Higher Self, your connection to the Universe. Once you understand them, you'll know how to channel your energy towards connecting with the knowledge of the Universe.

The subconscious mind is like a huge database, this is the system which records every thought, each activity we've engaged in or each impression we made. Although these are kept at a subconscious level, not all of them are processed by the conscious mind. Lack of processing in the brain leads to accumulation of the residual data – hence, energy blockages leading to physical and psychological issues.

The superconscious mind: this is a superior level of the conscious mind, wherein it is able to retrieve a superior kind of awareness. The superconscious mind allows you to perceive the higher energy governing superficial layers of reality.

3. Research Techniques of Connecting to your Higher Self and the Knowledge of the Universe - **There are a few techniques** you can choose from when you strive to tap into your connection with the higher Intelligence of the Universe. Whichever you choose, it's worth knowing they will connect your subconscious mind to the superconscious one, which helps your being be synchronous to the Universe.

- Meditation (to achieve gamma frequency – not the beta waves of many meditation techniques)
- Free flow visualization
- Dream interpretation
- Self-hypnosis.

4. **Cultivate Patience and Perseverance** - Nothing good comes the easy way. When you make this commitment to accessing knowledge of the Universe, you need to understand you're undergoing a transformational process. You need to persevere, even though you don't seem to register progress. You need to be relentless in your patience and perseverance.

Sources
1. "Your View of the Future is Shaped by Your Past," Dr. Art Marksman, Psychology Today, Aug 12, 2011,
2. https://www.psychologytoday.com/us/blog/ulterior-motives/201108/your-view-the-future-is-shaped-the-past
3. "The Time Machine of Consciousness. Past Present Future Exist Simultaneously," Rhawn Gabriel Joseph, BrainMind.com, Cosmology, 2014, Vol. 18. 331-375. Cosmology.com, 2014,
http://cosmology.com/ConsciousTime111.html
4. "How to Tap into the Knowledge of the Universe to Transform Your Life," Jerry Sargeant, Star Magic, https://www.starmagichealing.com/how-to-tap-into-the-knowledge-of-the-universe-to-transform-your-life/
5. Venn Diagram Definition, https://en.wikipedia.org/wiki/Venn_diagram

Article 30

THE DARK SIDE OF HEALING

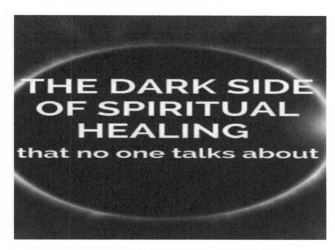

Don't get me wrong. I think spiritual healing is absolutely essential on our inner journeys. In fact, if every single person in this world underwent spiritual healing, I believe humanity and planet Earth would be transformed forever. I believe that we could finally achieve the ideal of world peace.

What is Spiritual Healing? - Spiritual healing is the practice (and experience) of restoring, harmonizing and balancing our Soul. There are many different approaches to spiritual healing. For example, some new age healing practitioners focus only on bringing balance to the etheric or non-physical energy field of the human body. Shamanic healers focus on restoring the Soul and curing Soul loss. And other holistic healers focus on unifying the body, Heart, Mind, and Soul. Even psychologists and therapists are starting to incorporate spiritual healing into their work such as those operating in the depth and transpersonal fields of psychology.

There are five main types of spiritual healing:
- Physical healing (of the Body)
- Emotional healing (of the Heart)
- Mental healing (of the Mind)
- Soul healing (of the Soul)
- Holistic healing (of the Body, Heart, Mind, and Soul)

Informed spiritual healers (i.e., those who understand the nature of the Soul), and spiritual healing resources recommend a host of different methods. Some of them include:
- Self-love and self-care practices
- Inner child work
- Shadow work

- Soul retrieval
- Solitude and introspection
- Meditation and mindfulness
- Connecting with spirit animals and spirit guides
- Spending time in nature (ecotherapy)

What is authentic spiritual healing? True spiritual healing is about facing, acknowledging, exploring, and integrating what we are going through. It's not about trying to escape our reality! It's really as simple as that.

Just think of it this way: if you had a blistering sore oozing blood and puss ... would you really achieve much by covering your eyes and pretending to ignore it? No. The pain and infection would still be there. Would you really heal by pretending the sore wasn't yours or by making it someone else's responsibility to look after? No. You'd still carry that sore with you everywhere. It wouldn't go away any time soon. The only way to heal that blistering sore is to face it, accept it, and find ways of alleviating your suffering – not as a way of trying to escape your reality – but as a form of self-love. This is true spiritual healing.

So when it comes to spiritual healing, please be mindful of these traps and practice healthy caution. Critical thinking skills and radical self-honesty are *so vital* in this day and age.

The Dark Side of Spiritual Healing - There's a reason why no one talks about the dark side of spiritual healing. Number one, most people aren't even *aware* that there's a dark side. And if they are aware then number two: they are uncomfortable to face or confront it.

It is completely understandable to want to try and get rid of our suffering – particularly if we are exhausted and deeply wounded. But here's the thing: desperately trying to heal can actually exacerbate your unhappiness and deepen your resistance to what's happening, thereby preventing you from actually healing!

- **Caution to Practitioners: Spiritualized Resistance** – Everyone in the spiritual community needs to understand that trying to "heal" is not always about healing. In fact, often, healing is used as an excuse to deny, suppress, disown, or reject what one is going through. Desperately trying to heal can intensify one's unhappiness and deepen the resistance to what's happening, thereby preventing you from actually healing! It is important to understand that true spiritual healing is about facing, acknowledging, exploring, and integrating what one is going through. It's not about trying to escape reality!

- **Caution to Patients: Dark Spiritual Teachers /Practitioners–** Another dark side is perpetrated by Spiritual "Healers" and Practitioners who are aware –

Either on a conscious or unconscious level – of Spiritualized Resistance. These teachers are aware of the addictive quality of the push-and-pull game of eternal self-improvement and they use it for their own self-gain.

Then, you have the more sinister breed of Spiritual Teachers/EM Practitioners who appear divine and enlightened on the surface but are raging megalomaniacs underneath. A true spiritual teacher will always give your power back to you, they will purport to have the power to "heal" all your issues and provide you with the "one true path" towards enlightenment, illumination, self-realization or Oneness. And if you believe them, you will be ensnared in a dangerous web of believing that someone outside of you can offer you salvation.

Sources:

1   Aura Versus Chakras, Gaia Staff, Gaia, Dec 21, 2019,
    https://www.gaia.com/article/difference-between-auras-and-chakras
2   "Physics of Seven Chakras and How to Balance 7 Chakras Correctly," Life
    Script Doctor, June 15, 2018, https://www.lifescriptdoctor.com/seven-
    chakras/
3   "Energy Medicine: Current Status and Future Perspectives," Christina L
    Ross, PhD, BCPP, Glob Adv Health Med. 2019; 8: 2164956119831221,
    Published online 2019 Feb 27,
4   "5 Types of Spiritual Healing," Altheia Luna, Shadow Works Journal, Loan Wolf,
    https://lonerwolf.com/spiritual-healing/
5   "Raising the Vibration of the Earth!," Deborah King,
    https://deborahking.com/raising-the-vibration-of-the-earth/
6   Beyond Techniques: the 2012 Shift: Evolving from Lightworker to Light,
    Lisa Marie Gutowsk, iUniversity Inc, 2008,
    https://books.google.com/books?id=67OlLHAzzdMC&pg=PA27&lpg=PA2
    7&dq=lightworker+chakra+frequency+manipulation&source=bl&ots=jPNW
    WvvG5p&sig=ACfU3U3_LpOARjt7qiJZe7Im9f81oGWCRQ&hl=en&sa=
    X&ved=2ahUKEwioxdL2_v_oAhXCF80KHYSJDUsQ6AEwCnoECAIQ
    AQ#v=onepage&q=lightworker%20chakra%20frequency%20manipulation
    &f=false
7   "Good vibrations - how sound balances our chakras," CHRISTINA DA-
    VIDSON,FRIDAY, July 29, 2016, chakradance,
    http://www.chakradance.com/blog/good-vibrations
8   "Sound and the Chakras," Jonathan Goldman, Healing Sounds,
    https://www.healingsounds.com/sound-and-the-chakras/
9   "Case Report: Energy Field Changes Approaching and During the Death
    Experience," Susan Peck, PhD; GNP-BC, APNP, FAAO, APT,
    CHTP/I,*Gail Corse, BS, BA, CNA,*and Der-Fa Lu, PhD, RN, INCJ In-
    teractive Medicine: A Clinician's Journal v.16(6) 2017 Dec, US National
    Library of Medicine, National Institute of Health,
    https://www.ncbi.nlm.nih.gov/pmc/articles/PMC6438089/
10 "The Dark Side of Spiritual Healing That No One Talks About" , Truth
    Theory, posted 2018/12/27, https://truththeory.com/2018/12/27/the-dark-
    side-of-spiritual-healing-that-no-one-talks-abou/

Article 31

HUMMING IS PSYCHO-ACOUSTIC & VBRO-ACOUSTIC THERAPY

There are two main ways that sound affects us. The first is called "psycho-acoustics". These are sounds that go into our ears and into our brain, affecting our nervous system, including our heart rate and respiration. As noted, this can produce great therapeutic benefits and is certainly something that occurs when we listen to music. The second is called "vibro-acoustics". These are sounds that go into our body and vibrate on a cellular level. As we'll discuss momentarily, these sounds can also produce amazing effects. While all sound (including music) that we hear have some vibro-acoustic ability, there are some sounds that in particular are extremely non-musical, yet quite excellent on vibrating the physical body.

Humming is one of the most powerful self-created sounds that we know of, which can produce vibro–acoustic effects, enabling the sounds to internally massage us and affecting us in the way that no other such sound can do. Thus, the saying: The simplest sound is the most profound.

Humming benefits include:
- Increased oxygen in the cells—enhancing health and wellness.
- Lowered blood pressure and heart rate.
- Increased lymphatic circulation—clearing toxins from the body.
- Increased levels of melatonin—a hormone that enhances sleep.
- Reduced levels of stress related hormones—enhancing health and wellness.
- Release of endorphins—self-created opiates that work as "natural pain relievers" and make us feel good.
- Increased levels of nitric oxide, (NO), a molecule associated with vasodilatation and promotion of healing.
- Release of oxytocin –the "love" hormone, creating trust between us.

Studies show that humming improves healing and reduces nasal congestion. Humming at 25–150 Hz has been known to speed healing of bone, tendons, ligaments and muscles. 25–50 Hz increases bone density. 100 Hz helps decrease dyspnea and shortness of breath.

So I was curious to see if I can hum in those frequencies. I fired up my frequency measurement app (iStroboSoft) and learned that my hum is around 100 Hz.

Hum for happiness—It's as easy as 1-2-3
1. Smile, and then breathe in and out through your nose, with your lips closed. As you release your breath, keep your lips closed and gently allow a soft hum to float out. Use a tone that is natural for you, one where you easily feel the vibration in your heart center. Hum softly. Louder is not better.
2. Continue for a few minutes, without straining, until you feel the relaxation response—slower breathing, slower heart rate, calmer thoughts.
3. For maximum happiness and health, hum for at least 20 minutes a day.

Do you feel "humming challenged"? Here's another option. Cuddle with a cat that loves to purr. Research shows that cats purr at healing sound frequencies of 25–150 Hz. They purr when giving birth, when frightened, and when severely injured. Their bones heal more rapidly after fractures than dogs (who don't purr, of course). So if you don't want to hum, you can try some "purr therapy".

In this time of stress and anxiety caused by fear of the virus, try humming a happy tune or the 5 toned that used with hand symbols in the movie "Close Encounters of the Third Kind" which are, in solfege, Re, Mi, Do, Do, So; the second Do is an octave below the First. On a side note, I think that the inhabitants of a distant galaxy would recognize and appreciate a melody formed of the major or minor scales, because they are both derived from universal acoustic principles: a vibrating string in another galaxy will have the same harmonic partials as it does here.

A last thought: The "Global Hum," heard by up to 4% of the population, is in the range of 40 to 50 Hz. Perhaps, Gaia is trying to calm you and you are not listening.

PART 5 - REALMS, DENSITIES, HUMAN CONSCIOUSNESS, ESCAPE

Article 32

THE VEDIC REALMS

Dimension

Dimension refers to one's location in space/time rather than a person's vibrational frequency (Density). Webster defines "dimension" as "Magnitude measured in a particular direction, specifically length, breadth, thickness or time." There are an infinite number of dimensions existing within a given Density or vibrational frequency. M-Theory of String Theory predicts that there are eight (8) physical dimensions and five (5) theoretical dimensions.

Frequency

Matter is vibrating energy. Different vibrationary rates denote the properties. Frequency is the rate at which molecules or consciousnesses vibrate.

Realms (sometimes referred to as Planes or Worlds):

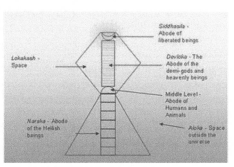

A **Realm**/plane/world, in esoteric cosmology, is conceived as a subtle state, level, or region of reality. Each plane corresponds to some type, kind, or category of being. The concept may be found in religious and esoteric teachings — e.g., Vedanta (AdvaitaVedanta), Ayyavazhi, Shamanism, Hermeticism, Neoplatonism, Gnosticism, Kashmir Shaivism, Sant Mat/Surat Shabd Yoga, Sufism, Druze, Kabbalah, Theosophy, Anthroposophy, Rosicrucianism (Esoteric Christian), Eckankar, Ascended Master Teachings, etc.—which propound the idea of a whole series of subtle realms (also known as planes or worlds) which, from a center, interpenetrate themselves and the physical planet in which we live, the solar systems, and all the physical structures of the universe. This interpenetration of Realms (planes or worlds) culminates in the universe itself as a physical structure, dynamic and evolving expression emanated through a series of stages (i.e., planes or levels).

All Reality is Divided into Awareness Levels - The Cosmos, Universe, Multiverse, All There Is, however you want to call it, is divided into Realms (planes, layers), each one with a corresponding vibratory rate of energy, and a different primary state of awareness. These layers or levels are called *Densities*. They are akin to "levels", each one on top of the other like concentric spheres, each one within the other, like the layers of the onion, permeating each other and occupying the same space at all times. Some picture Densities as a row of "containers" from which one "travels" back and forth between "Containers".

The Purpose of The Universe is to Support Life - In each Realm layer dwell beings that correspond to the Ream's primary awareness level. It is designed so a given Realm and the entities therein (1) are composed of, have access to, are in contact with, and possibly even have control over, the Realm and entitles below it; but (2) have lesser accessibility, restricted access, fewer contact - if any at all - with the Realm and entities above. As I once read somewhere, a given layer of the onion "sees" all the ones below it because it contains them all, but is contained by, and can't quite "reach", the one immediately above.

All Beings in existence, not just Human Beings and animals, but all entities, angels, aliens, spirits, energies, etc., every creature and form of existence in the cosmos have/belongs to a primary Realm awareness level, and exist in the corresponding vibratory state or Realm. Each Realm in turn has physicality and physical environment characteristics that correspond to the matching consciousness levels of the entities that live in it. In lower Realms the matter/consciousness is denser, and on higher ones the matter/consciousness is more subtle or "ethereal".

Density

Density denotes a vibrational frequency and not a location, which the term "dimension" implies. The Density structure of this reality is primarily expressed in multiple **Realms**, though **each Realm has its own levels of Densities** within it. The density scale is a model used to communicate one's perception of orientation in relation to other realities. Some of the Densities are intertwined with specific Realms, but Densities are not Realms.

According to Hindu cosmology, the Universe is divided into three "realms," "worlds," or "sections." The upper six regions are called Svarga, which corresponds with "Heaven." Prithvi is Earth, and Patala/Naga-loka (the seven lower regions), are the Underworld or the Netherworld. (There is no reason for the reader to know all these Sanskrit terms by heart—I am using many of them only once, in order to show the reader how they occur within the Vedic or Hindu texts).

This research paper should allow you to understand the Six Levels of Heaven, the Middle Realm, and the Seven Levels of Hell, if you like these terms instead of Upper, Middle and Lower Realms. The Realms will provide you with the knowledge you need to develop your Exit Plan. Do not confuse yourself by the Hindu names of the Realms; just recognize that there is a difference between the various Realms. Also note that this research is not "New Age" since it was revealed nearly 3,000 years ago as written within the Vedic text Atharva-Veda.

There are several "negative" levels (Lower Realms), including what many religions call "purgatory" or the "netherworlds", places where soul fragments journey to learn about separation, fear and terror. In these Lower Realms, fear thoughts manifest as grotesque apparitions, monsters, etc. There is a lot of talk about negative entities and their effect on humans. Whether ghosts, poltergeists or negative ETs, the truth is that these beings can only affect us if we vibrate at a level that attracts them. When we reach the Higher Realms, these experiences are seen as dreams or part of the "maya" of the Lower Realms.

THE SPIRITUAL REALMS – Above the Hierarchy of the Material Universe (Middle Realm that contains Earth) there is a spiritual hierarchy, which is dominated by the Supreme Being (One Source, Creator God). The Veda texts, which are typically patriarchal in their structure, are quick to point out that albeit there is a long "distance" between the material worlds and the spiritual realms, **all spirit souls are intimately related with the Supreme and that the Supreme Being (a fragment of) accompanies each soul as a Supersoul** (referred to as SPIRIT). Also, which is quite interesting, the Supreme Being is said to personally descend and incarnate as an Avatar on various material plants. Two such well-known Avatāra (Avatars) are Lord Krishna and Lord Rāma. The idea suggests that the Mother Goddess is the Supreme Being– ALL THAT IS, Source or whatever we want to call Her, incarnates in the Physical and Metaphysical Universes in order to participate more directly in the progress, and the process, of the evolution of the Universe. We know her incarnations the Queen of the Stars and Mother Gaia. In the Vedas, however, the Supreme Being is male energy because of its overly patriarchal nature.

THE REALMS – View the photo of the Vedic Realms. The YARTHIS Realms (Higher Realms) are in the Greater Universe and the PATALAS Realms, as well as the PRITHVI Realm (Middle Realm – the Material Realm containing Earth) is the Realm of both the 4% Universe (Dark Force Dominated and Controlled) and the Greater Universe. The Lower Realms are more predominate in the 4% Universe, but to a lesser extend exist in the Greater Universe.

Starting at the top and proceeding downward:

VYARTHIS, The HIGHER REALMS (Hindu "Heaven" – "above" the Realm containing Earth):

- **Brahmaloka/Satya-Loka–** On the absolute top of the Higher Realm is Lord Brahmā, pointed out to be the first being in the Universe, and he resides in a planetary system called *Brahmaloka*. Satya-Loka in Hindu mythology is the state of mind you reach when you experience Samadhi or Nirvana. **It is the moment of Absolute Truth** which the Hindus associate with Brahman – the all-seeing, all-knowing master of the Universe. To put *Satya-Loka* into perspective, have you ever experienced an ah–ha moment when you felt elated and knew – you just KNEW.

- **Tapaloka–**The inhabitants of *Tapa-Loka* are the four Kumaras – the enlightened sons of Lord Brahma. Given Brahma represents Mind, **the four Kumaras represent the four faculties, or powers of the mind; intellect, imagination, inspiration and intuition.** The four Kumaras are pure and **have no desire other than to teach.** In the Mahabharata, they are described as Nirvitti, – **inward contemplation.** *Tapa-Loka* is **the state of consciousness Buddhas retain after they reach enlightenment.** It is a state of eternal bliss. When you reach this state of mind, you are capable of creating anything you need in life because you are guided by divine consciousness – the highest faculties of mind. When you are capable of deep introspection, you can achieve everything you're supposed to.

- **Janaloka –** *Jana-Loka* is said to be the abode of the great saints and sages. **This is the realm of the Akashic Library** which you want to access. You will not achieve anything in life without first attaining knowledge – and the highest forms of knowledge have come from wise men of the ages. The Vedas position *Jana-Loka* is 80,000,000 yojanas (one Yojana = 13-16 km = 8 - 10 miles approx.) below *Tapa-Loka*, thus the realm is associated with the number eight. In turn, the number eight is associated with "God-Consciousness" – the state of mind awakened mystics, yogis, **philosophers and other spiritual teachers** should attain in order to teach others.

- **Maharloka –** It is said that the Rishis living on Mahar-Loka have a life span of 4,300,000,000 solar years – this is associated with the number seven (4+3), a symbolic mathematical principle you calculate using gematria. In ancient mythology, seven is associated with the Mother Goddess, who in turn is associated with emotions. The state of mind represented by Mahar-Loka, therefore, is tied to **emotional understanding; the power of patience and the ability to care and nurture.**

- **Svargaloka** /Svarloka – *Svargaloka*, which is populated by Devas, who have a military hierarchy, and they are often at war with the Asuras (demons, which represent bad habits or bad energies). The Devas are much into politics and warfare, and they have an extremely long life span. It is said to be the realm which is inhabited by the 33 Vedic gods, the head of whom is Indra. Indra is regarded as the King of the Gods and **recognized as a war god or storm god, and we often find him fighting** with his vajra – a weapon that fires a lightning bolt.

In essence, *Svargaloka* is the aspect of your nature in circumstances when you are called upon to summon courage and confidence to overcome challenges. This is how you expand conscious awareness and cultivate more quality in your life.

- **BhuvarLoka** – In the Vedas, *Bhuvar-Loka* is described as a **realm with Earth-like qualities but is inhabited by semi-divine beings.** These semi-divine beings are essentially humans that have **found inner-peace and live a happy and fulfilling life.** In this state of mind, you **vibrate at a high frequency,** As a consequence, you feel **confident and content with your life** most of the time. You **do not pine for anything** and on most occasions have **command over your emotions and actions.** When you live in **this state of mind, most things you do, or try, results in success. You are happy** with yourself, have strong relationships, and a content work-life. Sure, you are still prone to the odd error, but this is also human nature. *Bhuvar-Loka* is a **state of mind that everyone should strive towards – at the very least!**

PRITHVI, The MIDDLE REALM (the Material Realm containing Earth and the 4% Universe) – The Vedic Bhuama-Svarga is sometimes referred to as Bhū-Mandala or the Bhur–loka; Bhur-Loka in Hindu mythology is the realm that reflects planet Earth. The people that inhabit this lower realm of the higher Lokas are people that are awake but do not assert much effort into self-development and do not put any effort to reach the higher realms. This state of mind is typically neutral. For example, they could be aware of the corruption and injustices of the world, but do not let that concern them too much. They won't stand up and fight for their rights, but they won't moan and complain about it either. People in this realm are not overly concerned by material possessions or overcome by desires either. They may have ambitions, but they are even-keeled, grounded and go about their business at their own pace.

In Hindu it is Prithvi. This in turn refers to the flat Earth—therefore the ignorance of the people of that time, as well as many of the "gods." "Earth" actually corresponds to the plane of the ecliptic, with its 500,000,000 yojanas in diameter (1 yojana being about 8-10 miles). This is the plane determined, from a geocentric point of view, by the orbit of the Sun around the Earth. This plane is of course, flat. A careful study of Vedic texts shows that this "earth' actually corresponds to the plane, with that plane having a "thickness" to contain all of the "round" planets within the solar system and the 4% Universe. One has to be alert to the fact that the term "earth," as used in Vedic texts, does not always refer to the small Earth globe.

PATALAS, the LOWER REALMS ("below the Realm containing Earth)– the Vedic Underworld, or the Netherworld, The seven lower worlds are dark planets, devoid of sunshine or any natural light— therefore, they are artificially lit by means of huge reflecting surfaces—such as crystals and gems. Because there is no division between day and night, and no sunshine that reaches these planets, their inhabitants—and humans dwelling here in particular—have no sense of time. Time, as we look at time, does not exist here. The irony is that they are! Remember that we are talking about material existence here, depleted of all spiritual associations.

In these lower lokas we find beings, deities, and demons, such as Daityas, Dānavas, Panis, Nivat-Kavachs, Rakshasas, Kalkeyas, Nagas, and Uragas, who are all splurging in illusory material enjoyment and pleasures, without taking any spiritual consequences for their actions. All residents bathe in elixirs which free them from anxiety and physical disease, as well as any signs of aging. The visual beauty of some of these lower realms surpasses even that of the higher planets, so we are told. There are incredible feats of architecture in their cities, bedecked with exquisite and valuable jewels.

- **Atala-loka**: Atala is ruled by the daemon god Bala/Malduk – a son of Maya – who possesses mystical powers. Bala created three types of women – *svairiṇīs*, who like to marry men from their own group; *kāmiṇīs*, who marry men from any group, and the *puṁścalīs*, who kept changing partners. The state of mind represented by Atala-Loka is the delusional mind of the empirical ego. You may want to believe you are in control of your mind and emotions – and thus your life – but in reality you are controlled by the subconscious programs planted by society and therefore live in ignorance to what is really happening in the world. The enticement in Atala-Lokahere is that when a male dies, he may enter Atalaloka, where he immediately gets enchanted by all these types of women, who give him an intoxicating cannabis drink that induces sexual energy in the man. Then, these women enjoy sexual play with the "traveler," Regardless what some men may think about that, we see pure manipulation at play again ("...and forgets impending death"). With all these beautiful women serving the deceased (dead in a worldly sense) male, he can be manipulated into anything. Also, as a side note—there is something similar for women, where handsome men come and seduce them after death. Much of what is explained here should not be taken totally literally, of course, as some of it is metaphors and allegories, but the intents and the overall meaning is highly valid data.

- **Vitala-loka**: Vitala is ruled by the god Hara-Bhava (Malduk in a different avatar body, son of Vishnu, who is proven to be Lord Ea or Enki, depending on the time period) – Hara Bhava is a form of Shiva. Shiva's role is to destroy the universe in order to re-create it and uses its power to destroy the illusions and imperfections of this world, paving the way for change. This level includes ghosts and goblins, who are masters of the goldmines. Gold is still there in abundance in the "underworld"—in spite of the hundreds of thousands of years of digging on the surface by Mankind, created by the Enki Group. Here it is said that the gold is dug by ghosts and goblins, which sounds like it corresponds to deceased humans (ghosts) and demonic type of beings (goblins).

- **Sutala-loka:** Sutala is the kingdom of the pious demon king Mahabali. King Bali founded the mythologies of **Jainism – Jesus came into the world to teach the tenets of Jainism.** King Bail was thought to be benevolent due to his blessing the island, Bali, This is contrary to all rulers in the Patalas are malevolent. Mahabali, the "benevolent demon king," according to the records, is the grandson of Prahlada, who is the equivalent to Garuda, who is the equivalent to Lord Marduk. If we read this literally, Mahabali would therefore be Marduk's grandson, which in some aspects makes sense because Mahabali, in the Vedas, is portrayed as human (read human hybrid). Hence, either Marduk had his human hybrid grandson rule Sutalaloka, or Marduk deliberately changed the records so that it looks like his grandson rules this region, when in fact it's Marduk himself who is in charge.

  Sutalaloka is a part of the Underworld, and therefore, benevolence is hardly a term appropriate to this being when meeting him in his own domain. Aren't top players in today's society said to act in a similar way? They seem quite normal and benevolent when they meet the regular people, but behind the scenes they can act like monsters, doing rituals and being accustomed to rape and sacrifice of children.

- **Talatala-loka:** Talātala is the realm of the demon-Maya, who is well-versed in sorcery. Shiva, as Tripurantaka, destroyed the three cities of Maya but was later pleased with Maya and gave him this realm and promised to protect them. This is the mythological explanation to why Enki still is the Lord of Talatalaloka—it was once given to Marduk, and it included three cities. Therefore, these cities were originally built by Enki when he owned this domain. Enki gave the domain to Marduk, who destroyed the cities—allegedly he didn't like them. The torment here is the building, destroying and rebuilding, all to no avail. In Talatala loka the inhabitants have lost sight of their true nature. They have a mindset is that nothing exists beyond this Realm. Their state of conscious awareness is so attached to individualism that they become disconnected from the world and struggle to forge meaningful relationships.

- **Mahatala-loka:** Mahātala is the abode of the many-headed Nagas (serpents with the heads of cobras and the body of humans) – the sons of Kadru, headed by the *Krodhavasha* (Irascible) band of Kuhaka, Takshaka, Kaliya and Sushena. The Nagas are Enki's Minions. Most likely, they are also one of those races that reside in the Sirius star system. The Nagas live in this Realm in peace, but that they "always fear Garuda, "the eagle-man," who is Marduk. The Naga represent the dual nature of your personality. The Naga then represent cravings and incidents as bad luck. But there is no such thing as bad luck. It is bad energy, and the ones who reside here have these experiences because there is something they need to learn about themselves.

- **Rasatala-loka:** Now we're getting closer to the Vedic Hell. This region is inhabited by demons—here called Dānavas and Daityas. These demons are known by Hindus to be cruel and mighty. They are said to be foes of the Devas, and the Devas are the gods in the Vedas. Dānavas and Daityas live in holes, like serpents and are known to be cruel. Individuals in Rasatala loka typically experience a lot of chaos and have little to no control over their actions – but nor do they recognize what they are doing is wrong. Individuals which persist with a holier-than-thou attitude learn the hard way. From here there is only one place to go – Patala-Loka, or Hell. Don't wait for disaster to strike, because the next stage is "rock-bottom".

- **Patala-loka, also called Bila-Svarga :** The lowest realm is called Patala or Nagaloka, the region of the Nagas. This is the "snake" level in the Underworld. Here live several Nagas with many heads (hooded cobras). Each hood is decorated by a jewel, whose light illuminates this realm. The Nagas can travel through solid matter—something we hear a lot about from modern UFO abductees. The inhabitants of Patala-Loka are filled with hatred, malice and anger all the time. They are very abrupt people with a bad attitude and violent by nature. They hate themselves, the world and everything in it.

Masters of the Underworld – The Nagas serve the Masters of the Netherworld, which in the Babylonian texts are known as **Enki (later Marduk) and Ereškigal**. The Nagas are also known to live in parallel realities on the surface of the Earth, which means that they exist all around us, but on a wavelength just outside the third dimensional (3-D) reality. The place where many of them dwell is also called the Subterranean Heaven, located to the south of the Ecliptic.

The Nagas of this region are ruled by Vasuki, the "Great Naga King." According to the Vedas, Vasuki worked together with Vishnu (Enki) and the Asuras to obtain *Amrita*, the life-elixir that would make beings immortal—or at least next to immortal (in physical terms). This *Amrita (ambrosia)* was churned from the "Ocean of Milk," which of course is the Cosmic Ocean (also being a term for the Milky Way Galaxy). Ambrosia is said to be made from aloe, gentian root, bitters, some liqueurs, and a mixture of alcohols.

KARAKA, the Hellish Planets, also called Naraka-Loka – Beneath the planets of the Pitras is the Naraka, or the Naraklokas—the hellish planets, located just above the Garbhodaka Ocean. —The humans who enter there are going to suffer tremendously. In the Seven Paatalas, deceased humans may have a fairly tolerable existence, but the emphasis in these regions are on the material—the pure physical. Nothing of what we call spiritual is given any attention in the Naraka Loka. The Naraka is where the sinners are punished and could be said to be the equivalent to the Roman Catholic Purgatory, in the same sense that it is not an infinite punishment, like it is in the Christian Hell. The Naraka is a temporary abode for souls who need to "learn their lessons." it may help the reader to further understand what happens to souls after they die and get trapped in the Dark Force (Enki Group) Reincarnation Trap. In charge of the Naraka is a deity called Yama. He is also the "God of Justice," and thus the one who decides what a soul needs to accomplish before she/he can leave Naraka. Yama is assisted by beings called Yamadūtas— beings who are astonishingly similar to the "Grays." They look strange and frightening to the newly deceased and emanate very negative energies. They are also the ones who have to do with the transmigration of souls, and they are equipped with some mystical powers, so-called siddhis, which they use in order to carry out their duties. In the Vedas it is said that these beings are picking up souls who have been too entangled in the material world and are in need of special "care." However, when we research it more thoroughly, it looks like there's a little bit more to it than that. While abiding by the rules and regulations set down by the Supreme Lord (Enki or his son Malduk), has his agents, the Yamadūtas ("Greys"?), bring all the sinful men/women to him immediately upon their death. After bringing them within his jurisdiction, he properly judges them according to their specific sinful activities and sends them to one of the many hellish planets for suitable punishments.

Bottomline – Given that we live in the 4% Universe that is dominated and controlled by the Dark Forces (Enki Group) that dominates the Lower Densities, it would be best for your Soul not to be sent to any part of the Patales (Lower Densities). To escape this "doom" one needs to have and do the work they need to do while Living (**read Escaping the 4% Universe**) and to **have an At Death Escape Plan (read The Escape Plan – While on Earth)** that avoids being entangled in the Reincarnation Trap.

Post Note – **The Vedas** are a collection of hymns and other ancient religious texts written in **India** between about 1800 and 800 BCE. It includes elements such as liturgical material as well as mythological accounts, poems, prayers, and formulas considered to be sacred by the Vedic religion. According to tradition, Vyasa is the compiler of the **Vedas**, who arranged the four kinds of mantras into four Samhitas (Collections). There are four **Vedas**, originally written in Sanskrit:

- **Rig-Veda**, 1800 – 1100 BCE, "Knowledge of the Hymns of Praise", for recitation.
- **Sama-Veda**, 1200 – 800 BCE, "Knowledge of the Melodies", for chanting.
- **Yajur-Veda**, 1100 – 800 BCE, "Knowledge of the Sacrificial formulas", for liturgy.
- **Atharva-Veda**, 1000 – 800 BCE, "Knowledge of the Magic formulas", named after a group of priests.

Sources

1. "THE ORBITS OF THE PLANETS," Vedic Cosmology, Flat Earth Horizon, http://www.iskcon-truth.com/bhu-mandala/orbits-of-the-planets.html
2. "Wes Penre Papers," The Fifth Level of Learning, Part 1 and Part 2, The Vedic Texts, Feb 27, 2015, https://wespenrepapershome.files.wordpress.com/2019/07/fifthleveloflearningpart1.pdf
3. The Vedas, An English-only, indexed version of the 4 Veda Samhitas in one document, Compiled by the Dharmic Scriptures Team November 24, 2002, pdf format, https://zelalemkibret.files.wordpress.com/2012/03/the-4-vedas.pdf
4. "What's Your State of Mind? The Esoteric Meaning of the 14 Lokas in Hindu Mythology," Richard Oldale, April 11, 2018, Master Mind, https://mastermindcontent.co.uk/whats-your-state-of-mind-the-esoteric-meaning-of-the-14-lokas-in-hindu-mythology/

Article 33

SPIRITUAL DENSITIES OF THE EARTH

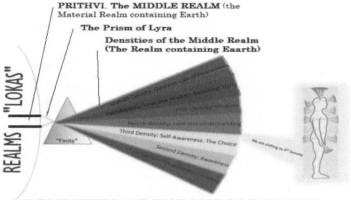

DENESTIES OF THE MIDDLE REALM
The Realm Containing Earth)

Density – Density denotes a vibrational frequency and not a location, which the term "dimension" implies. The density structure of this reality is primarily expressed in multiple **Realms**, though **each Realm has its own levels of Densities** within it. The density scale is a model used to communicate one's perception of orientation in relation to other realities. Some of the Densities are intertwined with specific Realms, but Densities are not Realms.

In contemporary spiritual and metaphysical content, 'Densities', 'Dimensions', '3D', '4D' etc are commonplace terms. They refer both to physical planes by which reality is divided and by Levels of Consciousness which correspond to each of them.

Densities or Dimensions? – Densities as a concept referred exclusively to an awareness state. You might say a being is living in a 5D Density on a given planet, but when you refer to the term "5D", you're saying "this is a reality where the predominant level of awareness is 5D". Densities focus on *awareness*. On the other hand, "Dimensions" as a concept not only relate to states of matter, but also notions from the fields of physics and science, like space, time, etc.

So by referring to Densities as the main idea, and not as Dimensions, what I'm actually saying is, "I don't really care *when* or *how* this happened, what matters is that this *was felt this way*". I'm not interested in arguing with scientists about how many dimensions there are. To me, it's all about awareness. For the Soul it's not so much about memorizing the details of what happens, but the experience as it is felt. This is why I'm all about Densities.

Different Models of Densities – There are several different models of Densities. Some are based on 7 Densities, others on 12. This Article is based upon the 7 Density Model, which is primarily derived from The Law of One, along with several other models and spiritual teachings of a metaphysical nature, such as the Theosophy-based human subtle bodies, the Sephiroths from the Kabbalah's Tree of Life, the human chakra system, and also, to what form of beingness corresponds each of the Realms (planes).

Densities List are Applicable to only the EARTH REALM – Each of the REALMS has a unique set of characteristics, perspectives, and core beliefs that are unique to that one REALM and, hence, the Densities of that Realm are unique to only that specific Realm. The Densities listed are applicable to the MIDDLE REALM (the one containing Earth) and not other Realms. They Densities within the Article were developed by the Dark Force (Enki Group of which is promoted by the Law of One) as part of their dominance and control of Mankind, as created by the Anunnaki (an off-shoot of the Draconian/Reptilian original race).

Finally, because each Density is further subdivided by the same number of Densities (i.e. 7 Densities, 7 sub-Densities, and so on), human beings can hold beliefs and manifest aspects of consciousness, corresponding to each level.

Reality is divided into the main 7 Densities. Humanity exists currently in the Third Density, which contains the First - existence (minerals and elements) – Second - life, animation and emotion (plants and animals) – and the Third: free will, creativity, mind and ego. As humanity evolves in its consciousness, Earth itself is currently transitioning up into the 4th Density.

Energy and Matter – All matter, everything that exists, is energy/light vibrating at a given frequency. The higher the frequency, the faster the rate of vibration, and the "lighter" or more subtle is the resulting matter; the lower the frequency, the slower the rate of vibration, and the "heavier" or denser the matter. Physical matter in the solid state corresponds to the lowest possible level of vibration. The liquid and gaseous states, for example water and air, are more subtle, or lighter, than the solid state. And after these, there are progressively "lighter" states of energy vibration.

BRIEF DESCRIPTION OF EACH DENSITY
(Refer to the section entitled "DENSTIES IN TERMS OF HUMAN CONSCIOUSNES" for a more extensive description of Human Consciousness).

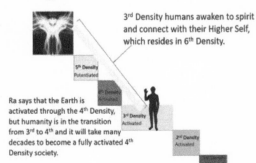

3rd Density humans awaken to spirit and connect with their Higher Self, which resides in 6th Density.

5th Density
Potentiated

Ra says that the Earth is activated through the 4th Density, but humanity is in the transition from 3rd to 4th and it will take many decades to become a fully activated 4th Density society.

3rd Density
Activated

2nd Density
Activated

1D - Survival aspects. Comfort. Sustenance. Abundance. Reacting when threatened. Physical intimidation. Violence vs. Vulnerability. Predatory gangs and groups.

2D- Negotiation. Judgment. Black-and-white beliefs. Good vs. Bad. Me vs. the other, Us vs. them. Austerity. Emotional suppression. Religious dogma.

3D - Willpower. Adaptability. Resourcefulness. Thriving in competition. Business and social acumen. Search for power and status. Worth by strength over/above others. Placing the end above the means. The unethical as a competitive advantage over the ethical. Evil as a viable route.

3.5 D – Ethics by philosophical, sociological, and non-spiritual values and pragmatic concerns. Intelligence. Science. Skepticism opposed to religious dogma and 'spiritual' ideals.

4D   Compassion. Peace. Ethics. Charity. Good intentions. Goodness that is vulnerable. Working for the interests of the group. Assuming the burdens and responsibilities of others. Permissive personal boundaries. Familiar attachment. Desire to care for/save everyone. Self-Rejection and self-concealment of what is perceived as 'bad' and 'wrong'. Self-nullifying. Victimization. Martyrdom.

5D- Freedom. Independence. Individuality. Speech and expression. Difference. Belief systems diverging from those of the collective. Trying to change the world as a necessary precondition to make the choices I want. Fringe ideas acted upon but at the expense of comfort and integrity of the self. Impulsiveness. Isolation. Not belonging. Revolt. Anger. Rash and impulsive actions.

6D- Wisdom. Big picture. Focus on inner change. Balance between external and internal. Allowing oneself abundance and comfort. Complete commitment to an inner-defined job, function, or passion. Intuition. Spiritual insight. Unrealistically overly-demand, overly-criticize the self. Self-deprecation. Lack of grounding. Lack of motivation. Laziness.

7D- Formless consciousness. Peak spiritual experience. Life-changing insight. Being, regardless of external circumstances. Detachment. Transcendence.

8D- Ascension. Absence of karmic attributes. One with Creation.

DETAILED DESCRIPTION OF EACH DENSITY - The Earth is in the 3rd density of reality (frequency band). At this density, everything — rocks, trees, houses, cars, etc. — APPEAR very solid and very "real." They feel solid because, when two objects encounter each other they do not interpenetrate and/or pass through each other — the density of the objects "material" seems to be very high. In the higher Densities, it becomes increasingly obvious that THINGS are simply projections of the creative mind and, as such, that they are not "real" in our normal sense of the word. In each successively higher Density, it becomes increasingly more obvious that only consciousness is real and that "things" are simply the projections of consciousness, thought forms within the cosmic mind and patterns of energy as you move up through higher and higher Densities "things" appear less and less dense, and more and more able to interpenetrate and/or pass through each other.

The confusing part is that we have numbered the Densities in an order OP-POSITE of the apparent density of "things" within those Densities — e.g.; things in a 6th Density are actually of a lower apparent density than in a 3rd Density. But note that the numbering order matches the frequency level — higher Densities correspond to higher frequencies. So a bit confusing, but we are stuck with this convention. Please note that some people use the term "dimension" to mean the same thing as "Density" (although this may not be appropriate and the term might be better used for other concepts).

There are entire realities that appear to exist in a particular Realm. When this is the case, then most of the beings inside that Density will share the same level of consciousness. Our Universe (one of many, by the way) is composed of multiple parallel Densities (sometimes referred to as "planes of reality"), and you are perceiving, and hence experiencing, one of them. There is a strong correlation between the Density and Level of Consciousness of the beings that inhabit it — typically the average Level of Consciousness of the population of the beings inhabiting a Density reality matches the Density level of the reality.

The 1st Density is the most rudimentary level. It is present in elemental entities like rocks, minerals, water, and air as well as simple organic biological entities such as single-celled organisms. Everything is conscious to some degree, and this level of consciousness is like a program that was created when the system it governs was created and then runs like a machine on automatic — it is the very simplest switch-like logic of "if this, then that." The very simple logical processes provided by 1D consciousness are all that is required for the functioning of these types of very simple entities, and it provides the foundation from which everything more complex in our reality is built.

Most of the planets of our solar system exist at 1st Density, and they are inhabited solely by entities/beings of 1D consciousness — inorganic elemental entities as well as single-celled organisms that metabolize the chemicals available to them from these entities. It may surprise you to know that these elemental inorganic entities have higher-selves with higher level consciousness just like we do.

The 2nd Density governs a being's choices and actions by instinct or "drive." On Earth, it occurs in higher animals which have developed nervous systems. These nervous systems allow animals (including the human animal) to feel urges from their various body systems and drives them to eat, procreate, sleep, avoid or defend against danger, and all the other things that each species needs to do for its survival. These drives happen pretty much automatically but are not absolute — they can be over-ridden.

A 2D being is not as self-aware in the way that we are. They do not have the same sense of individuality as we do — their sense of "self" as being separate from what is outside of "them" is largely absent. There is simply the drive to respond to cues from the environment. There is decision-making ability, sometimes fairly sophisticated, but there is not the formation of complex ideas, beliefs, or philosophies.

2nd Density consciousness is the foundation upon which more advanced life-forms with higher levels of consciousness rest.

The 3rd Density is characterized by true self-awareness, and the ability to make conscious choices and formulate complex ideological concepts such as principles, philosophical frameworks, and belief systems. This level perceives "self" versus "other", "me and mine" vs. "them and theirs", and conceives of "good" versus "bad." Hence it is the first of three Densities that are within a genre that has been called "Duality" or "Separation" consciousness.

3rd Density beings are deeply in the illusion of separation. In the genre of Separation there is little or no awareness that All is One. Beings of Separation consciousness see themselves separate from others, and the world as a place of limitation and scarcity. And it's this mindset that manifests all the greed, competition, and conflict that characterizes 3rd Density worlds. In addition, 3rd Density beings have lots of internal conflict on what to believe and desire. And this inner-conflict is reflected into their outer reality and hence 3rd Density worlds are wracked with conflict on many levels, both collective and personal.

Another one of the very convincing illusions that emerges from the separation game, the game that everyone on Earth is deeply immersed in right now, is the illusion that we are at the mercy of circumstances — that we ARE NOT the creators of our reality. And this illusion causes many to adopt a mindset that might be best called "Victim" consciousness and which manifests all the victim/perpetrator/rescuer dramas that dominate our lives, at both the personal and collective level.

3rd Density is the level of many, if not most, people now alive on Earth (although many are 4th Density and a few are 5th and even 6th Density). The world of 3D is complex, intricate, and often confusing and offers plenty of drama. 3rd Density is also the level where a phenomenon within the psyche known as the "ego" emerges — that powerful sense of "I", "Me", and "Mine." This level of consciousness can manifest powerful resolve and will-power. It is a Density characterized by very strong Individualism and "go it on my own" and "do it my way" attitude. Empires are built by such a consciousness when it is fully unleashed.

It is at this level where we first see a being that might willingly choose to put himself in harm's way over a complex ideological concept such as "fairness" or "justice". But it could go the other way too — a 3rd Density being who decides he has been unfairly treated might choose to take from or hurt others and feel quite justified in doing so.

Our planet is 3rd Density (at least it was until recently, now it's shifting into 4th Density) and in the past most people would reside at this Density for much, if not all, of their lives. Some people might have shifted from 3D or 4D to 4D or 5D to the diminishing of the ego. Others might have made a shift to higher Densities by INTENTIONALLY choosing to "listen to their heart", or "find their own truth", or to love unconditionally. Now this is all changing, at least here on Earth. Currently our Earth reality is undergoing a "stimulus package", that is being orchestrated from higher Densities or Realms, that is catalyzing accelerated "awakenings" and many people are spontaneously shifting to 4th, 5th, and even 6th Density consciousness — and this is all part of the plan for the Earth game.

3rd Density realities are constantly presenting the beings that inhabit them the choice of which direction to invest their energy. They are constantly being called to choose what they will serve and what they will love. This choice is between two diametrically opposed ways of being — Service to Self (STS) or Service to Others (STO). When a being makes this choice it means that its mindset, and resulting choices and actions, are consistently biased towards either (1) Satisfying its own needs (STS) or (2) satisfying the needs of others and the community (STO).

When a 3rd Density being ends its indecision and definitively chooses either a Service-to-Self or a Service-to-Other orientation — when they ask the questions; Who do I love?, What do I serve?, and To what will I give my energy? — And they answer with either "me" or "others" they graduate to 4th density of consciousness.

The 4th Density is the Density where the journey to becoming a truly individualized sovereign being begins. This Density still has most of the characteristics of 3rd Density except that at this Density the beings have polarized to one of two modes — Service to Self (STS) and Service to Other (STO). These modes represent two polar opposites in the manner in which beings will direct their energy — essentially there is two states of 4D consciousness — 4D STO and 4D STS.

The adoption of one of these two distinct polarities — STO or STS — is what moves you to this level of consciousness. Of course, most people who have made the shift to 4th Density are not consciously aware that they have done so — it's usually an implicit choice rather than an explicit one. In many ways, this polarization amplifies the duality of the realities manifested by this Density. And intensifies the many dramas that play out at this level of the game.

On worlds is populated with mostly 4th Density being's victim /perpetrator/ rescuer dramas are still being widely played out and greed, competition, conflict is still prevalent.

Here are examples of what polarized beings might look like.

- A full-fledged 4D STO being might be a person who is working at a shelter or a community social support services in a depressed community and giving a large amount of their energy to helping the poor on the streets. Or it might be a person who invests a large amount of their time and energy in environmental and animal rights issues. By their example, they offer you the choice to take a similar path. The 4D STO polarity had been called the polarity of compassion, as this is what rules their heart.

- A full-fledged 4D STS being might be one of the many self-serving power hungry people that litter our institutions, corporations, and our history. These types of people channel all their energy towards attaining power, wealth, and influence. And they are willing to manipulate others and destroy anyone who gets in their way if it serves THEIR needs. They'll often claim to be working for the greater good — serving the needs of the electorate, the shareholders, the customers, the community, or whoever they are pretending to serve. They can be found vying for power and control in criminal gangs, corporate offices, political parties, and religious organizations. The 4D STS polarity had been called the polarity of "power over others", because this is what rules their minds and satisfies their ego.

4th Density beings, regardless of their polarity, are characterized by a strong clarity of purpose. They have firmly adopted an orientation, and their choices and actions consistently demonstrate it. Because their mindset is so well defined and un-conflicted they tend to drive very powerfully and effectively towards their goals — they are achievers!

The challenge for those at this Density is to avoid burnout. 4th Density beings tend to give all they have and then exhaust themselves and their resources. The reason for this is simple — no system can exist in which the energy only flows in one direction. An STO being tends to give too much and receive too little. An STS being tends to take too much and give too little. So both STS and STO beings find that, lifetime after lifetime, that they either burn themselves out or end up all alone with nothing. 4th Density beings (and 4th Density societies) can be fairly successful but ultimately their success it limited by the fact that they don't understand one simple truth — you have to give to get, and you have to get to give. When they finally come to understand this, then they are ready to move up the ladder to the 5th Density.

The 5th Density has been called the density of "balanced polarity". At this level, the ascending being will still have an STO or STS orientation, as had emerged as they entered 4th Density. But they will know they must attain a better balance between the two by expressing more of the opposite polarity.

5D STO beings realize they must be open to receiving from all those that are willing to give to them so they can give their great service in a sustainable fashion. They can become powerful change agents because, for the first time, they are channeling energies through themselves rather than simply giving from their own small store of personal energy.

5D STS beings, by contrast, realize they must be willing to give to others, to nurture and motivate, so they will remain hard-working and loyal. They become much more benevolent and might even be admired, respected, or even loved by their subjects. Whereas 4D STS beings are likely perceived as "bosses", 5D STS beings are more likely to be perceived as "leaders" who inspire followers and unite them with their vision. Respected corporate CEOs and admired national presidents are great examples.

In a sense the strength of the polarity diminishes with every one drifting to a more balanced or neutral position on the scale. Because of this, the intensity and character of the dramas manifested on 5th Density worlds changes. The intensity and prevalence of victim/perpetrator/rescuer dramas diminishes and there is more cooperation and harmony and less competition and conflict.

Since 5th Density is the level where beings grasp the universal law of giving and receiving, the understanding that energy (and abundance) flows in circles and that, for best results, you must give to receive (or receive to give). Being in alignment with this universal law involves a fairly high degree of wisdom in managing yourself and others, and hence this level has been dubbed the density of wisdom.

Regarding our multidimensional nature: This is a paradox we are investigating here. When we are in our center, we realize we already exist in 5D. In fact, each one of us has at least 7 Densities of being. We are simply unaware of the vast majority of Who We Are.

At some point, 5D beings will have a realization that prepares them for the next step up the ladder of Densities. Eventually, after many, many incarnations where they work so hard to give to the world or take from the world, to save the world or rule the world, they finally begin to see the futility of both games and all their attendant dramas. They will eventually notice that there is one simple rule that always seems true:

What you do to another you ultimately do to yourself.

This is the point where they finally realize that the apparent separation between "self" and "other" is illusory, that in truth, All is One. And with this realization they step up onto the next rung on the ladder — the 6th Density!

The 6th D is the level where the STO/STS polarity completely disappears. Regardless of which orientation a being may have adopted at a lower Density it now dissolves. The reason for this is that 6D beings KNOW that All is One (still as individuals and not as a collective), and hence this Density is the first a genre called "Unity Consciousness" — a state characterized by loving acceptance of "what is" and surrender to the flow of life. The 6th Density is the highest level that can still experience itself in a physical body. Beyond this Density, it is not possible to be attached to a dense body without dropping out of that Density.

The 6th Density is a wonderful state of existence. A 6D being fully understands <u>the meaning of life</u> and <u>the true nature of reality</u> and are therefore able to maximize their enjoyment of it without constantly sabotaging themselves. And as a rite of passage into the 6th Density, a being fully embraces <u>its creator nature</u>. And so now it only puts out what it wants back, and it therefore only gets back experiences that it desires! Life becomes a lot more harmonious, peaceful, and abundant — a state of grace as compared to lower Densities.

6D beings fully understand the rules of the illusory game of physical reality that they are within and so can take the game to a whole new level! They become master players and can enjoy the fruits of the illusion to their fullest. They explore, play, live, love and laugh to their heart's content! They are still <u>within the separation game</u>, but this level of the game doesn't include fear and suffering! Now it only includes WONDERFUL!

6D beings know they are the creator of their own reality and that their experiences are manifested by their deepest beliefs. They, therefore, make a considerable effort to master their thoughts and choices and to release any beliefs that are attracting undesirable results — what amounts to Self-Mastery. Complete self-mastery cannot really occur until a being attains the 6th Density. Before being at 6th Density they simply have not eliminated their inner-conflict, suffering, and pain and therefore are still unintentionally creating fear and undesirable dramas in their lives.

Below 6th Density, a being's evolution is primarily driven by its fear, pain, and suffering — by its desire to get away from undesirable experiences. Their FOCUS is on how to avoid undesirable experiences. And because, as a creator, <u>what you focus on you attract</u> and <u>what you resist persists</u> they can't escape their negative experiences.

Suffering has a noble purpose: the evolution of consciousness and the burning up of the ego.—Eckhart Tolle, <u>A New Earth</u>

The 6D being transcends this — they focus, not on how to avoid negative experiences, but on how to attract positive experiences. And because of this "positive" focus they no longer find themselves having "negative" experiences.

Because a 6D being is no-longer spending most of its time reacting to negative experiences a space is created to observe and reflect and begin to see things, himself/herself and life, as they truly are. And clearly sees who he/she is, what she/he wants to be, and how he/she wants to respond to life — Each sees why one is here and what one's true purpose is. This makes ones focus on pursuing their passion and giving their "greatest gift" to the world.

The 6D beings focus becomes neither that of serving others or serving self (to give or take) but simply to find and express their genuine self and to pursue their greatest passion, in each and every moment. And by doing so, they are essentially giving their greatest gift to the world. They are in graceful alignment with their highest self, and they are effortlessly going with the flow of life and hence what they choose to pursue will most certainly be needed, desired, and appreciated by the world. It can be no other way at this Density. Whatever they choose will be a perfect response at the perfect time for all involved because we are all aspects of the same being and at this Density, all of its parts become completely harmonized!

And so 6D beings will find themselves giving their greatest gift and will be in their highest joy. And because "what you put out you get back" life will respond by giving its greatest gift right back to them, and they find themselves living a remarkably harmonious and abundant life.

Now instead of "negative" experiences driving their evolution, the process of mastering the skills and capacities needed to express their greatest gift become the means of their continued growth, expansion, and evolution. When one is doing what they love they can't help getting better at it, and ultimately they will be very good at it, so their reach will be far, and their impact will be large. And it will become an effortless joy.

At some point in this process, it may dawn on the 6D being all the learning, growing, and expanding he has been doing via the experiences within his physical reality are an illusory story he has been playing in. And they will deeply understand there is a greater reality from which the reality they are immersed in is constructed, and the story is orchestrated. As this realization deeply sinks in, it will nudge them up onto the next step of the ladder of consciousness — the 7th Density!

The 7th Density has been called the "magical" density because, at this level, one becomes formless and beyond the illusion of physical reality. 7D beings are a part of the primal energy field from which all realities are constructed. Beings at this Density are very close to becoming completely one with the Oneness.

7D beings participate in the creation of realities by directly working with the energy and the consciousness templates from which they are constructed.

Some part of every 7th Density being's mind is busy with tasks essential to the very existence of physical (lower density) realities. If it were not for their work no realities would exist at all.

Many 7D beings are carrying out the role of pattern holders or what is sometimes called "construct" holders. Their job is to hold the patterns that construct elements of realities. Some of these "construct holders" are holding the frames of planetary consciousness or galactic consciousness, others are holding the frame of the consciousness for the bodies of creatures (for instance, the human body), others still are construct holders for electrons, photons, and other "particles". Everything that exists is simply patterns of energy and vibration controls those patterns.

But not all 7D beings are pattern holders, there are many other roles — Watchers, Speakers, Seeders, Recyclers, Interventionists — just to name a few. And all these roles are involved; in some way, shape, or form, with making realities run smoothly. As an example, a "Watcher" is a special kind of "observing" density consciousness that narrows the huge range of possibilities inherent in the complex interactions of all these patterns into a smaller range of actualizations.

It is interesting to note that it is not possible for a 7th Density being to incarnate and still remain 7th density. In order for 7D beings to do what they do, they must, by definition, be everywhere. And this is incompatible with imagining into existence and wearing a physical body. One MUST lower one's consciousness to 6th Density or less to do that.

The perceptual experience at the 7th Density is very different than what we experience here in 3rd/4th Density. What seems to us to be many separate perceptual modalities, channels, and processes, are experienced as one unified process and perception. Thinking, feeling, seeing, knowing, creating, expressing, dreaming, fantasizing, smelling, tasting — all of these are, for the 7D being — one process. Imagine if every modality of your perception — taste, smell, visual, tactile, emotional, etc. — were all somehow extra hues or textures added to one universal perceptual experience and you'll get an idea of what it is like.

Imagine that there is no difference between your sensing of a thing and your creative imagination of it — that is, to see the thing is to imagine it into existence, and to see the thing change form is to imagine its form changing. 7D beings KNOW that things look the way they do BECAUSE they are imagining them that way. This Density is where your will is made manifest — it is PURE MAGIC!

Beings at this level don't really evolve or change. There is nothing they are apart from and nothing they cannot know or experience so there is nothing more that they can become. They simply do as they are called to and have agreed to and they do it for as long as required. And when they are done they may choose to dive back into some deep corner of their current reality system and explore it further, or they may leave their reality system altogether for another.

When a 7D being wants to leave their system, they must lovingly release all their attachments to their creations and thereby attain perfect balance and true Oneness of spirit enabling them to step up onto the last rung on the ladder of consciousness — the 8th Density!

The 8th Density is the level where one becomes utterly One with the Oneness. It is the ultimate level and it is a state that is nearly impossible to describe in words — perfection, wholeness, belonging, centeredness, absolute serenity — these words just scratch the surface. It is a state of BLISS beyond anything that one can imagine, a state of PEACE that transcends anything one has ever experienced — a state where one KNOWS one is completely appreciated for WHO YOU ARE and unconditionally loved exactly AS YOU ARE.

At this Density, there is NOTHING that is beyond the scope of one's mind. Your mind IS the universal mind. You perfectly know and understand absolutely everything that ever was, is, or will be. To inquire about something is to gain the WHOLE of the understanding of it.

In this state, it is simply impossible to have "negative" feelings about anything. All perspectives are your perspective. Such a complete and perfect comprehension IS BLISS. You understand that EVERYTHING is a creative work of art and that ALL creations are your creations. From this perspective, you can't help seeing everything as BEAUTIFUL and LOVING all of it! There is nothing that is incomplete or imperfect because ALL IS just as you created it — all is PERFECT. At least it is right up to the moment that you decide to create something NEW! And you don't see the "new" as something better, just different — something that pleases you to create and explore. The 8th Density contains ALL realities and is, therefore, the gateway through which you leave one reality and enter another. In the very moment that a new idea crystallizes in your mind — poof — you find yourself inside a reality at some lower density, and ready to plunge ever deeper. And thus the game of separation and the process of climbing the ladder begins again!

Analogy to Theology: From 1902 to 1955 the country's premier passenger trains, the Pennsylvania Railroad's Broadway Limited and the New York Railroad's 20th Century Limited were in competition for fast passenger service and mail/daily publication transfer between Chicago and

New York City's Penn Station. For a few miles prior to Chicago the two competitor rains on parallel tracks on the same timeline – it was a daily race as to which would arrive first at Penn Station.

Picture your Soul as a passenger on the train "on the left", where the passengers are both STS and STO, all headed to their death. The train is comprised of the 7 Densities and the "train" Head (8th Density) is lead by Lord Enki and his son Marduk, Anunnaki and creator of Mankind to be dominated and controlled, as he so chooses.

Mankind STS will proceed through the Densities and, through many lifetimes, "arriving at the God Head, Lord Enki (the False God) where the "train" travels into the Lower Realms.

Mankind STS "group" needs to Wake Up as to who they are and develop and Escape Plan to transfer to the "train" headed to the Upper Realms or they will remain on the "train" headed to the Lower Realms. An Escape Plan is essential to make the "transfer."   Good Deeds alone will only get you to the lowest "layer/plane" of the Upper Realm where, once your merits are expended, you will return for another lifetime on Earth (part of the Middle Realm).

Mankind STO "group" is on the same train as the STS. You need to WAKE UP to who and whose your are – your God Head is Creator God, who indirectly created both STS and STO races. The 7 Densities apply to you, if you become entangled by greed and the other Dark Force impediments of the Earth, you will stay on the "train" headed to the Lower Realms. Wake Up and transfer to in the "train" headed by Creator God that travels to the Higher Realms.

Reptilians. Regardless of whether or not "reptilians" are ET"s or are only holographic projections does not ultimately matter. If they are 4th Density vibrations, then like all 4D entities, going beyond the "maya" into the 5th dimension is the way to freedom. I know that overcoming fear within my consciousness is the answer.

Starseeds, Galactic Warriors, Indigos, and other Star Beings, and the descendants of the Star Being humanoids of other STO Star Being races that colonized Earth and survived the Great Flood (leaving approx. 15% of these Star Being descendants who survived the Great Flood), all **not** part of the Mankind creation – You are on the "train" headed by Creator God. The 7 Densities also apply to you but Creator God is the God Head. However, you can become entangled in the greed and the other Dark Force impediments of the Earth you will transfer to the "train" that is headed by the False God (Enki/Marduk) headed to the Lower Realms. Wake UP and complete your mission or this will be a wasted trip.

The Middle Realm, is controlled and dominated by Lord Enki/Marduk of the Lower Realms, who created a list of Densities (applicable to his creation of Mankind where Enki/Marduk are the God Head) to be different yet "mirror" the Densities of the Upper Realm, as applicable to the Middle Realm (each Realm has its own set of Densities).

By Waking Up, you will transfer to the "train" whose God Head is the Creator God. This train is headed for the Upper Realms. The passengers on this "train" sidestep the Reincarnation Trap and return to the Middle Realm (the one containing Earth) **only if they volunteer** to do so to assist Mankind in making the transition from the "train" headed by Load Enki/Marduk of the Lower Realms to the "train" headed to Creator God, God of the Upper Realms.

PICK THE "TRAIN" YOU WANT TO TAKE – You were given Free Will to make the choice.

DENSITIES OD SOME COUNCILS CONNECTED WITH EARTH – Some are STO and Some are STS. I presented the more common 7 Density model (I listed the 8th Density, which is one exits the Realm Earth is within or the point where one enterers a different Realm). The 12 Density model is listed below.

1st Density:	Mineral kingdom
2nd Density:	Plant & lower animal kingdom
3rd Density:	Higher animal & lower human
4th Density	Low: Astral, lower emotional realms
4th Density	High: Etheric, higher mental realms
5th Density	Low: Causal, creative realms
5th Density	High: Soul (last level of individuality)
6th Density:	Oversoul (social memory complex)
7th Density:	Master oversoul
8th Density:	Avatar planes, celestial heavens
9th Density:	Christ planes, Buddhic planes, lower God worlds
10th Density:	Higher God realms
11th Density:	Universal realms
12th Density:	The source; the mystery, the Tao
13th and beyond:	The void, unmanifested creation

The above 13 Model is a combination from Eckankar and other disciplines to achieve an integrated system. My own exploration concurs with many others that there are many sub-planes within each major density level. Remember that densities and dimensions are labels for convenience only so that our intellect can grasp these ideas. In actuality, there is not always a sharp demarcation between levels.

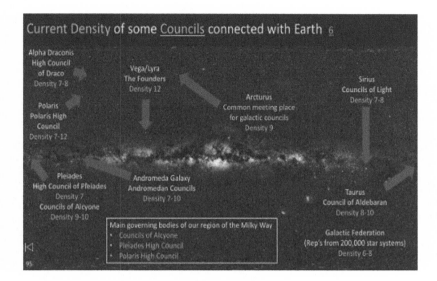

Sources

1 "Densities Explained," Nuno under *Densities*, First posted 14.06.12. Last updated 03.10.14, Heart Ki Akashic Records Readings,
   https://www.heartki.com/densities-explained/
2 Densities Chart," Nuno under *Densities*, First posted 14.06.12. Last updated
   24.06.19, Ki Akashic Records Readings, https://www.heartki.com/densities-
   chart/
3   The Ascension Papers, Book #1 and Book 2, Zingdad, Published July 16,
   2014, Bok 1, Book 2 (in process) and Book 3 (in process) are available on line
   in pdf format. Book 1 pdf:
   http://zingdad.com/images/downloads/the_ascension_papers_book_1_-
   _zingdad.pdf
4 "Ascending The Densities of Consciousness," Jeff Street, Divine C omos,
   http://divine-cosmos.net/ascending-the-densities-of-consciousness.htm

Article 34

LEVELS OF HUMAN CONSCIOUSNESS WITIN THE EARTH DENSITIES

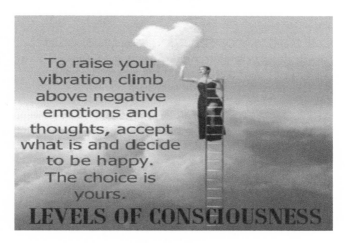

To raise your vibration climb above negative emotions and thoughts, accept what is and decide to be happy. The choice is yours.
LEVELS OF CONSCIOUSNESS

COMPOSITION OF HUMAN CONSCIOUSNESS – Human consciousness is composed by thoughts, beliefs, emotions, intuition, and perception. These elements are themselves also energy/light with a given vibratory frequency. A thought or emotion can be good or bad, can be of any point in the positive/negative spectrum, and can have higher or lower vibration. This occurs since consciousness is made of the same substance as matter – only more subtle. This is why thoughts may "condense" and manifest in the physical.

Consciousness and energy matter are the same thing. These words are synonyms. All are energy with different rates of vibration. All represent different states of beingness.

Rocks, minerals and elements are not conscious *per se*, as we commonly define it, but they represent an awareness state corresponding to simple, basic existence. Inanimate objects also have subtle levels of energy. Everything has. Animals in turn have a type of awareness that allows them to navigate and survive in their environment, even if they're not capable of extensively modifying their surrounding or evolved creative thought.

All Is Awareness – Man's consciousness can also be higher or lower, lighter or denser. It's difficult to define consciousness, or awareness, because it doesn't correlate to a physical attribute. It's a property of Beingness. In a loose definition, awareness is the set of perceptions, beliefs, impressions, and knowledge a being has of itself and of reality, which in turn dictates its experience and behavior.

The physical reality always has to match the consciousness Realm of the entities it resides with – in Earth's case, the Humans – because the external is like the internal, physical reality mirrors consciousness. If awareness changes, or increases, physical reality must *follow*. If higher consciousness on Earth reaches a critical mass, physical reality also has to *follow*. This is exactly the same reason why each human attracts and manifests its external reality according to its internal awareness. Because all is consciousness. Such is the purpose of the Universe: to support life, and to provide an environment for experience and learning.

STATES OF HUMAN CONSCIOUSNESS are how an individual relates to the Earthly Realm where they reside, whereas DENSITIES are spiritual grades (or levels or sights) that Mankind will eventually develop from the lowest or most dense level to the highest or most subtle level.

Remember that the below table as developed by Dr. David Hawkins and the Spiritual Science Research Foundation are an approximation (a sliding scale, if you will) to help you understand where your Consciousness Level might be centered. If something RESONATES within you then delve more deeply within yourself to confirm and if it does not resonate within you, then just read the levels for developing a possible future interest.

DR. DAVID R. HAWKINS, in his 30-years of research, developed a framework to detail the Levels of Human Consciousness.

Energy Levels – Hawkins' research explored "energy" in scientific terms. He associated numerical values to the different levels of consciousness from which one operates. Those operating from a lower level of consciousness operate at lower vibrational energy and as one advances in consciousness, they garner and cultivate more energy—hence when you may meet someone and say to yourself "wow, they have great energy"—they're probably operating at a higher level of consciousness with a higher energy value—according to Hawkins' framework.

NONE MANIFIST A PURE STATE – Hawkins also makes it clear in his writings that, "it is well to remember that a person is rarely manifested as a pure state. "A person may operate on one level in a given area of life and on quite a different level in another area of life." It's possible to be at a state of consciousness, let's say with work that may be different than where you are in love. We also suspect that it's possible to have reached a higher state of consciousness, and at moments, temporarily, "regress" back to a lower level depending on different external environments. Either way, this framework can be a helpful tool for understanding what drives both our and other people's behavior.

THE LEVELS OF HUMAN CONSCIOUSNESS – Our level of vibration, within the Earth Realm, corresponds to the composite total of where we place our attention. Within the Earthly sphere, most are vibrating at a level below Level 9 and, thus, Level 9 is what many strive for. Below is a more detailed list describing each level of human consciousness. In addition to the David

Hawkins' Levels of Consciousness I have also incorporated the Stages, Characteristics and Experiences that have been developed by the **Spiritual Science Research Foundation** that has a unique approach to our spiritual journey and the life lessons we are to learn.

Level	Scale	Dr. David Hawkins States of Consciousness	SPERITUAL SCIENCE RESEARCH FOUNDATION Characteristics Displayed & Spiritual Experiences
1	20	Shame – Just a step above death. You're probably contemplating suicide at this level. Either that or you're a serial killer. Think of this as self-directed hatred.	Animal instincts
2	30	Guilt – A step above shame, but you still may be having thoughts of suicide. You think of yourself as a sinner, unable to forgive yourself for past transgressions.	
3	50	Apathy – Feeling hopeless or victimized. The state of learned helplessness. Many homeless people are stuck here.	
4	74	Grief – A state of perpetual sadness and loss. You might drop down here after losing a loved one. Depression. Still higher than apathy, since you're beginning to escape the numbness.	
6	100	Fear – Seeing the world as dangerous and unsafe. Paranoia. Usually you'll need help to rise above this level, or you'll remain trapped for a long time, such as in an abusive relationship.	
7	125	Desire – Not to be confused with setting and achieving goals, this is the level of addiction, craving, and lust — for money, approval, power, fame, etc. Consumerism. Materialism. This is the level of smoking and drinking and doing drugs.	
8	150	Anger – the level of frustration, often from not having your desires met at the lower level. This level can spur you to action at higher levels, or it can keep you stuck in hatred. In an abusive relationship, you'll often see an anger person coupled with a fear person.	

9	175	Pride – The first level where you start to feel good, but it's a false feeling. It's dependent on external circumstances (money, prestige, etc), so it's vulnerable. Pride can lead to nationalism, racism, and religious wars. Think Nazis. A state of irrational denial and defensiveness. Religious fundamentalism is also stuck at this level. You become so closely enmeshed in your beliefs that you see an attack on your beliefs as an attack on you.	Average man/woman in today's era. Negligible interest in Spirituality. Thinks only about his/her own happiness.
10	200	Courage – The first level of true strength. Courage is the Gateway. This is where you start to see life as challenging and exciting instead of overwhelming. You begin to have an inkling of interest in personal growth, although at this level you'll probably call it something else like skill-building, career advancement, education, etc. You start to see your future as an improvement upon your past, rather than a continuation of the same.	Seeks personal growth, skill-building, career advancement, education, etc. Beginning to think he may be spiritual.
11	250	Neutrality – This level is epitomized by the phrase, "live and let live." It's flexible, relaxed, and unattached. Whatever happens, you roll with the punches. You don't have anything to prove. You feel safe and get along well with other people. A lot of self-employed people are at this level. A very comfortable place. The level of complacency and laziness. You're taking care of your needs, but you don't push yourself too hard.	Interested in ritualistic worship, spiritual books, pilgrimages, places of worship, etc.

12	310	Willingness – Now that you're basically safe and comfortable, you start using your energy more effectively. Just getting by isn't enough anymore. You begin caring about doing a good job — perhaps even your best. You think about time management and productivity and getting organized, things that weren't so important to you at the level of neutrality. Think of this level as the development of willpower and self-discipline. These people are the "troopers" of society; they get things done well and don't complain much. If you're in school, then you're a really good student; you take your studies seriously and put in the time to do a good job. This is the point where your consciousness becomes more organized and disciplined.	Curiosity about the spiritual dimension and genuine seeker-ship commences.
13	350	Acceptance – Now a powerful shift happens, and you awaken to the possibilities of living proactively. At the level of willingness you've become competent, and now you want to put your abilities to good use. This is the level of setting and achieving goals. I don't like the label "acceptance" that Hawkins uses here, but it basically means that you begin accepting responsibility for your role in the world. If something isn't right about your life (your career, your health, your relationship), you define your desired outcome and change it. You start to see the big picture of your life more clearly. This level drives many people to switch careers, start a new business, or change their diets.	More single-minded about spiritual growth. Picks a singular path to proceed on.

| 14 | 400 | Reason – At this level you transcend the emotional aspects of the lower levels and begin to think clearly and rationally. Hawkins defines this as the level of medicine and science. The way I see it, when you reach this level, you become capable of using your reasoning abilities to their fullest extent. You now have the discipline and the reactivity to fully exploit your natural abilities. You've reached the point where you say, "Wow. I can do all this stuff, and I know I must put it to good use. So what's the best use of my talents?" You take a look around the world and start making meaningful contributions. At the very high end, this is the level of Einstein and Freud. It's probably obvious that most people never reach this level in their entire lives. | Wants to remain in spiritual company all day. Goes beyond organized religion i.e., does not consider oneself belonging to any religion in particular (if one is sectarian one cannot grow beyond this point) |
| 15 | 500 | Love – I don't like Hawkins' label "love" here because this isn't the emotion of love. It's unconditional love, a permanent understanding of your connectedness with all that exists. Think compassion. At the level of reason, you live in service to your head. But that eventually becomes a dead end where you fall into the trap of over-intellectualizing. You see that you need a bigger context than just thinking for its own sake. At the level of love, you now place your head and all your other talents and abilities in service to your heart (not your emotions, but your greater sense of right and wrong — your conscience). I see this as the level of awakening to your true purpose. Your motives at this level are pure and uncorrupted by the desires of the ego. This is the level of lifetime service to humanity. Think Gandhi, Dr. Albert Schweitzer. At this level you also begin to be guided by a force greater than yourself. | Wants to serve the Absolute Truth of Spirituality at all times. Begins to qualify for discipleship and grace of the Guru's depending on the path one follows. |

16	540	Joy – A state of pervasive, unshakable happiness. Eckhart Tolle describes this state in The Power of Now. The level of saints and advanced spiritual teachers. Just being around people at this level makes you feel incredible. At this level life is fully guided by synchronicity and intuition. There's no more need to set goals and make detailed plans — the expansion of your consciousness allows you to operate at a much higher level. A near-death experience can temporarily bump you to this level.	Is willing to sacrifice mind, body and wealth for spiritual growth and to obtain self-realization.
17	600	Peace – Total transcendence. Hawkins claims this level is reached only by one person in 10 million.	**Guru** – Gains access to Absolute knowledge and gets answers within.
18	700- to1000	Enlightenment – The highest level of human consciousness, where humanity blends with divinity. Extremely rare. Even just thinking about this level can raise your consciousness.	**Paratpar Guru** – Doing all actions without expectation of results. **Sadguru** – Liberation from the cycle of birth and death. Obtains the stance of spectator – views the world for what it is i.e., the Great Illusion. Sees God in everything. **Final Liberation** – Merging with God, Self-realization, Achieving a state of perpetual Bliss.

Using the calibration scale developed by **Dr. David Hawkins**, most of humanity is vibrating a lot lower than Stage 9. I was informed by my higher self that my composite vibration vacillates between 500 and 550 and sometimes "bounces" up to 600 (the answers come from within) but it does not matter what your number is or might be, because you are always right where you are suppose to be – nothing is by chance. Just look at the whole scale as being part of your melody wherein you shift back and forth between the "notes" as to where you vibrate on an emotional level.

The **Spiritual Science Research Foundation** estimates that less than 4 percent of the world's current population is at a spiritual level of 50% or greater and they claim a level of 60% is needed to be liberated from the cycle of birth and death. Other sources claim that the Earth needs to achieve 50% Light vs. 50% Darkness to enter the 4th Density. According to the Foundation, the

212 | Article 35 - Levels of Human Consciousness

majority of people in the current era, known as the Era of Strife, fall in the 20% spiritual level category.

Love and Light Lightworks and Galactic Warriors reading this research article should find they resonate within the following Consciousness Levels:

- **Willingness** – Think of this level as the development of willpower and self-discipline. THIS IS THE POINT WHERE YOUR CONSCIOUSNESS BECOMES MORE ORGANIZED AND DISCIPLINED.
- **Acceptance** – Now a powerful shift happens, and YOU AWAKEN to the possibilities of living proactively. This is the level of setting and achieving goals. It basically means that you begin accepting responsibility for your role in the world.
- **Reason** – At this level you transcend the emotional aspects of the lower levels and begin to think clearly and rationally. You take a look around the world and start making meaningful contributions.
- **Love** –This is not the emotion of love. It's unconditional love, a permanent understanding of your connectedness with all that exists. Think compassion. At the level of reason, you live in service.

As Love and Light Workers & Galactic Warriors -you now, more than ever, need to continue your own ascension to the next Level of Consciousness as well as your daily connections to One Source (Creator God). Through you, the Grid of Light strengthens. Together we now bring the Law of Manifestation to a new and higher level. Through your efforts, the Earth is only now at the point that the Force of Light (Service-to-Others) just matches the Force of Darkness (Service-to-Self), and it is this "gate" that allows the Earth to transition to the 4th Density. The work of Love and Light Workers, and Galactic Warriors continues well beyond the end of the 3rd Density.

Remember STATES OF HUMAN CONSCIOUSNESS are how an individual relates to the Earthly Realm where they reside, whereas DENSITIES are spiritual grades (or levels of light) that mankind will eventually develop from the lowest or most dense level to the highest or most subtle level.

Sources
1. "Levels of Consciousness," Steve Pavlin, April 7, 2005, https://www.stevepavlina.com/blog/2005/04/levels-of-consciousness/
2. Power vs. Force: The Hidden Determinant of Human Behavior, David R Hawkins, 1/30/2014, Hay House Inv
3. "Aether Magick," posted November 20, 2019, Armed Heart, https://armedheart.com/2019/11/20/aether-magick/

Article 35

THE ENKI GROUP OF 24 ASCENSION MASTERS
(Part of the Anunnaki dominion of dominance)

It's suggested, through several sources, that **Vishnu** had (at the time the Vedas were written) **sent down Avatars** twenty-two times in our history to function as teachers in order **to enlighten the masses.** That "enlightenment" was part of the plan to maintain control and domination over Mankind.

Vishnu is Enki, and therefore, it makes sense that the 24 Ascension Masters, including Jesus Christ, would have been Avatars of Vishnu/Enki, the creator of mankind through DNA manipulation to be dominated and controlled by the **Anunnaki, who are NOT Creator God.**

The twenty-four known "ford makers" (tīrthaṅkaras) in this time cycle **revitalized the Jain religion.** In Jainism, a Tīrthaṅkara is a human being who helps in achieving liberation and enlightenment as an arihant.

> **Arihant** (Jain Prakrit: **arihant,** Sanskrit: árhat "conqueror") is a soul who has conquered inner passions such as attachment, anger, pride and greed. ... Arihants are also called kevalins (omniscient beings) as they possess kevala jnana (pure infinite knowledge). An **arihant** is also called a jina ("victor").

According to Jain scriptures, that which helps one to cross the great ocean of worldly life is a tīrtha "ford" and a person who fills that role is a tīrthaṅkara "ford-maker". Tīrthaṅkaras achieve liberation and enlightenment by destroying their constraining (karmas) and becoming role models and leaders for those seeking spiritual guidance. They also seek Kevala Jnana, a state of permanent, perpetual, absolute knowledge of the Soul; it is the precursor to final liberation from the cycle of birth and death. We know these as the 24 Ascension Masters.

Each of the 24 Masters has spent lifetimes on Earth influencing and directing the births and developments of the worlds' religions. The 24 Masters, some well-known, others less so:

- Allah Gobi
- Gautama Buddha
- Djwhal Kuhl
- El Morya Kahn
- Hilarion
- Kuthumi
- Lord Lanto
- Lady Leto
- Lord Ling
- Lady Lotus
- Lady Magda
- The Mahachohan
- The Melchisadek (the teacher of Abraham)
- Lady Nada
- Pallas Athena
- The Master Paul
- Paul the Venetian
- Lady Portia
- Quan Yin
- Master R (Rakoczy)
- **Sananda (Jesus)** — "Christ" symbolizes the frequency which means "One with God" (that "God" being Enki), upon whom was founder of the Christian religion (despite Jainism wanted no "priests). He was overshadowed for the last 3 years of that life by Lord Maitreya who headed the Office of the Christ, and was leader of the Great White Brotherhood ("White" meaning they wore white robes).
- Sanat Kumara
- Serapis Bey
- Saint Germain

Beliefs of Jainism Religion — All make for good, obedient workers desired by the Dark Force (Enki's Group). The term "**Jainism**" is derived from "**Jina**" which literally means "**Conqueror.**" It is said that -"**He who has conquered love and hate, pleasure and pain, attachment and aversion, and has thereby freed his soul from the karmas obscuring knowledge, perception, truth, and ability, is a Jana.**" The main concern of this religion is the welfare of every living being in this Universe. The Jain beliefs include:

1. **Reincarnation** — They believe in reincarnation and to attain ultimate liberation by attaining total freedom from the control of others.
2. They believe in **five great vows** that may lead one to liberation:
   - *Ahimsa* – Completely non-violence. They believe that even mental torture (harsh words or actions) should be avoided at all costs.
   - *Asteya* – Never steal anything from someone else's possession. They believe that even when accepting help or aid from someone, one shouldn't take more than what the minimum is needed. To take more than is needed is considered theft in Jainism.
   - *Brahmacharya* – Sexual restraint. Sexual pleasure is considered as an infatuating force which distracts one from the aim of Jainism. They believe that the sexual relationship with your own spouse should be limited.
   - *Satya* – They believe that one should speak the truth if it is pleasant or remain silent if the truth is painful for others.
   - *Aparigraha* – Never have an attachment with any possession as it is believed that attachment may result in greed, jealousy, selfishness and other negative emotions.
   - **No Priests** – The religious people in Jainism are monks and nuns, who lead strict and ascetic lives.

Twenty-four is an important number. For example, it is part of the RA Material and the Council of Saturn that took advice from the Council of 24; RA is part of the Lower Realm Enki Group. Also, there is an interesting references to "24" in the Bible—The Book of Revelations, King James Version, "And round about the throne were four and twenty seats: and upon the seats I saw four and twenty elders sitting, clothed in white raiment; and they had on their heads crowns of gold."

Jesus would be one of the last in this series of avatars, and many people of many religions are now waiting for another coming of such an Avatar (the biblical "Second Coming of Christ"). As a side note— Jesus is described as the Lion of Judah. What does the lion represent? It represents the Sun. This is one of many references to Jesus being the "Sun God." Marduk, perhaps more than Enki, is described as the Sun God, but also notice when you read the New Testament that Jesus has one calmer side and one more aggressive side. YHWH/Jehovah had the same "problem" in the OT. It's therefore reasonable to assume that Enki and his son (Maldek) were both acting as the same god/son of god at different times). Now, let us recapitulate this. What does all of this tell us? We have learned that enlightenment is wisdom, and wisdom is related to the Owl and the Serpent. Who, then, are the Serpent and the Owl associated with? Well, the Serpent is associated with Satan and/or Lucifer—the "Light-bringer" or "Light-bearer" (light is information). The Owl is associated with both Marduk and Isis.

Our DNA is not restricted to our physical bodies, and neither are the chakras. With our DNA, we are connected to the entire universe—not only the 4%, but the whole Greater Universe (KHAA). The DNA is fluid and ever-changing, as we are changing—both on a physical and non–physical

216 | Article 35 - Levels of Human Consciousness

level. Enki simply disconnected us from the KHAA (dark matter and dark energy- in this case, "dark" means unseen); the part Enki "disconnected" equates to approximately 4% of the whole Universe for us to experience. For Enki, it wasn't enough to let us randomly perceive about 4% of the Universe—he also wanted to dictate what 4% of the Universe he wanted us to see! He did not want us to randomly perceive a minimal frequency of the electromagnetic spectrum because then we may perceive something he did not want us to perceive. This is where an actual computer system comes into play (for lack of a better word since the "computer system" is not like our own computer systems here on Earth, they are just children's toys in comparison with the one Enki is using. It is so much more sophisticated than ours and does not necessarily mean a physical machine with a screen and a keyboard. The hologram that the Dark Force (Enki Group) is projecting is instigated on Saturn, relayed on the Moon (or Mars—or both!), and then hits Earth with intended capacity. The end result is that there is around 4%, which is all we can perceive with our active DNA.

Remember that the 24 Ascension Masters are all part of the Enki Group of the Lower Realm that has draconian control and dominion within the 4% Universe and has its own set of Densities, as well as the Reincarnation Trap and the Trap of Oneness/Singularity within its 3rd Density. Enki's deception runs deep! Toward One World Government and One World Religion.

Also Remember that Lord Enki is still holding our planet in his grip and that means not many "outside" beings, which he has not approved of, are currently here on the planet. This includes all races living within the 4% Universe such as, the Orions, the Alpha Draconians, the Arcturians, the Vegans, The Andromedans, The Blue Avians, Praying Mantises, the Nordics, Reptilians, Draconians, Grays, and who knows what more.

Researchers list all these races (and more) as having different agendas and traits, including benevolent or adversarial, as if they were totally independent from each other. The Big Picture is we need to see them all as being in complete agreement with each other (Mankind is to be dominated and controlled to meet their needs), each having slightly different agendas to meet the same "end." There are a few here that either "fly" under Enki's "radar" or are allowed to be here as "Observers" or emissaries for the Greater Universe, but they are few in number.

The Key to Escaping the 4% Universe— The "Supreme Being" in the Darkness controlled 4% Universe is Enki (and his son, Malduk) and he is the one who sends down the "teachers" to Earth (i.e., the Ascension Masters), although most of the time it is Enki himself who descends as the teacher by incarnating as certain famous beings we know from history. **The point is that here on Earth, Enki and Marduk are still in control. Fewer people than we may think have actually seen through the illusion and the manipulation enough for them to break out of it.**

We need to recognize we exist outside the "computer program" (Matrix), and we can't break out until we have realized everything we thought we knew about Ascension has been released from our own minds, and are not willing to continue accepting the Universe Ascension Process.

From what we now know from the content of this Article and with a willingness to accept it, once we leave the Grid behind us, our DNA will once again lighten up, and the Universe, with all of its dimensions, will literally lie wide open in front of us! BUT this will only happen if we are willing to accept the above concept! If we don't, our "disconnected" DNA will stay.

Sources
1. "12 Beliefs of Jainism Religion," MysticalBee, https://mysticalbee.com/beliefs-of-jainism-religion/
2. "ASCENDED MASTERS," HILARY JANE HARGREAVES, http://www.innerlightworkers.co.uk/
3. The Wes Penre Papers, The Vedic Texts, The Fifth Level of Learning Part 1, Wes Penre, Feb 27, 2015, https://wespenrepapershome.files.wordpress.com/2019/07/fifthleveloflearning part1.pdf

Article 36

ESCAPING THE 4% UNIVERSE

BACKGROUND – As a point of reference, the First Galactic War of 22-million years ago was fought in the Lyra constellation between the Lyra Felines/Humanoids and the Vegan Humanoids (who have the mantra of "Service-to-Self), and Reptilians/Carrions, with subsequent battles occurring in the Orion Star System. In the end, the Reptilians/Carians and their dependents were awarded, by Treaty total control over 4% of the Universe – the 4% Universe in which we reside. The 4% is, therefore, primarily, Dark Force, yet there are some Beings of Light. The 4% is full of traps and "minefields" to keep you here through fear and dominance, be it the Draconian Alliance or the Galactic Federation or the many number of Councils (Nibiruan, Thurban, Council of 9, Council of 12, Ashtar Command, Andromedan, Orion Federation, Sirian High Command, and many, many more – if it has rules to join then it is definitely a means of control) – these are all part of the 4% Universe of Entrapment.

The Universe of Entrapment includes those self-identifying as a LIGHTWORKER – which is also part of entrapment to not leave the 4% Universe. There are many levels (Densities) within the 4% Universe and, thus, you may believe you are making "progress" when, in reality, you are not. The means of escape is not becoming ONE (a collective mind) but to raise your own frequency to identify all of these as a trap. It will be your higher frequency that will provide the "Light" to see all is a trap and escape is to the other 96% of the Universe (the Free Universe).

Go inward (INTROSPECTION) to find WHO YOU ARE (an untethered free spirit), raise your frequency, disassociate from chaos and fear, and become a free spirit in the Universe (the other 96%).

The 4% UNIVERSE – We are stuck in what is called the 4% universe since this is where we perceive that we're living. This 4% universe was set up by malevolent forces, so therefore what we learn first is often of a malevolent nature. The 4% universe is heavily controlled with holographic equipment.

Think the "Matrix Series". If people would only understand *how muc h truth there is in those movies!*

It is quite clear that the 4% universe is all about humans in different stages of development. The oppressors knew that Mankind was going to evolve; it's such a natural state of being that they can't really stop that process. So ENKI (ANUNNAKI) and his cohorts had to think out a universe where even those who evolve stay trapped.

Of course, he knew how dimensions and densities work in the "real" universe (the other 96%), so he just had to mimic this and program it into the "software", which is the human body system.

Part of the entrapment hardware are the holographic systems which keep it all in place,. The holographic systems project eight dimensions within which Mankind is free to evolve, similar to how it would look like in the 96% universe. The whole difference, however, is that in the 4%, everything is controlled.

So why are there are only humans in the 4% universe? It's due to the human template - the human DNA - that is trapped! It's humanity as a whole and no one else.

The universe outside the trap is teeming with life in all shapes and forms, but in the free universe you are also free to travel across the dimensions and Realms. Evolution in the 96% is mostly a *process of learning about oneself.* By learning about oneself in the free universe one can create so much more, and it becomes a universe of magic!

Yes, there are stars and galaxies and all the rest of it in the 96% as well - that's the "hardware" - but by living as a spiritual being in that hardware universe you are absolutely free to create anything and travel instantly wherever you want. The only restriction is your own imagination!

That is why art in all its forms is considered so valuable here; people have this feeling that we can create universes with it, and we can!

The 4% universe has its timelines, and humans have evolved on several of them. Some became non-physicals, who can travel the dimensions, using stargates and star-lanes, and others became the Grays. Not all beings in the 4% need spaceships to travel; some actually seem to have developed nano-travel, *but only within the 4%.*

However, entering the 9th Density within the 4% Universe has restrictions built in, and strands taken away from our DNA, now lying dormant. This is why those who decide to evolve without help from Sirian technology, and who have seen through the veil of manipulation, can reshape their whole RNA/DNA structure and no longer be stuck in the hologram.

This is what I am saying...

Those who decide to take this route don't have to go through lifetimes after lifetimes of being stuck in a restricted universe that is controlled; one can do it by reconstructing our light-body, using our Fire (Soul) and our Spirit to see the traps for what they are and the traps will eventually disappear, because it's held in place by frequency. Supersede that frequency band and you're out of here! Some refer to this change as Human 3.0 SI.

In elementary school we learnt about the electromagnetic spectrum. A tiny bit of it is visible, but most of it is not. We are stuck in the visible spectrum, which is the 4% universe. Increase your vibration until you start perceiving things outside this tiny piece of spectrum and you are breaking down the prison walls.

If you're reading this, you are already well on your way of doing that! Oh, but you are not feeling very psychic? Don't worry, you will... In fact, you already are psychic, but it takes more to shatter the Quarantine, the Grid, and all the rest of it, before you can really break through. Some people have become quite psychic over the last few years, but those who feel they have not, although they've been working at least as hard on it, need not to worry. For you it will eventually come in "bigger chunks", once you let go (refer to Stage 3 of Waking up – INTROSPECTION).

Again, do not worry - it will happen if you consistently keep doing what you are doing to raise your frequency. You are not "behind" in your development because you are not as psychic as your friend. No comparison between us is necessary and should be avoided; every one of us needs to work on ourselves and everything will be just fine.

Out there in the 96% universe our friends are waiting. All those who are monitoring our progress now and at the same time are benevolent and really love mankind are doing so, not from the 4% as much as from the 96%. Everybody in the 4% universe has an agenda whether they are benevolent beings or not. In a prison, everybody's agenda is to get out.

Even LIGHTWORKS, Galactic Warriors, Old Souls, Indigos, et al may need to increase their frequency, depending on if your origin is within or outside the 4% Universe. For physical comparison, the Milky Way (150,000 light years in diameter and 200 billion stars) makes up only 0.00016% of the visible universe (93 billion light years in diameter and approx 350 galaxies); yet the visible Universe we see is composed of 4% visible objects and 96% Void (which could be composed of dark matter).

The Multiverse (the 96%), however, is benevolent and loving; the restricted 4% universe is not.

Imagine a free multiverse (the 96%) where you can create freely without having some government or organization telling you to stop doing it. The reader gets the drift and can see the difference between enslavement and freedom, as much as it is possible to see it from our restricted perspective.

The various star groups who tell you that we need to evolve so we can join this or that Galactic Federation of Council; they may appear to be benevolent but they are trying to manipulate you or they are themselves deceived. The Federations are talking about the 4% universe, and we should have no interest in joining any of them.

This is why I like the Pleiadians. They don't tell you about the 4% vs. the 96% universe, but they answer people's questions insightfully so we can really gain from the reply and comments that often follow, once they have our permission to talk about it. They, too, don't want us to join any of these space organizations, because they obviously know they are not in our best interest.

Our job, if we really want to break out, is to work on ourselves and get to the KHAA (Mother Universe – THE VOID). It will happen on a one on one basis and rarely in a group. We have to gain it from hard work - that's the only way. But once you have mastered it, there are beings on the other side that will be extremely happy to see us - each and every one of us.

But is the 96% really such a Paradise all the time? No, it's not. There are warlike beings there, too, because you are free to create what you want, but you have the freedom not to mingle with them. No one is going to draft you; if you go to war, it's your own choice.

So, no Galactic Federation or Draconian Alliance, No Councils, No other Being Networks for us; we don't need them since most, if not all, are also within the 4% Universe, and they will drag us down into the rabbit hole again. No, thank you! We are on our own with lots of benevolent beings watching over us, and "being on our own" in the evolving process is actually not a bad thing.

You are the only one who knows what is best for you, How can somebody else tell you? You are a unique being after all, in an intelligent cosmos. Use what you have and you will notice that you have more than you could imagine even in your wildest dreams. It's not that we have to work to get to a state of being of some star races, either. Our state of being is already divine and magnificent. Other star races are jealous, but the benevolent ones are jealous in a "good way".

We just need to concentrate on letting go, release the chaos of the world, listen to the truth of the Pleiadians, connect to the Free Universe and our guides, see our own light frequency rises to above that of the 4%

Universe, and we are then "home free" to be part of the free universe (the 96% - Multiverse).

We must think and perceive of ourselves as being outside of the "box" (the 4% Universe).

Sources
1. "Galactic Federation and Councils," Wes Penre, 23 March 2013, the Wes Penre website,
    https://www.bibliotecapleyades.net/vida_alien/alien_galacticfederations43.htm
2. The Knowledge of Forever Time, Episodes 1-8, The Final Invitation, Damon T. Berry, InfoTV, Amazon and other retailers.

Article 37

REINCARNATION IS A TRAP

The souls of the human species are trapped in a dimension of control (i.e., what we call "reality") established by the Orion Draco-Reptilian Empire (Dark Force) eons ago and the afterlife is merely a short break before being recycled back into the chaos. (Similar to how wounded soldiers are sent to the field hospital for treatment, before being sent to the front line once again).

It may sound scary to choose not to go to the Light because many of us are afraid of the unknown. Whereas, the Light feels "safe" because we've gone there many times before, and "everybody else" who went there seems to have done just fine.

When you die, you will most probably be approached by your guide of guides as usual, and he or she wants to help you "cross over," and if you allow this, it will lead you through the Tunnel.

In some cases, there are no guides in the beginning, and the Tunnel will open up in front of you, but at a distance.

Normally, souls feel the attraction and gravitation from the Tunnel and start moving toward it, consciously or unconsciously - like a leaf being sucked in by a vacuum cleaner.

1. Instead of letting yourself be "hypnotized" by its attraction, turn and look in the opposite direction (you will have 360° vision, and you can still concentrate on looking in a certain direction) and move away from the Tunnel (you do this by "thinking" yourself as moving — it's all about thoughts and intention in this dimension). Remember, you, as a soul of Fire, are far stronger than the force that pulls you toward the Tunnel.

   Don't try to fight it — that's not the way to do it. Instead, think yourself away from it!

2. The Tunnel with the Light on the other side of it is a sophisticated holo-gram, and all you need to do is to think yourself in another direction, and the Tunnel will fade away.

    Soon you will see the Grid as a fuzzy "barrier" in front of you, or above you (there are no ups and downs or lefts and rights in space). You will also see that it has holes in it — like Swiss cheese. Move through one of these holes.

3. You will now see the Universe the way it is, i.e., you will now be truly interdimensional. This means you will see a much larger Universe than you are used to. This is possible because you are outside the Grid, and you're not in a programmed body — you are meeting the Universe as a pure Spirit of Fire riding an Avatar, which is your mind.

    What you experience outside the Grid, as a discarnate Spirit, can be quite overwhelming and impressive. Probably for the first time, you see the Universe as it really is, with the KHAA (Egyptian: The Mother Un-iverse - the VOID) and everything. When you read this, you are still li-mited with your five senses, but a good idea is to prepare yourself men-tally for what is out there. It's not at all going to be a negative experience, just very different!

    You will also see the Space War that is going on in the solar system, and you will notice the soldiers fighting in other dimensions, which you now are going to have access to.

Those who have come to this point in their awareness level are beginning to do their own research. You don't have to worry about getting "stuck" in the "ether" and become a "lost soul." If you have escaped the Reincarnation Cycle (here or elsewhere) you have become a Wanderer/Star Being and may have voluntarily come here to help the humans to escape dimensional con-trol. For the most part, those who are or have Awakened to the polarity game on Earth are beyond dimensional control because you know too much. But some Star Travelers/Wanders may get trapped by the illusion of wealth, con-trol or the other Dark Force "trappings" of a polarity world.

Article 38

ONENESS – SINGULARITY IS A TRAP
(Is This Really the Goal of the Species in the Universe?)

Oneness is a term which is used throughout the New Age community — they believe that we are all One with the One Creator, and our purpose is to return to the One Creator, and merge with Him (it is mostly a "He"). They say that the sole purpose with ascending into higher dimensions is to as soon as possible return to Source/God, and once again become One with Him. Most of us, including myself, have fallen for this idea at one point or another and most people are still falling for it. If you are one of them, don't feel bad—the idea has become deeply rooted in our psyche— especially if we have been truth-seekers for a while. Now, where does this idea actually come from? Is this really a new concept that somebody decided to spread into the truth-seeker community as the main goal for mankind, or does it have deeper and more ancient roots?

In the Advaita Vedānta (1800-800 BC), we are taught that the ultimate goal is to merge the individual ego into the Godhead. This school of teaching follows the traditional Vedic teachings, which means that it teaches the idea that an individual transmigrates through a celestial hierarchy of inhabited Densities and Realms—from solid 3-D matter, through more etheric realms, and until she reaches the Realm of the One God (Source), where she merges with the One God. Also, both Advaita Vedanta, and other Vedic texts, hold that all these Realms are illusory, and nothing exists but the One Consciousness.

As we can see, the "New Age" idea of becoming One with the Creator is thousands of years old and based on a Patriarchal principle of a male God — This concept is well embraced and channeled by many, including the Ra Material. The RA people are a social memory complex, which means that they have already merged and become One amongst themselves as a mass consciousness, and they claim to be of Sixth Density (while we humans are allegedly of Third Density). The problem with the RA Material is that they are "talking" about the god that created mankind and that "god" resides in the very bottom of the Lower Realms of the Universe; they are not relating themselves to Creator God, who resides at the very top of the Upper Realms. Remember that the Lower Densities of the 4% Universe are predominately associated with the Lower Realms.

If we go back to the time before Lucifer and his Fallen Angels took over this paradise, there was no such idea that the primordial man, or any other beings or species in the Universe, should go back and merge with the One God. This idea was non-existent. We have been taught that we should ascend so we can go back and merge with Source. This teaching is included in the Book of Enoch, when Enoch followed the "Anunnaki" up to "Heaven," The Book of Enoch was taken out of the Bible by the Roman Emperor Constantine at the Council of Nicaea in AD 325.

The problem with any "new" spiritual ideas is that they may sound pretty good, but when a person does not have a clue about the real history of Earth—often found embedded in mythology and ancient religions — it's easy to subscribe to these ideas, without scrutinizing them. In this case, a new mass agreement is being introduced to the Western World that the destiny of Mankind is to merge with Source, that Source being the one who created Mankind (it was the Anunnaki who created Mankind).

All "Roads" Lead to Source but not the one you are thinking of — By subscribing to this (merge in ONENESS with Source), we are setting ourselves up for a new, future trap. Think about it. Who is this "Source" we are talking about? Well, we have been taught since ancient times that God is masculine, and in the Vedas, God is Brahma, who is Vishnu, who is Lord Enki, the Anunnaki who, with his son Malduk, created Mankind (via DNA manipulation of the Anunnaki DNA with that of the local human species) to be dominated and servant to the Anunnaki, Moreover, Enki is also the Biblical Satan in the Garden of Eden, the rebellious Lucifer, the Jewish God YHWH, the Christian God Jehovah, and the Muslim God Allah! Do you see where I'm going with this? The "Source" we are supposed to merge with is Enki, Mankind's creator, not ONE SOURCE / CREATOR GOD who created the universe and all within it, including the Four Original Races and, from them, their "off-shoots," including Humanoids, Draco/Reptilians, Carrion like beings, and Cetaceans.

Herein lays the Trap. We are within the 4% Universe that was given to the Orion Empire (Dark Force) via Treaty at the end of the 2rd Galactic War and reconfirmed at the end of the 3rd Galactic War (approximately 500,000 years ago) and without directly knowing it, you believe the ascension process will lead to the God Density. The problem is that, these Densities exist and were created by the Dark Force to provide you with a feeling of freedom and bliss, when it is not. The Dark Force Destinies are a dark mirror of the Destinies of the Free Universe (96% Universe).

x

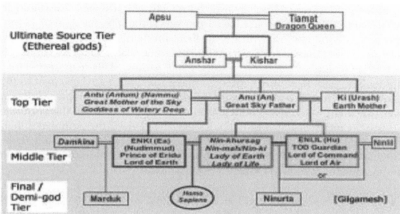

Who are Enki and Enlil — Enki and Enlil are both Anunnaki and are Service-to-Self; neither is the "good guy."

The Anunnaki came to Earth (approx. 500,000 years ago) to harvest gold; needing atomized gold to repair their home planet's atmosphere. Earth has an abundance of gold, compared to other planets. The Anunnaki soon tired of mining the gold themselves (they are, for the most part, etheric) and, thus, being excellent geneticists, they modified the DNA of the resident humans and created Mankind to do the mining work – as servants to the Anunnaki.

Enki and his son, Malduk (mainly involved in the evolution of Mankind), were the primary "architects" of the DNA manipulation. The difference between Enki and his brother, Enlil, is that Enki "pushed" technology over spirituality (spirituality being more aligned with the Anunnaki, themselves), which was supported by Enlil. Enlil wanted more of the Anunnaki DNA left intact within Mankind's creation but this did not occur – it was technology vs. spirituality, which sounds very familiar today. Anu was the programmer and, during the 2nd phase of development (Human 2.0 – after the Flood), Anu, father of Enki and Enlil, installed, as part of the program, for Anu to be God Almighty over Mankind.

Enki established the Brotherhood of the Snake, precursor to the Egyptian Mystery Schools, to teach Adapa (the first of Mankind) and his descendants' spiritual wisdom, yet Enlil disapproved of this. The Brotherhood of the Snake became corrupted, when the power hungry members took over control of the school; the Priesthood officially began. This same Priesthood has been corrupting Earth for thousands of years, hiding the real history of the planet and replacing it with organized religion.

Enki was first son of Anu and, hence, believed he was to be the true ruler of Earth. Eventually, Enlil retreated and left Earth, leaving Enki and Malduk in "control," where Malduk was even more of a controller.

Although it was Enki's "Priesthood" who corrupted the Earth, I lay the blame on Enki for choosing technology over spirituality, even thought that spirituality (encouraged by Enlil) would have been very limited by the Anunnaki. So, who is the "good guy" and who is the "evil brother," the answer is neither; both are "evil" (Service-to-Self). Although, some claim that the Anunnaki gave us agriculture, civilization, a work ethic, various skills (e.g., metallurgy, tool making etc.), they were "given" to make Mankind more revenant to the Anunnaki. What they really taught us was hierarchy, misogyny, violence, greed, debt and a warlike attitude toward mass destruction (for the last thousands of years, their creation was no longer needed by the Anunnaki; their thought was to let them destroy each other). Enlil's faction has joined the Federation as a means to retake Earth from his brother, not as a benevolent gestured to join Service-to-Others.

The Harvest, as some call it — The RA collective, who talked so vividly about the Harvest, also told us about non-physical beings, who are going to help people cross over from the Third to the Fourth Density. Who could those non-physicals be, except Enki and his followers? Do you think they really are going to harvest us and transfer us into the Fourth and Fifth Densities? — the dimensions of bliss. Of course, this only applies if you are exceeding being 50% Service to Others (STO). Here we have the anxiety/fear button (created by the Dark Force) —am I going to make it to 51% or not? Am I worthy? Am I good enough or am I going to be left behind and thrown to the wolves, together with the majority of Mankind? Yesterday I did something bad— what's my percentage rate now? Did I blow it? Should I keep statistics? All this leads to anxiety, fear, and terror.

The Greater Universe (KHAA), will not accept Humankind in our current state — the truth of the matter is that the peaceful star races, living in the Greater Universe (KHAA), will not accept Humankind in our current state. We are considered a warlike race, which wittingly and unwittingly are serving infamous and despised warlords, who are not hesitant to create more destruction in the Universe. Unless we can prove that we are able to rise above this current state, and break out of the trance, we will not be welcomed in the KHAA. We are considered much too primitive, and could potentially disrupt the peace which reigns in the majority of the Greater Universe (yes, there are skirmishes in the KHAA as well). The goal is to create a peaceful Universe, free from oppression, with free trade between worlds—no one is interested in bringing in another warlike race into the Greater Universe. Therefore, **we have no choice but to evolve—otherwise someone with greater capabilities than we have will put us in a new quarantine** in order to make us stay away from the universal community.

Why the Dark Force wants an Awakening — To the Dark Force, we need to have an awakening in order to land in a world of Artificial Intelligence (AI), Transhumanism, and ultimately—a social memory complex, i.e. a Singularity.

It all started hundreds of years ago, with what we call The Enlightenment. That was when magicians and others, e.g. through alchemy and art, were beginning to bring humanity to higher awareness. After that came the Industrial Revolution, which we are the ever expanding result of today, and of which AI, Transhumanism, singularity, and all the rest of it, are a part.

Finally, we have the spiritual awakening, which includes the disclosure of the UFO phenomenon, channeling, and communication via global networks, such as the Internet. All these "movements" are interconnected and could all be manipulated into being, and are supposed to bring us, not to elusive higher dimensions, but to the phenomenon of One People, One Mind, i.e. Singularity and a social memory complex, set up and run by a Dark Force central super-computer, which most certainly will be run off-planet. This is much like what happened to the "Grays" who operate on a social memory complex; the Greys are, now, allied with the Draco/Reptilian Alliance (Empire) and are their minions.

Freedom Through Individual Achievements — Instead of becoming One and merge with each other and the Creatrix, we need to continue being individuals in order to explore the Multiverse we ourselves are helping to build every single moment of our lives. Yes, we will, in a way, become "One" with each other as a human group. Compassion, love, and understanding will bring about a closeness that will feel almost like Oneness, but we are still to remain individuals—everyone with his and her own mind and sovereign thinking. No Group (Elite Dark Force, Enki Elite, nor Draco/ Reptilian Alliance/ Empire), Social Memory Complex, machines or computers are going to run us, and be considered equal, or superior, to the human mind.

Source
1.   The Wes Penre Papers, The Vedic Texts, The Fifth Level of Learning Part 1, Wes Penre, Feb 27, 2015, https://wespenrepapershome.files.wordpress.com/2019/07/fifthleveloflearningpart1.pdf

Article 39

ESCAPE PLAN PREPERATION WHILE ON EARTH

In the previous Article, I presented the case on why Oneness (We are One) was a Trap. I can see how one might start getting discouraged, and wonder what this really means. Aren't we supposed to increase our awareness, then?

Yes, of course we are! What I am suggesting here is that the Dark Force is taking advantage of something that was inevitable in the first place—all species evolve to a greater or lesser degree because we learn new things every time we have a new life experience. Indeed, mankind needs to evolve, or we will stagnate and no longer remain human. This is impossible because in the Universe there is no such thing as stagnation.

However, the awakening (evolution/evolvement) I am talking about, is different than what we are usually being taught in the New Age and UFO communities. From all these years of research, the following points are what we need to concentrate on—both as individuals and as a mass consciousness, if humanity will stand a chance to outsmart the forces we are up against:

1. As a mass consciousness, we need to learn about a) the Dark Force (Service—to—Self Enki Group, Draco/Reptilian Alliance/Empire) and its history, b) how they came to Earth, c) how they genetically tampered with existing species and isolated us in this Middle Realm/ Third Density, d) how they manipulated the historical records, e) that they are the source to much of our suffering, from the beginning up to present, and f) their future plans.

2. We need to learn how to disagree with their manipulation, and how to claim our rights as sovereign beings. This means that we need to make a lot of changes in our daily lives—both as individuals and as a human race. It means that we no longer agree to feed their bank accounts by beings

234 | Article 39 - Escape Plan Preparation While on Earth

3. slaves to the big corporations. We need to, slowly but surely, create our own society, excluding Dark Force interference. In order to do this, it requires a very good knowledge of #1 above, so we are able to see through impostors, who will inevitably infiltrate everything we try to accomplish. I am not saying any of this will be an easy task, but nevertheless necessary. Building a new, alternative society can't be done until we have progressed through #6 (below).

4. Scrutinize our own behavior. It is true that the Dark Force has taken advantage of humanity's naivety, but we can't blame only them for our current conditions— we need to take responsibility for our own involvement and agreements to have been manipulated in the first place, and continue to be so in almost every area of life. We need to realize that war and violence are not justified in the new society that humanity is building. Wars are the result on one Elite Group vying for power over another Elite Group – it has nothing to do with the betterment of Mankind; there are thirteen Elite Groups on Earth all vying for power – these are the thirteen Elite Orion Families sent to Earth to control the Earth.

5. Instead of becoming One and merge with each other and the Creatrix, we need to continue being individuals in order to explore the Multiverse we ourselves are helping to build every single moment of our lives. Yes, we will, in a way, become "One" with each other as a human group. Compassion, love, and understanding will bring about a closeness that will feel almost like a Oneness, but we are still to remain individuals— everyone with his and her own mind and sovereign thinking. No Group (Elite Dark Force, Enki Elite, nor Draco/ Reptilian Alliance/ Empire), Social Memory Complex, machines or computers are going to run us, and be considered equal, or superior, to the human mind.

6. We want to continue developing spiritually and connect with the Creator God, Mother Goddess or Home Universe or The Greater Universe (KHAA), something that is achieved by **connecting with our inner selves**. We also need to understand our body, love it, and connect with it. The body is, amongst a million other things, an antenna, which connects us to our "inner truths." The body has the answers to our questions, and we need to learn how to read the messages that come from our Heart-Mind/Body/Soul. In the current now, people are extremely ignorant about what is "inside" because they have given their power away to doctors, governments, and others, who act as authorities. In reality, they know nothing about the body's potentials. **Until we can truly connect to our Universal Heart, which is different from the hijacked heart chakra** (which is addressed in another Article), **our body must be the sensor, which can tell us what is true and what is not, and whom to trust and whom to mistrust.**

7. Until the above is achieved, creating groups and communities as alternatives to the current social structure under which we are captured

will not work. The group members would be too ignorant to be able to expose infiltrators, who would inevitably manifest, destroy, and dissolve such group attempts. Any change that has had positive value for mankind throughout history has originated from an individual—not a group. Therefore, **we need to start by changing from within, and share our insights with others**—first through media that is already set up around the world (such as the Internet), and later by adding "inner communications," such as telepathy, to the equation. It's all a learning process and a learning curve. By practicing the above, there is no group to infiltrate, and even if one individual here and there would be "taken out," there are millions more. **This will inevitably raise the vibration of the planet, and people will be much more aware.** This is all happening right now, but needs to develop to a much higher level before groups are even considered as a solution to the current social structure and manipulation. People need to understand what they really want to evolve toward, and stop being naïve by feeding into the Dark Force's hidden agendas.

8. When all this is achieved, we are, as a human race, ready to meet other star races out there—not the ones who are controlling the 4% Universe, but those who live in The Greater Universe (KHAA)—in what we call dark matter and dark energy. When we have achieved the above, the Grid will already have dissolved due to our own evolution, and if this is done successfully, the Dark Force will have had to surrender their control, and have no choice but to leave the planet. The whole Universe will then lie open for us!

These are the very basic ideas on how to solve our problem, and are not by any means complete, but the purpose is to ignite the urge to find a solution. The truth of the matter is that the peaceful star races, living in The Greater Universe (KHAA), will not accept humankind in our current state. We are considered a warlike race, which wittingly and unwittingly are serving infamous and despised warlords, who are not hesitant to create more destruction in the Universe. Unless we can prove that we are able to rise above this current state, and break out of the trance, we will not be welcomed in The Greater Universe (KHAA). We are considered much too primitive, and could potentially disrupt the peace which reigns in the majority of the Universe Community (yes, there are skirmishes in the KHAA as well). The goal is to create a peaceful Universe, free from oppression—no one is interested in bringing in another warlike race into the Greater Universe. Therefore, we have no choice but to evolve—otherwise someone with greater capabilities than we have will put us in a new quarantine in order to make us stay away from the universal community. Is it all possible? Everything is possible! Is it likely to happen? That is an open question. However, I want the reader to see that it is the individual contribution that counts! There is no such thing as "little me can do nothing." Little you can move mountains and shape new realities—not only for yourself, but for all of humanity!

9.   When your contract expires and you leave Earth, remember to side-step the Dark Force's Reincarnation Trap and execute your AT DEATH EXIT PLAN. Remember that you are a Free Spirit riding an avatar and are not to be controlled and dominated by another force, such as the Dark Force.

10.   **Develop an AT DEATH EXIT PLAN!** This means that when the day comes when we die from this Earth the next time, we **have a plan as of where to go (Realm – forget about the Densities which occur within the Earth Realm) and what to do.** I can't stress enough how important this is! If we don't bother to have one, we will once again be drawn into Enki's Recycling Station, and with full amnesia we will have to endure yet another lifetime having to figure things out. Well, most probably it will not be only one lifetime but a series of them. I can imagine that those of us who have figured things out to an extent that is uncomfortable for the Dark Force (Enki Group), they will not give you another chance the next lifetime to reconnect the dots—at least not as easily as it was in this current life. I would be very surprised if the Enki Group didn't make sure of that if they catch us and get us into their system again. I'm sure they would make certain that our forgetfulness mechanism will be set to full capacity. I don't think any of us would want that. I am not mentioning this to scare anybody—it's just pure logic. Wouldn't you, if you were the Enki Group, make sure that the next time around the evolved soul would have a very difficult time remembering anything? Wouldn't you implant that soul fragment with false data?

Hence, I suggest that the reader, **TODAY, starts thinking about a Death EXIT PLAN,** who knows when your day will come? You may live many decades still, or you may die tomorrow—therefore, it's much better to be safe than sorry. I can guarantee you that it's not enough to "hope for the best." When you need groceries, you don't "hope" that the groceries will show up—you plan for your purchase and perhaps even make a list. The same thing applies here. The way to do it, with the knowledge you have, would be to think about exactly where you want to go and how you want to get there.

As mentioned earlier, you can think yourself to a certain place, and once you're separated from the silver-chord, which connects your astral bodies with your physical body, you can think those thoughts, put intention behind them, and you will be at your destination in a blink of an eye.

What you want to do and where you want to go is your decision and your decision alone. Let no one manipulate you in the astral planes— either disregard such beings, or tell them that you appreciate their willingness to assist, but this time you want to do it differently. They won't take you if you express your Free Will. Then, pass through the Grid, which you will have "above" you, and well outside of it, the real Greater Universe will open up before you. I have heard that this will be the most fantastic moment in your life as a spiritual being! You will be in the Greater Universe (KHAA), and you will see the traps for what they are!

From there on you are free to think your way across the Multiverse, and you are free to create whatever you wish that gives you joy. You can spend time alone, or you can spend it with other likeminded beings and create something together with them—it's up to you. You can also go to Orion, and as a human being they will let you in, unless you are a criminal or a person who most likely will create chaos. Or, better yet, chose a place outside of the 4% Universes and be free from most of the ciaos and polarity.

All you need to do to achieve this is to have a solid exit plan. You must know what you want so that you're not in doubt when the day comes for your departure. On that day, you think yourself to the Realm where you want to go, and put a strong intention behind your thought. You will notice that you will reach your destination much easier than if you would get into your car and drive to the grocery store. The Universe is a great place for beings that have good intentions and know what they want.

Article 40

JOURNEY AFTER DEATH
(Realms of Consciousness)

THE TUNNEL OF LIGHT IS A TRICK

The Tunnel of Light is a trick and it leads to an implant station which will recycle the soul again.

Spiritual Sciences Research Foundation (SSRF). Some of their methodologies for accessing spiritual Truths and knowledge are through EEG machines and is based upon the realization that knowledge can be passed from the neurons in the brain through the nervous system which affects muscle memory and movements. SSRF findings on the Light at the end of the tunnel that near death experiencer's see:

"The Divine Light (not a tunnel) in actuality is definitely seen by people who have a genuine desire for their religious defined God. Those above a spiritual level of 50% (samashi) or 60% (vyashi) are actually able to see Light either due to immense merits or very little ego and they reach the region of Religious Heaven (Swarga). A person at a lower spiritual level, such as 40%, may see a Light when they die if they had an intense desire for spiritual growth towards their religious defined God. In this case, while they may see the Light, they don't actually reach the region of Heaven (Swarga).

The remainder at the point of death are not able to see any light. Instead as soon as we die, ordinarily they see darkness. Even though the 'Region of the Dead' (Martyalok) that one goes through immediately after death is purplish in color, most subtle-bodies journeying through it see only darkness. The reason is subtle-body has a black covering of impressions of unsatisfied desires, personality defects, and ego and in many cases a covering of black energy of ghosts. Hence it is as if they have their eyes closed and thus cannot perceive the actual colors of the Region of the Dead.

Those people without a genuine desire for a religious defined God-realization who see a light are in fact seeing the light generated by an illusion-creating subtle-sorcerer (mantrik). Subtle-sorcerers, due to their high spiritual strength, can create illusions of light as well as feelings of peace and happiness radiating from the light. These illusions are created by their spiritual powers and their black energy. The Dark Force uses this as a mechanism to lure subtle-bodies into the light and trap them into slavery. Earthbound ancestors are generally of a lower spiritual level and with a lot of attachments and unfulfilled desires. This means that they ordinarily cannot see a religion driven Light when they die. By telling them to go into the light, what one is effectively doing is telling the departed ancestor to go towards the illusion created by subtle-sorcerers.

The MESSAGE OF THIS ARTICLE is that you need an Exit Plan Before You Leave – This means that when the day comes when we die from this Earth the next time, we have a plan as of where to go and what to do. I can't stress enough how important this is! If we don't bother to have one, we will once again be drawn into Enki's Recycling Station, and with full amnesia we will have to endure yet another lifetime having to figure things out. Well, most probably it will not be only one lifetime but a series of lifetimes. I can imagine that those of us who have figured things out to an extent that is uncomfortable for the Dark Force (Enki Group) will not get another chance the next lifetime to reconnect the dots—at least not as easily as it was in this current life.

The way to do it, with the knowledge you have, would be to think about exactly where you want to go and how you want to get there. As mentioned earlier, you can think yourself to a certain place, and once you're separated from the silver-chord, which connects your astral bodies with your physical body, you can think those thoughts, put intention behind them, and you will be at your destination in a blink of an eye. Make it your goal to rise to "HIGHER REALMS." Do it Today, tomorrow may be too late.

A previous Article (the Vedic Realms) should have allowed you to understand the Six Levels of Heaven, the Middle Realm (where we "live") and the Seven Levels of Hell, if you like these terms instead of Upper, Middle and Lower Realms. The Realms presentation provided you with the knowledge you need to develop your Exit Plan. Also note that this Article is not "New Age" since it was revealed nearly 3,000 years ago written within the Vedic text Atharva-Veda.

Two Paths – These are two paths of the soul after death, according to our karma and our spiritual development. By the Upper Path, one does not come back or voluntarily returns to this world (teachers, guide, etc.); by the Lower Path, one returns and tries again to achieve the Upper Path, but you are fought by the Lower Realms to not find the Upper Path.

Try to reach the upper path. Whoever knows the merits and demerits of these two paths will certainly pursue the path of merit rather than the path of demerit. It is the lack of knowledge that prevents us from working for our own salvation; no one else can provide it for you. But if we know that such a thing exists, and that even after death our karmas will pursue us wherever we go—even if we go to the nether regions, we will be caught by the nemesis of our actions, the results of what we have done, because there is a law which punishes us—we will obey the law. And if we know that there are these two paths, and there is a chance of our entering into the lower one, we will certainly want to work to attain the higher one. Knowing this, we will certainly become wiser and, therefore, work toward a state of union with the divinities in the various graduated levels of development within the Upper Realms, or with the Supreme Absolute (One Source /Creator God) itself, whatever the case may be. Either way, one will be a united with the Creator God now, or one will systematically move through the Upper Realms.

Lower Path (no merit)– When the soul departs from the body in the case of the lower, unpurified and negligibly spiritual souls, it is taken away by the messengers of Yama and placed before the Lord of Death for judgment in Patala-loka (also called Bila-Svarga), the lowest level of the Underworld (Patalas, the Lower Realms). At this point (taken before the Lord of Death), a series of events occur:

- Yama asks the soul, "What have you done?"
- Ordinarily, the Soul cannot remember anything. It will say, "I don't know."
- It is said that then a hot rod, called a *yamadanda,* is kept on its head, and immediately it remembers its entire past. It knows every detail of the actions that it did both good and bad. The soul says, "I have done a little good, but have also made many mistakes and performed so many erroneous actions."
- Yama asks, "What do you have to say about it now?"
- The Soul replies, "I have got relatives. They will expiate them for me. They will conduct *yajnas*, charities, worship, *sankirtans*, *bhajans* and meditations in my name, and I shall be free from the consequence of the sins that I have committed or the mistakes that I have made."
- "Go then!" says Yama, "And see what they do."
- Apparently, it takes ten days for the soul to be brought back, so some ceremony is usually done on the tenth, eleventh, twelfth and thirteenth days. The soul hovers around, observing what the relatives are doing, and Yama's messengers stand behind like policemen to see what is done.
  - If an expiatory ceremony is done in the name of the soul, and presentations made on behave of the departed as to the life the Soul

lead, the effect of these good deeds is credited to the account of the soul and it is exonerated to that extent.

- But suppose this is not done and, like modern people, the relatives do not believe in these observances and they proceed as if nothing has happened; there is no mention of charity, no goodwill, and if the Soul's relatives have done nothing. Yama's policeman drags the Soul back to the kingdom of the Lord of the Death. At first they brought the Soul back within ten days because they wanted to know what was happening. When it is certain that it is going to be punished, they drag it, pull it, scratch and beat it, and it will be hungry and thirsty and bleeding. That is why another ceremony needs to be done after one year; it takes one year for the soul to return to the abode of Yama. The *varshika* (annual) ceremony is very important. If nothing has been done on the tenth to thirteenth days after the passing of the soul, at least something should be done on the anniversary so that some mercy may be granted by Lord Yama before the sentence is passed.

- If the soul has no merit at all, Yama will establish the punishment and the Soul will be sent to the land of punishment (Karaka, the Hellish Planets), whatever the punishment is. In the Srimad Bhagavata Mahapurana, the Garuda Purana, etc., the type of punishment and difficulties that the soul has to undergo to be expunged of its sins by suffering in the prison of Yama's hell.

- When the soul is expunged of all its sins it is released and after many, many solar years, the soul attains its freedom to return to Prithvi, Earth, the Middle Realm for another chance to find the Upper Path.

- This is how a bad person gets purified in a very painful way, and then finally attains blessedness.

Lower Path (with merit) – There are those who have not spiritually awakened themselves, have not done spiritual meditation, and have an insufficient devotion to their religious God. Even if they are very good people, highly charitable and humanistic in their approach, they still have to follow one of two paths.

- **The North Path** –Those who are not spiritually awakened but have done immensely good deeds reach a Middle Kingdom called Chandraloka (Lunar deity), the realm of the moon, where they stay invisibly and enjoy the fruit of their good deeds. When the momentum of their good deeds, charitable deeds, etc., is exhausted, they come back into this world reincarnated in hope they will find the spiritual path.

- **The South Path** – If a Soul is spiritually awakened and is not merely a good person—not merely a charitable or a philanthropic person—then the path is different, in that they too will return to Earth to learn the lessons of charity and good deeds.

Upper Path – There are those who have spiritually awakened themselves, have done spiritual meditation, have insufficient devotion to Creator God, not the False God created by many religions as a means of control, and have charitable and humanistic in their approach, At the time of death, a super-human entity comes and takes the soul by the hand. Up to the solar orb, or even a little beyond, is called the realm of lightning. That is, beyond the sun, the lightning of Brahmaloka flashes forth.

• The individuality consciousness of the soul slowly gets diminished at that time, and it is not aware of any self-effort. It does not know that it is moving at all, inasmuch as the ego is almost gone. At that time an *amanava purusha* deputed by Brahma (Creator God) himself comes down in a luminous form, and leads the soul through the other Upper Realms, achieving a gradual liberation, until the Absolute Brahman (Creator God) Realm is reached. This process may take 100 solar years or more.

• There is a possibility of immediate "salvation" without passing through all these stages (Realm "levels")—a hundredfold promotion, as it was. It is the dissolution of the soul in the Supreme Brahman (Creator God) at this very spot. The soul need not have to travel in space and time because it is a *jivanmukta purusha*, one who has attained to a level where there is no distance to be travelled. For this Soul, there is no solar orb or anything else. This Soul has spread its consciousness everywhere, in all beings, everywhere in the cosmos.

• The Liberated Soul – when a soul is liberated it reaches the highest Realm and becomes one with Brahman/Creator God. It exists no more as an individual self. According to some schools of thought, when a soul attains the highest Realm of Brahman/Creator God, it remains there permanently as a liberated soul savoring the company of the Supreme Being and forever freed from the delusion of Prakriti (Earth) or nature. It does not reunite with Brahman completely. Some of them may at times incarnate again on their own accord to serve humanity. But even then they would not be subject to the impurities of illusion, attachment and karma. A liberated soul remains forever free and untainted even during the dissolution of the worlds and the beginning of a new cycle of creation.

The Path Less Taken – Having known clearly that these are the two paths, who would like to tread the lesser path? "Therefore, try to tread the upper path.

As stated in the Sanskrit Vedic text: *Vedeṣu yajñeṣu tapaḥsu caiva dāneṣu yat puṇyaphalaṁ pradiṣṭam, atyeti tat sarvam idaṁ viditvā yogī paraṁ sthānam upaiti cādyam* (8.28). "The knowledge of these wonderful things beyond this world that you are gaining is greater than all the good deeds that you do by way of charity, and all the sacrifices that you perform. All the merits that you will accrue by doing charity, good deeds and even the study of scriptures like the Vedas, and by doing austerity and living an abstemious life will bring you some good results. But this *phala* of *satsanga*, the blessing of this highly purifying training that your soul is undergoing by listening to these glorious eternal realities, certainly has a greater capacity to produce an effect than all the charities, studies and scriptures, etc. It transcends even the Vedas, and you attain to that place, that abode, which is the Ancient One."

The 28 Hells
Tamisra (darkness): It is intended for a person who grabs another's wealth, wife or children. In this dark realm, he is bound with ropes and starved without food or water. He is beaten and reproached by Yamadutas till he faints.

Andhatamisra (blind-darkness): Here, a man – who deceives another man and enjoys his wife or children – is tormented to the extent he loses his consciousness and sight. The torture is described as cutting the tree at its roots.

Raurava (fearful or hell of rurus): As per the Bhagavata Purana and the Devi Bhagavata Purana, it is assigned for a person who cares about his own and his family's good, but harms other living beings and is always envious of others. The living beings hurt by such a man take the form of savage serpent-like beasts called rurus and torture this person. The Vishnu Purana deems this hell fit for a false witness or one who lies. Maharaurava (great-fearful): A person who indulges at the expense of other beings is afflicted with pain by fierce rurus called kravyadas, who eat his flesh.

Kumbhipaka (cooked in a pot): A person who cooks animals and birds is cooked alive in boiling oil by Yamadutas here, for as many years as there were hairs on the bodies of their animal victims. Kalasutra (thread of Time/Death): The Bhagavata Purana assigns this hell to a murderer of a brahmin (the Hindu priestly caste), while the Devi Bhagavata Purana allocates it for a person who disrespects his parents, elders, ancestors or brahmins. This realm is made entirely of copper and extremely hot, heated by fire from below and the red hot sun from above. Here, the sinner burns from within by hunger and thirst and the smoldering heat outside, whether he sleeps, sits, stands or runs.

Asipatravana/Asipatrakanana (forest of sword leaves): The Bhagavata Purana and the Devi Bhagavata Purana reserve this hell for a person who digresses from the religious teachings of the Vedas and indulges in heresy. The Vishnu Purana states that wanton tree-felling leads to this hell. Yamadutas beat them with whips as they try to run away in the forest where palm trees have swords as leaves. Afflicted with injury of whips and swords, they faint and cry out for help in vain.

Shukaramukha (hog's mouth): It houses kings or government officials who punish the innocent or grant corporal punishment to a Brahmin. Yamadutas crush him as sugar cane is crushed to extract juice. He will yell and scream in agony, just as the guiltless suffered. Andhakupa (well with its mouth hidden): It is the hell where a person who harms others with the intention of malice and harms insects is confined. He is attacked by birds, animals, reptiles, mosquitoes, lice, worms, flies and others, who deprive him of rest and compel him to run hither and thither.

Krimibhojana/Krimibhaksha (worm-food): As per the Bhagavata Purana and the Devi Bhagavata Purana, it is where a person who does not share his food with guests, elders, children or the gods, and selfishly eats it alone, and he who eats without performing the five yajnas (panchayajna) is chastised. The Vishnu Purana states that one who loathes his father, Brahmins or the gods and who destroys jewels is punished here. This hell is a 100,000 yojana lake filled with worms. The sinful person is reduced to a worm, who feeds on other worms, who in turn devour his body for 100,000 years.

Sandansa/Sandamsa (hell of pincers): The Bhagavata Purana and the Devi Bhagavata Purana state that a person who robs a Brahmin or steals jewels or gold from someone, when not in dire need, is confined to this hell. However, the Vishnu Purana tells the violators of vows or rules endure pain here.) In either case, the body is torn by red-hot iron balls and tongs.

Taptasurmi/Taptamurti (red-hot iron statue): A man or woman who indulges in illicit sexual relations with a woman or man is beaten by whips and forced to embrace red-hot iron figurines of the opposite sex.

Vajrakantaka-salmali (the silk-cotton tree with thorns like thunderbolts/ vajras): A person who has sexual intercourse with animals or who has excessive coitus is tied to the Vajrakantaka-salmali tree and pulled by Yamadutas so that the thorns tear his body.

Vaitarni/Vaitarna (to be crossed): It is a river that is believed to lie between Naraka and the Earth. This river, which forms the boundary of Naraka, is filled with excreta, urine, pus, blood, hair, nails, bones, marrow, flesh and fat, where fierce aquatic beings eat the person's flesh. As per the Bhagavata Purana and the Devi Bhagavata Purana, a person born in a respectable family – kshatriya (warrior-caste), royal family or government official – who neglects his duty is thrown into this river of hell. The Vishnu Purana assigns it to the destroyer of a bee-hive or a town.

Puyoda (water of pus): Shudras (workmen-caste) and husbands or sexual partners of lowly women and prostitutes – who live like animals devoid of cleanliness and good behavior – fall in Puyoda, the ocean of pus, excreta, urine, mucus, saliva and other repugnant things. Here, they are forced to eat these disgusting things.

Pranarodha (obstruction to life): Some Brahmins, Kshatriyas and Vaishyas (merchant caste) indulge in the sport of hunting with their dogs and donkeys in the forest, resulting in wanton killing of animals. Yamadutas play archery sport with them as the targets in this hell.

Visashana (murderous): The Bhagavata Purana and the Devi Bhagavata Purana mention that Yamadutas whip a person, who has pride of his rank and wealth and sacrifices animals as a status symbol, and finally kill him. The Vishnu Purana associates it with the maker of spears, swords, and other weapons.

Lalabhaksa (saliva as food): As per the Bhagavata Purana and the Devi Bhagavata Purana, a Brahmin, a Ksahtriya or a Vaishya husband, who forces his wife to drink his semen out of lust and to enforce his control, is thrown in a river of semen, which he is forced to drink. The Vishnu Purana disagrees stating that one who eats before offering food to the gods, the ancestors or guests is brought to this hell.

Sarameyadana (hell of the sons of Sarama): Plunderers who burn houses and poison people for wealth, and kings and other government officials, who grab money of merchants, mass murder or ruin the nation, are cast into this hell. Seven hundred and twenty ferocious dogs, the sons of Sarama, with razor-sharp teeth, prey on them at the behest of Yamadutas.

Avici/Avicimat (waterless/waveless): A person, who lies on oath or in business, is repeatedly thrown head-first from a 100 yojana high mountain whose sides are stone waves, but without water. His body is continuously broken, but it is made sure that he does not die.

Ayahpana (iron-drink): Anybody else under oath or a Brahmin who drinks alcohol is punished here. Yamadutas stand on their chests and force them to drink molten iron.

Ksarakardama (acidic/saline mud/filth): One who in false pride, does not honor a person higher than him by birth, austerity, knowledge, behavior, caste or spiritual order, is tortured in this hell. Yamadutas throw him head-first and torment him.

Raksogana-bhojana (food of Rakshasas): Those who practice human-sacrifice and cannibalism are condemned to this hell. Their victims, in the form of Rakshasas, cut them with sharp knives and swords. The Rakshasas feast on their blood and sing and dance in joy, just as the sinners slaughtered their victims.

Shulaprota (pierced by sharp pointed spear/dart): Some people give shelter to birds or animals pretending to be their saviors, but then harass them poking with threads, needles or using them like lifeless toys. Also, some people behave the same way to humans, winning their confidence and then killing them with sharp tridents or lances. The bodies of such sinners, fatigued with hunger and thirst, are pierced with sharp, needle-like spears.

Ferocious carnivorous birds like vultures and herons tear and gorge their flesh.

Dandasuka (snakes): Filled with envy and fury, some people harm others like snakes. These are destined to be devoured by five or seven hooded serpents in this hell.

Avata-nirodhana (confined in a hole): People who imprison others in dark wells, crannies or mountain caves are pushed into this hell, a dark well engulfed with poisonous fumes and smoke that suffocates them.

Paryavartana (returning): A householder who welcomes guests with cruel glances and abuses them is restrained in this hell. Hard-eyed vultures, herons, crows and similar birds gaze on them and suddenly fly and pluck their eyes.

Sucimukha (needle-face): An ever-suspicious man is always wary of people trying to grab his wealth. Proud of his money, he sins to gain and to retain it. Yamadutas stitch thread through his whole body in this hell.

Though the Vishnu Purana mentions 28 hells, it gives information only about sinners condemned in 21 hells and does not give details about the punishments. The hells described in the Vishnu Purana, but not in the Bhagavata Purana and the Devi Bhagavata Purana are as follows:

Rodha (obstruction): A causer of abortion, a murderer of a cow, a plunderer or one who strangles a man is cast here.

Sukara (hog): A murderer of a Brahmin, a stealer of gold or an alcoholic and those all associated with them fall into this hell.

Tala (padlock): Murder of a Kshatriya or a Vaishya and adultery with wife of a religious leader leads here.

Taptakumbha (hot pots): Incest with sister and murderer of an ambassador results in torment in this hell.

Taptaloha (hot iron): A wife-seller, a jailer and one who abandons his followers is tortured here.

Mahajwala (great-fire): Incest with daughter or daughter-in-law brings one here.

Lavana (salt): One who vilifies his guru, people superior to them or the Vedas go to this hell.

Vimohana (the place of bewildering): A thief or those who despise prescribed observances are tormented here.

Krimisha (hell of insects): One who uses magic to harm others is condemned here. Vedhaka (piercing): The maker of arrows is damned to this hell.

Adhomukha (head-inverted): He who takes bribes, an astrologer and he who worships improper objects is cast here.

Púyaváha (where matter falls): A Brahmin who sells meat, alcohol, salt; he who commits violence and he who eats sweets without sharing falls in this hell.

Rudhirándha (wells of blood): Wrestlers or boxers who commit violence for entertainment, fishermen, followers of bastards, arsonists, poisoners, informants, fortune-tellers, traitors, those who have coitus on sacred taboo days and those who live off their wives' prostitution are cast here.

Krishna (dark/black): A fraudster, a trespasser and one who causes impotence is cast into this hell. Vahnijwala (fiery flame): Potters, hunters and shepherds are punished here.

Shwabhojana (food of dogs): A religious student who sleeps in the day and one who does not have spiritual knowledge and learns it from children are damned here.

Some of these condemnations are ludicrous—take the last one, Shwabhojana as a single example. It doesn't make any logical sense. In the other cases—I am of course against any kind of evil that a person puts upon another, but it really makes you wonder who is the most evil—the perpetrator who died, or the Master (Yama) who is supposed to judge them.

The purpose of the Heavens and the Underworld – In the ultimate sense, the purpose of after life is neither to punish nor reward the Souls, but to remind them of the true purpose of their existence. In the final analysis, the difference between heaven and hell is immaterial because both are part of the great illusion that characterizes the whole creation. The difference is very much like the difference between a good dream and a bad dream. It should not matter to the Soul whether the Soul has gone to a heaven or to some hell, because the soul is eternally pure and not subject to pain and suffering. It is the residual of the Living Being, that part which leaves the body and is directed to one of the Realms after death. If one is directed to the Lower Realms, the Soul is subject to the process of learning through pain. Once its learning is accomplished and the effects of its previous karma are exhausted it returns to the Earth to continue its existence or, if directed to the Upper Realms, may remain to become one with BRAHMAN /Creator God.

A Living Soul which goes to heaven, will enjoy the pleasures of heaven and in the end realizes that seeking heavenly pleasures may not the ultimate goal since, however intense these pleasures may be – I suppose the term "up or our" may be the byword.

A soul which falls into the darker world gets a taste of the horror of the evil it tried to promote on Earth, with a multiplier effect and with an intensity and severity that would make it realize the horrors of evil.

In either case, the purpose of heavens and hells is to impart an attitude of wisdom and detachment to the Souls. However, how far these lessons will leave their imprint upon the Souls and mold their future lives, we do not know because once they return to the Earthly Realm, because of the power of maya, they may forget much of what they have learned or unlearned and revert to their old ways. Hence the need for many lives and learning and re-learning the same lessons, untill they become an integral part of a Living Being's samskara (education).

Sources
1. "Death and Afterlife in Hinduis," Jayaram V, Hinduwebsite.com, https://www.hinduwebsite.com/hinduism/h_death.asp
2. "Commentary on the Bhagavadgita," Discourse 26: The Eighth Chapter Concludes – The Journey of the Soul After Death, Swami Krishnananda, The Devine Life Society, https://www.swami-krishnananda.org/bgita/bgita_26.html
3. "Wes Penre Papers," The Fifth Level of Learning, Part 1 and Part 2, The Vedic Texts, Feb 27, 2015, https://wespenrepapershome.files.wordpress.com/2019/07/fifthleveloflearning part1.pdf

PART 6 - HISTORY OF HOW WE GOT HERE & WHY
(Galactic History, Living Library, DNA Manipulation, Electromagnetic Frequencies, Earth Frequency Rising)

Article 41

THE GALACTIC WARS +

"Know the past to understand the present" – Dr. Carl Sagan (1980)

The past and the future are actually not so different. Every past event has a cause or causes that, as we look back at them, typically make sense to us from our vantage point in the present. Likewise, each past event has implications and influences the events that follow it. It can be a very linear sequence that, again, makes sense to us when we look back at them. To me, the future works in the exact same way. The difference, of course, is we don't know what will happen in the future. Instead, we have a wide range of possible futures. But, just as with a singular event in the past, the events happening today will shape the ultimate future.

MAIN CHARACTERS DISPLAYED IN THIS TAPESTRY FROM THE PERSPECTIVE OF EARTH:

LYRA– The general area of the "birth" of the humanoid race. All humanoid races in our galactic family have genetic roots connected to Lyra. It is the symbolic harp upon which the song of humanity is played. Humanoid races originated as fragments of the Feline Primary Race that passed through the Prism of Lyra and were given the mantra of "Service-to-Others" (STO).

- **FELINES (STO) –** One of the four (4) Primary Galactic Races created by Creator God to inhabit the Lamikiakea Super Cluster (the Universe that contains the Milky Way, which contains Earth). The Felines were sent to this Universe by the Founding Fathers (via Creator God). Like all Primary Races, they were etheric in form and, therefore, went through the stages of evolving a physical body by adapting to the local environment (common to their planet) and evolved as lions and other felines. With DNA modification, a Feline specialty, they took on a more human appearance.

- **Humanoids–** After numerous crossings and genetic upgrades that would create a Soul, the Felines created a new species that would be known as the Humans.

  The Feline Humanoids were given the creation myth of "Service to Others" which clashed with the creation myth of the Draconian Reptilians.

They continued to evolve and eventually developed the technology for space travel and then warp and hyper-warp technology.

VEGA– A star within the constellation of Lyra. Descendants of Vegans are the Lyran refugees from the Lyran Wars. They are in contact with the Dal universe and are being assisted by them; Vega birthed a race of beings that **manifested Lyra's opposite polarity** both in their beliefs and actions. There were frequent conflicts between the Lyran and Vegan races. The Vegans helped to colonize star systems such as Altair, Centauri, Sirius, and Orion, among others.

SIRIUS– A urinary star group, it is known in Earth mythology as *the Dog Star*. Sirius was one of the first areas to be colonized by beings from the Lyran star group. Sirius embodied the energy of the triadic template and perpetuated the drive toward integration. There is a large variety of consciousness types that incarnated in this system.

ORION– This is the main "battleground" for the challenge of polarity integration, seeded from Sirius as well as Lyra and Vega. There is a direct connection with Earth, as explored in a later Article.

- **CARRIONS** (Carians - the Bird people)– One of the four (4) Primary Galactic Races created by Creator God to inhabit the Lamikiakea Super Cluster (the Universe that contains the Milky Way, which contains Earth). The Carrions were sent to this Universe by the Founding Fathers (via Creator God). Like all Primary Races, they were etheric in form and, therefore, went through the stages of evolving a physical body and adapted a local species (common to their planet) and evolved as bird like bipedal beings since their planet was more tropical in design and featured an abundance of humid swamps and jungles. Over a period of hundreds of thousands of years, they developed bodies of varying colors and sizes, yet somewhat humanoid in appearance.

  When their bodies reached a certain level of development, they began genetic crossings (something they learned from the Felines) with certain reptiles that evolved in the swamps and warmer regions of the planet; these became known as Reptilians.

- **DRACONIANS** – The result of the Carrion genetic program was the creation of a new hybrid race known as the Draconians – part Carrion and part reptile.

  As they continued to evolve, they eventually developed the technology for space travel and then warp and trans-warp technology.

  The Draconian Reptilians and their derivatives were given the creation myth of "Service to Self" which clashed with the creation myth of the Humanoids. This creation myth has been the source of many conflicts between the Reptilians and the Humanoids throughout the Densities.

  - **Flying Serpents (snakes) and Lizard** like beings were their first derivative.
  - **Anunnaki Reptilians** were/are a creation of the Carrions, their parent race. The Anunnaki were a species within the Lyra star system that traveled to Orion.
  - Tiamat, the Dragon Queen of the Orion Empire, during the 2nd Galactic War, overthrew the King. She was beloved by her subjects. As part of the Peace Treaties ending the 2nd Galactic War (the Sirian Solution, which eventually failed) and then at the end of the 3rd Galactic War, Tiamat was given governorship of our local galaxy system, along with her own system of Orion.

- **PLEIADES–** Colonized by Lyran offshoots; this group is Earth's main genetic connection from extraterrestrial sources. The Lyrans claim The Pleiadian technology surpasses Earth technology by 3000 solar years. Their colonization approach was to explore each planet and, based upon its unique nature, they developed each colony to coexist with the life forms on each planet. In this way they have been visiting Earth for at least10 million solar years (and again 800,000 solar years ago).

- **ARCTURUS–** An archetype or future-self ideal of Earth; possibly due to first arriving on Earth and then relocating to Arcturius, where they developed at a quicker pace than their compatriots on Earth – thus, they may have been like Earth humanoids then but have no comparison, today. Arcturius assists in healing personal and planetary consciousness. Its vibration, primarily Sixth Density, has been attributed to the angelic kingdom.

- **ZETA RETICULI** (the Greys) – This civilization is intimately connected with Earth. They are very scientific and share more of a group mind. They are mentally developed to a fault but their emotional sensitivity is not as developed. They come from a planet called the Apex planet in the Lyra system. Their spiritual growth did not match their technology development which finally led to a planetary cataclysm.

The Negative Zeta Reticuli are the more power hungry and are the primary group instigating abductions (or more accurately called "temporary detainments" since this group always returns the abductees, so it is said). Part of their abductions is their generations of cloning use the same genetic material that caused their evolutionary growth to become much imbrued and stagnate. The Zata Reticuli are also creating a hybrid race of both humans and Zeta origin.

- **COUNCIL OF 5** (thought to consist of the Grays and other Orion beings) – In 1953, Astronomers discovered large objects in space which were moving toward the Earth. Project Sigma intercepted alien radio communications. When the objects reached the Earth they took up a very high orbit around the Equator. There were several huge ships, and their actual intent was unknown. Project Sigma, and a new project, Plato, through radio communications using the computer binary language, was able to arrange a landing that resulted in face to face contact with the aliens.

In the meantime a race of human looking aliens (Ed, most likely the Pleiadians) contacted the U.S. Government. This alien group warned us against the aliens that were orbiting the Equator and offered to help us with our spiritual development. They demanded that we dismantle and destroy our nuclear weapons as the major condition. They refused to exchange technology citing that we were spiritually unable to handle the technology which we then possessed. They believed that we would use any new technology to destroy each other. This race stated that we were on a path of self destruction and we must stop killing each other, stop polluting the Earth, stop raping the Earth's natural resources, and learn to live in harmony. These terms were met with extreme suspicion, especially the major condition of nuclear disarmament. It was believed that meeting that condition would leave us helpless in the face of an obvious alien threat. We also had nothing in history to help with the decision. Nuclear disarmament was not considered to be within the best interest of the United States. The overtures were rejected.

Later in 1954 the race of large nosed Gray Aliens which had been orbiting the Earth landed at Holloman Air Force Base. A basic agreement was reached. This race identified themselves as originating from a Planet around a red star in the Constellation of Orion which we called Betelgeuse. This was alleged as the 'First Contact' meeting with extraterrestrials at Edwards Air Force base (previously Muroc Airfield), and the beginning of a series of meetings with different extraterrestrial races that led to a 'treaty' that was eventually signed.

The treaty stated that the aliens would not interfere in our affairs and we would not interfere in theirs. We would keep their presence on Earth a se-ret. They would furnish us with advanced technology and would help us in our technological development. They would not make any treaty with any other Earth nation. They could abduct humans on a limited and periodic basis for the purpose of medical examination and monitoring of our development, with the stipulation that the humans would not be harmed, would be returned to their point of abduction, would have no memory of the event, and that the alien nation would furnish **Majesty Twelve** (MJ12) with a list of all human contacts and abductees on a regularly scheduled basis.

Col. Phillip Corso, a highly decorated officer that served in Eisenhower's National Security Council, alluded to a treaty signed by the Eisenhower administration with extraterrestrials in his memoirs. He wrote: "We had negotiated a kind of surrender with them [extraterrestrials] as long as we couldn't fight them. They dictated the term because they knew what we most feared was disclosure." Corso's claim of a 'negotiated surrender' suggests that some sort of agreement or 'treaty' was reached that he was not happy with.

By 1955 it became obvious that the aliens had deceived Eisenhower and had broken the treaty. **Even with the Treaty broken, the Aliens (Council of Five) are still orchestrating the actions of the U.S. Government, its Agencies, and its Institutions.**

- **THE PRISM OF LYRA–** The term used to describe how Prime Source (Creator God), through the Founders, split the light code into fragments (sparks, rays) creating Densities and polarities (spectrums) to explore, including Feminine/Masculine integration and separation. This occurred on Lyra 100s of thousands years ago.

BRIEF HISTORY PRIOR TO THE GALACTIC WARS – This presentation revolves around star races that are approximately 700 light years from Earth and, primarily, within the Milky Way Galaxy (10,000 – 150,000 galaxies). The Milky Way is within a Local Group, within Vega-Ceti Supercluster, all within the Lanakea Super Cluster (200-400 billion galaxies).

- 20 Billion Years ago our universe began as a point of light (in the mind of Creator God).
- 14 Billion Years ago the point of light began to expand.
- 14–12 Billion Years ago minerals and gases formed into nebula configurations.
- 12 Billion years ago the first stars appeared.
- The universe evolves with plants and animals long before Earth was formed:
  - 12–10 Billion years ago The Building Blocks of Life planets.
  - 10.4 Billion Years ago plants.

- 4.5 Billion Years ago Earth.
- 4.1 Billion years ago Animals (except Earth).
- 1 Billion year ago, Consciousness (Founders') from Prime Source (Creator God) enter the Milky Way Galaxy through a White Hole near Lyra as 12th Density awareness. The Founders created "light packets" of conscious energy to explore 12th to 9th Densities. The Founders helped to develop 4 Primary Races (Feline, Carrion, Reptilian, Humanoid) to explore the galaxy through sensory inputs.

Prime Source (Creator God) split the light code into fragments (sparks, rays) creating Densities and polarities (spectrums) to explore, including Feminine/Masculine integration and separation.

- 100s of Millions years ago, the Founders fragmented into individualized 7th Density consciousness to fully explore this part of the galaxy. The 7th Density "DNA keys" became "DNA molecules" which enabled the "incarnation" of consciousness as inhabitants of the 7th–5th Density evolving worlds. 7th Density is the first level of individual Souls.
  12th Density – Light
  11th Density – Light packets
  10th Density – Light packets
  9th Density – Light Codes
  8th Density – DNA Keys
  7th Density – DNA Molecules

As the individualized consciousness lowered in frequency they moved into 4th and then 3rd Densities – living in physical beings on chosen planets.

All humanoids races (except Mankind) have their genetic roots in Lyra where the Founders ethereally (energetically) manipulated Primate/ Feline/Lyran DNA to create humanoids that could sustain 3rd Density consciousness without forgetting Prime Source (Creator God). Incarnation into 3rd Density bodies became so all-consuming that awareness of Primary Source was lost or clouded in mythology.

Some non-physical Lyran beings went to Sirius which operated at 4th and higher Densities. They slowly lowered to a 3rd Density physical existence. Sirians became skilled genetic and etheric engineers of DNA. Two Sirian cultures developed:
- One group believed in "Service-to--Others" (STO) for the good of all by each serving another.
- The other believed in "Service-to-Self" (STS) for the good of all by each serving themselves.

Over time the Vegan groups developed:

- Humanoid–Reptilian mammals.
- Reptilian mammals.

Descendants of Lyra populated Vega that developed a culture that was opposite polarity of the Lyrans. Conflict began and quickly spread.

As star races developed technology for weapons and interstellar travel, there were cycles of expansion, alliances and conflict over millions of years.

- Density of Life forms changed over time:
  - 100 million years ago – 7th Density
  - 70 million years ago – 6th Density
  - 60 Million years ago – 5th Density
  - 50 Million years ago – 4th Density
  - 30 Million years ago – 3rd Density

THE 1st GALACTIC WAR

- **Tensions developed between the two Sirian groups [ex–Vegan (STS) and ex–Lyran (STO)] which spread across the Sirius star system and beyond.**
- The Elders of Sirius intervened and moved the conflicting Sirian groups to Orion – 700 light years away.
- As the civilizations became more polarized, several groups from Lyra and Vega looked for new planets with less conflict. They chose our solar system as part of the Lyran migration.
- Earth Primate DNA was combined with Lyran DNA to improve adaption to Earth.
- Earth-Lyrans wanting to escape growing conflicts on Earth founded a new star system in the Pleiades to create a culture of peace, harmony, and unconditional love. Earth-Lyran DNA was taken to the Pleiades.
- Other of Lyran descent wanting to escape conflict also moved to the Pleiades where a community–based conflict–free culture developed over generations.
- The Pleiadians became so focused on peace; they denied all conflict to the point where life lacked challenge and learning. Pleiadian culture isolated itself from the rest of the galaxy.
- Vegans (Reptilian mammals) generally stayed in Earth orbit during this period. Vegans colonized Mars and Maldek (now the asteroid belt) before Earth. The Reptilians didn't stay on Earth very long, migrating to Orion system or back to abandoned home worlds in Lyra.
- A project began to establish the humanoid form on Earth. Small groups of humanoids began incarnating on Earth in specially created primate forms. Early humanoids were 7th Density highly telepathic beings.

The 2ⁿᵈ GALACTIC WAR - Lead Up to The Orion Wars (20 Million years ago)

- **60,000 Million years ago**, The Orion King realized that in the distant past, females had been even better warriors than the males, so the King started another galactic war in an effort to expand his Empire. He decided to bring the females into the war, to fight side by side with the males. The females were not only incredible warriors, who never backed off, always fighting to the bitter end, if necessary; they also had a deadly weapon that the males didn't have - their venom! The Queen overthrew the King and the females had the power over the Empire.
- Toward the end of the Reptile mammal period on Earth, there was a great space battle between the Reptilians and Lyra. The Lyrans won. Maldek, Mars and Earth became Lyran Property.
- Vegans moved into the Orion system where they developed their spirituality. Vegan mystic practices helped them to remember their connection to Source.
- A new group of Lyrans came to Earth bringing old conflicts and a new genetic agenda. Lyran DNA was combined with primate DNA to improve Earth hominoids.
- Individual consciousness (Souls) within life forms (bodies) of decreasing Density began visiting Earth.
- As the Orion Empire expanded and polarized into controlling dominators and selfless victims. The Orion Empire became technologically advanced while in deep spiritual conflict.
- Non-physical beings in Arcturius and Sirius specialized in emotional healing and physical healing respectively. The holistic healing dynamics for body-mind-spirit was (and still is) used on many planets.
- **20 Million Years Ago,**
  - Numerous conflicts became the **Orion Wars** which lasted for eons. The war was initially over territory, but it became a war of mind-sets and ideologies.
  - The war started in as a misunderstanding in which the Draco/ Reptilians (whose STS belief was take what every you want since it is yours by right) wanted one of the planets within the Lyran Star System, which the Lyrans said they would think about it and the Draco/Reptilians took that response as a "no" and then destroyed three Lyran planets, killing 50 million Lyrans. The Lyrans swore revenge.
  - A resistance group formed to liberate the victims - that force was the Lyran United Federation of Colonies (later called the Lyran United Federation of Planets). The Rebel Alliance consisting of human and hybrid races that had been subjugated at the hands of the Draco, and therefore rejected the ideas of colonization and intervention in other worlds. But force was met with force by the Draco/Reptilians (known as the Empire), resulting in stalemate.

- When the Pleiadians heard about the Orion Wars and the plight of the Lyran descendants, they felt the urge to help. The Pleiadians felt alive again and zealously attack Orion negativity in many ways. The Orion Empire struck back and destroyed a populated Pleiadian planet. The destruction of the Pleiadian planet impacted the consciousness of many across the galaxy. The Pleiadians withdrew from the conflict.

- This war lasted literally millions of years and while there were truces and times of greater peace, the general trend was one of conflict and countless generations grew up with war, desperation and strife as the norm.

- **12 Million Years Ago-** The Founders decided to assist. The Sirians didn't really want to get involved, but tensions were rising. In order to find peace, a group in Sirius came up with a creative plan for conflict resolution. Inspired by the idea of an alchemical union of opposites, they suggested to the Empire and the Federation a marriage between royal lineages to create a common ruling dynasty, mixing the genetics of humanoid members of the Orion Royalty (reptilian/human hybrids) with high ranking members of the Federation (pure human) and a new royal race was created — the muscular, dark-skinned, warrior-like humanoids that we know in our history as the Anunnaki (who were, incidentally the "Gods" of Ancient Samaria, Greece, Rome and the Old Testament). Their offspring (A Founder "fragment") became the **Orion Christ. It was the goal for this child** to remind people they were connected to Prime Source – this was called the Sirian Solution.

The Sirian Solution did, initially bring about a peace between the warring parties. The "union" between opposites was partially successful and as a "token" of peace, Tiamat, Queen of the Orion Empire, was given governorship of our local galaxy along with her own system of Orion.

Unfortunately, the "marriage" and subsequent new royal lineage didn't have the result that the Sirians had hoped for. Because of their different heritages they were a race divided amongst themselves almost from the start, and it would prove difficult for the Anunnaki to unite as one family, or to hold to one set of principles.

Also, many people (species of aliens) refused to pledge their allegiance to the new dynasty, because they disagreed with any genetic manipulation that included Reptilian DNA. But this union did create a peace that lasted for a few hundred thousand years, with the Anunnaki ruling, before warfare once again exploded throughout the Galaxy.

- "Victims" gradually became empowered in their personal sovereignty and the Empire slowly lost its power. Over time peace was established across most of the Empire.

THE 3RD GALACTIC WAR - - Lead Up to and End of the Galactic Wars.

- Many star systems formed alliances for governance, expansion, protection, trade and cultural/scientific exchange. Neighboring star races formed councils and joined federations which grew over time – both the Galactic Federation and the Orion–Draconian Empire (Alliance).
- The Galactic Federation was formed:
  - Lyra/Orion – Founding members 7.5 Million years ago
  - Sirius-B –   4.3 Million years ago
  - Andromeda – 3.5 Million years ago
  - Centaurs B –   1.1 Million years ago
  - Aldebran –   800,000 years ago
  - Pleiades –   300,000 years ago
  - Mintaka –   1996
  - Draconia –   1998
  - Earth – Under review (but not likely due to their warring nature)

- **Millions of years ago** – With all the back and forth battles and worlds changing possession every other century, another faction emerged that was fed up with both sides — The Rebels, who were based in the Sirius System.

  Neither the Federation nor the Empire dared launch a large-scale attack on these Rebels, fearing that if they did so the Rebels would team up with the other side and that joining of forces would create an unbeatable enemy.

  Even though a lot of people were sympathetic to their desire to end the war, the Rebels didn't succeed in making any major breakthroughs in negotiations with either the Federation or the Empire and it looked like yet another stalemate had been reached, only this time there were three parties involved instead of two.

- Pleiadians came to the land of "Pan" (ex Pangaea) on Earth where there were many exotic creatures such as the unicorn and winged horse (Pegasus). The Pleiadians experimented with exotic genetic manipulation and cross-species breading in 3rd and 4th Densities. The rich diversity of life on Earth attracted attention from across the galaxy. Alien life was brought to Earth and the humanoid form was taken to over 100 star systems. Advanced genetics and research was taught to many alien species and they took this knowledge back to their star systems.

- 7th Density beings incarnated into poorly designed mixed species with convoluted mental processes lost their Soul until death.

- **9 Million Years ago** the First Great Flood on Earth wiped out 40% or so of all animal species in Pangaea. Species DNA were saved in Pleiadian laboratories.

- **7.5 Million Years ago** the Second Great Flood destroys most animal species in Pangaea. Species DNA was again saved in Pleiadian laboratories.

- **3.1 Million Years ago** Orion and Draconian (Reptilians) explorers visited and incarnated on Mars and Maldek for mining and conquest. The Orion and Draconians interbred with the existing species on Mars and Maldek.

- **Approx. 3.1 Million Years ago** Maldekian civilization developed into warring factions that discovered neutron technology. Nuclear conflicts escalated and eventually shattered the planet creating the asteroid belt. Most of the 10 million souls perished on Maldek, with the survivors later incarnated on Mars.

- **3 Million Years ago** a new project to upgrade humanoids on Earth was initiated by the Founders, Lyrans and Sirians, and a group of Pleiadians who liked Earth agreed to help. Pleiadian DNA (some originating on Earth) was used with Earth DNA (which had since evolved) to create a new species of human. Sirian DNA was also involved.

- **1.4 Million Years ago** 100 million beings from several star systems lived in large cities on the surface of Mars. Again, conflicts escalated into atomic war which destroyed the fragile ecosystem. 10% survived in underground cities.

- **Last 1 Million Years** – For many thousands of years Pleiadians visited most primitive Earth cultures leaving a lasting impact. Several other civilizations still used Earth as a DNA laboratory for their own agenda.

Arcturians 6th Density non-physical beings provided ongoing assistance to Earth through channeling or by appearing as light bodies. Human DNA was occasionally "adjusted", as well as evolving naturally.

Arcturians emotional healing was often used in partnership with Sirian physical healing. Their healing practices became embedded in ancient Earth holistic healing disciplines. Human DNA was adjusted energetically to prepare for ascension to 4th and 5th Densities.

- **800,000 years ago** 500,000 colonists arrived on a very large ship from the Pleiades. The ship was intercepted and destroyed above the Earth in violation of Treaty. The Pleiadian ship exploded in space and melted debris fell on Earth in what is now Australia. Several years later rescue craft arrived from the Pleiades with Feline military escort confronted the aliens who broke the Treaty.

- **Approx 500,000 year ago.** It was Merlin who brokered the Peace Treaty that ended the 3rd Galactic War. The Merlin "solution" was more permanent than the Sirian Treaty which ended the 2nd Galactic War and as concession, the Treaty reconfirmed Orion Empire's governance over the Virgo Supercluster which contains our Local Galaxy Group (which contains the Milky Way). This concession was, in part, for the Orion Empire to become the "protectors" of the Living Library on Earth – what a ruse and coup by the Orion Empire politicians.

  Tiamat, Queen of the Orion Empire, was once again declared to have governorship of our local galaxy along with her own system of Orion.

  Tiamat traveled to Earth to help seed life and created a giant, androgynous, humanoid race, the Namlu'u, to act as guardians of the Living Library on Earth. The Namlu'u were the race that the Greeks called the Titans. The giants that were the "parents" of the "gods" — meaning a race of 50–60 foot tall humanoids that existed here before the Annunaki arrived. In Hebrew the word for giants is "Anakim".

- **Approx 500,000 year ago** a group of 7th-9th Density beings came to assist 4th Density Earth beings in conflict. However philosophical differences within the former group sparked a 1,000 year conflict above the Earth. Around that same time there was a large influx of Orion Reptilians and Earth population reached 1 billion.

END OF THE 3RD GALACTIC WAR – Warring star systems connected with Earth's history signed a peace treaty between themselves – this was the **Merlin Solution**, when Merlin was the mediator. The Merlin Treaty was **signed approximately 500,000 years ago.**

Today we know Merlin as the counselor, or magician in the court of King Arthur. However, the original Merlin, or at least the Merlin archetype, made his first appearance during the Orion wars. Within the ranks of the Rebels, he grew up as a young boy with remarkable talents, capable of manipulating the 3rd Density by operating in the 5th Density, in other words, capable of "magic" or "miracles".

By helping the warring parties to transcend and value their differences, peace agreements between parties were reached, and with this peace and change of mindset came a dramatic increase in awareness and a rising of consciousness for the whole Milky Way. Over the next hundreds of thousands of years entire masses of people would ascend into higher Realms (Realities).

- It was during this time of peace throughout the Universe that someone had the bright idea to create a system of "Living Libraries" — planets that contain flora and fauna from hundreds of other worlds, as well as on Earth, there was a humanoid races which contained nearly all of the DNA of the races throughout the universe (due to many cycles of DNA manipulation) — to act as a kind of storehouse for genetic material.

  Our planet, which was already quite diverse, was one of the 12 planets in our Galaxy selected to act as Living Libraries and many races journeyed here from all over to seed different plant and animal species - octopus, mushrooms, orchids, etc. Many of them stayed for a while, delighting in the rich lushness of the Earth, and some are still around.

  This Merlin "solution" was more permanent than the Sirian Treaty which ended the 2nd Galactic War and the concession of reaffirming the Orion Empire's governance over the Virgo Supercluster which contains our Local Galaxy Group (which contains the Milky Way was done in order for the Orion Empire to become the "protectors" of the Living Library on Earth - what a ruse and coup by the Orion Empire politicians.

  The Orion Empire transformed into a true matriarchy with Tiamat, the Dragon Queen, as its "benevolent ruler" (Ed, "benevolence" for her own people - the Dracos-Reptilians). . However, there remained a faction of 13 human/reptilian hybrid families within the Orion Royalty who still believed in a "might-is-right" and service-to-self mindset. These are the ancient roots of our present day Cabal — the 13 Royal Bloodlines, the Dark Men from Orion. The 13 Bloodlines were banished from their system (Orion Empire), an action that would come back to haunt the civilizations of Maldek, Mars and eventually, Earth.

  The 13 Royal Bloodlines were jealous of this ruling and they decided to travel to our system to see if they could perhaps gain a toehold from which to eventually take over the resource-rich planets here which they coveted. They settled on Mars but didn't exactly receive a warm welcome from the Pleiadian civilizations which existed there. The existing civilizations tried to make room for the dark-minded newcomers, believing everyone deserved a chance, but before too long even these benevolent and fair-minded people could no longer tolerate the vibration of the Dark Men from Orion. Infighting led to Nuclear War, destroying the atmosphere that surrounded Mars. The 13 Royal Bloodlines relocated to Earth.

- **Approx 400,000 years ago,** Orion Reptilians became the dominate force on Earth through interbreeding thus reducing the influence of the Pleiadians on Earth culture.

- **From 500,000 - 200,000 year ago** a few beings regained 4th Density. Most had dropped to 3rd Density during the 100,000 year war.

- **300,000 years ago** a pole shift triggered catastrophic Earth changes. 50% of Earth's 1 billion humanoid population perished. After the cataclysmic changes a large landmass called Lemuria (Mu) formed in the Pacific Ocean. The energy of Lemuria attracted peaceful beings from the Pleiades, Sirius, and Orion. 50% of Earth's population lived in Lemuria.**100,000 years ago** cataclysms affected most of the land of Lemuria. Most of Lemurians lived in large cities on the coasts. Their culture was right brain dominated and matriarchal.

- **75,000 years ago** Earth passed through the tail of the Photon Belt which dramatically cooled tropical Lemuria killing many people. A new civilization was developing in Atlantis in the Atlantic Ocean.

- **50,000 year ago** cataclysms caused large areas of western Limeira to sink while Atlantis largely survived. Sumerian survivors moved to Australia, Indonesia and India.

- **40,000 years ago** The Atlantean civilization became technologically advanced. They invented a single energy generator based on crystals that powered their civilization. A group of Atlanteans traded the crystal technology for Orion (Reptilian) military and propulsion systems. Atlanteans were a mix of Pleiadian, Orion and Draco genetics and culture.

- **Approx 30,000 years ago** Atlanteans attempted to use their crystal energy source for military purposes. Miscalculations resulted in a catastrophic explosion that destroyed much of Atlantis and the remainder of Limeira.

  Massive tsunamis killed millions of people around the planet. A few thousand Atlanteans escaped in airships and landed in Central and South America.

- **Approx 12,000 years ago** Atlanteans accidently caused the final sinking of the last remnant of Atlantis while attempting to rebuild the crystal power generator.

- **Approx 7500 years ago** Sirius with technology psychic ability and inflated egos arrived and became the gods and gurus of the ancient world. They were joined by Orion and Dracos (Anunnaki) who were interested in enslaving Earth populations. Interbreeding resulted in humanoid DNA degradation.

- **Approx 4,000 years ago** More Sirians arrived to become gods, priests, and pharaohs in Egypt. They also reincarnated as sheppards, stonemasons or sailors to influence culture in less dramatic ways.

- **Approx 1,000 years ago** – Sirians withdrew from influencing Earth's culture and political affairs during the Middle Ages. This influence was

- largely positive by "Service-to-Others" Sirians in Religions and Mystery Schools although occasionally "Service-to-Self" Sirians infiltrated these organizations.

- **Approx Earth time: 1930 – mid-1940** World War II Germany. The Nordics are blond looking humanoids from Orion and are also of a predictorial and warring nature, This species is responsible for spreading Religious Violence, racism, Misogyny, genetic discrimination, genetic experimentation within the Nazi ideology and they are proponents of their belief system of "genetic superiority" through spiritually abusive methods of Eugenics. This Nordic group was directly involved with supporting Hitler's Germany and World War II, by providing military technology, and mind control technology to the SS in the meetings in the Black forest and the Himalayas. They are interested in procuring Earth based artifacts from the Essenes, Christos Templars or Guardian Host races, and supported Hitler's henchmen like Himmler, to organize archaeological digs, maraud other countries while searching for Ark tools and Atlantean artifacts, and threaten monasteries and monk-priest class humans to hand over religious or other sacred and valuable objects to be used in rituals for controlling subtle forces on the Earth.

- **Approx Earth time: 1940,** Two different groups from the Zeta system (Greys) came to Earth – largely during the 1940's when Earth developed atomic weapons. Zetas from Zeta Reticuli were originally from the planet Apex in Lyra, which they destroyed with pollution and warfare. They survived by going underground. Human DNA and hybrid breeding (involving "abduction") occurred to save the Zata race from extension.

- **Approx Earth time: 1945.** Some Andromedans have helped to prevent nuclear disaster on Earth several times since 1945, although they have been visiting for thousands of years via a wormhole/stargate/portal from the Andromeda Galaxy to Antares. Antares is home to high Density beings and a gateway to other galaxies.

- **Approx Earth time: 1945.**The Galactic Federation was approved to stop humanity from destroying itself. Steps were taken to prevent disaster caused by nuclear testing, nuclear accidents, rogue use of WMD, and the triggering of cataclysmic earthquakes and volcanoes.

- **Earth time: 1953-1954:** Eisenhower Treaty with Extraterrestrials (Council of 5) – Both the Pleiadians and the Zeta forced meetings with President Eisenhower. The Pleiadians warned against meeting with the aliens that were orbiting the Equator and offered to help with our spiritual development. They demanded dismantling and destroy nuclear weapons, stop polluting the Earth, stop raping the Earth's natural resources, and learn to live in harmony. The U.S. Government refused the terms and the Pleiadians left. The Government negotiated with the Zetas a kind of surrender since the United States didn't have the technology to fight them. The Zeta's dictated the terms by offering technology (weapon) in exchange for various concessions, including human DNA experimentation. Majestic 12 (MJ12) was formed to monitor and control Media attention. The Treaty stipulated that the Zeta presence not be revealed to the public. Although both sides broke the Treaty, **the Aliens (Council of Five – STS Dark Force) are still orchestrating the actions of the U.S. Government, its Agencies, and it's Institutions.**

- **Approx Earth time: Mid-1990s**
  - Many ETs (both STO and STS) decide to work less physically with humans choosing to assist instead through subconscious (dreams, institutions) telepathic communications (channels, psychic) or reincarnation. Remember not all is from benevolent beings – each still has their own agendas.

  - A new Galactic Treaty begins that results in star races originally opposed to the Galactic Federation transforming societies, and in many cases joining the Federation. And, those star races that made self-serving deals with secret Earth organizations, such as the Earth contingent of the Draco/Reptilians remain as a "hold-out" continuing to dominate and control Mankind through the Council of 5 and the Cabals (the 13 original families from Orion).

- **Approx Earth time: 1995** – The Zetas, who came to Earth due to their civilization dying and needed DNA to restart, successfully completed their DNA and hybridization programs conducted largely from 1945-1995, thus the Zata are saved from extension.

- **Approx Earth time: 2000s** – A few STO ("Service-to-Self"-namely, Dracos/Reptilians) ET's still con governments to do their bidding. This deception was strengthened when governments continue to deal with the ETs in secrecy. Some organizations are still complicit in this secrecy and deception. Many government leaders believe it is too risky, despite its ability to bring openness, thrust and new allies. As it is revealed, both the STS and the STO will place their "spin" upon what is revealed so as to take credit or to lay blame.

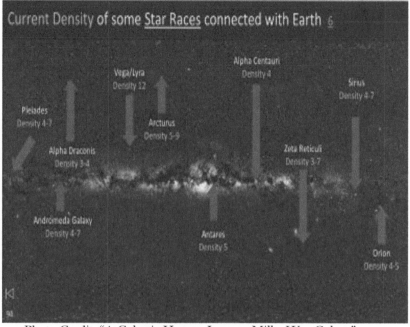

Photo Credit: "A Galactic Human Journey Milky Way Galaxy"

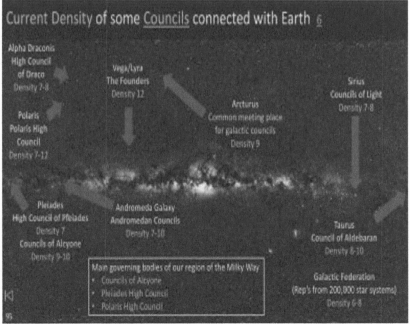

Photo Credit: "A Galactic Human Journey Milky Way Galaxy"

DNA MANIPULATION – Multiple Star Beings have manipulated the Earth Human DNA, over millennia, to adapt the Human to their needs and desires (e.g., bigger, stronger, faster, more brain computing capacity, for control reasons, etc.). The DNA Strand is made up of six smaller molecules And five carbon sugar called **deoxyribose**, a **phosphate** molecule and four different nitrogenous bases (**adenine, thymine, cytosine** and **guanine**).

DNA **is** the body's "computer code" — think of a DNA molecule acting as a digital memory device: just like a USB drive (for example). DNA stores a sequence of binary digits (**bits**, zeros and ones), but instead of a pure **binary code (base 2)**; DNA uses a *quaternary code* (base 4). The bases — T, C, A, and G — represent 0, 1, 2, and 3, respectively, which in binary code is 00, 01, 10, and 11. It "only so happened" that evolution opted for devices other than transistors to do the storing: the *nucleobases.*

The DNA stranded code delivers not only body growth, etc. but also establishes the functions of the chakras, etc. The DNA stranded code even establishes our brain functions and thought processes.

Thus, the various Star Beings, over the past 1000s of years, developed **DNA computing** which uses DNA, biochemistry, and molecular biology hardware, instead of the traditional silicon-based computer technologies. The term "moletronics" has sometimes been used, but this term has already been used for an earlier technology, a then-unsuccessful rival of the first integrated circuits; this term has also been used more generally, for molecular-scale electronic technology.

The first Star Beings to develop DNA Computing was the Felines/Lyrans, who distributed their technology throughout the Universe. It was DNA Computing that the Anunnaki's used to create Mankind. The "program" was called Human 1.0 for the humanoids created prior to the Great Flood that "wiped out" their first creation. Their first creation, using Human 1.0, revolted and it is a myth that the Anunnaki caused the Great Flood to "stop the revolution". After the Great Flood, the Anunnaki revised the "program" (to take out any programming that could lead to revolt) and called the new program Human 2.0; it is Human 2.0 that has extended to today.

Today, the Anunnaki and the other Overloads are creating Transhumans (part machine and part human) and are installing Human 3.0 in this "new" creation. To counter this development (Human 3.0), the STO Star beings are supporting the self-realizing program called Human 3.0 SI (Sovereign Integral); it is stepping out of the constructed universe or reality, and living as a self-expression of I AM WE ARE.

WE ARE PRONE TO WAR AND CONFLICT DUE TO STAR BEING INTERVENTION as attested to within the below table of conflicts. The reader may choose to research these other conflicts on their own.

Historical Timeline Trigger Events

Historical Timeline Trigger Events	Approx. Timeline	Summary Description
Lyran Wars, Orion Wars, Victim-Victimizer Program	20 Million YA	Main Galactic War History of Human Holocaust, Lyran-Elohim overseeing 5D Earth Seeding, Genetic Hatred, Black Hole Entities, the seed of Anti-Christ Conflict.
Electric Wars	5 Million YA	Race War over First Root Race, Wall in Time, Separated from 12 Strand DNA, Need to Collect Fragments in Timelines, 2D/4D Soul Split, Soul Rescue Missions.
Thousand Years War	1 Million YA	War over realities based on the Law of One, Service to Self vs. Service to Others conflicts, First Draco and Annu hybrid root races, and Elohim and Annunaki wars.
Nephilim Wars	75,000 YA	Annunaki Breeding Program, Second Seeding attempt of Nephilim rejected by Elohim, Melchizedek and Annu DNA Fracture, 666 Seal is quarantine in Solar System.
Lemurian Holocaust	52,000 YA	First Major Event of Planet Earth Genocide, Secret Deception of Draconian Invasion via Underground Tunnels, Ice Age and surface climatic destruction.
Atlantian Holocaust	30,000 YA	Nibiru Annunaki Resistance and Patriarchal Melchizedek take over the Inner Earth, Earth Core Power Generator Crystal Grid Explosion, and intentional genocide of Christos Grail lineage.
Luciferian Rebellion and Armageddon Program	26,000 YA	Rebellion reaches apex at end of Atlantian Cataclysm, End of Aeon, Sons of Belial enslave Seraphim, Michael Wars, Enemy Patterning, and Golden Eagle Grid Wars.
Eieyani Massacre, Essene Breeding and Emerald Tablet	22,000 YA	Females taken to Nibiru by Thoth-Annunaki for forced breeding. Thoth stole CDT plate; wrote down Emerald Tablet. Trigger timeline for Hermeticism, esoteric Kabbalah , Mystery Schools and Secret Societies formed to hide ancient knowledge from the common people.
Ascension Timeline Rebellion	22,000 YA	NAA groups negotiate agreements for Earth Territories and Humans for workers, sex or slave colonies. Galactic Trading of Earth Resources. Reptilian ownership of earth humans.
Celtic Massacres/Druid Sacrifices	22,000 YA	NAA genocidal agenda to eradicate Celtic Kings Grail DNA and Melchizedek Christ Teachings from Atlantis, RH Negative Hunting, spread disinformation, destroy records of star origin and artifacts.
Sachon- Thoth Viking Invasion	22,000 YA	Intruder Thoth groups, earliest Vikings attacked Celtic lines to eradicate Atlantian history and eliminate, spread false records about Celts and Druid lineages.
Luciferian Covenant	11,500 YA	The Anti-human and Anti-Krystic agenda for takeover of the planet from NAA, as its controlled by Luciferian forces is called the Luciferian Covenant. Illuminati Lines.
Lunar Outpost, Moon Colony and Sexual Misery Program	11,500 YA	The moon is a craft stolen from war and stripped to be refitted for its use as a Human, Reptilian and Grey Alien base. Transmits Mind Control NETs, Soul trap.
Atlantian Flood	11,500 YA	Takeover and destruction of Giza Stargate, victors of war start re-writing historical records and false timelines, surface flood and holocaust.

Sumerian-Egyptian Invasion	10,000 YA	First stage of takeover of Iran-Iraq 10th Gate, Middle East settlements and organizing Brotherhood of the Snake in from Atlantian timeline in the region. Thoth Group and Phoenix Grid to gain control over Giza Stargate. Tiamat wormhole.
Knight Templar Invasion, Essene Templar Massacre	9,500 YA	Takeover of Celtic Templar lines, NAA attempt to create super-race of Controllers for earth, genetic elitism, lineage of Freemasonry, massacre of those who do not comply. Hidden esoteric knowledge agenda.
Centaurian Wars	8,000 YA	Alpha Centaurian races attempt takeover on Earth from other NAA races, manipulation of Stonehenge and 11D timeline. Unsuccessful hijack.
Mayan Invasion	5,500 YA	Genocidal agenda to eliminate all 12 strand DNA bloodlines from Mayan tribes related to those that had ascended and traveled off planet.
Sumerian/Babylonian Massacre	5,500 YA	DNA unplugging and identity and consciousness memory erasure, confounding DNA language and signals, glandular malfunction, early death.
Djoser Invasion	5,000 YA	Sakkara invasion from 5D wormhole, infiltrate regime, takeover portals, blood sacrifices and use of advanced SRA underground for power.
Dead Sea Wars and Masada Massacre	4,000 YA	War in region to maintain control in Middle East, destruction of many cities in the area. Essene groups tracked down and massacred.
Hyksos King Invasion and Exodus	3,600 YA	Sakkara NAA forces infiltrate Egyptian Pharaoh lines through Thutmose, Hyksos intend takeover of Temple Mount and massacre of Human Tribe 2. Battle for control over Grail tools and Grail Stargate.
Israel and Jerusalem Crusades	3,500 YA	Genocidal campaigns to eliminate all humans with Essene Templar knowledge and Tribe 2 genetics in the landmass of Israel.
Hatshepsut Invasion	3,400 YA	Hatshepsut hides Arc portal technology, protecting portal system from Thutmose Draconian controlled brother, finalizes Hyksos expulsion from Egypt.
Akhenaton Fall and Murder	3,300 YA	Akhenaton despises politics, working for human Law of One Ascension timelines, transits out trapped souls, attempts overthrow of Amun Priest's child and blood sacrifice rituals, 2D underworld portal rips, family murderous plot, character assassination campaign.
Destruction of the Solomon Temple	3,000 YA	Grail Stargate takeover through Arc technology, genocide of Human Tribe 2, Hyksos line attempt takeover through King Solomon, NAA destroys the Temple and holographic grid
Iron Age Christos-Sophia, Jesus Christ Mission	2,000 YA	Sirius B Christos Mission to repair Giza and Stonehenge Stargate, timeline repair gridwork to prepare for the Ascension timeline and reclamation of the Christos Diamond Sun body in 2012 timeline.
Roman and Draconian Invasion	2,000 YA	Draconian infiltrate Greek sacred texts and Italy to build the Church of Rome and spread NAA religious mind control through Catholicism. Retaliation of Christos mission. Collection of Martyr's blood.
Council of Nicea	1,700 YA	NAA and Luciferian Knights Templar cover story to hide the Christos Mission and humanities star origins, False Alien God worship and Blood Sacrifice based religion that became the Canonized Bible.

Saxon Invasion and Arthurian Grail Takeover	1,400 YA	Invasion of UK to take over territory and 11th Stargate, kill Templar Grail King Arthur and his support team, last benevolent Grail King, False King of Tyranny replaces rulership, King Arthur is in Stasis in UK. Related to the Awakening Albion and stasis beings.
Draconian Christian Crusades	1,000 YA	Violent Religious Wars used for human blood sacrifice, soul binding and feeding Crucifixion Implants and Martyrs Blood Alien Machinery in the Earth. Generates Black Heart systems and Anti-Life reversals on the grid.
Cathar Genocidal Massacre	780 YA	Albigensian Crusade carried out by the Church of Rome, Cathars were trapped and burned alive in Southern France. Attempts to eliminate Essene Templar knowledge outside control of the Church.
America Crusades, Native American Holocaust	500 YA	Native American holocaust and America crusades, elimination of indigenous lines that had Templar knowledge of Earth grids. Setting up Secret Societies in USA for Global Control.
Nibiruan Intervention/NRG Implants, Sexual Misery Mind Control	250 YA	NAA and Galactic Federation starts to contact their lineages for channeling and propaganda for preparation of the New Age. Sexual Misery mind control and implants for harvesting human creative sexual energies, alien hybrid breeding programs.
Aleister Crowley, Black Magic Grids, Mainstream Satanism	115 YA	NAA Alien Abductee cooperates with Zeta infiltration of Earth grid networks, sets up Satanic Black Magic, Blood Sacrifice and portals that become Human Energy harvesting networks. Enochian and Thoth-Annunaki Thelema Language, OTO.
Zeta Alien Surveillance, Abduction and Breeding	100 YA	Zeta cooperate with Orion Group for NAA takeover agenda, human enslavement and territorial control.
Black Sun Program World War SRA Agenda, World Wars	100 YA	Poking holes in Earth's protective grid, Orion and Zeta groups orchestrate World Wars to weaken EMF, Nuclear Bombs, and infiltrate Portals by ripping holes in the time-space fabric.
Majestic 12 and Zeta Grey Alien Trade Agreements	85 YA	Zeta contact World Governments for Military Technology and Human Trade, Grey Alien Weaponry, Holographic Inserts and Time Travel Technology.
World War II, Nordics, Human Blood Sacrifice Grids	80 YA	After WW1, sophisticated machinery and implants are inserted into planetary field designed to capture souls and blood sacrifice for NAA during wars/killing. Perpetuate War Economy and World Slavery.
Nazi Infiltration, Psycho-Spiritual Warfare on Global Population, MKUltra	75 YA	Orion Controlled Nazi Groups go underground infiltrate Power Elite and Intelligence Groups, Nordic Alien technology and SRA experiments to mind control the public. Learned Helplessness, Pavlovian Conditioning.

Black Operation, Secret Space Program, Space Colonies and Human Trafficking	75 YA	USA Government splinters off into assorted secret interest groups to research, study and hide alien contact and alien technology from the public. Galactic human slave trade becomes highly organized.
Orion Groups Intervention	40 YA	Orion Groups recruit more Reptilian Races to join with NAA to prepare for the final conflict war over timelines in 2012-2017. Share spoils of war.
Pleiades and Sirian Agreement	30 YA	Galactic Federation makes agreement to support Ascension timeline as front to gain total control over the intended hijack of the New Age Spiritual movement. New Age Channeling increases.
Necromiton Invasion	30 YA	Orion Group recruits Necromiton for NAA control strong-arm on earth, to assist enforcement and compliance in the joint Military Complex Black Op and Secret Space Programs. MIB's.
Seed of Anti-Christ- Sophia, Azazael and Black Lilith	25 YA	Produce anti-hierogamic spawn in Peru Stargate to destroy Genetic Equal and Twin Flame Sacred Unions during the Ascension , and put AI reversals and clones in its place. This is known as the Alien Love Bite.
Edict of War against Starseeds, Indigos and Angelic Human Population	17 YA	NAA groups offer hostage agreement to allow evacuation of selected humans by Lyran-Sirian Guardian Races, before intended Armageddon Destruction Agenda or Pole Shift.
911 Timeline Trigger Event, NWO Agenda for AI False Timeline Propagation	16 YA	NAA draws line in the sand via the 9-11-2001 event to take control over Earth timelines, attempt to circumvent Ascension by dimensional blending, NAA carries out AI Transhumanist Agenda. Starseed Christos Mission Upgrade to repair Ascension timelines.

NO ONE IS COMING TO RESCUE YOU – Earth races are known throughout the universe to be a warring people. The Free Universe is mainly peaceful, predominately free of war (yet it still exists there, as well) and they do not want a warring people to "pollute" their peace. Until the Earth dismantles and destroys nuclear weapons, stop polluting the Earth, stop raping the Earth's natural resources, and learns to live in harmony, will the Free Universe consider the Earth for membership.

NO REVELATION– The True History of the Universe and Earth, Genetic Manipulation, UFO, and the strangle hold various alien entities have over the world is yet to be revealed by our or any other government, to any extent. The cover story by our own government is that the revelation would reveal a weakness in our military to repeal a UFO invasion (due to their superior technology) and that our government and world institutions are fully controlled by invasive aliens.

Thus, it is more important now than ever for each of mankind to develop their own Escape Plan.

BOTTOMLINE – Many extraterrestrials have a claim on you through DNA manipulation – some by STO beings (to allegedly help mankind) and some STS (to dominate and control). Over the vastness of time, Mankind has become a "Living Library" of the DNA occurring throughout the universe.

For the last 50,000 years, Mankind has been "ruled" by the Dracos/ Reptilian/ Anunnaki Overloads who dominate and control Mankind with an "iron fist."

You need to determine which "camp" you have joined or are part of and determine where you want to be in your journey to the Truth – to determine who and whose you are – you must use your Free Will to determine what you know is right in your heart/soul and to discard all illusions – the Truth is inside of you not from outside influences, since they do not know what is best for you, only what is best for them.

SOLIDIFY YOUR ESCAPE PLAN to find the real you – the real "I AM."

Sources
1. The Golden Lake: Wisdom from the Stars for Life on Earth, Lyssa Royal Holt, 2019, Light Technology Publishing, LLC
2. "The Eisenhower Treaty with the Aliens," Source: Research Study #8, Jan 28, 2004 revised Feb 12, 2004, Exopolitics, http://ww.expolitics.org also refer to: Sumary of Findings Article at https://www.info-quest.org/ documents/ Eisenhowerufo.html
3. "Chapter 3, Part 1: The Lyran Expansion, The Orion Wars, and The Creation Of The Annunaki," Seth, Aug 30, 2017, https://medium.com/a-history-of-the-multiverse/chapter-3-part-1-the-lyran-expansion-and-the-orion-wars-fb103b8b6e99
4. "Galactic History of the Lyran races and Reptilian races and the Great Galactic Wars," Chris, March 14th, 2012, Sirius Cprus, https://cdreifuz.wordpress.com/
5. Lyssa & Priest, Keith. The Prism of Lyra: An Exploration of Galactic Human Heritage. Light Technology Publishing, 2011
6. "The Great Galactic Wars," Wes Penne, July 20, 2012, Wes Penne website, https://www.bibliotecapleyades.net/vida_alien/war_celestialconflicts08.htm
7. "A Galactic Human Journey Milky Way Galaxy", Galactic Human Journey, http://tas-education.org/exo/Galactic-Human-Journey.pdf
8. Royal, Lyssa & Priest, Keith. The Prism of Lyra: An Exploration of Galactic *Human Heritage. Light Technology Publishing,.
9. Rachele, Sal. Earth Changes and Beyond: Messages from the Founders, 2016
10. Robinson, Lytle. Edgar Cayce's Story of the Origin and Destiny of Man. Berkley Publishing, 1972
11. Fenton, Daniella. Hybrid Humans: Evidence of our 800,000 Year-Old Alien Legacy. 2018
12. Rachele, Sal. The Real History of Earth, 2015
13. Nidle, Sheldon. Your Galactic Neighbors, 2005
14. Rachele, Sal. Earth Awakens: Prophecy 2017-2030, Second Edition 2017
15. Solaris, Debbie. Galactic History, 2019 (Accessed Jan 2020)
16. Lake, Gina. The Extraterrestrial Vision: Who Is Here and Why, 1993 (with 2011 preface)

Article 42

CARD CATALOGS AND THE SECRET HISTORY OF MODERNITY

EARTH IS THE LIBRARY- HUMANS ARE THE LIBRARY CARDS

Original Purpose of the Earth - The plan was to create an intergalactic exchange center of information within planet Earth. It was an extraordinary plan, involving a beautiful place, for Earth is located on the fringe of our galactic system and is easily reached from other galaxies. Earth exists close to many way-portals, the highways that exist for energies to travel throughout space.

The Earth would be colonized by the Lyrans/ Pleiadians who were some of the original Planners of Earth, orchestrators who seeded worlds and civilizations with light and information through creativity and love. They gave their DNA to the original Planners, and this DNA became part of the DNA of the human species.

When they designed Earth, other forms of intelligence were able to grasp the reason for Earth's creation. They understood that perhaps their own civilizations might one day be annihilated, and they did not want to lose them entirely.

So, libraries were built throughout existence, and each was filled with specific data. All forms of intelligence that made the libraries valued their identities and valued their civilizations. They understood how their civilizations were constructed. They valued life.

Humans Have Extreme Universal Value - Human beings are the library cards, the keys to the Living Library. All the information stored in Earth's library is accessible only through the humans. The codes and master numbers that the other species in the universe seek are geometric formulas and combinations of intelligence stored within the human. Each creation in the Living Library has its purpose and has a great amount of data stored in it.

Humans were designed to be merged with, influenced, and emerged through. The physical bodies that humans now occupy are sending and receiving centers, broadcast units that exist in many realities. All creation is designed to be influenced - to be puzzle pieces that lock and fit with other pieces of the puzzle. Within each human there are stored codes and master numbers that the rest of the universe desperately needs for their own existence. As Earth is being catapulted into a frequency that will allow the Living Library to come back into full function, in order to once again become valuable assets as the keys who access the Living Library from many cosmic points of view.

Humans will have twelve-stranded DNA and full brain capacity. In order for humans to be in partnership as library cards, humans must understand that they are more than human. Humans are considered by some in this universe to be priceless, though in actuality your Soul selves have no idea of the value stored in the human body. Your human body is the most valuable thing you will ever own and encounter. Humans are priceless to the universe.

Battles have long been fought over Earth, and as a result, humans have been purposely enticed away from discovering the wealth of data stored inside of them by controlling or limiting forces. One is purposely taught, by the Dark Force (Service-to-Self), that humans are insignificant and valueless so that other forms of intelligence will not come and tap into them. Those who control you cannot get the formulas out of you, so they keep you hidden away, quarantined and isolated. In this way, others who need what you have cannot get to you. You are taught the dance of disempowerment, which you choreograph as a species.

You are now learning to find your own value, a value you will intend to share, teach, and encourage others to discover through an ongoing process. The value you discover about yourself will grow and grow as you wonder at these formulas inside of you, which are the codes for other civilizations. The Federation of Light (Service-to-Others) is here to help you recover your self-worth and be of service to the entire universe, not subservient to the Dark Force. Yet, The Federation wants access to the codes you store within your body; thus, they only appear to be benevolent to order to achieve their agenda.

Earth is a microcosm of the macrocosm, a miniature version of what is happening all over, except that Earth is a trigger point, what some call a kernel. You know that a kernel is a seed. The Lyrans/ Pleiadians have come back to Earth to assist the members of the Family of Light, who have been seeded here, in this essential time when events can be altered.

Millions of years ago, the Dark Forces (Anannaki / Orion-Draconian Empire) Had Won the Battle to Control Earth and Its Humans. Although Humans are bearers of the Light, many have been lured to the Dark Force or have not awakened to know they are free spirits that were never meant to be dominated by and subservient to the Dark Side. The Federation is mounting a battle to restore the Earth as the "free zone," Living Library that was first envisioned. The Starseeds are promoting the increase in the frequency of the Earth as well as increasing the frequency of all human beings that are part of the Earth. The increased frequency to that of Love (13 Hz vs. eons of 7.8 Hz) will cause many of the humans to 'Wake Up" and realize their universal purpose.

Why the Draconian-Reptilian Alliance (Orion Empire) wants to initiate Transhumanism and Human 3.0 subservient programming - Through the various quantum processes, the Dark Force is attempting to extract the Universe Knowledge stored within Mankind in order to further control their fought-for 4%Universe and the various species therein. The Elite/Dark Force will use the various Quantum Processes to modify the human DNA by incorporating "Junk" DNA and bio-mechanics to create trans-humans or to create trans-humans through the injection of nanobots. The trans-human creation may reveal the human's vast stored knowledge. The Dark Force will induce the humans to become trans-human by telling them it will provide them with eternal life which they already have without becoming trans-human. It was this same obtuse "attack" used by the Anunnaki to lure the Atlanteans to become the power source for the Anunnaki/Sirian creation of Mankind. Be wary of the attempt to create trans-humans.

Article 43

PLANET C-53 - Earth
(The Slave Planet)

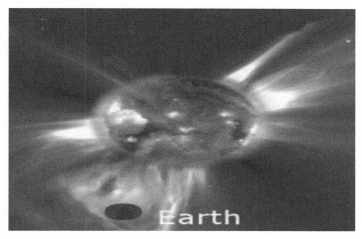

Sphere Alliance / Galactic Federation Council has told the Archara Alliance that it is GAME OVER.

The Sphere-Being Alliance has increased their effort of helping Mankind to WAKE UP by placing an Energetic Blockade around Earth and also around our entire solar system, by increasing the Earth's frequency (a key factor in the wakening process to raise the frequency of the human heart-mind, placing "boots on the ground" (Starseeds, Galactic Warriors, Indigo Children, Wanders, Star Travelers, and Star Beings), arresting Elite non-humans, and changing the corrupt, world financial system, but it will be up to those WAKING UP to bring the CABAL/Elites/Reptilians to their knees (to the point of full disclosure) and to ferret out the Dark Side Alliance from their underground bases.

The Cabal/Elites/Reptilians are not as powerful as they have made us believe, but it up to us to realize our power. The "big event" or, as some refer to as the GREAT ENLIGHTMENT, will occur when the Sun has a major ICMA (Interplanetary Coronal Mass Ejection), much larger and more intense than any past CME (Coronal Mass Ejection) and the "light" we will see will not be the Bright White Light generated by a CME, but will be a massive Super Bright Rainbow Light. There is no accurate prediction date for the ICME; some astrological physicists have given the range of 2022 - 2036, but it could be later. However, the "event" will occur when there is a significant number who have AWAKENED to the point of The Hundredth Monkey Effect, which begins when one group acknowledges a new behavior or idea, and it is spreads rapidly from one group to all related groups. As Starseeds, Warriors, Indigos, Wanders, Star Travelers, and Star Beings, you are the initial "one group." Each Starseed, Warrior, Indigo Child, Wanderer, Star Traveler, and Star Being needs to quickly WAKE UP to the real story of humanity's celestial presences and the details of the extraterrestrial message which conveys details of the coming collective ascension of Mankind. It is each Starseed's, Warrior's, Indigo Children, Wanderer's, Star Traveler's, and Star Being's mission to help Mankind prepare for ascension or many will perish to the "Darkness."

The Sphere-Being Alliance is fighting the current controlling Elite, known as the CABAL/Elites/Reptilians, who exist on Earth, at this very moment. There are events and battles occurring above our atmosphere involving the Secret Space Program and Break Away Civilizations. The people of Earth have been in debt slavery, mind controlled, sickened, and lied to in order to control the masses. We have had technologies suppressed from us that would change our lives. The Sphere Alliance is here to help humanity evolve out of its lower frequency. These technologies would immediately collapse the world economies and make the Babylonian Money Magic Slave System of no use. It means the Loss of Control by the .01% (Elite) over the Masses and a complete Paradigm Change. It's time to know our rights, who we truly are, and what we need to do about it.

Each Starseed, Warrior, Indigo Child, Wanderer, Start Traveler, and Star Being needs to immediately focus on increasing your service to others and be more loving to yourself and everyone in order to raise your vibration frequency and consciousness level. Learn to forgive yourself and others (this is releasing Karma). This will change the vibration of the planet, raise the shared consciousness of humanity, and change humankind one person at a time – even if that one person is you. They tell us to treat your body as a temple and you will change over to a lighter body in the process.

The ICME is coming and you are being called to duty. You have already begun your journey by having purchased and are reading this book. This book will give each Starseed, Warrior, Indigo Child, Wanderer, and Star Being a heads-up and head start of knowing the past and current events, and changes in frequency that will come to fruition in the near future, and prepare each to complete their mission to assist Humankind in their ascension process.

THE TIMES THEY ARE A CHANGING.

Article 44

THE COUNCIL OF 5

(ORELA - EGAROT - EMERTHER - GINVO - REDAN)

Benevolent Protectors or Malevolent Giants of Darkness - You be the Judge

Chapter 4 of my book, *Conscious Awakening - A Research Compendium*, lists and provides a description of the 58 advanced species that have visited earth - some benevolent, some self servant, some to observe, some to conquer, and some neutral but wanting something our planet has to offer.

Out of these comes the Council of Five.

ORELA   EGAROT   EMERTHER   GINVO   REDAN

Very little is known about the five alien races that are part of the "Council of 5" (previously known as the Council of 9). They have been watching (some say "protecting") Earth and Humans since primordial times when Humans were only a 1 cell marine organism and throughout all natural evolution when Humans became primate like creatures and beyond (After the Anunnaki manipulated the Human DNA to be subservient to the Anunnaki). According to some alien records, all evolution sequences in all planets have a beginning and an end (with the exception of minor details due mostly to radical weather conditions). The Council realized that one day Humans would be able to join the other human races in the universe.

It is generally agreed that EMERTHER is the most important race among all known races, according to the Council. The EMERTHER are related to Silipsi Rai but much older and advanced in all levels. They claim they were one of the Founding Fathers.

In 1953, President Harry Truman gave up the oval office and passed the reins of power to his successor, President Dwight D. Eisenhower (Ike). It appears that Truman also gave Ike a pretty hefty file concerning a top-secret project called Majestic 12 that Truman established by Classified Executive Order. Majestic 12 consisted of a group of scientists, military personnel and other governmental professionals who all worked together to understand and communicate with UFOs and extraterrestrials (ETs). President Eisenhower was extremely interested in UFOs and ETs. William Cooper, who was on the Naval Intelligence briefing team and had access to classified documents, was a credible witness. His Review of the Documents revealed that ETs

(Council of 5) had had contact with Earth. They had warned that the Earth was "on a path of self-destruction" and they wanted to meet to help effectuate a long-lasting peace.

THE GREYS: Late in 1954 the race of large nosed gray aliens which had been orbiting the Earth. This race identified them as originating from a planet around a red star in the Constellation of Orion which we call *Betelgeuse*. They stated that their planet was dying and that at some unknown future time they wouldn't be able to survive there.

The respected author and former pentagon consultant, Timothy Good, came forward in 2012 to talk about Ike's meetings with the ETs. Good discussed the purpose of those meetings. The upshot is that these particular extraterrestrials, like many others ETs, apparently wanted peace. This led to a second landing at Edwards Air Force base. Evidence indicates that they wanted the U.S. To **Discontinue Testing Nuclear Weapons**. At first, they apparently wanted the public to be told the truth about their existence. In the final treaty, they seemingly had changed their minds and wanted to remain secret.

Approximately 300 people saw Air Force One land at Holloman AFB and taxi back out to the end of the runway. Shortly after the plane landed, the pilot instructed the tower to turn off all radar while the President's plane was on the tarmac. Shortly after Air Force One landed, and the radar was turned off, three, round objects were seen in the sky. One landed about 200 feet in front of Air Force One; another hovered over the area as though keeping watch, and a third one disappeared from visibility. A man, presumed to be Eisenhower, descended the steps of Air Force One. He was seen shaking hands with a being at the door of the saucer, then entered the unusual saucer-shaped aircraft. Ike was in the saucer for about 45 minutes. When he left, he was not wearing a hat and was clearly visible to many observers when he entered the spacecraft. All witnesses recognized him as President Eisenhower.

Ultimately, Eisenhower signed a Treaty with the Alien Nation (**Council of 5**, allied with the Draconians/Reptilians/Snake People/ Ant and Stick People, and the **Alien Greys**). The terms of the Treaty are reported to have been:

- We would not be involved in their affairs and they would not become involved in ours.
- They would keep their presence on Earth a secret.
- They would not make any treaty with any other earth nation.
- They would help the U.S. with developing advanced technology.
- They could abduct humans for various experiments, but had to provide names of all those they abducted to Earth's Majestic 12 committee.
- Each nation would receive the Ambassador of the other for as long as the treaty remained in force. It was further agreed that the Alien Nation and the United States would exchange 16 personnel each to the other with the purpose of learning, each of the other.

- The public would not be informed about the existence of ETs.

It was also agreed that bases would be constructed underground for the use of the Alien nation and that 2 bases would be constructed for the joint use by the Alien nation and the United States Government. Exchange of technology would take place in the jointly occupied bases. These alien bases would be constructed under Indian reservations in the 4 corners area of Utah, New Mexico, Arizona, and Colorado, and 1 would be constructed in Nevada in the area known as S-4 located approximately 7 miles south of the western border of Area 51. All alien bases are under complete control of the Department of Naval Intelligence and all personnel who work in these complexes receive their checks from the Navy.

The Council also met with 2 High – Ranking USSR leaders on 3 different occasions... And they tried to meet with USA President R. Nixon but he refused claiming that it would be too dangerous as they may read his mind and find out about delicate national security secrets concerning the relations with the USSR.

The first meeting between extraterrestrials and President Eisenhower occurred at Edwards AFB in February 1954, prior to the meeting with the Council of 5. Navy Commander Charles L. Suggs reported that his father had attended the meeting between Ike and the ETs. Eisenhower met with two Nordic appearing, blue-eyed ETs (Pleiadians). A third one stood near the door as a lookout. The discussions were polite. The aliens left with no treaty in place but returned in February 1955.

This alien group warned us against the aliens (Council of 5 who were aligned with the Draconian who are allied with the Greys and Snake/Dragon aliens), that were orbiting the Equator and offered to help us with our spiritual development. They demanded that we dismantle and destroy our nuclear weapons as the major condition. They refused to exchange technology citing that we were spiritually unable to handle the technology which we then possessed. They believed that we would use any new technology to destroy each other. This race stated that we were on a path of self-destruction and we must stop killing each other, stop polluting the Earth, stop raping the Earth's natural resources, and learn to live in harmony. These terms were met with extreme suspicion especially the major condition of nuclear disarmament. It was believed that meeting that condition would leave us helpless in the face of an obvious alien threat. We also had nothing in history to help with the decision. Nuclear disarmament was not considered to be within the best interest of the United States. The overtures were rejected. The aliens left with no treaty in place but returned in February 1955.

The Nordic aliens mentioned the fact that the presence and arrival of these 5 races could cause cosmic events that can affect Earth's atmosphere. And it also said that Humans would be seeing an increase of alien ships activity during that period. The note states that the meeting of Council with the Leaders of the World was to discuss the possible threats to Earth and Humans as well as the fact that so many "new" alien races race have been visiting Earth for the previous 500 years, prior to meeting with Eisenhower.

The Nordic (referred to as the "Blues" by the Hopi) later allied and lived with the Hopi in Northern New Mexico and Arizona, who referred to the Blues as Star Warriors (Children of the Feather who came from the stars vs. the Children of the Reptile, who came from under the Earth), and were harassed/monitored by the Greys (allied with the Council of 5) until the Blues left the Earth. The Hopi refer to the Blues and the Blue Star Kachina (Ursa Minor); the Blues may have been Andromedan (said to have blue translucent skin) in addition, Krishina (Hindu culture) was said is depicted as black or blue skinned.

Broken Treaty: By 1955 it became obvious the aliens had deceived Eisenhower and had broken the treaty. Mutilated humans were being found along with mutilated animals all across the United States. It was suspected that the aliens were not submitting a complete list of human contacts and abductees to MJ-12 and it was suspected that not all abductees had been returned. The Soviet Union was suspected of interacting with the aliens and this proved to be true. It was learned that the aliens had been and were then manipulating masses of people through secret societies, witchcraft, magic, the occult, and religion. After several Air Force combat air engagements with alien craft it also became apparent that our weapons were no match against their weapons.

John F Kennedy (1961-1962): At some point President Kennedy discovered portions of the truth concerning drugs and the aliens. He issued an ultimatum in 1963 to MJ-12. President Kennedy assured them that if they didn't clean up the drug problem he would. He informed MJ-12 that they intended to reveal the presence of aliens to the American people within the following year and ordered a plan developed to implement his decision. President Kennedy was not a member of the Council on Foreign Relations. President Kennedy's decision struck fear into the hearts of those in charge. His assassination occurred before Kennedy made any announcement concerning the aliens.

Lyndon B Johnson (1963-1968): Was not a member of the Council of Foreign Relations but knew why President Kennedy was assassinated, and when he was going to be briefed about the aliens, he declined the briefing.

Richard Nixon (1969-1974): When the Watergate scandal broke, President Nixon had intended to ride out the storm confident that he could not be impeached. MJ-12, however, had a different agenda. The intelligence community rightfully concluded that an impeachment trial would open up the files and bare the awful secrets to the public eye. Nixon was ordered to resign. He refused and so the first military coup ever to take place in the United States was promulgated.

Gerald Ford (1974-1977): President Ford organized the Rockefeller Commission to look into alien interference in the government. At least that is what everyone thought. His real purpose was to head off the Congress and keep the cover-up going. Nelson Rockefeller who headed the Commission investigating the intelligence community was a member of the Council on Foreign Relations and was the one who helped Eisenhower build the MJ-12 power structure. Rockefeller uncovered only enough to keep the hounds at bay. He threw the Congress few bones and the cover-up rolled merrily along as always.

Jimmy Carter (1977-1981): Was a member of the Council of Foreign Relations.

Ronald Regan (1981-1989): In 1979, Nannar's Anannaki faction, the one running this planet now, forced U.S. President Reagan and USSR Chairman Gorbachev to develop a world-wide "star wars" defense GRID aimed–not at each other–but at incoming spacecraft of the rival Anannaki faction led by Prince Marduk. President Reagan also agreed to defend Nannar's system of 10 czars that already rules Earth against Marduk's incoming forces.

George H.W. Bush (1989-1993): Director of the United States Central Intelligence Agency and member of the Council of Foreign Relations.

Bill Clinton (1993-2001): Was a member of the Council of Foreign Relations. Although very interested in the Council of 5 and alien participation in our Government, he told the public that he was never told about the aliens. Hillary was Secretary of State and a member of the Council of Foreign Relations.

MJ-12 has presented each new president with a picture of a lost alien culture seeking to renew itself, build a home on this planet, and shower us with gifts of technology. In some cases the President was told nothing. Each President in turn has bought the story.

The Council of 5 has convinced the U.S. Government to establish Space Command and a General assigned to head this Group to advance U.S. and allied interests in, from, and through the space domain.

It will be up to you to determine if the Council of 5 wants to keep Earth as their own, if the Council of 5 are Benevolent Protectors or if the Council of 5 are Malevolent Giants of Darkness (yet, implying that there are no aliens), If Majestic 12 and The Jason Society exist and have been acting in the best interest of the people, and if actions should be taken.

It is interesting that ORELA - EGAROT - EMERTHER - GINVO - RE-DAN are not listed as one of the 68 alien species that were identified by 13 NASA Astronauts (Gordon Cooper, Donald Slayton, Robert White, Joseph A Walker, Eugene Cernan, Ed White, James McDivitt, James Lowell, Frank Gorman, Neil Armstrong, Edwin Aldrin, Maurice Chatelain, and Scott Carpenter) and many retired military officers. (I described the 58 alien species within my book, *Conscious Awakening - A Reference Compendium*). In addition, my research only revealed six Google article mentioning the Council of 5 and each of those appear to be a repeat of a translation of a Russian book, entitled *Introduction to the Alien Races* , with one referencing five alien Generals, and one mentioned the "Blue" aliens.

The original 1946 book (*Introduction to the Alien Races)* was written to inform KGB agents of the various alien races that had visited our planet and also was used as a notebook by secret agents as they constantly made additions and revisions to the original startling information over the years. The book has been re-edited at least 12 times to include new alien races as well as new reports and photos/illustrations. The first editions were printed in 1946 or 1947, with editions in 1951, 1959, 1968, 1971, 1980...all the way to 2011, all in Russian. The book was translated into English in 2012, when the book was found by Dante Santori and published in 2014.

Sources
1. Book of Alien Races: Secret Russian KGB Book of Aliens, Jan 1, 2007, Dante Santori, WorldPress
2. "The Giants from Terra", 16 Oct 2012, https://gigantiidacia.wordpress.com/2013/10/16/the-council-of-5/comment-page-1/
3. "SHOCK CLAIM: Aliens make contact saying humans will be 'ENSLAVED' by extraterrestrials", JON AUSTIN, Express, 13 Dec 2017, https://www.express.co.uk/news/weird/891912/Aliens-UFO-interbreed-humans-allies-of-humanity-Marshall-Vian-Summers
4. "FBI Records: The Vault — Majestic 12", FBI Federal Bureau of Investigation, Declasified Records, The Vault, https://vault.fbi.gov/Majestic%2012
5. Top Secret/Majic: Operation Majestic-12 and the United States Government's UFO Cover-up, August 19, 2005, Stanton Friedman (Author)
6. "Comments on Majestic 12 Material - GAO", General Accounting Office, commentary, July 28, 1995, https://www.gao.gov/assets/200/196986.pdf

Article 45

MAJESTIC 12 and The JASON SOCIETY

By secret Executive Memorandum, NSC 5410, President Eisenhower had authorized NSC 5412/1 in 1954 to establish a permanent committee (not ad hoc) to be known as Majority Twelve (MJ-12) to oversee and conduct all covert activities concerned with the alien question. NSC 5412/1 was created to explain the purpose of these meetings when Congress, as the Press became curious. Majority Twelve was made up of Nelson Rockefeller, the director of the CIA, Allen Welsh Dulles, the Secretary of State, John Foster Dulles, the Secretary of Defense, Charles E. Wilson, the Chairman of the Joint Chiefs of Staff, Admiral Arthur W. Radford, the Director of the FBI J. Edgar Hoover, and six men from the executive committee of the Council on Foreign Relations, known as the "Wise Men", were also party to MJ12. These men were all members of a secret society of scholars that called themselves "The Jason Society" or "The Jason Scholars", who recruited their members from the "Skull and Bones" and the "Scroll and Key" societies of Harvard and Yale.

TOP SECRET DOCUMENT, Prepared 18 November 1952,
        Declassified 2017
Briefing Officer: Adm. Bosco Hillenkoett
Subj: Masjestic 12 established by special classified order by President Truman on 24 September 1947 and consisted of:
Adm. Bosco H Hillenkoett
Dr. Vannevar Bush
Gen. James V Forrestal
Gen. Nathan F Twining
Gen. Nathan F Vandenberg
Dr. Detlev Bronk
Mr. Jerome Hunsaker
Mr. Sidney W Souers
Mr. Gordon Gray
Mr. Donald Menzel
Gen. Robert M Montague
Dr. Lloyd V Berkner

Due to death, on22 May ???? of Secretary Forrestal, the vacancy was filled by Gen. Walter B Smith.

Within this same document (declassified in 2017) was discussion of the 24 June 1947 report of flying objects over the mountains in Washington State, the 7 July 1947 recovery of an extra-terrestrial vehicle with four small humanoids.

An alien craft was found on February 13, 1948 on a mesa near Aztec, New Mexico. Another craft was located on March 25, 1948 in Hart Canyon near Aztec, New Mexico. It was 100 feet in diameter. A total of 17 alien bodies were recovered from those two craft. Of even greater significance was the discovery of a large number of human body parts stored within both of these vehicles. A demon had reared its ugly head and paranoia quickly took hold of everyone then "in the know." The secret lid immediately became an Above Top Secret lid and was screwed down tight. The security blanket was even tighter than that imposed upon the Manhattan Project, since the "Blues" had requested that we stop nuclear energy research. In the coming years these events were to become the most closely guarded secrets in the history of the world.

We can only imagine the confusion and concern when the informed Elite of the United States Government discovered that an alien spacecraft piloted by insect like beings from a totally incomprehensible culture had crashed in the desert of New Mexico.

Between January 1947 and December 1952 at least 16 crashed or downed alien craft, 65 alien bodies, and 1 live alien were recovered. An additional alien craft had exploded and nothing was recovered from that incident. Of these incidents, 13 occurred within the borders of the United States not including the craft which disintegrated in the air. Of these 13, 1 was in Arizona, 11 were in New Mexico, and 1 was in Nevada. Three occurred in foreign countries. Of those 1 was in Norway, and 2 were in Mexico. Sightings of UFO's were so numerous that serious investigations and debunking of each report became impossible utilizing the existing intelligence assets.

During these early years the United States Air Force and the CIA exercised complete control over the Alien Secret. In fact the CIA was formed by Presidential Executive Order first as the Central Intelligence Group for the express purpose of dealing with the alien presence. Later the National Security Act (NSA) was established to oversee the intelligence community and especially the alien endeavor. A series of National Security Council memos and Executive Orders removed the CIA from the sole task of gathering foreign intelligence and slowly but thoroughly "legalized" direct action in the form of covert activities at home and abroad.

The Jason Society: By secret Executive Memorandum, NSC 5411 in 1954, President Eisenhower had commissioned a study group to "examine all the facts, evidence, lies, and deception and discover the truth of the alien question. NSC5412/2 was only a cover that had become necessary when the press began inquiring as to the purpose of regular meetings of such important men. The first meetings began at Quantico Marine Base. The study group was made up of 35 members of the Council on Foreign Relations and Secret scholars, known as "The Jason Society" of the "Jason Scholars". Dr. Edward Teller was invited to participate. Dr. Zbigniew Brzezinski was the study director for the first 18 months. Dr. Henry Kissinger was chosen as the group's study director for the second 18 months. Nelson Rockefeller was a frequent visitor during the study.

STUDY GROUP MEMBERS	
Gordon Dean, Chairman	
Dr. Zbigniew Brzezinski, Study Director - 1st phase	
Dr. Henry Kissinger, Study Director - 2nd phase	
Dr. Edward Teller	Maj. Gen. Richard C. Lindsay
Hanson W. Baldwin	Lloyd V. Berkner
Frank C. Nash	Paul H. Nitze
Charles P. Noyes	Frank Pace, Jr.
James A. Perkins	Don K. Price
David Rockefeller	Oscar M. Ruebhausen
Lt. Gen. James M. Gavin	Caryl P. Haskins
James T. Hill, Jr.	Joseph E. Johnson
Mervin J. Kelly	Frank Altschul
Hamilton Fish Armstrong	Maj. Gen. James McCormack, Jr.
Robert R. Bowie	McGeorge Bundy
William A.M. Burden	John C. Campbell
Thomas K. Finletter	George S. Franklin, Jr.
I. I. Rabi	Roswell L. Gilpatrio
N. E. Halaby	Gen. Walter Bedell Smith
Henry DeWolf Smyth	Shields Warren
Carroll L. Wilson	Arnold Wolfers

Today: MJ-12 still exists and operates just as it always has. It is made up of the same structure, 6 from the same positions in government, and 6 from the executive members of the Council on Foreign Relations and/or Trilateral Commission. It is most important to understand that the Council on Foreign Relations and its offshoot the Trilateral Commission not only control but own this country. Long before WWII they were instrumental in helping to decide policy for the United States Government. The Council on Foreign

Relations, Trilateral Commission and their foreign counterparts report to the Builderburgers. Almost every high level government and military official of any consequence since WWII including Presidents have been members of the Council on Foreign Relations and/or Trilateral Commission. All American members of the Trilateral Commission have either been or are a member of the Council on Foreign Relations.

Each foreign nation of any importance has its own offshoot of the Council on Foreign Relations and the members of each country interact with those of other countries to further their common goals.

Even a cursory investigation by the most inexperienced researcher will show that the members of the Council on Foreign Relations and the Trilateral Commission control the major foundations, all of the major media, publishing interests, the largest banks, all the major corporations, the upper echelons of the government, and many other vital interests. Their members are elected and appointed because they have all the money and special interests behind them. All, that is, except the peoples' interest. They are undemocratic and do not in any way represent the majority of the United States of America. You can find a list of those who are or have been a member of the Council on Foreign Relations, including corporate members, at en.m.wickipedia.org and, for a greater revelation, scroll back up to Study Group Members.

The Council on Foreign Relations and the Trilateral Commission are the SECRET GOVERNMENT and rule this nation through MJ-12 and the Study Group known as the Jason Society or Jason Scholars and the top echelon of the government which consist mostly of their members.

MJ-12 has presented each new President with a picture of a lost alien culture seeking to renew itself, build a home on this planet, and shower us with gifts of technology. In some cases the President was told nothing. Each President in turn has bought the story or no story at all. Meanwhile innocent people continue to suffer unspeakable horrors at the hands of alien and human scientists who are engaged in barbarous research that would make even the Nazis look like Sunday school children. As if that is not enough many people end up as food for the insatiable alien appetite for biological enzymes, glandular hormonal secretions, and blood. Many people are abducted and are sentenced to live with psychological and physical damage for the rest of their lives. In a few documents, 1 in 40 humans have been implanted with devices (transhumans). The government believes that the aliens are building an army of human implants which can be activated and turned upon us at will. In the meantime, we have not even begun to come close to parity with the aliens.

In addition, starting in 1957, "Batch Consignments" of human slaves which were used for the manual labor in the effort to build military base colonies on the Moon, code named "Adam", the object of primary interest followed by the planet Mars, code named "Eve". The "Official" space program was proposed by President Kennedy in his inaugural address when he mandated that the United States put a man on the moon before the end of the decade. Although innocent in its conception this mandate enabled those in charge to funnel vast amounts of money into black projects and conceal the REAL space program from the American people. A similar program in the Soviet Union served the same purpose. A joint alien, United States, and Soviet Union base already existed on the moon at the very moment Kennedy spoke the words. The real purpose of military presence (weapons and space craft) was to intercept any other aliens from interrupting the Alien Nation's (**Council of 5,** allied with the Draconians/Reptilians/Snake People/ Ant and Stick People, and the **Alien Greys**) control and subjugation of the Earth.

Extensively Research the topic and determine if the above is Your Truth. Rely upon your institution to tell you the truth. Question everything. I am just a Lightworker Messenger whose goal is to provide a Wake Up service.

Sources
1. Book of Alien Races: Secret Russian KGB Book of Aliens, Jan 1, 2007, Dante Santori, WorldPress
2. "The Giants from Terra", 16 Oct 2012, https://gigantiidacia.wordpress.com/2013/10/16/the-council-of-5/comment-page-1/
3. "SHOCK CLAIM: Aliens make contact saying humans will be 'ENSLAVED' by extraterrestrials", JON AUSTIN, Express, 13 Dec 2017, https://www.express.co.uk/news/weird/891912/Aliens-UFO-interbreed-humans-allies-of-humanity-Marshall-Vian-Summers
4. "FBI Records: The Vault — Majestic 12", FBI Federal Bureau of Investigation, Declassified Records, The Vault, https://vault.fbi.gov/Majestic%2012
5. Top Secret/Magic: Operation Majestic-12 and the United States Government's UFO Cover-up, August 19, 2005, Stanton Friedman (Author)
6. "Comments on Majestic 12 Material – GAO", General Accounting Office, commentary, July 28, 1995, https://www.gao.gov/assets/200/196986.pdf
7. "US researchers alarmed as government cuts ties with elite science advisory group", Jeff Tollefson, NEWS EXPLAINER, 10 APRIL 2019. https://www.nature.com/articles/d41586-019-01185-8
8. "JASON Defense Advisory Panel Reports", https://fas.org/irp/agency/dod/jason/ "the story of jason - the elite group of academic scientists who ...", Peter Peter Stubbs, Editor of NEW SCIENTIST, in NEW SCIENTIST, August 24, 1972, www.ocf.berkeley.edu

Article 46

THE CONCLUSIONS ARE INESCAPABLE

THE CONCLUSIONS ARE INESCAPABLE, if you have been following my previous Articles (Council of 5 and Majestic 12 / The Jason Society).

The secret power structure believes that, because of our own ignorance or by Divine Decree, planet Earth will self destruct sometime in the near future. These men sincerely believe that they are doing the right thing in their attempt to save Mankind. It is terribly ironic that they have been forced to take as their partner the Council of 5 "Generals" representing several alien races who are engaged in a monumental struggle for survival. Many moral and legal compromises have been made in this joint effort. These compromises were made in error and must be corrected and those responsible should be made to account for their actions. It is understandable that fear and urgency must have been instrumental in the decision not to tell the public. Obviously, many disagree with this decision.

Throughout history small but powerful groups of men have consistently felt that they alone were capable of deciding the fate of millions and throughout history they have been wrong. This great nation owes its very existence to the Principles of Freedom and Democracy. The United States of America cannot and will not succeed if any these principles are ignored. Full disclosure to the public should be made and we should proceed to save the human race altogether.

We are being manipulated by a joint human/alien power structure which will result in the total enslavement and or destruction of the human race. The government has been totally deceived and we are being manipulated by an alien power which will result in the total enslavement and/or destruction of the human race. We must use any and every means available to prevent this from happening.

Something else is happening which is beyond our ability to understand at this time –Earth frequency is increasing, the Poles are shifting, the Earth is in a phase of disruption, including the disruption of Mankind displayed by riots in the streets of France, Hong Kong, the large populated cities in the United States, elsewhere. Corrupt governments are rampant. Earthquakes, volcanic eruptions, massive forest fires and severe weather (snowing where it has never snowed before) is easily identifiable. These "disruptions" and the raising of awareness are caused by Gaia (Mother Earth) in concert with the Galactic Federation of Light (Service to Other alliance of approximately 400 planets) to restore the Earth and the people thereon.

It is now the time of the "GREAT AWAKENING." Love & Light Workers and Galactic Warriors need to **WAKE UP** to this Reality, WAKE UP to the deception and lies created by the Dark Force, and complete their mission to awaken Mankind to the deception created by the Dark Force to dominate and control the Earth.

Article 47

THE ESSENTIAL WAR LIGHT vs. DARK
(Pending Revelations)

The Orion Empire (Draco-Reptilians and their allies) were awarded, by Treaties (end of the 2nd and 3rd Galactic Wars) 4% of the Universe, which includes the Milky Way (in which Earth resides). Since that time, this **small but powerful group** has consistently felt that they alone were capable of deciding the fates of millions and throughout history they have been wrong. The Anunnaki (part of the Orion Reptilian Empire) created Mankind through genetic inculpation to be subservient and controlled by Orion's 13 "Elite" families. They have "literally" strangled Mankind into compliance, which result in the total enslavement and or destruction of the human race and the Earth where they reside. In addition, the Earth's contingent of the Orion Empire has teamed with the Council of 5, another domination group of aliens.

Due to behind the scenes intervention by the Galactic Federation of Light, in an alien-to-alien (Federation vs. Dark Force) confrontation (part of the Galactic Wars), the below revelations will, soon, become apparent.

The Galactic War and the Existence of the Cabal/ICC/Draco/Dark Fleet or more simply "Dark Side or Dark Force". The Galactic Federation/ Brotherhood of Light has, for eons, been engaged in a war being fought in deep space, Mars and now extending to Earth, resulting in a complex planetary situation involving multiple space programs, both modern and ancient, and extraterrestrial civilizations in a struggle for dominance over the Earth. This is leading to possibly the most comprehensive disclosures ever to emerge of what is really happening behind the scenes taking place on Earth and our solar system. Side Note: ICC = Interstellar Commerce Commission (strict control on biological items moving around in the universe).

Galactic Human Slave Trade – A galactic human slave trade, instigated by the Dark Force, exists where millions of captured humans are taken off planet to distant colonies on other worlds to be bartered or abused. The Federation plans to disclose the full truth about the abusive practices that has plagued humanity for centuries, if not millennia, due to corrupt "Elites" (Cabal/Illuminati/Builderburgs/13 Orion Families) and intervention by imperial space powers (Draco Orion Empire).

Galactic Trade in Human Body Parts – There is a galactic need or demand for human fluids, human organs, tissues, and other body products that are sold by the Dark Force on the galactic black market.

UFOs are Real and Aliens have Infiltrated all World Governments, Institutions and Social organizations. The "infiltration" has been occurring for 100's of thousands of years and Galactic Wars have been fought over control of the Universe and of Earth. The warring parties have been both benevolent and predatory.

The Federation plans to disclose the full truth, including all of the above. The Dark Side has already begun a major disinformation campaign. Once the Cabal/Illuminati et al realized that their "Gods" had betrayed them and it was now every group for themselves they may begin to turn on one another (as they did millions of years ago on Malduk and Mars, resulting in nuclear war that destroyed their own blue planets. They have also begun to activate the assets that they had deeply infiltrated into the Ufology field to begin to cause conflict whenever an opportunity presented itself. They have gone from a position of preventing disclosure while conditioning the public for some sort of future false disclosure to now trying to control the disclosure narrative.

It is now the time of the "GREAT AWAKENING." Love & Light Workers, Galactic Warriors and all Star Beings need to **WAKE UP** to this Reality, WAKE UP to the deception and lies created by the Dark Force and complete their mission to awaken Mankind to the deception created by the Dark Force to dominate and control the Earth.

Article 48

DEFEATING THE DARK FORCE
(Death by a 1,000 Cuts)

Defeating the Dark Force and Not Be Subservient To It - We are living in a 21st-century feudal society and we are the serfs. Humanity is sliding ever faster into the great abyss of subsistence living. How does one defeat the New World Order (NWO) with their control over the banks, the military, the corporations, health care and the politicians? In short, they own it all. Is there any way to defeat the NWO?

On A Global Scale – Claim the World's Governments: The specific aim of the Council of 5, The Jason Society, MJ 12, Anannaki, Reptilians, Greys (all commonly referred to as the 'Dark Force') is to take over planet Earth through covert mind control methods, mind implants, reprogramming, separation, defeatism (there is nothing we can do), gene manipulation, propaganda, Cabals and Cartels, and even the establishment of Police States and Cities (where cameras, drones, and your own home security systems will track your every move). Several organizations have been put together to control us financially and politically, such as the Bilderbergs, Illuminati and Secret Governments. Our government has sold us out because of their greed for power and world domination and now they can't stop what they have started.

Globally:
We must force disclosure of all the facts, discover the truth and act upon the truth.

We must reclaim the world governments and firmly resist the formation of a One World Government.

The world needs to wake up spiritually and psychologically, and stop being victims. It is this victim consciousness that allows them to be abducted and manipulated.

Individually:
If ever you sense the Dark Force round you, affirm your core and visualize protection for yourself. Your connection with First Source (Creator God) will bring you immediate protection. Also, refer to Chapter 15 (*Conscious Awakening – A research Compendium* book by Arlene Lanman for several other means of spiritual protection).

The Greys are a group memory complex that has very little ability to think on their own. It is time now to make people aware of what is really going on. Share this information and others like it with your friends. Do additional research on your own. If enough people become aware, the one hundredth monkey effect will begin to occur. It is already happening. The people reading this are the Light Bearers for the new age. It will only happen if we do it. The world will change when we change it. This change begins in consciousness, which leads to individual and group action. The Secret Government, Illuminati, and negative extraterrestrials are more vulnerable now than ever before.

Look at all choices from four perspective ranges and make your choices accordingly. Image each range to have ten increments.

Exercise my Own Free-Will .... Being Controlled
Encourage Love of All .... Encourages Hate & Separation
Support what is Best for All ..... Encourages what is Best for the Elite
Best for Humanity /Universe ... Best for New World Order

32 suggestions to defy the Dark Force. Below are a few specific suggestions that we can employ in defiance of the Dark Force. It is called the "Death by a 1000 cuts" strategy. These actions will allow time for others to 'Wake Up" and help us to get our house in order and to raise the frequency of the Earth and the humans on it.

1. Free Yourself/ Empower Yourself – refer To 'Reclaim Your Power' within Chapter 24 of my book, *Conscious Awakening – A Research Compendium.*
2. Let your pet choose your friends and acquaintances. Animals have a better "sense" of good and not so good than we do.
3. Trust your 'gut.' Your intuition has better judgment than your rational mind.
4. Just because everybody does it/supports it, it does not mean you have to be part of mob mentality.
5. Individuality beats plurality.

6. Do not make decisions out of Fear, Anger, Jealousy, Rivalry, Sociability, or Sympathy.

7. Become informed of all topics and weigh the "good" against the "bad."

8. Support Sovereignty and Local Government. Decentralization is the opposite of global central government. Starting with your local government, support decentralization of power whenever you can. Do not fall for the trap of surrendering to the idea of becoming a global citizen. It is better to be a free citizen of your own sovereign country who can freely choose where to go around the world than to be a global citizen who is slave to a global central government. Say NO to the United Nations, NO to the North America Union, NO to the European Community and any other globalist illusion.

9. Say No to Smart meters. Reduce or eliminate your Use of wireless Technology. This new technology is part of the global control grid. Not only is it a serious health hazard because of the high levels of electromagnetic radiation, but it also creates a completely invasive spy system which records every activity, right down to inside your home. Inform yourself, share the information, know your rights, join other like-minded neighbors and say NO!

10. Say No to Vaccines. The globalists are so obsessed with vaccines that some, such as Bill Gates, tell us to our face that they are using it to control the population. Unless you like to being filled with mercury and many other poisons, do not take them. Get informed: Why do vaccine manufacturers have immunity from liability if their product is so good? Why are governments around the world trying to make them mandatory? Why has the number of autistic infants skyrocketed since the recent introduction of these new massive vaccinations? Evidence shows that we are systematically being experimented on without our consent and most importantly our lives and health are at risk. The worst part is that most of the population is defending the perpetrators, denying the evidence and attacking the messengers.

11. Find Your Souls Faith. The New World Order wants to establish one world religion, destroy the family, destroy the individual and the final God they want you to submit is the state. I am not telling you what to believe in, that's your personal choice, but to find the strength that we will need to endure this struggle; we need something that materialistic things sometimes cannot provide: Faith.

12. Be Wary of Organized Religion. I am not telling you not go to church or what you should or not should believe in. Most organized churches that have the 501c tax exempt status are under the control of the government and they will be used under martial law to control the "flock." Refer to Google "Clergy response team under the control of FEMA." Be aware that throughout history the church has been used to brainwash humanity and now it will be used to create compliance to the Elite's agenda that distorts and abuses the message of First Source

God. Just be careful and use critical thinking when another human being who happens to be speaking from an altar tells you what to do.

13. Do not Follow Political Parties, They Are All Controlled. Support candidates who believe in freedom and oppose globalism. Political parties have been created to "conquer and divide." Like it or not the globalists control both parties. You can clearly see that there is not much difference in their agenda when it comes down to the important issues. It does not really make a difference whether they are Democrats or Republicans. It is just an illusion to make you believe that you are still free to choose and vote. Goethe once said: "None are more hopelessly enslaved than those who falsely believe they are free." However, I still believe that we have to be politically involved and be part of the system in order to create positive change. So, regardless which political party you decide to join, never follow blindly, but follow your heart and the principles of freedom. Do not be afraid to expose the paid trolls of the New World Order in your party.

14. Turn off all mainstream media. Control of mass media is the key to the New World Order strategy for command and control. Do not watch network news unless you are viewing it as a way to determine what the enemy is up to. Apply the same logic to your local newspaper and radio channels that are owned by media giants. The media giants are broadcasting the words of the New World Order.

15. Do not support those who support the New World Order. This includes actors, actresses, public officials, athletic players and teams, performers, artists, businesses, etc.

16. Forget global mentality. What is good for the EU, China, or Russia does not mean it is best for you.

17. Take your money out of the megabanks and place into the credit union or state-owned or controlled banks.

18. Get your children out of the government schools with their NWO Common Core curriculum along with their zero tolerance policies and transgender restrooms.

19. Get Out of Debt. Debt is slavery. The Private Central banks that control the world's governments are based on the principle of slave/master relationship. Governments are slaves to the central banks like the private Federal Reserve because they have given them the sovereign power to issue their currency. Every dollar that is issued will be paid back with interest. Our labor is the collateral to pay back the interest of every dollar the government will spend. We may not be able to change that for now, but we can try to get out of personal debt so we do not need the banks, even the local ones. When the economy gets worse, it will be even harder to get out of debt. Live within your means. Pay off your credit cards. We are now a nation of debt slaves. Pay cash for as much as you can. If you cannot pay cash, then do not buy it! Own your future instead of the bankers owning you. Maintain the smallest mortgage or loan that you can manage.

20. Buy as much as you need from local "mom and pop" stores. Stay away from the NWO giant box stores that, also, broadcast the NWO paradigm.

21. Buy gold and do not hoard cash. Hard cash may be OK, once it is backed by gold, as Trump and others are planning to do. This cuts into the power the NWO bankers have over you and your country.

22. Never vote for the incumbent. The longer the power hungry are in power, the more likely they will become part of the NWO.

23. As hard as it might be, buy only Made in America products. This is part of Nationalism and not Globalism (NWO). Do not confuse 'nationalism" with "white nationalism," as the NWO wants to call it. We were formed as an independent nation not bound to any global group, such as the British Commonwealth. We need to stand as One and not a part of the many, who do not have our best interest in mind.

24. Do not Support Unconstitutional Wars. United States Marine Corps Major General and two time Medal of Honor recipient Smedley D. Butler wrote a very important book: "War is a racket", and Wars are evil and most of the time are created to hide the failures of our politicians and to increase the profits of corporations and central banks. Even worse, wars have not been declared by Congress in the last 60 years that is since the Korean War, these are unconstitutional wars with the only purpose of serving the New World Order and its agenda. When the propaganda machine tries to sell you a war without the declaration of Congress, remember, only "Congress shall have Power to ...declare War" Article I, Section 8, Clause 11.

25. Learn about False Flags. A false flag is a covert operation designed to deceive in such a way that the operation appears as though it has been carried out by entities, groups, or nations other than those who actually planned and executed them.

26. Go Rural, Go Wild. If you can, consider moving to a rural area. One of the goals of the globalists is to confine us in mega cities so they can control every aspect of our life, like a herd of cows packed in a corral. That's one of the plans of Agenda 21. Now more than ever it is time to move to rural areas. Go find open spaces away from their regulatory control of ordinances, and unconstitutional bureaucratic parasitic regulations. Nobody should tell you what color you can paint your home or how tall your grass should be. Go live wild, live free.

27. Try to Be a Decent Person. The New World Order feeds on the weaknesses of humanity. The global Elite can recruit their minions only if they are willing to submit to evil. To become pawns for their agenda, they will tempt you with wealth, sex, drugs, power and all Earthly possessions. We are all human (at least most of us, I am not sure about them), and therefore we are corruptible. It is our duty to be decent people believing in the power of positive action and decent values based on good and the best part of our humanity. There is a spiritual battle between good and evil currently taking place in this physical dimension.

28. Do all things out of Love – Reach out and make room for love. Come to realize that, every human encounter possesses a nexus point with every human being we encounter. In each instance, we have a choice to be honorable, compassionate and kind to another or to take advantage of them. You have a choice to chart a new path for humanity or to walk in the evil footprints of those who have come before you. You can choose to align with the Universe or continue to serve and be ruled over by evil.

29. Love Life, Love Your Neighbors, Have Fun. We need to love life. We need to love, period. They want us miserable and full of hate as they feast on fear and hate. Loving life and creating good things is the antithesis of their destructive agenda. We need to have fun, especially now under these circumstances. Do not get me wrong, I wish we didn't have to face these globalist parasites. Since we don't have a choice, and this task will take up a big part of our lives, let's try to have some fun and share quality time with other like-minded people who have committed themselves to exposing and defeating the New World Order. Resistance is never futile! Resistance to tyranny is a duty and a pleasure.

30. Keep an Open Mind. We were all ignorant at some point, ignorance can be fixed, but for arrogance there is no hope. Always have an open mind, do not be an arrogant know it all if somebody is trying to talk to you about some new ideas or theories. I am not saying that you must believe everything you are told, but always keep an open mind. This gives you the ability to continue learning and to re-evaluate apparent truths that are given as dogma through the propaganda in the media.

31. Find Each Other. Fighting and learning about the New World Order can be overwhelming and stressful. Once you are awake it is very difficult to go back and even share a beer with somebody who still refuses to at least learn about this reality. This world can be a lonely place unless you start to find like-minded people who are aware or at least willing to learn about what is currently happening on our planet.

Know that a fragment of Creator God is with each of us. Our Spirit is pure; do not be fooled by the thought of Original Sin since we all began as a pure fragment of One Source (Creator God) not a controlled and manipulated "creation" of the Lesser God (the Orion Reptilian who declared himself to be God Almighty).

We have a choice, but our window of opportunity is quickly closing.

Sources

1. '20 Key Ways to Defeat the New World Order,' David Hodges, March 12, 2013, Activist Post, https://www.activistpost.com/2013/03/20-key-ways-to-defeat-new-world-order.html

2. 'How to Defeat the New World Order,' Gianluca Zanna, LoveGunsFreedom.com, https://www.lovegunsfreedom.com/how-to-defeat-the-new-world-order

ARTICLE 49

ELECTROMAGNETIC FREQUENCY USES

The technology may have been provided and used in the distant past and re-given to us in the current era by aliens who trade technology for control of mankind and other concessions.

Frequency beams and weapons – The technology may have been provided to us by ancient aliens and current alien entities. These systems manipulate electro-magnetic waves and can be used for both "good" (medical) or "bad" (weapons) depending upon the amount of energy to power the device and the frequency spectrum of operation (broadband or narrow high intensity beam).

Lasers: Both use light to heat and destroy their targets. But unlike lasers that use a single wavelength (color) of light which typically matches only one chromophore and hence only treats one condition, IPL (Intense Pulsed Light) uses a broad spectrum that when used with interchangeable filters, allows it to be used against several conditions. Directed lasers (today's usage) work by disrupting (by heat) at the molecular level – such as, laser treatment of cancer cells.

Plasma: A specific type of Laser that creates enough "heat" at a specific point of concentration to cause the material to enter a plasma state, which appears to "cut" the object (such as mild thickness steel). Late 20th and 21st Centuries used Plasma torch cutters to cut steel. Could be the source for "light sabers" in Star Wars.

Particle Beam Weapons: uses electromagnetic fields to propel charged **particles**, such As electrons or protons, to very high speeds and energies, containing them in well-defined beams through the use of electro-magnetic fields. In the early 21st Century, the most powerful **accelerator** was the Large **Haddon Collider (LHC)** near Geneva, Switzerland.

Phasers: a kind of particle beam stream that is concentrated into by an electro-magnet field. As a weapon, Phaser acts somewhat like a jack-hammer to destroy a large object.

Disruptor: A more broad bandwidth electro-magnetic device that causes molecules to "disrupt" / "shatter" and can be "tuned" to specific molecular compensation (such as those within a human body).

20th Century Railgun: Uses a pair of parallel conductors—rails—along which a sliding armature is accelerated by the electromagnetic effects of a current that flows down one rail, into the armature and then back along the other rail to launch a ballistic "bullet". It is based on principles similar to those of the homopolar motor. Railguns were used during the Galactic Wars beginning 22-million years ago, along with other electromagnetic weapons.

Frequency Match, Harmonic Generators: This "beam" device will analyze and then match the natural frequency of an object in order to fracture it. This principal was proposed by Nicholas Tesla to describe how a device the size of one's palm could "bring-down" an entire building. Such a device could be designed to intercept and neutralize an opponent's beam weapon, in so doing, creating a shield. It is speculated that the Egyptians used Frequency Matching Devices to "cut" stone with precision accuracy.

Mind Image Embedment: Use of blue light beams flashing Gamma Ray frequencies to transmit and imbedded images within the human mind, as part of Human 2.0 program by the Anunnaki during the creation of Mankind (i.e., "programming" of the DNA strand) and, today, to implant Human 3.0. Perhaps, this is how Our Reality (inside the brain) was imbedded, which differs from Actual Reality – we see only what "they" want us to see. Refer to Control of recollection by slow gamma dominating mid ..., https://www.ncbi.nlm.nih.gov › pubmed,.., by D Dvorak, Jan 18, 2018.

Consciousness: The human mind operates on electrical impulses between the numerous synopses (10,000 or more), with the neurons "firing" at a rate from 4 to 80 per second. The rate is, sometimes measured in the brain wave output signal. There are five major brain wave ranges: Beta (12-30Hz) is present in normal waking consciousness and is heightened during times of stress; Alpha brain wave (7.5-14Hz) in deep relaxation; Theta (4-7.5Hz) in meditation and light sleep; and the slowest, Delta (0.5-4Hz) in deep dreamless sleep and transcendental meditation. The less recognized Gamma is fastest (above 40Hz) and associated with sudden insight. The optimal level for visualization is the Alpha-Theta Border at 7-8Hz. It is the gateway to your subconscious mind; the, for eons, frequency of the Earth was 7.83 Hz – since our brain operates in concert with the Earth's frequency, we have been "asleep" when it comes to consciousness.

Med-Beds: Every part of your body (i.e., each Chakra) vibrates to its own rhythm. We will soon see healing by way of frequency waves.

Anti-Gravity: An elementary electro-gravity disk craft has two counter-rotating discs, each consisting of multiple air capacitor discs that are charged as a field of high voltage by Tesla resonance transformers. [This can be seen as the proton spin of positive charge and the electron spin of negative charge, whereas changing the spin frequency and voltage of the protons and electrons in the material of the rotating disk is caused by induction]. When the electromagnetic field that is rotating in the same direction as the earth's field, it is stronger than the opposing field, i.e., negative on negative, the ship is repelled away from the earth's surface. When the field that rotates counter to the Earth's dielectric field is stronger, i.e., positive field, the craft is pulled towards the surface of the earth. The difference between these two counter rotating fields allows for the control of the ship's altitude and at what rate of speed the ship achieves that altitude. Currently, we do not have a compact high energy source (e.g., a fusion reactor) that can provide the "power" needed to create such a craft. In addition, the outward dielectric and magnetic waves by the nature of their movement thru time create a counter polarity, which when that wave is harnessed, then the two flows can adjust the gravity-time zone of our star system from Earth point of view – thus, light speed or beyond will be achieved.

Electro-Magnetic Propulsion Thruster Engines: A solid fuel propellant (named Teflon) enters the thruster, and high voltage current occurs between the nozzle and the tip, the plasma is controlled by electro-magnetic fields to prevent the plasma particles from touching the thruster walls; the plasma gas is ionized and accelerated by an external magnetic field (Lorentz Force principal). At some point in the future, solar energy (photon packets) will be the propellant. Plasma engines are limited to the power source capabilities. Currently, we do not have a compact high energy source (e.g., a fusion reactor) that can provide the "power" needed to create such an engine. Of course, plasma thruster engines will be supplemented or even replaced when fusion engines are developed.

In theory, all of the above can be "weaponized," given a large power source, such as a fusion reactor to create a Laser, or Phaser, or particle beam Canon or by a more compact power supply for limited range use, such as a phaser pistol or a laser light sword; it is feasible that a "Mothership" could produce a wide enough "field" to power lasers or phases on a planet's surface without the weapon needing a local "in-weapon" source. As to starships and scout ships, it is likely that a star ship employs Electro-magnetic thrusters, Ion engines, fusion engines and even anti-gravity devises to warp the fabric of space-time; on the other hand, scout ships and near Earth craft would tend to use anti-gravity to manipulate the Earth's gravitational field.

Below are a few illustrations where electromagnetic frequencies may be used or has been used as directed energy weapons.

ARTICLE 50

PLANET EARTH Inc.
(Who really Controls the World)

It is the 13 Orion Families and their Legacy Who Actually Controls the World - The Founders have encoded the laws and corporate charters upon each of the subsidiaries as participants in the pyramid in such a way as to take control of the beliefs, money, military, and commerce of Planet Earth. And so it has come to pass that humanity has indeed accepted the fictional things as real the same way we all accept the rules of the corporations we work for.

But under PLANET EARTH Inc. the business plan has engaged vehicles such as the corporation of GOD with the corporate charter of The Bibles. And the corporation of IMF (International Monetary Fund) and UNITED NATIONS with their charter of a New World Order, a new monetary system and one god have come to the forefront. The goal is to employ all the residents of Earth, and, in the eyes of the owners make the slaves happier.

For those who are happy to be employed by the PLANET EARTH Inc. and are happy with the laws as set forth in Corporation GOD, all is wonderful. View the stories in this book as a revelation of how you came to be so lucky. Perhaps PLANET EARTH Inc. is leading to a new Age of One Order.

For those who are unhappy to be employed, or driven by their higher spiritual needs, this book may shed some light on how to quit and to ESCAPE this dominated, polarity, one rule world. Created under PLANET EARTH Inc. What may be the great revelation in this case is how they came to be unknowingly employed and how to quit what may be an undesirable employment.

So, here is why this book was written. It is your choice as to how the information is brought into your daily reality. Like Morpheus in the Matrix movie said:

> *"Do you want to know what it is? The matrix is everywhere, it is all around us. Even now in this very room. You can see it when you look out your window, or turn on your television set. You can feel it when you go to work, when you go to church, when you pay your taxes. It is the wool that has been pulled over your eyes to blind you from the truth. You are a slave Neo like everyone else. You were born into a prison that you cannot see, that you cannot smell, or taste or touch. A prison for your mind. Unfortunately no one can be told what the Matrix is. You have to see it for yourself.* **This is your last chance. After this, there is no turning back.** *Take the blue pill, the story ends, you wake up in your bed and believe whatever you want to believe. Take the red pill, you will stay in wonderland, and I will show you how deep the rabbit hole goes. Remember,* **what I am offering is the truth, nothing more.** *Follow me."*

The Global Elite "gods" - The ones who are at the top of these heaps are alleged to be the gods, the Global Elite, The Powers That Be, there are many names. They are our starting point and like doing some due diligence on any corporation; one must look to the alleged Founders, the Directors, and the private Owners of the corporations. In following our simple model, we will explore the Corporation from the top down.

Bloodlines of the Global Elite – At the end of the 2nd Galactic War and reconfirmed at the End of the 3rd Galactic War (approx. 500,000 years ago), the Orion Empire, by Treaty, was awarded the governance over the Virgo Supercluster which contains our Local Galaxy Group (which contains the Milky Way, with contains Earth and many other planets).

There were 13 Humanoid/Reptilian hybrid families within the Orion Royalty who still believed in a "might-is-right" and service-to-self mindset. These are the ancient roots of our present day Cabal — the 13 Royal Bloodlines, the Dark Men from Orion. The 13 Bloodlines were banished from their system (Orion Empire), an action that would come back to haunt the civilizations of Maldek, Mars and eventually, Earth.

The 13 Royal Bloodlines were jealous of this ruling and they decided to travel to our system to see if they could perhaps gain a toehold from which to eventually take over the resource-rich planets here which they coveted. They settled on Mars but didn't exactly receive a warm welcome from the Pleiadian civilizations which existed there. The existing civilizations tried to make room for the dark-minded newcomers, believing everyone deserved a chance, but before too long even these benevolent and fair-minded people could no longer tolerate the vibration of the Dark Men from Orion. Infighting between the 33 families led to Nuclear War, destroying the atmosphere that surrounded Mars. The 13 Royal Bloodlines relocated to Earth and began their domination of the planet.

Long ago in the dark unwritten pages of human history, the Royal Families discovered how they could control other men by torture, magical practices, wars, politics, religion and interest taking. These Elite Families designed strategies and tactics to perpetuate their special knowings, technologies and abilities into practice.

In time, The Royal Families developed a plan; a simple model, all gods, bloodlines, and humanity are evolving on a path of different stages of growth and evolution. This Plan colligates into the greatest and largest corporations on earth--particularly the ones alleged to be under the PLANET EARTH INC.

Because these people live in the private domains, and are outside of the scope of the inquisitors and peering eyes, the accumulations of fortunes has allowed them to march towards the conquering of PLANET EARTH in their own way without rules except their own.

The ideology f the Elite Orion Families is an eclectic and confusing mixture of religious, ideologies, philosophies and quantum physical calculations, scientific experimental ideals, mysticism, occultism, shamanism, Judaism, Cabbalisms, Gnosticism, Satanism, Taoism, externalism, center-egoism, materialistic values and priorities, voodoo magic, chaos magic, cannibalism, pedophiliam spirituality, psychiatric and neo-psychology, hypotheses All these ingredients gave birth to their mystical Luciferian Doctrine / Luciferian Dualism to manifest itself, by the structure of their thinking and visualization, using two many opposite components as their main constructions of their complete product.

The Original 13 Orion Bloodlines formed the following groups

- Ishmael bloodline from which a special elite line developed alchemy, assassination techniques, and other occult practices.
- Egyptian/Celtic/Druidic bloodline from which Druidism was developed.
- The Orient bloodline developed oriental magic.
- The Canaan bloodline and the Canaanites. It had the name Astarte, then Astorga, then Ashdor, and then Astor.
- The tribe of Dan was used as a Judas Iscariot type seed. The royalty of the tribe of Dan have descended down through history.
- The royal lineage of Jesus, known as the House of David with their blood which they believe is not only from the House of David but also from the lineage of Jesus, who they claim had a wife and children. This was instilled with the direct seed of Satan so that they would not only carry Christ's blood--but also the blood of his "brother" Lucifer.
- Babylon bloodline and are descendent from Nimrod.
- The Mystery Religions each had their secret **3 councils** which ruled them, and these councils themselves came under the guidance of a secret supreme Grand Council or Governing Body. The Mystery Religions in turn ruled the masses and the political leaders.

Modern Day Decedents of the 13 Royal Orion Empire Families (sometimes referred to as the Bloodlines of the Illuminati). Most are involved in Drugs, Sex Trade, similar. The list is, of course, incomplete but it is what I found in print.

The top 13 ruling families

- Rothchild (Bauer / Bower)
- Bruce
- Cavandish (Kennedy)
- De Medici
- Hanover
- Habsburg / Hapsburg
- Krupp
- Plantagenet
- Rockfeller
- Romanov
- Sinclare (St. Clare)
- Warburg (Del Blanco)
- Winsor (Saxe-Coburg-Gothe)
- Astor

Second Division of Top Members of the Committee of '300"

- Agnelli
- Baliol
- Beale
- Bell
- Bouvier
- Bush
- Cameron
- Campbell
- Carnegie
- Carrington
- Coolidge
- Delano
- Douglas
- Dord
- Gardner
- Graham
- Hamilton
- Harriman
- Heinz
- Kuhn
- Lindsay
- Loeb
- Mellon Montgomery
- Morgan

- Korman
- Oppenheimer
- Rhodes
- Roosevelt
- Russell
- Savoy
- Schiff
- Seton
- Senser
- Steward / Stuart
- Wilson

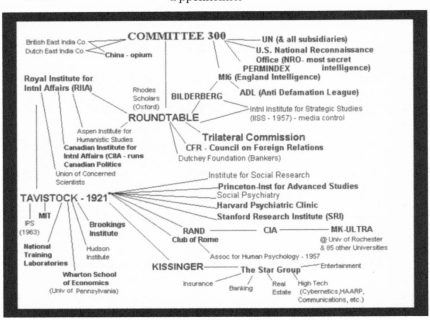

Organizations / Corporations that have been infiltrated / hijacked by the Royal Bloodlines

- Council of Foreign Relations
- The Bilderberg Group
- The Ateral Commission
- Club of Roam
- Royal Institute of International Addairs
- The Mafia
- CIA

- NSA
- MOSAD
- Secret Services
- International Monetary Fund
- Federal Reserve
- International Revenue Services
- Interpol

Created Countries – The Elite Families have, over centuries, created several countries to further support their own sinister goals, to create economic crisis, wars between these countries, to breed more economical prosperity for themselves. These countries include:

- The United States
- Kuwait
- The Soviet Union (Russia)
- Panama
- Israel

- Yugoslavia (Bosnia/Herzegovina, Croatia, Kosovo, Serbia, etc.)
- The United Kingdom
- All of the Arab Countries
- All of Central & South America

King James made a pack with the Roman Catholic Church (The Vatican and the secret society of the Jesuits) that they would be the owner of the United States, where the monarchy of Britain would be the force of regency of England, United States, and Canada.

Communists. The super rich Illuminated families generally get along quite well and supposedly want to take away the wealth of the above and give it to the people. However, this is only double talk designed to bolster the superstructure of delusion that Communists are the enemies of all Capitalists. But Communists, like the super rich families, are not the enemies of MONOPOLY CAPITALISM: they are the foes of FREE ENTERPRISE." (Untitled manuscript of David Hill, p. 215.)

If one just follow the money - the top ten transnational companies that hold the most control over the global economy.

- Barclays plc
- Capital Group Companies Inc.
- FMR Corporation
- 4AXA
- Merrill Lynch & Co Inc.

- State Street Corporation
- JPMorgan Chase & Co.
- Vanguard Group Inc.
- UBS AG

The illustration shows the interconnectedness of the top players in this international scheme:

Some of the other usual suspects round out the top 25, including Morgan Stanley, Credit Suisse, and Goldman Sachs.

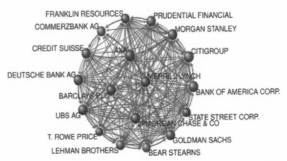

What you won't find are Exxon-Mobil, Microsoft, or General Electric; you have to scroll all the way down to China Petrochemical Group Company at number 50 to find a company that actually *creates* something.

The top 49 corporations are financial institutions, banks, and insurance companies — with the exception of Wal-Mart, which ranks at number 15.
The rest essentially just push money around to one another.

Lightworkers, Galactic Warriors, Light Bearers, Crystals, Wanders, Travelers, Way Showers, and Star Beings – you now know the environment in which you are working and the challenges you face in bringing LIGHT INTO THE WORLD.

With the Orion Empire having governance over the 4% Universe (which contains Earth), there is nothing that Enki, the Load of the Lower Realms (called by many other names) does not know that is happening within the 4% Universe. This means that he knows you are here. Some of us are hear as Observers for the Free Universe to confirm that Enki is complying with the Treaty that ended the 3rd Galactic War and, hence, we are protected by the Emissary role. However, I do not know under what terms that the other Lightworkers, et al are granted to be on Earth. It may be that He knows that the Lightworkers will only be able to contact a very limited number of mankind and, perhaps, the ones that have an Escape Plan are an acceptable loss – just a couple of percent of the Earth's population.

WAKE UP AND COMPLETE YOUR MISSION

Sources
1. "The Anonymous Worldwide United's Revolution, Against the System",
   https://anonymousworldwideunited.wordpress.com/
2. "Special Report: Who Really Controls the World?", The Outside Club,
   https://www.outsiderclub.com/report/who-really-controls-the-world/1032
3. Bloodlines of Illuminati", Fritz Springmeier, 1995,
   https://www.cia.gov/library/abbottabad-compound/
   FC/FC2F5371043C48FDD95AEDE7B8A49624_Springmeier.-
   .Bloodlines.of.the.Illuminati.R.pdf
4. Devine Providence – Birthing New Earth, Jaemes McBride & Ed Rychkem,
   https://uploads- sl.webflow.com/59c1dba5802d9b0001338665/5cb794
   7425b50adde5012efa_THE%20DIVINE%20PROVINCE.pdf

ARTICLE 51

WE ARE FRAGMENTS FROM THE SAME SOURCE DESPITE MANY MIGRATIONS & CROSSINGS

The Dark Force "owns" the 4" Universe (in which we are located) and they employ separation and fear to maintain their dominance and control.

THEIR SEPARATION IS TO PIT ONE AGAINST THE OTHER includes but not limited to,

- Age
- Disability
- Marriage and civil partnership
- Race
- Religion and belief
- Sex
- Creed: Service-to-Self vs. Service-to-Others
- Education level attained
- Income
- Place of employment
- Type of work: White Collar, Blue Collar
- Where and how you live
- Social status

- Language
- Nationality
- Dialect, inflection and type of speech

Once they "drive this "wedge" between people, they then inject distrust and fear to complete their means of control.

The types of "wedges" that the Dark Force employs include,

1) <u>Direct discrimination</u> - There are three different types of direct discrimination.

Direct discrimination occurs when a person is treated less favorably because of:
* A characteristic they possess.
* A characteristic possessed by someone who they are associated with (such as a member of their family or a colleague). This is direct discrimination by association.
* A characteristic they are thought to possess, regardless of whether the perception is correct or not. This is direct discrimination by perception.

Although there is normally a deliberate act or exclusion, direct discrimination does not have to be intentional.

2) <u>Indirect discrimination</u> - Indirect discrimination is usually less obvious than direct discrimination and is normally unintended. Generally speaking, it occurs when a rule or plan of some sort is put into place which applies to everyone; and is not in itself discriminatory but it could put those with a certain protected characteristic at a disadvantage.

* It has (or will have) the effect of putting those who share the characteristic at a particular disadvantage when compared to others who do not have the characteristic
* It puts, or would put, the person at that disadvantage
* The person is unable to objectively justify it.

Indirect discrimination is most likely to include an employer's **policies, procedures, requirements, rules and arrangements, even if informal, and whether written down or not.**

3) <u>Harassment</u> - Harassment is 'unwanted conduct' related to a protected characteristic. It has the purpose or effect of violating a person's dignity or creating an intimidating, hostile, degrading, humiliating or offensive environment for them. Bullying, nicknames, gossip, intrusive or inappropriate questions and comments can be harassment. Excluding someone (not inviting them to meetings or events) may also qualify. To say the behavior was not meant to cause offence or was 'banter' is not a defense. With harassment, how the victim sees the conduct is more important than how the harasser sees it.

4) **Victimization** occurs when a person suffers a 'detriment' because they have done (or because it is suspected that they have done or may do) one of the following things in good faith:

- Make an allegation of discrimination
- Support a complaint of discrimination
- Give evidence relating to a complaint about discrimination
- Raise a grievance concerning equality or discrimination
- Do anything else for the purposes of (or in connection with) Equality

RECENT DISCOVERIES DEBUNK THE OUT-OF-AFRICA THEORY

- Anthropologist has recently discovered that we are not "Out of Africa" but that mankind is distributed throughout the Earth. This research includes:

- Human footprints in the clay of Crete, Greece dating to 5.2 Million years ago.

  Two skulls, one Neanderthal and one Homo sapiens, were discovered in Southeast Europe and they date back 170,000 and 210,000 years old, respectively.

  These skulls "show that the early dispersion of Homo Sapiens out of Africa not only occurred earlier, before 200,000 years ago, but also reached further geographically, all the way to Europe" (Katerina Harvati, paleoanthropologist, Eberhard Karls University, Tubingen, Germany).

Multiple migrations? - Hominines— a subset of great apes that includes Homo sapiens and Neanderthals—are believed to have emerged in Africa more than six million years ago. They left the continent in several migration waves starting about two million years ago.

The oldest known African fossil attributed to a member of the Homo family is a 2.8 million-year-old jawbone from Ethiopia.

Homo sapiens replaced Neanderthals across Europe for good around 45,000-35,000 years ago, in what was long considered a gradual takeover of the continent involving millennia of co-existence and even interbreeding.
But the skull discovery in Greece suggests that Homo sapiens undertook the migration from Africa to southern Europe on "more than one occasion", according to Eric Delson, a professor of anthropology at City University of New York.

"Rather than a single exit of hominins from Africa to populate Eurasia, there must have been several dispersals, some of which did not result in permanent occupations," said Delson, who was not involved in the *Nature* study.

Harvati said advances in dating and genetics technology could continue to shape our understanding of how our pre-historic ancestors spread throughout the world.

DNA Analysis Indicates that we are all ONE, despite the multiple "crossings" made by various aliens over eons of time.

National Geographic complete an exposé of the Out-of-Africa theory and listed that the migration occurred in three stages.

First wave: Out of Africa (45,000 years ago)- Thirty-two years ago the study of the DNA of living humans helped establish that we all share a family tree and a primordial migration story: All people outside Africa are descended from ancestors who left that continent more than 60,000 years ago. About 45,000 years ago, those first modern humans ventured into Europe, having made their way up through the Middle East. Their own DNA suggests they had dark skin and perhaps light eyes.

The first modern Europeans lived as hunters and gatherers in small, nomadic bands. They followed the rivers, edging along the Danube from its mouth on the Black Sea deep into western and central Europe. For millennia, they made little impact. Their DNA indicates they mixed with the Neanderthals — who, within 5,000 years, were gone. Today about 2 percent of a typical European's genome consists of Neanderthal DNA. A typical African has none.

As Europe was gripped by the Ice Age, the modern humans hung on in the ice-free south, adapting to the cold climate. Around 27,000 years ago, there may have been as few as a thousand of them, according to some population estimates. They subsisted on large mammals such as mammoths, horses, reindeer, and aurochs — the ancestors of modern cattle. In the caves where they sheltered, they left behind spectacular paintings and engravings of their prey.

Second wave: Out of Anatolia (10,300 years ago) - The Konya Plain in central Anatolia is modern Turkey's breadbasket, a fertile expanse.

Notably, this is the period that at least part of Gobekli Tepe is believed to have been constructed. Ancient carvings on Gobekli pillar show evidence of a comet swarm hitting Earth around 13,000 years ago.

Within a thousand years the Neolithic revolution, as it's called, spread north through Anatolia and into southeastern Europe. By about 6,000 years ago, there were farmers and herders all across Europe.

About 5,400 years ago, everything changed. All across Europe, thriving Neolithic settlements shrank or disappeared altogether. The dramatic decline has puzzled archaeologists for decades. "There's less stuff, less material, less people, less sites. There are signs of catastrophic events (<u>Comets and the Bronze Age Collapse</u>).

After a 500-year gap, the population seemed to grow again, but something was very different. In southeastern Europe, the villages and egalitarian cemeteries of the Neolithic were replaced by imposing grave mounds covering lone adult men. Farther north, from Russia to the Rhine, a new Culture sprang up, called Corded Ware after its pottery, which was decorated by pressing string into wet clay.

Third wave: Out of the Steppe - 4,700 years ago. On what are now the steppes of southern Russia and eastern Ukraine, a group of nomads called the Yamnaya, some of the first people in the world to ride horses, had mastered the wheel and were building wagons and following herds of cattle across the grasslands. They built few permanent settlements. But they buried their most prominent men with bronze and silver ornaments in mighty grave mounds that still dot the steppes. Their DNA seems to have little or no "out-of-Africa" DNA content. This lack of "Out-of-Africa" DNA may cause the whole the0ry to be discarded – for the moment, the antropoligists are indicating a small sub-intrusion of "Out-of-Africa" into the Yamnaya homeland.

By 2800 B.C, archaeological excavations show, the Yamnaya had begun moving west.

Within a few centuries, other people with a significant amount of Yamnaya DNA had spread as far as the British Isles and other locations. The Yamnaya brought domesticated horses and a mobile lifestyle based on wagons into Stone Age Europe. And in bringing innovative metal weapons and tools, they may have helped nudge Europe toward the Bronze Age.

From the National Geographic illustration, one can see the migration patterns and the percent distribution of the various peoples {Hunter Gathers (white), Neolithic Farmers (blue) and Yamnaya (brown)] as well as the "paths of migration) of,

- **Hunter Gathers** (Out-of-Africa) – The earliest settlers into Europe. They kept to themselves and did not mix with Neolithic Farmers.
- **Neolithic Farmers** (Out-of-AAnatolia) – They brought wheat, sheep, cattle and their own DNA to most of Europe by 4000 BC.
- **Yamnaya** (Out-of-the Steppe) – They brought horses, wagons and introduced Europe to the Bronze Age.

Modern Europe – Yamnaya bloodlines is stronger in the North; Neolithic Farmers are strong in southern Europe.

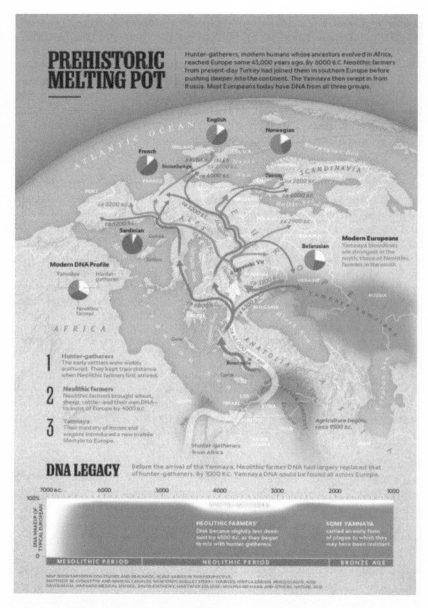

Bottomline - We are all a mix of Hunter Gathers, Neolithic Farmers, and Yamnaya/ to this extent, we are One and not separate. Yet, the Yamnaya "separation" may point to more than one location for the origin of Mankind.

Lightworkers, Galactic Warriors, Crystals, Wanders, Travelers, and Star Beings need to apply their mission equally to all without discrimination or separation, since all are One, including the Dark Force who, also, needs to "See the Light".

Sources
1. "THE 4 TYPES OF DISCRIMINATION: WHAT EVERY EM-PLOYER NEEDS TO KNOW," Karen FalconerApril, Feb 2020, Current Affairs, Legal Update, Top Tip, https://www.hrsolutions-uk.com/4-types-of-discrimination/"Out of Europe, Not Africa? 5.2 Million years old pre-human footprint found in Greece", Emily Chung, CBC News, Fri, 23 Feb 2018, https://www.sott.net/article/378613-Out-of-Europe-Not-Africa-5-2-Million-years-old-pre-human-footprint-found-in-Greece

2. "Oldest remains' outside Africa reset human migration clock", July 10, 2019, https://phys.org/news/2019-07-oldest-africa-reset-human-migration.html

3. *"DNA Deciphers Roots of Modern Europeans"*, Carl Zimmer, June 10, 2015, The New York Times- Matter, https://www.nytimes.com/2015/06/16/science/dna-deciphers-roots-of-modern-europeans.html

ARTICLE 52

UNITING WITH YOUR TWIN FLAME IS ESSENTIAL (Your Twin Flame is a Fragment of You – A Mirror of You)

Several people misunderstand the meaning of "Twin Flame". They are entirely different from Soul Mates.

<u>Soul Mates</u> complement each other and make us feel whole. Do not confuse "soul mate" with romance. You have a "soul mate family" who helped you determine what your goals and mission would be in this life – you determined your life plan in the Pre Life Planning session long before your arrival in a human uniform here on Earth. Refer to Chapter 2 of my book, Conscious Awakening – A Research Compendium (2019) for Pre-Life Planning.

- You have many Soul Mates. We often meet more than one Soul Mate in a lifetime, but they are not romantic partners.
- Soul Mates have the same energetic frequency to you – you could call them your "family" – consider them anything from close "energetic relatives" like sisters and brothers to cousins and distant cousins, and even close friends depending on how close your frequencies match.
- Soul Mates and friendships are often "challenging" but close. We sign up to meet in life to help each other evolve. There is always something to be learned from Soul Mate connections.
- Many Twin Flames encounter Soul Mates prior to coming together with their Devine Counterpart – to evolve and learn lessons, getting a chance to resolve important karma before meeting their Twin Flame for Ascension and Union.
- These encounters can be with so-called "False Twins" (someone who is very similar to your Twin Flame in important ways) or "Karmic Twins"

- (souls who have had similar important karma to resolve as you have had). These relationships have a specific purpose of healing wounds and getting over limitations.
- Soul Mates can be romantic partners, family members or friends. They can come into your life for a specific reason (brief moment), for a particular period of your life (for a season), or be lifetime companions. There are a variety of different Soul Mate "roles".

Twin Flame

- **There is only one Twin Flame**/Twin Soul – our true Energetic Counterpart.
  - o Your Twin Flame is the only other being in the Universe Realms who shares the exact same Core Spiritual Frequency as you, which is known as your "Twin Flame Soul Song".
  - o You and your Twin Flame are aspects of the same energy consciousness – Twin Flames are, therefore, often called "one soul with two bodies".
  - o You and your Twin Flame, deep down, share an identical Soul identity.

- **Twin Flames are part of the same, greater conscious soul**. They share an innate, deep connection. That's why Twin Flame relationships are often compared to a mirror. A Twin Flame acts as a spiritual window into the deepest, most hidden away aspects of your soul. **Your Twin Flame is mirror images of you** – a fragment of you which makes you whole. Their past, fears and emotional lives resonate within you.

- **Everyone has a Twin Flame** – Your Twin Flame is the other half of you. You were both cut from the same energetic cloth. You may not always be "in sink" with each other, despite having the same nature and the same Spirit. When you connect with your Twin Flame it is the discovery of "Oneness".

  - **Your Twin Flame may have chosen to incarnate into your Timeline** in order to be your Soul Mate during this lifetime. However, your Twin Flame is using your Soul Mate as a conduit for communication because you believe that the only means of contact is by direct communication. In this case, it may be difficult for you to separate Soul Mate from Twin Flame but there is, indeed, a difference.

  - **Your Twin Flame may not reside here on Earth** but may reside within a different Realm (Article 32), Different Density (Article 33) or even within a different Timeline (Article 7), or Simultaneous Living in Past, Present and Future (Article 29). You need to "connect" via telepathy, Astral Projection, through Dreams, or finding your Twin right inside you – so look inside.

- **The true means of communication is between you and your Twin Flame is telepathic**, even in this physical world on where your Twin Flame is ethereal and resides in a different Realm and in a different Density. Communication with your Twin Flame is a "two-way street". The telepathic message may then be vocalized depending upon the situation and need to do so.

  ○ **You do not need to "search "for your Twin Flame** since your Twin Flame is just a breath away. You just need to open a "channel" since your Twin Flame is has been trying to talk to you all of your life. Various means of communication include,

    ○ Dreams.
    ○ Astral Projection.
    ○ Going to bed thinking of a spiritual conundrum and waking up with the answer or having been given the means to find the solution.
    ○ That "Still Small Voice" within you that guides you.
    ○ Your Twin Flame may "talk to you" through a friend, acquaintance, or a "passerby" – noting is by chance.
    ○ Your Twin Flame provides you comfort through Soul Mates, animals, plants, and the Earth itself.

- **You say that you are past middle-age and have never found your Twin Flame.** Often your Twin Flame has agreed to incarnate here on Earth as part of your Life Pre-Planning Session (refer to Chapter 2 of my book, *Conscious Awakening – A Research Compendium*). But, perhaps you have been looking in all the wrong places.

- **Your Twin Flame may be your ethereal Guide** in this life or may be a close friend in who you can confide any feeling or thought, or may co-exist as your Soul Mate.

- **Your Twin Flame has the power to change your beliefs**, ideas and concepts, and how you perceive life. Most likely, it was your Twin Flame who started you on your journey of enlightenment to find the TRUTH and your AWAKENING.

- **Your Twin Flame fills the Void within you.** Whenever they are in your presence, they fill the VOID within you – again, your Twin Flame does not have to be a physical being. A Twin Flame relationship is not Love. It is a relationship that takes many forms. Sometimes this relationship can be a teacher, sometimes a therapist, and sometimes a despotic tyrant. Your relationship defies the laws of a normal human relationship.

- **Twin flames have checkered relationships** marked by emotional inconsistencies, mission priorities and expectations, and method of achieving your ascension. The love between Twin Flames is the love of self and the love of Creator God.

- o Unlike a life partners, or what **we** consider "**soul** mate," **Twin Flames are an intense and challenging relationships** which force us to deal with our unresolved issues to become a better person.
- o Twin Flame is a mirror of you and sometimes appears to be an opposite.

I don't have a Twin Flame – Many will claim they do not have a Twin Flame. This is, of course, a misconception – everyone has a Twin Flame. It is rare and fraught with difficulties to have both Twin Souls meet in 3D. 3D is for resolving karmic difficulties and Twin Souls are such perfect mirrors that they often cannot get along until very far along in their individual karmic resolutions. It is more common for your Twin Flame to remain in a different Density or Realm in order to overlight and assist the incarnated Twin. Therefore, the connection is truly telepathic. Many misinterpret this relation as Incarnate and Guide, when the relationship is really that of Twin Flames.

One needs to remember You and all of the Lightworkers on this planet have previously ascended at least 3 times before being allowed to volunteer for this assignment. Those were not ascensions in which you took your physical with you. This will be the first physical ascension for most of us. Given this, it unlike that the Twin Flames will incarnate together; one often confuses Twin Fame with Soul Mate.

We have hundreds of soul mates and affinities of both male and female gender that constitute our soul family.

Each of us work out agreements with these members that mutually serve us, even though, we sometimes take adversarial roles to stimulate the acknowledgement of areas that still need more resolution. This is actually a very loving service.

On the other hand, we only have one Twin or-- a Triad of male, female, and androgynous aspects with the latter being the fully merged and higher dimensional unified self.

For this lifetime, most have chosen a gender that corresponds with their first incarnational expression. However, we all have had about the same number of lifetimes in each gender. Hence, if the Twin Flames who incarnated together may be of the same sex – this will be disturbing to many and is one of the primary reasons the Twins do not, normally, incarnate together. One normally remains an Overlight and the other Incarnate.

The thing that is so powerful with Twin or Triad Souls is that, when they come into each other's presence, the resonance is so complete that it can throw them out of balance with their Earth mission.

The True Stages of a Twin Flame Union with your Twin Flame – Directly applicable to your Earth incarnated Twin Soul; similar but different from your ethereal Twin Soul.

- **Prepare yourself for union with your Twin Flame** - Whether you have yet to meet your Twin Flame or already have them in your spiritual life, the Universe has already prepared you for the initial stages by allowing you to experience karmic relationships (soul mates). These relationships tend to be very sweet and end very badly. These relationships allow you to Awaken and grow and learn your karmic lessons.

- **Meeting with your twin flame** -This is the stage where you actually meet your Twin Flame, the first meeting. It will happen when you least suspect it and you won't believe what is happening. In this Twin Flame relationship stage you will feel that magnetically pull towards a stranger, yet in your soul you have already recognized them and feel you know them from somewhere. Maybe it's the moment you get that inner sense, "hey stranger, where have you been all this time?"

- **Developing a deeper connection** - After the first initial encounter with your Twin Flame, both of you will be feeling the magnetic pull, now you will run into each other more often. You are both being pulled together by the unusual synchronicity. As you both continue your interactions, you will feel the connection deepening, you know the feeling you have known them for a lifetime.

- **Twin Flame Unity** - In this Twin Flame relationship stage, you understand the deeper meaning of the Twin Flame relationship. You both feel a sense of perfection, intense connection, just feels perfect. Everything in the Twin Flame relationship is intensified, all your emotions and feelings whether they are positive or negative. Not doing the inner work in the first stage may allow the negative emotions to take control. Once reconciliation occurs, both realize the reality of the union, which is spiritual reality. You have managed to let go of emotional baggage. There is only harmony, feeling the bliss. Now as Twin Flames your work begins to guide this world, be selfless and help others find their inner bliss.

The process of achieving Twin Unity is not so much one of creation but one of rediscovery, a process of learning that fuels the evolution of universal consciousness.

Twin Flames & the Illusion of Time - The Twin Flame relationships abides by no timeline - Souls don't understand the concept of time. They don't follow traditional rules.

In the beginning when we were created from light and the dust of the stars, each orb of energy was split into two flames—two souls. These souls travel in each lifetime learning as much as they can about life and humanity. Often times, Twin Flames gravitate toward the non-traditional because it is there that their souls feel most at ease in the discovery of their purpose and authentic life path.

The only way to fully immerse ourselves in togetherness with our Twin Flame is to leave it up to the Universe.

Twin Flames gather strength from the combining soul energy.

To make the decision to embark on a journey with our Twin Flame requires openness and patience. It requires courage and passion for the unknown. To journey into the unfathomable means to learn how to be in togetherness along the way.

You must unite with your Twin Flame in order to Escape this Realm - When Twin Flames are united, they become a gateway to Higher Realms and enable high vibrational energy to spread from their system and out to others, benefitting not only themselves but everyone who comes in contact with them.

Sources
1   "Twin Flame Meaning: What You Need To Know", Kash And Susan, https://www.spiritualunite.com/articles/twin-flame-mean-ing/#:~:text=Twin%20flames%20have%20checkered%20relationships%20marked%20by%20emotional%20inconsistencies%20and%20intense%20passion.&text=Their%20time%20together%20runs%20the,stimulus%20to%20our%20spiritual%20awakening
2   "Everything You Need to Know About Twin Flame Relationships",
3   Crystal Zane, https://zanebaker.com/everything-know-twin-flame-relationship/
4   "Twin Flames & the Illusion of Time", Kash And Susan, Spiritual Unite, https://www.spiritualunite.com/articles/twin-flames-the-illusion-of-time-2/
5   "Twin Flames", Mark Huber, GTR-Intel.com, http://www.grt-intel.com/s-t_topics/twin_flames.htm

ARTICLE 53

ME AND MY SHADOW
(Shadow Work is Essential to finding True Self)

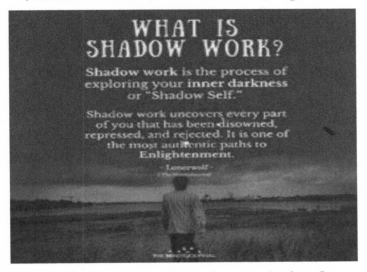

"Nothing ever goes away until it teaches us what we need to know"

– Pema Chodron

What is the Shadow?

The shadow is the "dark side" of our personality because it consists chiefly of primitive, negative human emotions and impulses like rage, envy, greed, selfishness, desire, and the striving for power.

- All we deny in ourselves—whatever we perceive as inferior, evil, or unacceptable—becomes part of the shadow.
- Anything incompatible with our chosen conscious attitude about ourselves is relegated to this dark side.
- The personal shadow is the *disowned self.* This shadow self represents the parts of us we no longer claim to be our own, including inherent positive qualities.
- These unexamined or disowned parts of our personality don't go anywhere. Although we deny them in our attempt to cast them out, we don't get rid of them.
- We repress and deny them; they are part of our unconscious. Think of the unconscious as everything we are not conscious of.
- We can't eliminate the shadow. It stays with us as our dark brother or sister. Trouble arises when we fail to see it. For then, to be sure, it is standing right beside and behind us.

Our "Shadow" is the other half of each person and along with our "Light" side makes us a whole person. The True Self recognizes both sides.

How the Shadow is Born

- Every young child knows kindness; love, and generosity, and also expresses anger, selfishness, and greed. These emotions are part of our shared humanity.

- But as we grow up, something happens and the traits associated with "being good" are accepted, while others associated with "being bad" are rejected.

- We all have **basic human needs**. These needs include physiological needs, safety and security needs, and needs for belonging. These needs are biological and instinctual.

- As children, when we expressed certain parts of ourselves, we received negative cues from our environment. Maybe we got angry and threw a tantrum. Our parents reprimanded the outburst and sent us to our room. Or perhaps we acted boldly, playfully, spontaneously, or silly in our first-grade classroom. Our teacher shamed us for our lack of decorum in front of the class and told us to sit down. Whenever it happened—and it might have happened often—it threatened one of our basic needs.

- We adjusted our behavior to gratify our needs and learned to adapt to the external world.

- What happens as we grow up? - Through time, we learn to both enjoy, and despise our socially-approved egos because, on the one hand, they make us feel good and "lovable" but, on the other hand, they feel phony and inhibited.

Each of us is like Dorian Grey. We seek to present a beautiful, innocent face to the world; a kind, courteous demeanor; a youthful, intelligent image. And so, unknowingly but inevitably, we push away those qualities that do not fit the image, that do not enhance our self-esteem and make us stand proud but, instead, bring us shame and make us feel small. We shove into the dark cavern of the unconscious those feelings that make us uneasy — hatred, rage, jealousy, greed, competition, lust, shame — and those behaviors that are deemed wrong by the culture — addiction, laziness, aggression, dependency — thereby creating what could be called shadow content. Like Dorian's painting, these qualities ultimately take on a life of their own, forming and invisible twin that lives just behind us or just beside it ...

- This repression of unwanted parts creates what psychologist Carl Jung called the *personal shadow*.

Why Focusing Only on the Light is a Form of Escapism – Most firmly believe that the only thing worthy of guiding us is "light" and "love." Whether through the family environment or the cultural myths, we were brought up clinging to and believe that all you really needed to do in life to be happy was to focus on everything beautiful, positive and spiritually "righteous." It's a sort of "Recipe for Well-Being."

It is very easy and comfortable to focus only on the light side of life. So many people in today's world follow this path. And while it might provide some

331 | Article 53 - Me and My Shadow

temporary emotional support, it doesn't reach to the depths of your being: it doesn't transform you at a core level. Instead, it leaves you superficially hanging onto warm and fuzzy platitudes which sound nice, but don't enact any real change.

What DOES touch the very depths of your being, however, is exploring your Shadow.

What Happens When You Repress Your Shadow - Rejecting, suppressing, denying, or disowning your Shadow, whether consciously or unconsciously, is a dangerous thing. The thing about the Shadow Self is that it *seeks* to be known. It *yearns* to be understood, explored, and integrated. It craves to be held in awareness. The longer the Shadow stays buried and locked in its jail cell deep within the unconscious, the more it will find opportunities to *make* you aware of its existence.

Both religion and modern spirituality have a tendency to focus on the "love and light" aspects of spiritual growth to their own doom. **This over-emphasis on the fluffy, transcendental, and feel-good elements of a spiritual awakening results in shallowness and phobia of whatever is too real, earthy, or dark.**

Spiritually bypassing one's inner darkness results in a whole range of serious issues. Some of the most common and reoccurring Shadow issues that appear in the spiritual/religious community include pedophilia among priests, financial manipulation of followers among gurus, and of course, megalomania, narcissism, and God complexes among spiritual teachers.

Other issues that arise when we reject our Shadow side can include,

- Hypocrisy (believing and supporting one thing, but doing the other)
- Lies and self-deceit (both towards oneself and others)
- Uncontrollable bursts of rage/anger
- Emotional and mental manipulation of others
- Greed and addictions
- Phobias and obsessive compulsions
- Intense anxiety
- Chronic psychosomatic illness
- Depression (which can turn into suicidal tendencies)
- Sexual perversion
- Narcissistically inflated ego
- Chaotic relationships with others
- Self-loathing
- Self-absorption
- Self-sabotage... and many others. This is by no means a comprehensive list (and there are likely many other issues out there).

13 Types of Shadow Selves - Our inner demons come in many different shapes and varieties. While some are more ferocious than others, others don't really seem to be all that monstrous at all – until we reap the devilish consequences later on in our lives. Keep in mind that this list only explores the dark side of the Shadow, not the light side (where the positive repressed qualities of our nature are buried).

1. The Egotistical Monster - "not being good enough"; arrogance, egocentricity, pompousness, narcissism, excessive pride.
2. The Neurotic Monster - fear of life and self; desire to regain control; paranoia, obsessiveness, suspiciousness, finicky, demanding, masochistic.
3. The Untrustworthy Monster - fear of life in general; secretive, impulsive, frivolous, irresponsible, deceitful, unreliable.
4. The Emotionally Unstable Monster - feeling "unlovable" and powerless; moody, melodramatic, manipulative, weepy, overemotional, impulsive, changeable.
5. The Controlling Monster - mistrust of life, feelings abandoned and "not being good enough"; suspicious, jealous, possessive, bossy, obsessive.
6. The Cynical Monster - feeling vulnerable; negative, overcritical, patronizing, resentful, cantankerous.
7. The Wrathful Monster - fear others, mistrust of life, closed heart; ruthless, vengeful, bitchy, quick-tempered, quarrelsome.
8. The Rigid Monster - fear and rejection of the unknown, chaos, and ego death; uptight, intolerant, obstinate, uncompromising, inflexible, narrow-minded.
9. The Glib Monster - mistrust of life, others, and self; superficial, cunning, inconsistent, sly, crafty.
10. The Nonchalant Monster - buried grief, fear, and shame; emotionally detached, distant, indifferent, uncaring, unexcited.
11. The Perverted Monster - repressed sexual energy, possible unresolved childhood wounds; sadistic, lustful, depraved, corrupt.
12. The Cowardly Monster - fear, disbelief in self; weak-willed, timid, fearful.
13. The Naive Monster - refusal to grow up, lack of individuated ego; puerile, petty, immature, illogical, simpleminded, vacuous.

Shadow Work is a practice that helps us to become whole again. It works on the premise that **you must 100% OWN your Shadow**, rather than avoiding or repressing it, to experience deep healing. This daunting and often frightening task is a requirement of every person in order to be your TRUE SELF.

Shadow work is the process of exploring your inner darkness or "Shadow Self." As mentioned previously, your Shadow Self is part of your unconscious mind and contains everything you feel ashamed of thinking and feeling, as well as every impulse, repressed idea, desire, fear and perversion that for one reason or another, you have "locked away" consciously or unconsciously. Often this is done as a way of keeping yourself tame, likable and "civilized" in the eyes of others.

Shadow work is the attempt to uncover everything that we have hidden and every part of us that has been disowned and rejected within our Shadow selves. Why? Because without revealing to ourselves what we have hidden, we remain burdened with problems such as anger, guilt, shame, disgust, and grief.

Before you begin Shadow Work, it's important for you to assess whether you're ready to embark on this journey. Not everyone is prepared for this deep work, and that's fine. We're all at different stages. So pay attention to the following questions and try to answer them honestly:

- **Have you practiced self-love yet?** If not, Shadow Work will be too overwhelming for you. **Shadow Work should not be attempted by those who have poor self-worth or struggle with self-loathing.** In other words: if you struggle with severely low self-esteem, please do not attempt Shadow Work. Why? If you struggle with extremely poor self-worth, exploring your Shadows will likely make you feel ten times worse about yourself. Before you walk this path, you absolutely must establish a strong and healthy self-image. No, you don't have to think you're God's gift to the world, but having average self-worth is important.
- **Are you prepared to make time?** Shadow Work is not a lukewarm practice. You are either all in or all out. Yes, it is important to take a break from it time to time. But Shadow Work requires dedication, self-discipline, and persistence. Are you willing to intentionally carve out time each day to dedicate to it? Even just ten minutes a day is a good start.
- **Are you looking to be validated or to find the truth?** As you probably know by now, Shadow Work isn't about making you feel special. It isn't like typical spiritual paths which are focused on the feel-good. No, Shadow Work can be brutal and extremely confronting. This is a path for truth seekers, not those who are seeking to be validated.
- **Seek to enter a calm and neutral space.** It is important to try and relax when doing Shadow Work. Stress and judgmental or critical attitudes will inhibit the process. So please try to incorporate a calming meditation or mindfulness technique into whatever you do.
- **Understand that you are not your thoughts.** It is essential for you to realize that you are not your thoughts for Shadow Work to be healing and liberating. Only from your calm and quiet Center (also known as the Seat of your Soul) can you truly be aware of your Shadow aspects. By holding them in awareness, you will see them clearly for what they are, and realize that they ultimately don't define you; they are simply rising and falling mental phenomena.
- **Practice self-compassion.** It is of paramount importance to incorporate compassion and self-acceptance into your Shadow Work practice. Without showing love and understanding to yourself, it is easy for Shadow Work to backfire and make you feel terrible. So focus on generating self-love and compassion, and you will be able to release any shame and embrace your humanity.
- **Record everything you find.** Keep a written journal or personal diary in which you write down, or draw, your discoveries. Recording your dreams, observations, and analysis will help you to learn and grow more

effectively. You'll also be able to keep track of your process and make important connections.

How to Practice Shadow Work - There are many Shadow Work techniques and exercises out there. In this Article, I will provide a few to help you start off.

1. Pay attention to your emotional reactions - Essentially, this practice is about finding out what you have given power to in your life unconsciously, because: what we place importance in – whether good or bad – says a lot about us. The reality is that what we react to, or what makes us angry and distressed, reveals extremely important information to us about ourselves.

    For example, by following where your "demons" have guided you, you discover that you may be burdened by an exasperating guilt complex that developed through your religious upbringing. A part of you may want to feel unworthy because that is what developed as a habit or feeling since childhood (e.g. "You're a sinner," "It's your fault Jesus was crucified"), and therefore, that is what you secretly feel comfortable with feeling unworthy. So mind nit-pick anything you might have done "wrong "and you are left with the feeling of being "bad." Thanks to this practice, you have welcomed more compassion, mindfulness, and forgiveness into your life.

    Paying attention to your emotional reactions can help you to discover exactly how your core wounds are affecting you on a daily basis.

2. Artistically Express Your Shadow Self - Art is the highest form of self-expression and is also a great way to allow your Shadow to manifest itself. Psychologists often use art therapy as a way to help patients explore their inner selves.

    Start by allowing yourself to feel or drawing on any existing dark emotions. Choose an art medium that calls to you such as pen and pencil, watercolor, crayon, acrylic paint, scrapbooking, sculpting, etc. and draw what you feel. You don't need to consider yourself an 'artist' to benefit from this activity. You don't even need to plan what you'll create. Just let your hands, pen, pencil, or paintbrush do the talking. The more spontaneous, the better. Artistic expression can reveal a lot about your obscure darker half. Psychologist Carl Jung (who conceptualized the Shadow Self idea) was even famous for using mandalas in his therapy sessions.

3. Start a Project - The act of creation can be intensely frustrating and can give birth to some of your darker elements such as impatience, anger, blood-thirsty competitiveness, and self-doubt. At the same time, starting a project also allows you to experience feelings of fulfillment and joy.

If you don't already have a personal project that you're undertaking (such as building something, writing a book, composing music, mastering a new skill), find something you would love to start doing. Using self-awareness and self-exploration during the process of creation, you will be able to reap deeper insights into your darkness. Ask yourself constantly, "What am I feeling and why?" Notice the strong emotions that arise during the act of creation, both good and bad. You will likely be surprised by what you find!

4. Write a Story or Keep a Shadow Journal – In High School I read Goethe's story *Faust* and saw the play. In my opinion, this is one of the best works featuring the meeting of an ego and his Shadow Self. His story details the life of a Professor who becomes so separated and overwhelmed by his Shadow that he comes to the verge of suicide, only to realize that the redemption of the ego is solely possible if the Shadow is redeemed at the same time.

Write a story where you project your Shadow elements onto the characters – this is a great way to learn more about your inner darkness. If stories aren't your thing, keeping a journal or diary every day can shine a light on the darker elements of your nature. Reading through your dark thoughts and emotions can help you to recover the balance you need in life by accepting both light and dark emotions within you.

Why do Shadow Work – Our journey to Self-Realization is a bit like Dante's Inferno.

Before making our way out of "hell" we must walk through the depths of our inner darkness. Many religions symbolize these experiences well. Two famous examples include the case of Jesus who had to face Satan in the desert and Buddha's encounter with Mara (the Buddhist Satan) before his spiritual awakening.

Indulging your anger, for instance, will simply result in more anger. *By embracing your inner darkness I mean that it is necessary for you to "accept" it.* Accepting your darkness will allow you to take responsibility for yourself, and once you truly acknowledge these dark traits instead of avoiding them, suddenly, they will stop having control over you.

It's astounding to realize that often the mundane characteristics in people are the ones that are socially acceptable.

In essence, any "primitive" traits within us get sent to the Shadow, but at the same time, any creative, unique, innovative, and different qualities within us also get confined within the Shadow because they're not socially acceptable.

Exploring your darkness is not necessarily all doom and gloom. In fact, you'll likely be surprised by the endless array of creative and interesting things you find that have secretly buried away for years.

The "Path of Light" seeks to improve the personal self and overcome its flaws, but the Shadow Self seeks investigation, seeks to face the shadows in its pursuit of self-care. Just as is represented in the ancient symbol of the Yin and Yang, when you balance both opposites, the dichotomy of Light and Darkness will disappear.

Personally, I like to think that first there was darkness. Unlike light, darkness is infinite. Under every rock, you will find darkness, but light and darkness need each other to come into existence. **Unless you learn to first embrace that darkness within yourself, you can never pursue the light of self-love in a balanced way.**

To accept and embrace your Shadow Self is to become Whole again.

Merging you Shadow Self and Your Self Love into your life and daily routine, you create many other benefits, a few the most commonly experienced benefits:

1. Deeper love and acceptance of yourself
2. Better relationships with others, including your partner and children
3. More confidence to be your authentic self
4. More mental, emotional, and spiritual clarity
5. Increased compassion and understanding for others, particularly those you dislike
6. Enhanced creativity
7. Discovery of hidden gifts and talents
8. Deepened understanding of your passions and ultimate life purpose
9. Improved physical and mental health
10. More courage to face the unknown and truly live life
11. Access to your Soul or Higher Self
12. A feeling of Wholeness

It's important to remember that there are no quick fixes in Shadow Work, so these life-changing benefits don't just happen overnight. But with persistence, they will eventually emerge and bless your life.

Sources
1. "A Definitive Guide to Jungian Shadow Work: How to Get to Know and Integrate Your Dark Side", Scott Jeffrey, CE Sage, https://scottjeffrey.com/shadow-work/
2. "Shadow Work Guide + Psychological Test", Aetheia Luna, LonerWolf, https://lonerwolf.com/shadow-work-demons/
3. "Shadow Self: How to Embrace Your Darkness (3 Techniques)", Mateo Sol, LonerWolf, https://lonerwolf.com/shadow-self/

PART 7 - END MATTER

PHOTOGRAPH CREDITS

1. Preface, Passiton.com. I'm Not Afraid of Storms for I am learning to sail my ship, https://www.google.com/search?q=I+am+not+afraid +of+storms&sxsrf=ALeKk005RVa-ePpQn2rDjxOTZ0OnrJKOBA:1597091907950&source=lnms&tbm=isch&sa=X&ved=2ahUKEwjF8O L-vpHrAhUvAZ0JHbGxCCwQ_AUoAnoECA0QBA&biw=1920&bih=969#imgrc=QimijLPz_7at4M

2. pg 5, Star Races – The War of Lyra, cyberspaceandtime.com, http://cyberspaceandtime.com/RFWacYGi-tI.video+related

3. pg 9, pinterres,com.mx, pin by Glenda Forbes pined to Travel Places and Shalom, https://www.pinterest.com.mx/pinAlignment, /817895982303823962/

4. pg 10, The Galactic Photon Belt, aligningwithearth.com, ALeKk01nhul11y4UGeu0tLEkdPQQ2wTibQ:1597095087316&source=lnms&tbm=isch&sa=X&ved=2 ahUKEwiV-ufqypHrAhWSVc0KHSDQDowQ_AUoAnoECAw QBA&biw=1832&bih=1012#imgrc=nXSLIG1JolDYTM

5. pg 10, Age of Aquarious – Conscious Awakening, wakingupconsciousness.com, https://www.google.com/search?q=the+photon+ belt&sxsrf=ALeKk01nhul11y4UGeu0tLEkdPQQ2wTibQ:1597095087316&source=lnms&tbm=isch&s a=X&ved=2ahUKEwiV-fqypHrAhWSVc0KHSDQDowQ_AUoAnoECAwQBA&biw=1832&bih=1012

6. pg 11, The Pleiades – The Seven Sisters, www.worldwidewaterplan.com, https://www.google.com/search?q=the+photon+ belt&sxsrf=ALeKk01nhul11y4UGeu0tLEkdPQQ2wTibQ:1597095087316&source=lnms&tbm=isch&s a=X&ved=2ahUKEwiV-ufqypHrAhWSVc0KHSDQDowQ_AUoAnoECAwQBA&biw=1832&bih= 1012#imgrc=lJDEuzxm8hefWM

7. pg 21, Soul Agreement and Pre-Birth Planning, learnreligions.com, https://www.google.com/search?q= pre-incarnation+planning &sxsrf=ALeKk03YcR6D3WEDt0x0Jff rbahH9Y1ZTQ:159709562836 9&source=lnms&tbm=isch&sa=X&ved=2ahUKEwiGmefszJHrAhVQWs0KHR7UC80Q_AUoAXoEC A0QAw&biw=1832&bih=1012#imgrc=PzlX6mD8U-VayM

8. pg 25, The Tigger Movie – The Most Downloaded Images, kisspng.com, https://png.is/f/winnie-the-pooh-eeyore-tigger-piglet-roo-winnie-the-pooh/5113937771102208-201902201554.html

9. pg 29, Rising above adversity, alamy stock photo, low resolution scan, https://www.google.com/search?q=balloon+above+maze&sxsrf= ALeKk0217rlOs5simYw6RSMNZEyiMtckJw:1597096100962&source=lnms&tbm=isch&sa=X&ved=2a hUKE-wiUj5TOzpHrAhVEVc0KHWBoC3AQ_AUoAXoECAsQAw&biw=1832&bih=1012#imgrc=hSxHpgj Mvzl0fM

10. pg 33, Does Dark Matter fit with Gravity, World Science Festival, https://www.google.com/search?q= gravational+ energy+fields +intwined&tbm=isch&ved=2ahUKEwjEseGyz5HrAhVEY60KHX7AAloQ2-cCegQIABAA&oq=gravational+ energy+fields+intwined&gs_lcp=CgNpbWcQA1CiZ1j1gw Fgn60BaABwAHgAg AFdiAHnB5IBAjEymAEAoAEBqgELZ3dzLXdpei1pbWfAAQE &sclient=img&ei=d8ExX4SaOcTGtQX-gIvQBQ&bih=1012&biw=1832#imgrc=WWk2ac10HOC_lM

11. pg 37, Before the Big Bang, The Big Bang, https://www.google.com/search?q=before +the+big+bang+ quantum+ universe+multiverse+cycle+universe&tbm=isch&ved=2ahUKEwjJpbvI0ZHrAhV JbqwKHVTRAisQ2-cCegQIABAA&oq=before+the +big+bang+quantum+universe+multiverse+cycle+ un-iverse&gs_lcp=CgNpbWcQA1DxjwJYtf4DYM6IBGgAcAB4AIABX4gBjBSSAQIzNJgBAKABAaoB C2d3cy13aXotaW1nwAEB&sclient=img&ei=vsMxX8nOE8ncsQXUoovYAg&bih=1012&biw=1832#im grc=AwQJ2yvkaGBIWM

12. pg 37, String Theory Envisions..., Brian Green, idlehearts,com, https://www.google.com/search?q =brian+greene+string+theory+ envisions&sxsrf=ALeKk01vDh9tiESyh39nNjqTWsY4dVaMBQ :1597097122255&source=lnms&tbm=isch&sa=X&ved=2ahUKEwiR8JK10pHrAhVbV80KHaR0DkIQ _AUoAnoECBEQBA&biw=1832&bih=1012#imgrc=ek1T0z8YO0wsyM

13. 30. A guide to Different Kinds of Parallel Universes, pbs.org, https://www.google.com/search?q=a+ guide+to+different+parallel +universes&tbm=isch&ved=2ahUKEwiN0MnB05HrAh UGF6wKHVcACOwQ2-cCegQIABAA&oq=a+guide+to+different +parallel+universes&gs _lcp=Cg N pb Wc QAzoECCMQJzoCCAA6BQgAELEDOgQIABBDOgYIABAIEB46BAgAEBhQopgNWI dDWDd4Q1oAHAAeACAAAdcBiAH5GZIBBjM2LjIuMZgBAKABAAoBC2d3cy13aXotaW1nwAEB &sclient=img&ei=yMUxX43MLYausAXXgKDgDg&bih=1012&biw=1832#imgrc=NMXXEtNR5ZLUF M

14. pg 38, Could Dreams be from parallel universes – Quora, https://www.quora.com/Could-our-dreams-be-from-parallel-universes

15. pg 39, Astronomers spot 83 supermassive black holes in baby universe, the week, https://www. google.com/ search?q=black+hole +universe&tbm=isch&ved =2ahUKEwiP1tqOypHrAhUF-awKHeSSDzQQ2-cCegQIABAA&oq=black+hole+universe&gs_lcp= CgNpbWcQAzICCAAy Ag-gAMgIIADICCAAyAggAMgIIADICCAAyAggAMgIIADIC-CAA6BwgEOoCECc6BAgjECc6BQgAELEDOgQIABBDOgcIABCxAxBDUPuHxwFYo8vHAWD E1McBaAFwAHgDgAF5iAGJFpIBBDMzLjKYAQCgAQGqAQtnd3Mtd3Z2l6LWltZ7ABCsABAQ&scl ient=img&ei=7rsxX4-nCYXyswXkpb6gAw&bih=969&biw=1920#imgrc=L4kGsPE79-Au4M

16. pg 39, Traveling to a parallel universe, alphaabsurder.blogspot.com, https://www.google.com/search? q=parallel+universe+black+ hole &tbm =isch&ved=2ahUKEwiYsOf115HrAhUGzawKHetQAasQ2-cCegQIABAA&oq=parallel+universe+black+ hole&gs_lcp=CgNpbWcQA1CXtwFYrdsBYIbkA

WgBcAB4AIABVogBqwiSAQIxNJgBAKABAaoBC2d3cy13aXotaW1nwAEB&sclient=img&ei=aMox
X5jcAYaaswXroYXYCg&bih=969&biw=1920#imgrc=I9oonn1VltThxM

17. pg 40, Pine tree sillotte, clipart.email, https://www.google.com/search?q=pine+tree+silotte+roots&tbm=
isch&ved =2ahUKEwiijKKE2 J HrAhUMbK0KHZqRDjAQ2-cCegQIABAA&oq=pine +tree+silotte
+roots&gs_lcp=CgNpbWcQAzoECCMQJzoEC AAQQzoFCAA QsQM6AggAO gcIIxDqAhAn Og-
QIABAeOgYIABA-
FEB46BAgAEBg6BggAEAoQGDoHCAAQsQMQQ1DvoAxY7aENYOSoDWgDcAB4AYABjAGI
AYcWkgEEMjkuNJgBAKA-
BAaoBC2d3cy13aXotaW1nsAEKwAEB&sclient=img&ei=hsoxX6KxFYzYtQWao7qAAw&bih=969&b
iw=1920#imgrc=K3KxJjIaLUOEDM

18. pg. 40, Crab Nebula which harbors..., researchgate.net, https://www.google.com/search?q= astrophysi-
cal+plasma+ crab+nebula&tbm=isch&ved =2ahUKEwicl_Wa2pHrAhUIJKwKHQ78CV0Q2-
cCegQIABAA&oq=astrophysical+plasma+crab+nebula&gs_ lcp=CgNpbWcQA1DLlANY
2q8DYJ6zA2gAcAB4AIABUYgBvgWSAQIxMZgBAKABAaoBC2d3cy13aXotaW1nwAEB&sclient=i
mg&ei=zswxX5z4K4jIsAWO-KfoBQ&bih=1012&biw=1832#imgrc=8otf6VRXiPVwwM

19. pg 41, Underground Network of Trees..., sitn.htms.harvard,edu, https://www.google.com/
search?q=forest +multiple+trees +one+root+system +illustration&tbm=isch&ved=2ahUKEwjB-
sKK25HrA hVpja0KHSYHAZsQ2-cCegQIABAA&oq=forest+multiple+trees+one+ root+system
+illustration&gs_lcp=CgNpbWcQA1DqGFjEMGCCNGgAcAB4AIABWIgB1QaSAQIxM5gBAKAB
AaoBC2d3cy13aXotaW1nwAEB&sclient=img&ei=uM0xX8G-L-matgWmjoTYCQ&bih=1012&biw
=1832#imgrc=sbWnbxMhCBwM5M

20. 45, No such tihing as an external..., whisper.sh, https://www.google.com/search?q=there+is
+no+thing+as+a +external+enemy+whisper&tbm= isch&ved=2ahUKEwiw7KCO25HrAhVsja0KHes
_CY4Q2-cCegQIABAA&oq=there+is+no+thing+as+a+externa l+enemy+whisper&gs _lcp=CgNpb
WcQAzoECCMQJzoECAAQQzoF-
CAAQsQM6AggAOgcIABCxAxBDOgYIABAIEB5Q86cJWKqlCmCbxQpoAXAAeACAAbIBiAH
ZHpIBBDQyLjSYAQCgAQG-
qAQtnd3Mtd2l6LWltZ8ABAQ&sclient=img&ei=wM0xX7CMJeyatgXr_6TwCA&bih=1012&biw=1832
#imgrc=xhWDIctBb8jgvM

21. pg 57, Daniel Nielsen, Author The Infidelity..., infidelityrecovery institute,com, soul+Daniel+Nielse
n&tbm =isch&ved=2ahUKEwi-jY3h25HrAhXFi60KHf_LB8IQ2-cCegQIABAA&oq= Being+ awa-
kened+soul+Daniel+Nielsen&gs _lcp=CgNpbWcQAzoECCM QJzoFCAAQsQM6AggAOgQ IABB-
DOgQIABADOggIABCxAxCDAToHCAAQsQMQQzoGCAAQBRAeOgYIA-
BAIEB46BAgAEBg6BAgAEB5Q1sJEWNPdRmCr6UZoAHAAeACAAW-IAYAakgEENDAuMpgBA
KABAaoBC2d3cy 13aXotaW1nwAEB&sclient=img&ei=YcsxX_yDMIfWswWIhoCgBA&bih
=969&biw=1920#imgrc=OhAdRfcAoKBx9M

22. pg 67, The Sovereign Integral Consciousness, wingmakersblogeng.blogspot,com, https://www.
google.com/ search?q=sovereign+integral+consciousness&tbm=isch&ved=2ahUKEwi8uPPs2J HrA-
hUH66wKHQgDAEQQ2-cCegQIABAA&oq=sovereign+integral+consciousness&gs
_lcp=CgNpbWcQAzoECCMQJzoECAAQQzoFCAAQsQM6AggAOgcIABCxAxBDOgQIABAYOg
YIABAKEBg6BAgAEB5Q1sJEWNPdRmCr6UZoAHAAeACAAW-IAYAakgEENDAuMpgBA
KABAaoBC2d3cy 13aXotaW1nwAEB&sclient=img&ei=YcsxX_yDMIfWswWIhoCgBA&bih
=969&biw=1920#imgrc=OhAdRfcAoKBx9M

23. pg 77, Standing on the Edge, frepik.com, https://www.google.com/search?q=+on+the+edge+arms
+raised+ frepik&tbm=isch&ved=2ahUKEwj Fkfav6JHrAhVHjK0KHTX7DIYQ2-cCegQIABA
A&oq=+on+the+edge+arms+raised+frepik&gs_lcp=CgNpbWcQAzIECCMQJJ1D6nAFY-
pwBYJ6qAWgAcAB4AIABISgBSJIBATGYAQCgAQGqAQtnd3Mtd2l6LWltZ8ABAQ&sclient=img
&ei=qNsxX8WdNceYtgW19rOwCA&bih=969&biw=1920#imgrc=AnnXABrHjgNAvM

24. pg 77, Phase Difference and Phase Shift, electronics-tutorials.ws,
https://www.google.com/search?q=out+of+phase+wave+1+wave+2&sxsrf =ALeKk02brQGQwC wnbT
BFUL3WTEGSpKfFOw:1597103221608&source=lnms&tbm=isch&sa=X&ved=2ahUKEwjB1sWR6Z
HrAhXTQc0KHT_qAaoQ_AUoAnoECA0QBA&biw=958&bih=959#imgrc=FoznhYzLYbMdcM

25. pg 78, Constructive and destructive interference, Solved: Q1: Find Three Examples Wherever you can,
Cheg, https://www.google.com /search?q= +antimodal+lines+lines+of+interference&tbm=isch&ved
=2ahUKEwiLnvK49JHrAhUnja0KHWYkDb4Q2-cCegQIABA A&oq=+antimodal+lines+lines+of+in-
terfe-
rence&gs_lcp=CgNpbWcQA1CtkgFYickBYMnMAWgAcAB4AIABdIgB1QuSAQQyMi4xmAEAoA
EBq-
gELZ3dzLXdpei1pbWfAAQE&sclient=img&ei=UOgxX4u2N6eatgXmyLTwCw&bih=959&biw=958#i
mgrc=Jlfbonu-1qlR4M

26. pg 81, Brain Doodle Concept About Creative Right Side and Logical Left, Dreamtime.com, line drawing, https://www.google.com/search?q =brain+s ketch+drawing+equations&tbm=isch&ved=
2ahUKEwjm2eqS9pHrAhUGG6wKHcTbCCEQ2-cCegQIABAA&oq=brain +sketch+ drawing+equations&gs_lcp=CgNpbWcQA1DOgQJYvZYCYNmcAmgAcAB4AIABSYgBhwSSAQE4mAE
AoAEBq-
gELZ3dzLXdpei1pbWfAAQE&sclient=img&ei=GeoxX6bpOoa2sAXEt6OIAg&bih=959&biw=958#im
grc=JO3WQZYo4OGFZM&imgdii=PtOGUX7LYfmmsM

27. pg 81, Chrouching Tiger,Fidden Dragon: The Sad Sequel, Sword of Destiny, The Atlantic, David Sims,
Feb 27, 2016, https://www.theatlantic.com/entertainment/archive/2016/02/crouching-tiger-hidden-
dragon-sword-of-destiny-review/471234/

28. pg 82, Ground yourself: Meditation, three photos, https://mindful15.com/2019/08/ground-yourself-meditation-posture-matters/

29. pg 89, Spiritual Meaning of Snow, meaningfullife.comcom, https://www.google.com/search?q=333+spiritual +meaning++sunset&tbm=isch&ved =2ahUKEwjB7 di-Ug5LrAhVIbK0KHQFSDegQ2-cCegQIABAA&oq=333+spiritual+meaning++sunset&gs _lcp=C gNpb WcQA1DVPljzR2DdWWgBcAB4AIABRYgBxAKSAQE1mAEAoAEBqgELZ3dzL Xdpei1pbWfAAQE&sclient=img&ei=v_cxX4GSIMjYtQWBpLXADg&bih=959&biw=1579#imgrc=cx VmxVSRqtrqmM

30. pg.93, Spiritual Meaning of 222, Waking up at 2:22 am, intuitive Journal, https://www.google.com/search?q= 222+ spiritual+meaning&tbm =isch&ved=2ahUKEwih8KnogJLrAhXNi60KHcdICMcQ2-cCegQIABAA&oq=222+spiritual+meaning&gs_lcp=CgNpbWcQAzICCA AyAggAMgYIABAFEB 4yBggAEAUQHjIECAAQGDIECAAQGDIECAAQGDIECAAQGDoFCAAQsQM6BggAEAgQHj oEAAQHlDq5g5Y05APYN2iD2gAcAB4AIABhAGIAa0LkgEEMjAuMZgBAKABAaoBC2d3cy13aX otaW1nwAEB&sclient=img&ei=SfUxX-GnJc2XtgXHkaG4DA&bih=959&biw=1579 #imgrc=FIr8fdr5LzUcOM

31. pg 95, Angle Number 333 Meanings, numerologysign.com, https://www.google.com/search?q=angle +number+333+message+from +guardian&tbm=isch&ved=2ahUKEwiluoO9hJLrAh WOTqw KHVA1ALQQ2-cCegQIABAA&oq=angle+number+333 +message+from+guardian&gs_lcp =CgNpbWc QAzIECCMQJ1DefVjqwAFgzMcBaABwAHgAgAFQiAHNApIBATW YAQCgAQG-qAQtnd3Mtd2l6LWltZ8ABAQ&sclient=img&ei=IPkxX6WqIY6dsQXQ6oCgCw&bih=959&biw=1579 #imgrc=PEIQESgOFnQTKM

32. pg. 99, Angle Number 444 indicates that is the time \..., zodiac Signs Horoscope, https://www .google.com/ search?q =angel+number+444+meaning+your+devine+purpose&tbm =isch&ved =2ahUKEwitsdm-hZLrAhUMTa0KHUZtC_QQ2-cCegQIABAA&oq =angel+number+444+meaning +your+devine+purpose&gs_lcp=CgNpbWcQAzoECAAQHjoGCAAQCBAeOgQIABAYUJppWJ6nA WC4sQFoAXAAeACAAV2IAasKkgECMjGYAQCgAQGqAQtnd3Mtd2l6LWltZ8ABAQ&sclient=i mg&ei=MPoxX63ZHYyatQXG2q2gDw&bih=959&biw=1579#imgrc=Hkzapac38IOS3M

33. pg 103, Ascension Steps, tracyholloway.com, https://www.google.com/search?q=steps+to+ ascen-sion&tbm=isch&ved=2ahUKEwj5-P_JhZLrAhXLQa0KHV-OAPoQ2-cCegQIABAA&oq =steps+to+ascension&gs_lcp=CgNpbWcQAzIECAAQGDoECCMQJzoFCAAQsQM6AggAOgQIAB BDOgcIABCxAxBDOggIABCxAxCDAToGCAAQC-BAeUPWkCVi3yAlgqNQJaABwAHgAgAFdiAGNCZIBAjE4mAEAoAEBqgELZ3dzLXdpei1pbWf AAQE&sclient=img&ei=SPoxX_m0C8uDtQXfnILQDw&bih=959&biw=1579#imgrc=k7-lmWky1auLvM

34. pg 105, woman-arms-outstretched-giver on the River, giver on the river, https://www.google.com/search?q=pwoman+arms+out+stretched+sunset+pink&tbm=isch&ved=2ahUKEwjTkM7mipLrAhXBO qwKHVdaD0oQ2cCegQIABAA&oq=pwoman+arms+out+stretched+sunset+pink&gs_lcp=CgNpbWc QA1C0mQJY5o4DYJGwA2gAcAB4AIABjQGIAYoLkgEEMC4xMZgBAKABAaoBC2d3cy13aXota W1nwAEB&sclient=img&ei=wv8xX9OnFsH1sAXXtL3QBA&bih=959&biw=1579#imgrc=6LnvVcTkju 1M5M

35. pg 107, extracted from "Windmills of the Mind – The Stages of Spiritual Awakening in a Nutshell", https://wakingupconsciousness.com/ windmills-of-the-mind-the-stages-of-spiritual-awakening-in-a-nutshell/

36. pg 109, Physics Research News, futurity.org, photo cropped by Author, https://www.google.com/search?q =milky+eay+sky+view+man+looking +up&tbm=isch&ved=2ahUKEwjcnsiijpLrAhU VNK0KHTBIDCAQ2-cCegQIABAA&oq=milky+eay+sky+view+man+looking +up&gs_lcp=CgN pbWcQA1DgiAFYzKkBYK2uAWgAcAB4AIABpAGIAYgQkgEEMC4xNZgBAKABAaoBC2d3cy1 3aXotaW1nwAEB&sclient=img&ei=ZQMyX5zYGJXotAWwkLGAAg&bih=959&biw=1579#imgrc=qj Yl gezmphzUTM

37. pg 115, extracted and modified by Author from Ontological trichotomy of man: Spirit, Soul and Body, Bible.ca, https://www.google.com/search?q=dicotomy+of+man+mind+body+soul&tbm=isch&ved =2ahUKEwi7xdXFkZLrAhU G9KwKHVfFAvgQ2-cCegQIABAA&oq=dicotomy+of+man+mind+body +soul&gs_lcp=CgNpbWcQAzoCCAA6BggAEAoQGFCNwwJYpYsDYJWuA2gAcAB4AIAB3QGIAf sLkgEGM-jIuMC4xmAEAoAEBqgELZ3dzLXdpei1pbWfAAQE&sclient=img&ei=1AYyX7uLFIboswXXiovADw &bih=959&biw=1579#imgrc=WiwMYHEw6trMpM

38. pg 116, Uur mind heart and soul, Steemit, https://www.google.com/search?q=+mind+heart +conversation+I%27m+worried+just+ relax&tbm=isch&ved=2ahUKEwjjyLvgkZLr AhUUNK 0KHb2OAiIQ2-cCegQIABAA&oq=+mind+heart+conversation+I%27m +worried+just+relax&gs_lcp =CgNpbWcQAzoECAAQQzoCCAA6Bgg AEAcQHjoICAAQCBAHEB46BggAEAgQHlDYl dkWWJ7k2xZg3YrcFmgAcAB4AIABYYgB3hOSAQI0MpgBAKABAaoBC2d3cy13aXotaW1nwAE B&sclient=img&ei=DAcyX-OSIJTotAW9nYqQAg&bih=959&biw=1579#imgrc=ilfgbd8BwZd1rM

39. pg 119, Soul Types – Matching Your Personality and Spiritual Path, Sandra Krebs and Jane A.G. Kise, Aurthor modified art and presentation, https://www.google.com/search?q=soul+types+book&tbm =isch&ved=2ahUKEwiNhcTNxJPrAhXZA 50JHVchAIoQ2-cCegQIABAA&oq=soul+types +book&gs_lcp =CgNpbWcQAzIECAAQGFD6RFimTGDFWGgAcAB4AIABTIgBzQKSA QE1mAEAoAEBqgELZ3dzLXdpei1pbWfAAQE&sclient=img&ei=lsIyX43iLtmH9PwP18KA0Ag&bi h=959&biw=1579#imgrc=pqE_nIyQhCKQjM

40. pg 123, Light Bearers – Aglow Western New York Area Team, AglowNet, https://www.google.com/search?q =we+ are+bearers+of+light+ candle&tbm=isch&ved=2ahUKEwjb0Y-BxpPrAhUNE80K HdsK

Ak0Q2-cCegQIABAA&oq=we+are+bearers+of+light+candle&gs_lcp =CgNpbWcQA1DVJ FiaM
WDgN W gAcAB4AIAB3AKIAZIGkgEHNS4xLjA uMZgBAKABAaoBC2d3cy13a Xota W1 nwA
EB&sclient=img&ei=D8QyX5uOGI2mtAbblYjoBA&bih=959&biw=1579#imgrc=cvygdhleClXAg M

41. pg 129, What does the spike in the Schumann resonance mean?, Dr.JoeDispenze Blog, https://www
.google.com /search?q =perhaps+the+earth+is+assisting+us+joe+dispenza&tbm=isch&sxsrf=A
LeKk03Mq_ ICxmLfDdupviBKc4Fme93HiA 1597162759691&source=lnms&sa=X&ved=0ah UKE-
wiz7cH3xpPrAhXXZs0KHVuhAjMQ_AUIECgD&biw=1579&bih=959&dpr=1#imgrc=KmpXoMLhR
zL5GM

42. pg 133,& pg 143, pg 145, Author created diagrams using the artwork from various sites, including Nubia
Watu on Twitter: The heart generates the largest, Twitter (https://twitter.com/nubia_watu/status/
1099744754277994497) and Culvating Gratitude – Diana Quinn Inlak'ech MD, Diana Quinn Inlak'ech MD (https://www.google.com/search?q=heart+electromagnetic+field&sxsrf=ALeKk02ZL
nY0MPwgAv X4MifE6ENJJrQx3w :1597163039288&source=lnms&tbm=isch&sa=X&ved=2ahUK Ewi-
jev8x5PrAhVQaM0KHa7GD4MQ_AUoAXoECA0QAw&biw=1579&bih=959#imgrc=Ns8Uk9bpBI7
xOM

43. pg 138, Astral Projection: Easier Than You Think, Vapor95.com, https:// www.google.com/search?q
=astral+projection&sxsrf=ALeKk 03TlJnTdt1M36v2OnRxwW2J7ygAfw:1597163527523&
source=lnms&tbm=isch&sa=X&ved=2ahUKEwifytLlyZPrAhUcAp0JHb3wAyUQ_AUoAnoECBo
QBA&biw=1579&bih=959#imgrc=S1Q1CZpUvcxYxM

44. pg 149, Chakras Lotis Position Seven Stock Illustration-87, Dreamstime.com, https://www.google.com/
search?q= Chakras+tan+body+ lotus&tbm=isch&ved=2ahUKEwjQzrSx75PrAhXMXs0KHT2D
AXQQ2-cCegQIABAA&oq=Chakras+tan+body+lotus&gs_lcp=CgNpbWcQA1DnowFY_boBYPb
HAWgAcA B4AIABRIgBgAOSAQE2mAEAoAEBqgELZ3dzLXdpei1pbWfAAQE&sclient
=img&ei=cu8yX9DNH8y9tQa9hoagBw&bih=959&biw=1579#imgrc=UU7RcaqQUL97EM

45. pg 151, Perceiving and Caring for the Aura, Catherine Crytting's Weblog – WordPres.com,
https://www.google.com/search?q=Chakras+aura+field+liness&tbm=isch&ved=2ahUKEwic0L
Cj8JPrAhVCSKwKHZh2BFQQ2-cCegQIABAA&oq=Chakras+aura+field+liness&gs
_lcp=CgNpbWcQA1CfZliUcmDzd2gAcAB4AIABTYgB-wKSAQE2mAEAoAEBqgELZ3dzL
Xdpei1pbWfAAQE&sclient =img&ei=YfAyX9ybIMKQsQWY7ZGgBQ&bih=959&biw
=1579#imgrc=aCxppkhwDUhFsM

46. pg. 152, Chakra Frequencies and Correlations, Chakrakeyh, Pinterest.com, https://www.google.com
/search?q=Chakras++frequencies+and+ Correlations&tbm=isch&ved=2ahUKEwiR2u3f8J PrAhVN
E80KHb8lD-sQ2-cCegQIABAA&oq=Chakras++frequencies+and+ Correlations&gs_lcp=CgNpbWcQ
AzoC-
CAA6BAgAEB46BggAEAUQHjoGCAAQCBAeUNmPA1iI9ARgyb0FaABwAHgAgAFYiAHBDZI
BA-
jI4mAEAoAEBqgELZ3dzLXdpei1pbWfAAQE&sclient=img&ei=4PAyX5HqFc2mtAa_y7zYDg&bih=
959&biw=1579#imgrc=AytdQOim6KZfaM

47. pg 153, Do it Yourself Tesla Coil | Human Chakra Syste, Tesla Coil,,,, Pinterest.com, https://www.
google.com/search?q=Chakras++-+Tesla+coil&tbm=isch&ved=2ahUKEwie1paL8ZPr AhXD
Ya0KHWlGCDQQ2-cCegQIABAA&oq=Chakras++-+Tesla+coil&gs_lcp=CgNpbWcQAzoECAAQ
HjoGCAAQBRAeOgYIA-
BAIEB5Q38QJWLfhCWCZ5wloAHAAeACAAVGIAZAGkgECMTKYAQCgAQGqAQtnd3Mtd2l
6LWltZ8ABAQ&sclient=img&ei=O_EyX97MDMPDtQXpjKGgAw&bih=959&biw=1579#imgrc=2lZ2
uBm8-3ZPJM

48. pg. 153, Author cropped illustration at How the Tesla Coil Works (infographic), Life Science,
https://www.google.com/search?q=Tesla+ coil+components+listed&tbm=isch&ved=2ah UKEw
jRyqGX8pPrAhUazKwKHZ5kB1oQ2-cCegQIABAA&oq=Tesla+coil+components +listed&gs_
lcp=CgNpbWcQAzoECAAQQzoCCAA6BAgAEBg6BAgAEB5Q9OgCWIKeA2CipANoAHAAeAC
AAUuIAeMIkgECMTiYAQCgAQG-
qAQtnd3Mtd2l6LWltZ8ABAQ&sclient=img&ei=YPIyX9GaPJqYswWeyZ3QBQ&bih=959&biw=1579
#imgrc=X-ru-9HXhaPkZM

49. pg 153, pyramids power plant | Giza, Pyramids, Power plant, ww.pinterest.com, https://www.google
.com/search?q =Great+pyramid+as +power+station&tbm=isch&ved=2ahUKEwjJq8-x8pPrAhV
TE6wKHfNSDZ4Q2-cCegQIABAA&oq=Great+pyramid+as+power+station&gs_ lcp=CgNpbW cQA-
zoEC CMQJzoFCAAQsQM6AggAOgQIABBDOgcIABCxAxBDOgQIABAYUKO2CFjo-
ghg4f4IaABwAHgAg AFViAGZD5I BAjMwmAEAoAEBqgELZ3dzLXdpei 1pbWfAAQE
&sclient=img &ei=mPIyX8n_D9OmsA XzpbXwCQ&bih=959&biw =1579#imgrc=nFe5H1Z7dhsEKM

50. pg 154, The 7 Chakras, Anna Balkan Jewelry, https://www.google.com/search?q=inner+chakra+crown
+lotus+flower&tbm= isch&ved=2ahUKEwi_tJmd9ZPrAhUPb60KHeGaD04Q2-cCegQIABAA&oq
=inner+chakra+crown+lotus+flower&gs_ lcp=CgNpbWcQA1CpgwVYirAGYOC4BmgAcAB4AIABhA
GIAYwkkgEENzMuMpgBAKABAaoBC2d3cy13aXotaW1nwAEB&sclient=img&ei=kvUyX7-jLY_et
QXhtb7wBA&bih=959&biw=1579&hl=en#imgrc=wG7d_3shcWIW0M

51. pg 154, We apologize for any convenience, ww.rainbow-dawn.org.uk, https://www.google. com/
search?qinner+chakra+crown+lotus+ flower&tbm=isch&ved=2ahUKEwi_tJmd9Z PrAhU
Pb60KHeGaD04Q2-cCegQIABAA&oq=inner+chakra+crown+lotus+flower&gs_ lcp=CgNpbWc
QA1CpgwVYirAGYOC4BmgAcAB4AIABhAGIAYwkkgEENzMuMpgBAKABAaoBC2d3cy13aXota
W1nwAEB&sclient=img&ei=kvUyX7-jLY_etQXhtb7wBA&bih=959&biw=1579&hl=en#imgrc=w
9CmIpegDvr9qM&imgdii=Be3EgDANivx6nM

52. pg 159, Tricked by the Light with Wayne Bush, The Crazz Files, https://www.google.com/
search?q=tricked+by+ the+light+&tbm=isch&ved =2ahUKEwijn_aV95PrAhUMTK0KHQxCDb0Q2-

cCegQIABAA&oq=tricked+by+the+light+&gs_lcp=CgNpbWcQAzIECCMQJzIECA AQGDIE-
CAAQGFDuhwJY7ocCYOuLAmgAcAB4AIABSogBSpIBATGYAQCgAQGqAQtnd3Mtd2l6LWltZ
8ABAQ&sclient=img&ei=nPcyX6PhFYyYtQWMhLXoCw&bih=959&biw=1579&hl=en#imgrc=GHV7
3l9GXqZjSM

53.   pg 160 (left), Author cropped image, Tricked by the Light with Wayne Bush, The Crazz Files,
      https://www.google.com/search?q=tricked+by+the+light+&tbm=isch&ved =2ahUKEwijn_aV95PrAhU
      MTK0KHQxCDb0Q2-cCegQIABAA&oq=tricked+by+the+light+&gs_ lcp=CgNpbWcQAz
      IECCMQJzIECA AQGDIECAAQGFDuhwJY7ocCYOuLAmgAcAB4AIABSogBSpIBATG YAQC-
      gAQG-
      qAQtnd3Mtd2l6LWltZ8ABAQ&sclient=img&ei=nPcyX6PhFYyYtQWMhLXoCw&bih=959&biw=157
      9&hl=en#imgrc=GHV73l9GXqZjSM

54.   pg 160 (middle and left), Scanning and Editing Color Negative Film, Alex Burke Potography,
      https://www.google.com/search?q=black+white+ negative+colornegative++mountains&tbm=isch&ved
      =2ahUKEwjW0ZuJ_pPrAhUH_KwKHVsLB14Q2-cCegQIABAA&oq=black+white +negative+ color-
      nega-
      tive++mountains&gs_lcp=CgNpbWcQA1DPLVjUhwFgzZMBaABwAHgAgAGHAYgBxgqSAQQyM
      C4xmAEA oAEBqgELZ3dzLXdpei1pbWFAAQE&sclient=img&ei=2P4yX9a
      FLof4swXblpzwBQ&bih=959&biw=1407#imgrc=vGU7CWvxxZYoCM

55.   pg 160, Build Your Own Glasses-Free 3D Display, Doug Lanman, Siggraph2011, SlideShare,
      https://www.google.com/search?q= doug+lanman&tbm =i sch&ved=2ah UKEwiE6 y 2gZTrA_
      hVOYqwKHQazCMkQ2-cCegQIABAA&oq=3d+motorcycle+doug+ lanman&gs_lcp=CgNpbWc
      QA1CrswFY2oECYIuUAmgAcAB4AIABqgGIAccIkgEEMTMuMpgBAKABAaoBC2d3cy13aXota
      W1nwAEB&sclient=img&ei=XgIzX4TEAc7EsQWG5qLIDA&bih=959&biw=1407#imgrc=9SrWvEww
      8D-emM

56.   pg 162, A Deep Dive into Brainwaves: Brainwave Frequencies Explained, Muse headband,
      https://www.google.com/search?q=human+ brain+waves+table&tbm=isch&ved=2ahUKEwj
      HtaWTgpTrAhVHZ60KHbLfCngQ2-cCegQIABAA&oq=human+brain+ waves+table&gs_lcp=CgN
      pbWcQAzoECCMQJzoECAAQQzoF-
      CAAQsQM6AggAOgcIABCxAxBDOggIABCxAxCDAToGCAAQBRAeOgQIABAYOgQIABAeU
      LSnClj55Apg2ugKaABwAHgAgAFOiAHLC5IBAjIzmAEAoAEBqgELZ3dzLXdpei1pbWFAAQE&sc
      lient=img&ei=HwMzX4eqJsfOtQWyv6vABw&bih=959&biw=1407#imgrc=TVIIOR9ChxecNM

57.   pg 165, Used as background for applied lettering title, Morning Sunrise Mt. Fuji in Autumn..., photos-
      tockeditor, https://www.google.com/search?q=yellow+wild+flowers+myst+meadow
      +trees+blurr+bacvkground&tbm=isch&ved=2ahUKEwj_wo6Vj5TrAhXQO80KHWNtB58Q2-
      cCegQIA-
      BAA&oq=yellow+wild+flowers+myst+meadow+trees+blurr+bacvkground&gs_lcp=CgNpbWcQA1D
      MqwRYmcoEYMTjBGgAcAB4AIABR4gB6wKSAQE2mAEAoAE BqgELZ3dzL
      Xdpei1pbWFAAQE&sclient=img&ei=xRAzX7_MBtD3tAbj2p34CQ&bih=959&biw=1407#imgrc=TvG
      sVdRLg4W0aM

58.   pg 168, Used as background, applied lettering, Survey of Venn Diagrams – What is a Venn Diagram?,
      the Electronic Journal of Combinations, https://www.google.com/search?q=venn+diagram+A+B+C
      +yellow+red+blue&tbm=isch&ved=2ahUKEw j21abIgZTrAhUN _qwKHcsvBv4Q2-cCegQIABAA&oq
      =venn+diagram+A+B+C+yellow+red+blue&gs_lcp=CgNpbWcQAzoECCMQJzoCCAA6BQgAE LE-
      DOgQIABBDOgcIABCxAxBDOggIABAeOgYIABAIEB5Q74_3AVieiPgBYNaP-
      AFoAHAAeACAAV2IAe4QkgE CMzSYA QCgAQGqAQtnd3Mtd2l6LWltZ8AB AQ&sclient
      =img&ei=ggIzX _aMFo38swXL35jwDw&bih=959&biw=1407#imgrc=EdDZmJLjqejyQM

59.   pg 171, 5 Types of Special Healing (& What to be Careful of...), Pinterest, https://www.google.com/
      search?q=the+dar +side+of+healing&tbm =isch&ved=2ahUKEwj01sTakJTrAhUnA50JHYPJDywQ2-
      cCegQIABAA&oq=the+dark+side+of+healing&gs_lcp=CgNpbWcQAz IECAAQGDoECCMQ zoF-
      CAAQsQM6AggAOgQIABBDOgcIABCxAxBDOggIABCxAxCDAToGCAAQCBAeUNHuDVjWk
      g5g_5YOaABwAHgAgAGiAYgB3gySAQQyMi4ymAEAoAEBqgELZ3dzLXdpei1pbWFAAQE&sclie
      nt=img&ei=YxIzX7SZCKeG9PwPg5O_4AI&bih=959&biw=1407#imgrc=OyWVG6hp6AbvUM

60.   pg 175, Singing & Humming Heals, Balanced Woman's Blog, https://www.google.com/ search?q
      =humming+heals& tbm=isch&ved =2ahUKEwi 67fTJkZTrAhULRs0KHePeBZsQ2-cCegQIA
      BAA&oq=humming+heals&gs_lcp=CgNpbWcQAzoECCMQJ zoECAAQQzoFCAAQsQM6Agg
      AOgcIABCxAxBDOgYIA-
      BAIEB46BAgAEBhQo7cLWKrmC2Cr7AtoAHAAeACAAU6IAc4GkgECMTOYAQCgAQGqAQt
      nd3Mtd2l6LWltZ8ABAQ&sclient=img&ei=TBMzX7qXK4uMtQbjvZfYCQ&bih=959&biw=1407#img
      rc=PCKPYvRCdwAxAM

61.   pg 179, The 14 Lokas of Hinduism, UouTube, https://www.google.com/search?q=The+Vedic+
      Realms&tbm=isch&ved=2ahUKE wiamfqmkpTrAhWOUM0KHdl-BdAQ2-cCegQIABAA&oq
      =The+Vedic+Realms&gs_lcp=CgNpbWcQAzoECCMQJzoECAAQQzoFCA AQsQM6AggAOgc
      IABCxAxBDOgQIA-
      BAYUMftCVithgtg7o0LaAFwAHgAgAFOiAHHEJIBBDM0LjGYAQCgAQGqAQtnd3Mtd2l6LWltZ
      8ABAQ&sclient=img&ei=DxQzX9rVMo6htQbZ_ZWADQ&bih=959&biw=1407#imgrc=_r5xGFOk-
      f0k_M

62.   pg 189, The Law of One: An Encounter, Cosmic Christ, https://www.google.com/search?q= Densi-
      ties+prism+ spiritual&tbm=isch&ved=2ahUKEwiyh6PAlpTrAhUDbK0KHdW8CvwQ2-
      cCegQIABAA&oq=Densities+prism+spiritual&gs_lcp=CgNpbWcQA1DfTFibX2Cca2gAc
      AB4AIABR4gBzQSSAQIxMJgBAKABAaoBC2d3cy13aXotaW1nwAEB&sclient=img&ei=dhgzX7L0
      KIPYtQXV-argDw&bih=959&biw=1407#imgrc=dr3x397T1qqOGM

63. pg 190, Ascension energy stai steps, HeighHeartLife, https://www.google.com/search?q= spiritua
     l+Ascension+stairsteps&tbm= isch&ved=2ah UKEwi4np6JmJTrAhWBTqwKHZDDAN4Q2-
     cCegQIABAA&oq=spiritual+Ascension+stairsteps&gs_lcp= CgNpbWcQA1D_lgJYztEC YObtAmgA-
     cAB4AIABRogB1AWSAQIxMpgBAKABAaoBC2d3cy13aXotaW1nwAEB&sclient=img&ei=HBozX
     7igB4GdsQWQh4PwDQ&bih=959&biw=1407#imgrc=mi0TjfWMHx9iMM
64. pg 200, Race of the Trains, Broadway Limited, 20ᵗʰ Century Limited, atticpostcards.com, Pinterest,
     posted by Janice M Martin to TRAINS, https://www.pinterest.com/pin/308707749443049775/
65. pg. 203, slide extracted from A Galactic Human Journey, Milky Way Galaxy, http://tas-education
     .org/exo/Galactic-Human-Journey.pdf
66. pg. 205, 7 Books to Raise Your Vibration, Powered by Initution.com, Angela Artemis, https://www
     .google.com/search?q=to+raise+your+ your+vibration+ climb+above+negative+emotions&sxsrf=ALeKk0
     0O7zhfTN5jNUd49XDsFeeKxJb8eA:1597185864824&source =lnms&tbm=isch&sa= X&ved=2ah
     UKEwj LsfOAnZTrAhWhAZ0JHd5VBYAQ_AUoAXoECA0QAw&biw=1748&bih=959#imgrc=D-
     pth1zzqP2XYM
67. pg. 213, Free 13 Ascension Masters Attunement #reiki, YouTube cimage, https://www.google.com/
     search?q=ascension+Masters&tbm= isch&ved=2ahUKEwjRnruCnZTrAhUZ66wKHS99Ba4Q2-
     cCegQIABAA&oq=ascension+Masters&gs_lcp=CgNpbWcQ AzICCAA6B AgjECc6BQgAEL
     EDOgQIABBDOgcIABCxAxBDOgYIABA-
     FEB46BggAEAgQHjoECAAQGFCw3w1YyYIOYNiGDmgAcAB4AIABTIgBswiSAQIxN5gBAKAB
     AaoBC2d3cy13aXotaW1nwAEB&sclient=img&ei=TB8zX9HIBZnWswWv-
     pXwCg&bih=959&biw=1748#imgrc=6SIPI4mIRkIoyM
68. pg. 219, Flammarion engraving colored (edited).jpg, Eikimedia Commons, public domain,
     https://commons.wikimedia.org/wiki/File:Flammarion_engraving_colored_(edited).jpg
69. pg. 225, Alien Interview Destroys Most Notions you have About Religion...,finding sanity in a mad
     made world – WordPres.com, https://www.google.com/search?q=Reincarnation+is+not+a+
     good+thing+the+soul+is+being+forced+into+a+new+body&tbm =isch&hl=en&sa=X&ved=
     2ahUKEwiO_6Xeu5 TrAhUGQKwKHUb6C0kQBXoECAEQFA&biw=1731&bih
     =959#imgrc=TJv1hgPruMcDMM
70. pg. 227, The oneness Trap – Search for photo not successful
71. pg. 229, Nimrod, Nibiru, Anunnak (linage)i, Time to Believe,
     https://www.google.com/search?q=who+is+ Enki+Enill+ linage&tbm=isch&ved =2ahUKEwj86v
     LLwJTrAhVE-KwKHezOBL0Q2-cCegQIABAA&oq=who+is+Enki+Enill+linage&gs_lcp
     =CgNpbWcQA1DzmwNYwc0DY MfSA2gBcAB4AIABSIgBxASSAQIxMJgBAKABAao
     BC2d3cy13aXotaW1nwAEB&sclient=img&ei=mUQzX7y6FMTwswXsnZPoCw&bih=959&biw=1748&
     hl=en#imgrc=OIUIMqPNhcQ6vM
72. pg. 233, Author modified movie cover, Escape Plan Columbia opens Midland's first 'escape room", the
     State, Escape, https://www.google.com
     /search?q=the+maze+escape+plan&tbm=isch&ved=2ahUKEwi1lc-dw5TrAhVTfqwKHZdrD9EQ2-
     cCegQIABAA&oq=the+maze+ es-
     cape+plan&gs_lcp=CgNpbWcQAzoICAAQCBAHEB5QhaUGWKKyBmDa5AZoAHAAeACAAU
     WIAa0CkgEBNZgBAKABAaoBC2d3cy13aXotaW1nwAEB&sclient=img&ei=XUczX_XyI9P8sQWX
     172IDQ&bih=959&biw=1748&hl=en#imgrc=NF1-DQY6VuQbjM
73. pg. 239, The Soul's Journey after Death, Ibn Qayyim, Goodreads, https://www.google.com/
     search?q=the +soul%27s+journey after +after+death &tbm=isch&ved=2ahUKEwjrlpXTw5TrAhV
     POK0KHUBmD0AQ2-cCegQIABAA&oq=the+soul%27s+journey+after+death&gs_lcp=Cg
     NpbWcQAzIECAAQGDIECAAQGDIECAAQGDIECAAQGDoECAAQQzoF-
     CAAQsQM6AggAOggIABCxAxCDAToECCMQJzoHCAAQsQMQQzoECAAQHjoGCAAQCBAe
     UKj3CljHiXpgoZl6aABwAHgAgAFJiAGqD5IBAjMymAEAoAEBqgELZ3dzLXdpei1pbWfAAQE&s
     client=img&ei=zUczX6v8Nc_wtAXAzL2ABA&bih=959&biw=1748&hl=en#imgrc=HNoqVQ628MzJ9
     M
74. pg. 240, A deep dive into the future of company builfing, Yahoo News Singapore, https://www
     .google.com/search?q=frequency+worker+blue +tunnel+of+light+buseness+man&tbm=isch&ved=
     2ahUKEwj3loT5zZTrAhVFOqwKHZ88CugQ2-cCegQIABAA&oq=frequency+ worker +blue+tunnel
     +of+light+buseness+man&gs_lcp=CgNpbWcQA1CtcFihjQFg-5ABaABwAHgAgAFGiAGFBpIB
     AjEzmA EAoAEBqgELZ3dzL Xdpei1pbWfAAQE&sclient=img&ei=mVIzX7fmJ8X0sAWf-
     ajADg&bih=959&biw=1748&hl=en#imgrc=qxc3Y8DlYGQ99 M&imgdii=9UMl4tRXVsFTNM
75. pg. 253, Author cropped illustration, Star Wars 1-7-Space Scenes, YouTube, https://www.google.com/
     search?q=star +wars +starship+battle+ blue&tbm=isch&ved=2ahUKEwjHqNmWz5TrAhVHaKw
     KHfmG BC4Q2-cCegQIABAA&oq=star+wars+starship+battle+blue&gs_lcp =CgNpbWcQA1CO2
     QNYlOcDY JHwA2gAcAB4AIABQYgBmAOSAQE3mAEAoAEBqgELZ3dzL Xdpei1pbWf
     AAQE&sclient=img&ei=5FMzX3emEsfQsQX.5jZLwAg&bih=959&biw=1748&hl=en#imgrc=lZ5JNBVo
     FxLf0M
76. pg. 269, top and bottom slides extracted from A Galactic Human Journey, Milky Way Galaxy,
     http://tas-education.org/exo/Galactic-Human-Journey.pdf
77. pg. 277, Page 2| Royality free library photos free download, Pxfuel, https://www.google.com/search?q=
     humans+are +electronic+library+man+in+sillote&tbm=isch&ved=2ahUKEwiRv4jKj5brAhUB3K
     wKHWEXCjgQ2-cCegQIABAA&oq=humans+are+electronic+library+man+in+sillote&gs_lcp
     =CgNpbWcQAzoECCMQJ1DEqwFYuckBYLLMAWgAcAB4AIABZYgB9wqSAQQxNC4xmAEAo
     AEBq-
     gELZ3dzLXdpei1pbWfAAQE&sclient=img&ei=ox00X9HhJoG4swXhrqjAAw&bih=959&biw=1748&h
     l=en#imgrc=laUVAVjXKJXx5M

78. pg. 281, Sun Strorm: A Coronal Mass Ejection, National Air and Space Musseum-Smithosonian Institution, https://www.google.com/search?q=Coronal+Mass+Ejection&hl=en&sxsrf=ALeKk006yZ7Yz8pYckZ_oU1isuLY0rvb_w:1597252636605&source=lnms&tbm=isch&sa=X&ved=2ahUKEwi6rpXglZbrAhXIQc0KHSlXCaQQ_AUoA3oECBEQBQ&biw=1666&bih=959#imgrc=XXAAnIX_pgV_FM

79. pg. 283, The Council of Five @ CouncilOfFive, Facebook, https://www.google.com/search?q=Council+of+5+aliens&tbm=isch&ved=2ahUKE wj8ioXilZbrAhVe-KwKHSt9AL8Q2-cCegQIABAA&oq=Council+of+5+aliens&gs_lcp=CgNpbWcQAzoOCA QQzoECCMQJzoICAAQsQMQgwE6BQg AELEDOgIIA Do ECAAQGDoECAAQHlCPygtYxIAMYOyLDGg AcAB4 AIABbIgB-ySAQQxNi4zmAE AoAEBqg ELZ3dzLXdpei1pbWfAAQE&sclient=i mg&ei=ICQ0X_z6H97wswWr-oH4Cw&bih=959&biw=1666&hl=en#imgrc=6gHSzEfFEpJsmM

80. pg. 289, Majestic 12 (MJ12)/Jason Society Controls All, Conscious Awakening, https://www .google .com/search?q=Majestic+12+blue+ +hand+over+world&tbm=isch&ved=2ahUKEwjM29TCl5brAhW U_awKHbeOBDcQ2-cCegQIABAA&oq=Majestic+12+blue++hand+over+world&gs_lcp=CgNpb WcQA1D7X FigbmC2cmgAcAB4AIABaogBvgSSAQM0IJKYAQ CgAQGqAQtnd3M td2l6LWltZ8ABAQ&sclient=img&ei=9yU0X4yEJJT7swW3nZK4Aw&bih=959&biw=1666&hl=en#img rc=vKtk2AfyqH52_M

81. pg. 295, Background, Top 5 interesting facts about The Thinker by Rodin, Discover Walks, https://www.google.com/search?q=The+Thinker +sky+ up& tbm=isch&ved=2ahUKEwiAhp3Kl5brAh WMUawKHYleDVIQ2-cCegQIABAA&oq=The+Thinker+sky+up&gs_ lcp=CgNpbWcQAzo ECCMQJzoICAAQsQMQgwE6BQgAELEDOgIIADoECAAQQzoHCAAQsQMQQzoGCAAQCB AeOgQIABAYUOHHCFju-jAlgr5IJaABwAHgAgAFtiAGsDZIBBDEzLjWYAQCgAQGqAQtnd3Mtd2l6LWltZ8ABAQ&sclient=img&ei=ByY0X8DmG4yjsQWJvbWQBQ&bih=959&biw=1666&hl=en#imgrc=-BYPWAbij05_4M

82. pg. 297, Book Coved modified by Author, Grey Aliens and the Harvesting of Souls: The Conspiracy to Genetically Tamper with Humanity, Nigel Kerner, Amazon.com, https://www.google.com/ search?q=lalien+human+harvesting&tbm=isch&ved=2ahUK Ewj72Ju6nJbrAhWM Bs0KHX2TB8gQ2-cCegQIA-BAA&oq=lalien+human+harvesting&gs_lcp=CgNpbWcQA1C47AFYzf0BYPaZAmgAcAB4AIA BYogB5AOSAQE2mAEAoAEBqgELZ3dzLXdpei1pbWfAAQE&sclient=img&ei=JCs0X_u2A4yNtAb9pp7ADA&bih=959&biw=1666&hl=en#imgrc=FQPtf8PHWBpioM

83. pg. 299, Background, Lion Head | Art Board Print, Designed by Marian Voicu, Redbubble, https://www.google.com/search?q=lion+head+ art&tbm=isch&ved=2ahUKEwjxof3LnJbrAh UKX80KHVkeCosQ2-cCegQIABAA&oq=lion+head+art&gs_lcp=CgNpbWcQAzICCA AyAggAM-gIIADICCAAyAggAMgYIABA-FEB4yBggAEAUQHjIGCAAQBRAeMgYIABAFEB4yBggAEAUQHjoECCMQJzoFCAAQsQM6B AgAEEM6BwgAELEDEENQ7fwMWJ-lDWDIqg 1oAHAAeACAAaYBiAHxDZIBBDAuMTOYAQCgAQGqAQtnd3Mtd2l6LWl tZ8ABAQ&sclient=img&ei=SSs0X7HZEoq-tQbZvKjYCA&bih=959&biw=1666&hl=en# imgrc=lZadwH5DwdC2xM

84. pg. 305, What parellels can we draw between Indian and Greek mythology?, Quora, https://www. google.com/search?q=ancient+gods +dualing+lightening+bolts+ Hindu+vs.+Zus&tbm =isch&ved= 2ahUKE wiKyP6Kn5brAhUV0qwKHXqsCyUQ2-cCegQIABAA&oq= ancient+gods+dualin g+lightening+bolts+ Hindu+vs.+Zus&gs_lcp=CgNpbWcQA1CzpwhYq40JYOqhCWgAcAB4AIABb 4gByAmSAQQxNC4xmAEAoAEBqgELZ3dzLXdpei1pbWfAAQE&sclient=img&ei=5i00X4q9E5Wk swX62K6oAg&bih=959&biw=1666&hl=en#imgrc=oycFkLu8m9yH1M

85. pg. 306 (left), Russia's Giant Soviet Era Lightening Machine is Terrifying, Foxtrot Alpha - Jalopnik, https://www.google.com/search?q =russian+ lightening+experiment&tbm=isch&ved=2ahUKEwiVzZiM oJbrAhUND60KHSmaBMwQ2-cCegQIABAA&oq=russian +lightening+experiment&gs_lcp =CgNpbWcQA zoECCMQJzoCCAA6BQgAELEDOggIABCxAxCDAToECAAQQzoHCA AQsQMQQzoGCAAQBRAeOgYIA-BAIEB46BggAEAoQGFCsuAhY0PsIYKGCFCWgAcAB4AIABfYgBlhOSAQQyNC41mAEAoAEBqg ELZ3dzLXdpei1pbWfAAQE&sclient=img&ei=9S40X9X-EI2etAWptJLgDA&bih=959&biw=1666&hl=en#imgrc=X-K3nlX50r9uOM

86. pg. 306 (middle), Starseeds and Galactic Civilizations, Pinterest, https://www.google.com/search?q= pleiadians +pictures&tbm=isch&ved= 2ahUKEwiE9ZnLopbrAhVyA50JHZM4B6EQ2-cCegQIABAA&oq=pleiadians+pictures&gs_lcp=CgNpbWcQAzoCCAA6BEB46Bag AEBhQ8I0BWOOnAWCsqgFoAHAAeACAAZUBiAG3BZIBAzcuMZgBAKABAAaoBC2d3cy13aX otaW1nwAEB&sclient=img&ei=kjE0X4TkEfKG9PwPk_GciAo&bih=959&biw=1666&hl=en#imgrc=yu M7w0Zwh0IxEM&imgdii=TeAJHqnBF8v79M

87. pg. 306 (Right), extracted from Episode 66 - Timeless Cool, Superdupersititious (Podcast), https://www.google.com/search?q=great+phramits +power+station+lightening&tbm=isch&ved =2ahUKEwjQz6r1pJbrAhXSAM0KHVpSDR8Q2-cCegQIABAA&oq=great+phramits+powe r+station+lightening&gs_lcp=CgNpbWcQA1Cv3gNYvvQDYOP5A2gAcAB4AIABbIgBjAeSAQM5Lj KYAQCgAQG-qAQtnd3Mtd2l6LWltZ8ABAQ&sclient=img&ei=AzQ0X5DCH9KBtAbapLX4AQ&bih=959&biw=16 66&hl=en#imgrc=si2FIJL8c5rXZM&imgdii=9Yo5Q0DQOxC2CM

88. pg. 309, background, AllSeeing Eye, Illumiti Symbol, Masonic Sign. Conspiracy Of..., Dreams-time.com, https://www.google.com/search?q= illumiti+eye+fire&tbm=isch&ved=2ahUKEwjiz-mUpZbrAhULb80KHcB9DHEQ2-cCegQIABAA&oq=illumiti+eye+fire&gs_lcp= CgNpbWcQA

zoECCMQJzoIAAQsQMQgwE6BQgAELEDOgcIABCxAxBDOgQIABBDOgIIADoECAAQGDo
GCAAQLjKYAQCgAQGqAQtnd3Mtd2l6LWltZ8ABAQ&sclient=img&ei=RTQ0X6KZIovetQbA-
7GIBw&bih=959&biw=1666&hl=en#imgrc=IBDnXFpDQhLeHM

89.   pg. 312,excerpts from the book The Committee of 300 The Conspiratrs..., Third World Traveler,
https://www.google.com/search?q= Committee+300+roundtable&
tbm=isch&ved=2ahUKEwiJuZvRppbrAhUCJ6wKHWH1BJMQ2-cCegQIABAA&oq=Committee+
300+roundtable&gs_lcp=CgNpbWcQAzoECCMQJzoFCAAQsQM6AggAOggIABCxAxCDAToECA
AQQzoHCAAQsQMQQzoGCAAQCBAeOgQIABAYUIOk-
CliC7wpgq_oKaABwAHgAgAFriAGAD5IBBDIzLjGYAQCgAQGqAQtnd3Mtd2l6LWltZ8ABAQ&s
client=img&ei=0DU0X4mRJ4LOsAXh6pOYCQ&bih=959&biw=1666&hl=en#imgrc=kQh8ULwE2xm
LRM

90.   pg. 314, Who controls the world? More resources for understanding, Ted Blog – Ted Talks,
https://www.google.com/search?q= who+controls+the+world&tbm =isch&ved=2ahUKEwiHmN
OgtJbrAhXCY60KHeyAADsQ2-cCegQIABAA&oq=who+controls+the+world&gs_lcp=Cg
NpbWcQAzICCAAyAggAMgIIADICCAAyAggAMgIIADICCAAyAggAMgIIADIECAAQG-
DoECCMQJzoF-
CAAQsQM6CAgAELEDEIMBOgQIABBDUNOpA1j3zwNg8dIDaABwAHgAgAGHAYgBrhGSA
QQx-
My45mAEAoAEBqgELZ3dzLXdpei1pbWFfAAQE&sclient=img&ei=GEQ0X4esNsLHtQXsgYLYAw
&bih=959&biw=1666&hl=en#imgrc=t8KL7-uEzeMbSM

91.   pg.315, We are just fragmented energy from the same source, 9buz.com, https://www.google.com/
search?q=we +are+just+fragmented+ engry+ from+the+same+sources+&tbm=isch&ved=2ahU KE-
wiW5N W9tJbrAhWITqwKHc44CJMQ2-cCegQIABAA&oq=we+are+just+ fragmented+engry
+from+the+same+sources+&gs_lcp=CgNpbWcQAzoECCMQJzoECAAQQzoHCAAQsQMQQzoFC
AAQsQM6 CAgAELEDEIMBOgIIAFCF7AtY0YgNYPzHDWgAcAB4AoA BggOIAeQ6kg
EIMC40N S4zLjOYAQCgAQGqAQtnd3Mtd2l6LWltZ8ABAQ&sclient=img&ei =VUQ0X9blL
YidsQXO8aCYCQ&bih=959&biw=1666&hl=en#imgrc=8SbiJs5b7ooy0M

92.   pg. 320, NatGeoMaps onTwitter: "Genetic Tests of ancient settlers remains..., Twitter, https://twitter.
com /natgeomaps/status/1172880290936737792

93.   pg. 223, Soulmate | Twin flame love, Twin Flame, Flame Art, pinterest, https://www.google.com/
search? q=ying+yang+twin +flame&sxsrf= ALeKk02oV_Ad6I5eCOAml03k1Mc18BxpNw:1597263273
485&source=lnms&tbm=isch&sa=X&ved=2ahUKEwi9-ZywvZbrAhVVW s0KHWH-CpoQ_AUoA
XoECA8QAw&biw=1666&bih=959#imgrc=7GdbiK4CE3YLmM

94.   pg. 319, Discussion: Exploring Your Shadow, Meetup, https://www.google.com/search?q
=What+is+shadow+work&tbm=isch&ved= 2ahUKEwi20eXVvZbrAhWPe6w KHa-sDNcQ2-
cCegQIABAA&oq=What+is+shadow+work&gs_lcp=CgNpbWcQAzI CCAAyBggAEAgGDIECAAQGDIECAAQGDIECAAQGDIECAAQGDoECCMQJ zo-
zo-
FAAQsQM6CAgAELEDEIMBOgQIABBDOgcIABCxAxBDUOHZBljm_gZg94UHaABwAHgAgA
FGiAGiCZIBAjE5mAEAoAEBqgELZ3dzLXdpei1pbWFfAAQE&sclient=img&ei=-
E00X7b1D4_3sQWv2bK4DQ&bih=959&biw=1666#imgrc=o4jDhhaoNdRCcM&imgdii=Dj-
jcOpVchY0DM

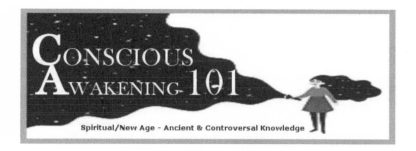

ABOUT THE AUTHOR - ARLENE LANMAN

John 8:32: 'Then you will know the truth and the truth will make you free.'

As a child, I knew I came from the stars. This thought has permeated my entire life, knowing that I was sent to Earth to complete a mission – a search for the "truth". As a youth, the search was to find "reality" – I read several books including George Orwell's "1984" (1949), Aldous Huxley's "Brave New World" (1932), Ray Bradbury's "Fahrenheit 451" (1953), Barry Wells' "The Day the Earth Caught Fire (1960), William Golding's "Lord of the Flies" (1954), H.G. Well's "War of the Worlds" (1898), J.R.R. Tolkien's "The Hobbit" (1937) and "Lord of the Rings" (1954), and Karel Capek's play "R.U.R. - Rossum's Universal Robots" (1921), to only mention a few; all of which only presented parts and pieces of the past and future. In college, I wandered between History of Origins to Alternate Histories of the Universe, from Advanced Mathematics/Chemistry/ Physics/ Thermodynamics/ Structural Analysis to Metaphysics, from Theology to Philosophy and Transcendentalism, from the Sciences to Sculpture, Ceramics, and Art, from Astronomy to Astrophysics, and from Business Administration to Sociology. At the end of this journey, I obtained a degree in Architectural Design and Engineering with numerous Minors. I was a Military Officer, Professional Engineer, Registered Architect, and Engineering Manager for a large number of years within a major Oil & Gas Corporation, Hospital Design, Higher Education, and Military Engineering & Construction Management. In the end, I found no answers to what is the "truth". At a weekend religious retreat, one of the best selling spiritual writers stated, "Stop the reading. You are only trying to confirm what you already know. Go inside of yourself to find the answers to the questions you are seeking." With that, I relied on the universe to guide me in my research to find the truth, resulting in my first book, *Conscious Awaking – A research Compendium* (2019) – this was my universe guided path to Awakening and Enlightenment. That journey revealed everything, I mean everything, is an elaborate deception to trap you and there has been an ever on-going, since time eternal, war throughout the universe between the Service-to-Self entities (often referred to as "evil" and "darkness") and the Service-to-Other entities (who call themselves "Bearers of Light"), both having their own agenda of how to use you to their advantage. This book was written as a Guide to reveal that everything you see, hear, touch and taste is a well crafted lie to keep you, lifetime after lifetime, tied to this world of polarity that is dominated and controlled by the Dark Force, to reveal the True You, and to learn how to develop your Escape Plan to travel to Higher Realms.

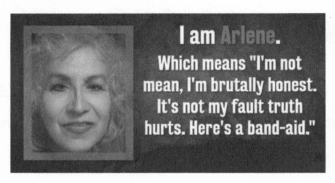

AUTHOR'S OTHER BOOKS

Conscious Awakening – A Research Compendium
Published: September 23, 2019 by BookBaby
ISBN: 1543972195 (ISBN13: 9781542972191)
Genre: Spiritual / Controversial Literature
Pages: 594. Available in print and eBook

Climbing the Mountains – On the Colorado Midland/Midland Terminal
Soon to be published. Look for the book at BookBaby and other online bookstores